PC/Computing Guide to Shareware

PC Computing

PC/Computing Guide to Shareware

Preston Gralla

ZIFF-DAVIS ZD PRESS

Ziff-Davis Press
Emeryville, California

Development Editor	Leslie Tilley
Copy Editor	Winnie Kelly
Technical Reviewer	Mike Callahan
Project Coordinator	Sheila McGill
Proofreader	Pat Mannion
Cover Design	Michael Yapp
Book Design	Laura Lamar/MAX, San Francisco
Word Processing	Kim Haglund and Howard Blechman
Page Layout	Kevin Shafer & Associates and Bruce Lundquist
Indexer	Julie Kawabata

This book was produced on a Macintosh IIfx, with the following applications: FrameMaker®, Microsoft® Word, MacLink®*Plus*, Aldus® FreeHand™, Adobe Photoshop™, and Collage Plus™.

Ziff-Davis Press
5903 Christie Avenue
Emeryville, CA 94608

ISBN 1-56276-036-X
Manufactured in the United States of America
10 9 8 7 6 5 4 3

For Elliot, whose good works live on, and who knew about the spirit of shareware before it even existed.

CONTENTS AT A GLANCE

TABLE OF CONTENTS

Part 2 The Programs

In the early days of shareware just ten years ago, a book such as this would have been easy to write. There were only a handful of shareware programs available.

But doing a complete review of shareware today is a daunting task, as Preston Gralla has discovered. There are now, by my conservative estimate, 15,000 shareware and public-domain programs floating around the 25,000 bulletin boards devoted to distributing software. At least ten companies take in over a million dollars a year in shareware registration fees. Some 60 other companies are providing a living for shareware authors.

Here are just a few of the major advances on the shareware scene:

- The command-line editor DOSEdit evolved through CED and Anarkey to 4DOS.
- PC-Write acquired all the trappings of the most fully featured word processor.
- PC-Calc evolved into As Easy As.
- The fledgling flat-file database PC-File re-emerged as SR-Info and Wampum, with all the capabilities of dBASE III.
- The little picture-drawing program PCPG became Desktop Paint 256, with more features than the current PC Paintbrush.
- The original Rogue game merged with the arcade graphics of FlightMare to become Captain Comic, Commander Keen, Duke Nukem, and a whole raft of new-generation games.

In recent months, the shareware arena has also seen a rush of Windows programs that have actually preceded similar programs in the retail marketplace. This happens because tools can be developed more quickly by a talented individual than by a team of programmers in an office working to a marketing plan.

PC/Computing Guide to Shareware is your source for all you need to know about the diverse and ever-changing shareware marketplace. If you're new to shareware, use this book as a reference instead of running down to the friendly neighborhood retail software store to shell out your hard-earned cash for software that may or may not do the job. If a program in this book seems to fit your bill, get it, try it out, and then pay for it only if it works for you.

If you're already a shareware enthusiast, use this book before spending the time to get the software and test it. Remember that time is money. You can spend days looking at the many alternatives in some categories of software. Preston Gralla has done that for you with this book.

It seems that shareware is still in its infancy because there is so much potential yet to be explored. Sounds like the microcomputer industry 10 years ago, doesn't it? The shareware arena is an exciting and creative place to be. With this fine book from Preston Gralla, you have the best guide available.

Bob Ostrander
Founder, Public Brand Software
December 1991

ACKNOWLEDGMENTS

This book has survived despite hurricanes, power blackouts, and illnesses, in addition to the usual disasters normally associated with the writing and producing of a book. That it has flourished is a testament to the many people who helped me put it together.

I'd like to thank everyone at Ziff-Davis Press for their help, particularly Cindy Hudson for supporting the idea; Cheryl Holzaepfel for holding the whole thing together; Leslie Tilley and Winnie Kelly for fighting inconsistency and bad grammar at every turn; and Jeff Green and Sheila McGill for ushering it through the production process.

I'd also like to thank Nelson Ford of the Public Software Library for his help, as well as PC-Sig. And one of the biggest thanks goes to Public Brand Software, who provided me with unlimited access to their excellent shareware library and sent programs to me by overnight mail to bail me out of many emergencies.

The Association for Shareware Professionals was a great help as well. And the real heroes of this book are the shareware authors who, despite all odds, continue to write superb programs.

Finally, I'd like to thank my family. My daughter Mia proved an invaluable reviewer of children's programs. Mia and my son Gabriel helped rejuvenate my spirits when I thought the writing would never end. And through it all, my wife Lydia put up with a glassy-eyed husband who spent far too much time online and in front of a monitor. Without her support, I'd probably still be writing.

INTRODUCTION

How would you like to save thousands of dollars in software costs every year? How about keeping up with the latest in cutting-edge programs? Or finding great utilities that save you untold hours of frustration at the keyboard? Wouldn't it be great to know about undiscovered software gems before everyone else finds out about them? And do you like the idea of trying out dozens—even hundreds—of programs for free, before deciding whether you'd like to buy any of them?

If you answered yes to any of those questions, this book is for you. It's a guide to the best in shareware. Whether you're a novice user just learning to put finger to keyboard, or you're a power user who's trained his PC to jump through hoops, you'll find it to be invaluable.

I've looked at thousands of shareware programs. Then I've picked more than 250 of the best ones and reviewed them all for you. And I've done more than just list and describe them. I've also told you on what jobs they work best, and given tips and advice on how to use them. And I've included screen captures from many of them so you can get the look and feel of the programs as well.

Shareware, for the uninitiated, is the ultimate in "try-it-before-you-buy-it" marketing: You try the program out for free, and if you decide you want to keep using it, you pay the author. And that fee is generally far less than you'd pay for more traditionally marketed software.

The book also gives you a comprehensive guide on the best places to find shareware, and on how to use any piece of shareware, fast. And it tells you how to avoid viruses, which is something most everyone is worried about these days.

But wait, as they say in the late-night TV ads, there's more! I've also searched out the best in shareware and made it available on the two disks that accompany the book. You'll find half a dozen shareware programs there that are absolutely top-notch, and that will help you do everything from manage your hard disk, to dial into bulletin boards to make Windows run better.

How to Use This Book

There are two parts to this book. The first section, made up of the first two chapters, covers the basics of how to obtain and to use shareware and how to avoid viruses.

The second, which makes up the bulk of the book, reviews more than 250 of the best shareware programs. It does so by program category, so if you're looking for a shareware word processor, you'd look under Chapter 3, for example. Also in these chapters are overviews of the software categories, so that if you want to know more about shareware databases in general, for example, you would turn to Chapter 6. Within the reviews of individual programs are addresses and phone numbers of the shareware authors, followed by one or more $ symbols, which indicate the price range of the registration fee for the program. (If the program is free, I've told you so.) Here's the key to the price range symbols:

$	$1–$35
$$	$36–$75
$$$	$76–$125
$$$$	Over $125

The appendices round out the book. They give a comprehensive listing on where to get shareware, detail the disks included with this book, give advice on putting together a complete shareware toolkit, and tell you how to log onto PC/Contact, *PC/Computing*'s online service, which is part of the ZiffNet online service.

You can read this book from cover to cover, starting at the beginning and ending at the back, but you might also like to use it to browse. I'd suggest reading at least the first chapter before doing that, though, to give you the best sense of what shareware is and how to use it. Read Chapter 2 for guidance in how to avoid viruses, no matter what kind of software you use.

Browsing will be easy: Look in the Table of Contents for the type of software you're interested in, then go directly to that chapter. I've covered both DOS and Windows shareware in the book. To find a Windows *application,* look to the chapter that covers that type of application. So, for example, to find a Windows checkbook manager, turn to Chapter 7, which covers finance and business programs. But to find Windows *utilities*, such as replacements for Program Manager, turn to Chapter 10.

What's Inside?

There are 16 chapters in the book and a set of appendices. Chapter 1 gives a rundown on what shareware is, how to find it, and how to use a typical shareware program. It explains the benefits of shareware, the basics of using it, where and why to register shareware, and places to get it. This chapter's not just for novices—even advanced users could benefit from reading it.

Chapter 2 gives advice on how to avoid viruses. It details the symptoms of infection, tells you what to do if you're infected, and gives guidelines for practicing safe computing so you'll avoid infection in the first place.

Chapter 3 covers the most heavily used applications on the PC—word processors, text editors, and add-ins to those programs. It reviews the best word processors and text editors and gives advice on how to use them. It also details outliners, style checkers, and dictionaries, as well as shareware programs that will make commercial programs such as WordPerfect and Word for Windows more powerful or easier to use.

Chapter 4 is about communications and compression programs, one of shareware's greatest strengths. In it, you'll find general communication programs, as well as software to automate access to online services. There's also software to set up your own bulletin board, and to do a variety of communications tasks, such as sharing a single phone line among a fax machine, modem, and answering machine. The chapter also covers a wide variety of compression software.

Chapter 5 covers spreadsheets. You'll find excellent shareware spreadsheets here, as well as templates, add-ins, and utilities to make the ubiquitous Lotus 1-2-3 easier to use.

Chapter 6 reviews databases and database utilities. Here you'll find surprisingly powerful shareware databases, as well as utilities to enhance the power of dBASE. And you'll find a number of miscellaneous databases that do things such as create a database of images.

Chapter 7 talks about the best in finance and business programs. You'll find everything here from business and accounting programs to personal finance programs. Whether you want to run a business, manage your checkbook, or do your taxes, you'll find a piece of software to your liking.

Chapter 8 covers DOS shells and menu programs. Here, you'll find ways to shield yourself from the unfriendly DOS prompt, and to make your PC do tricks you never thought possible. You'll find out that shells and menus don't just help out novices—they'll also help the most powerful of power users.

Chapter 9 reviews a wide variety of general utilities that can make your computing life easier. Here you'll find programs that help you manage files better, make your life at the command line easier, and give extra power to your batch files. It also includes utilities to give you commands that DOS—even DOS 5—doesn't include.

Chapter 10 covers the world of Windows utilities. Here you'll find programs to improve on the way that Windows works. You'll find things such as replacements for the Windows Program Manager, Task Manager, and File Manager. There also are icon and wallpaper utilities, graphics utilities, and uncategorizable utilities that do things such as give you batch-file power in Windows.

Chapter 11 details hard-disk enhancers, backup programs, and formatters. Look here if you're searching for programs to keep your hard disk in tip-top shape. With them, you'll make it run faster, last longer, and hold more files. And you'll be able to back it up with ease. You'll also find programs to do complicated floppy-disk formatting chores.

Chapter 12 lists a wide variety of antiviral programs. Here you'll find shareware to detect viruses and disinfect your PC if they're found. You'll also find software to prevent you from being infected in the first place.

Chapter 13 lets you know how to get the most out of your printer. It covers printer programs and utilities. With them, you'll be able to make your printer do things such as create booklets, address envelopes, print on labels, create letterhead, and download fonts. Whether you have a laser, ink-jet, or dot-matrix printer, you'll find something here to make it do remarkable things.

Chapter 14 takes a look at the lighter side of computing—games. There are a lot of great shareware games out there, and this chapter details the best. Whether you're looking for a shoot-em-up, an adventure game, an arcade game, a game of logic, or a Windows game, you'll find something here to your liking.

Chapter 15 covers a grab bag of programs. There are graphics programs, memory utilities, personal information managers, and programs that just don't fit into any recognizable category.

Chapter 16 is my personal pick of the best of shareware—*PC/Computing*'s Ten Top Shareware Picks. Read it to find out the absolute best in shareware.

Appendix A lists the programs on the disks and explains how to use them. Appendix B helps you put together a complete shareware toolkit. Appendix C is a comprehensive listing of places to obtain shareware. Appendix D tells you how to log onto PC/Contact, the online service of *PC/Computing,* and ZiffNet, the online service owned by Ziff-Davis.

Disks with the Book

As a bonus for buying this book, you get two free disks containing six programs: the communications program {COMMO}; the superb file viewer List; the Windows utility METZ Task Manager; the popular compression program PKZIP; the hard-disk manager Treeview; and the virus detector ViruScan. Individually each of these programs is absolutely superb, and taken together as a suite they're a great shareware toolkit.

Happy Hunting!

I hope you'll use this book in the spirit it was written: that shareware not only means greater productivity and big savings, it's also a concept that should be nurtured and supported. It's one of the last bastions of individual creativity left in the world of computing. Shareware authors tend to be individualistic, freedom-loving, and downright quirky. When you support them and participate in the shareware world, you're doing more than supporting individuals, you're also helping keep alive the original spirit of the earliest days of the PC, when marketing took a back seat to technology, and when sharing ideas and friendship was more important than commerce. So browse through the book, try out as many shareware programs as you can get your hands on, and then register them with their author. You'll find that a little bit of the magic of those early days will rub off on you as well.

PART 1

Shareware Basics

CHAPTER

1

Introducing Shareware

What Is Shareware?

The Benefits of Shareware

Using Shareware: The Basics

How and Why to Register Shareware

Where to Get Shareware

IMAGINE YOU COULD BRING HOME A NEW CD PLAYER AND USE IT FOR AS long as you'd like before buying it—and if you weren't pleased with it you wouldn't owe a cent. What if you could bring home a car, and pay for it only if it's the auto of your dreams? Or imagine you were able to read a book first, and buy it only if it educated or entertained you. Does this sound too good to be true? In the PC world, at least, it's not. That's the idea behind shareware.

What Is Shareware?

Shareware is the ultimate in "try-it-before-you-buy-it" purchasing. You test drive a shareware program first. If you decide to keep using it, you pay for it by sending the author a *registration fee,* generally a small fraction of what you would pay for commercial software. Full-blown commercial word processors cost $400 or more, whereas many shareware word processors—often just as capable as their higher-priced commercial cousins—sell for $80 or less.

There are thousands of shareware programs out there, and thousands more written every year. You'll find everything from complete applications, with as many bells and whistles as commercial programs, to one-trick ponies that perform a single task exceedingly well (for example, sniffing out and reporting on every duplicate file on your hard disk). There's far more variety among shareware programs than among commercial software, too. You'll find high-powered spreadsheets, databases, and graphics programs, as you would in the commercial world, but you'll also find computerized tarot card readers and databases full of recipes for raccoon and opossum. There are some remarkable gems among them, and some fool's gold as well. That's this book's purpose: to help you find the gems hiding among the thousands of shareware programs available, and give you advice on how to find and use them.

You won't find shareware in the same places you buy traditional software. Instead, look for it through on-line services (such as CompuServe), electronic bulletin boards, PC user groups, or from commercial disk vendors. User groups and disk vendors often sell shareware programs, or groups of programs, for $6 or less per disk. They're free from bulletin boards and on-line services—you only pay the cost of the phone call and connection charges, if any. (See Appendix C for phone numbers and addresses of shareware sources.)

When you obtain a piece of shareware, you typically get a disk or set of disks without a bound manual or any other printed documentation. Instead, the documentation is on the disk, along with the program and information on how to register the program with the author. Should you decide to send in money and register the program, you usually get the complete set of printed documentation (if there is any), technical support from the shareware author, and notices about program updates.

In all other respects, shareware is the same as more traditional forms of software, with a major difference: With shareware you only pay for the good programs. The bad ones are free.

What Shareware Isn't

The term *shareware* may be one of the most misused terms you'll ever encounter. It's often referred to as *freeware*—software given away for free. Since shareware authors need to make a living just like any other software writer, that's certainly not the case. If you use a shareware program, authors expect you to register.

True freeware is *public-domain software*—uncopyrighted programs that are free to all takers and have been put into the public domain by their authors. These programs are often utilities, rarely full-blown applications like spreadsheets, databases, or word processors. They're often, though not always, technical in nature or are system-wide, hard-disk, or file utilities. Some public-domain programs include the original programmers' code, so that they can be rewritten and customized by anyone who wishes to do so.

Sometimes authors will make their programs available for free, but will still retain the copyright, with an eye to turning them into shareware eventually. If such a program becomes really popular, for instance, its author may decide to release the next version as shareware. Should that happen, the original freeware versions of the program are still free, whereas the later shareware versions carry a registration fee.

There is also a whole group of quasi-shareware programs, which are like normal shareware in every respect but one: They're not fully functioning programs. Until you pay the author and obtain a complete program from him or her, not all the features are available. A spreadsheet, for example, may have a limited number of cells it can create. Or a word processor may have no printer drivers, and so can't be used to print out a file. An interesting variation on the theme are programs that are completely functional—for a time, that is. After a certain period of time, or a specified number of uses, the program simply stops working.

Some of these types of programs, sometimes called *crippleware,* became a nuisance several years ago. In 1987, an influential group of shareware authors banded together and formed the Association of Shareware Professionals (ASP). All ASP members have to live by a code of ethics, which says among other things that their programs must be fully functional when downloaded or obtained from a user group or disk vendor. The ASP has over 300 members at the time of this writing. Not all shareware authors, however, are members of the ASP and so may not feel obliged to follow that code. Many non-ASP authors do follow the code, however.

Another type of program has come to be termed *nagware*. Nagware is fully functional shareware that repeatedly reminds you to register with the author. In its most extreme form, nagware will unexpectedly remind you in the middle of an operation to register, or force you to hit a key acknowledging the nag before you can continue. The ASP didn't quite do away with nagware: It allows its authors to flash a promotional screen when you load the program. But the screen can only appear that once, and not again. Non-ASP authors aren't bound by this stricture, of course, but they often follow it.

Finally, you may find free demonstration versions of commercial programs on bulletin boards. Some of these are little more than advertisements for a commercial program—animated demonstrations of the program. Others are crippled versions of the commercial packages. There's nothing wrong with these, as long as you use them in the spirit in which they've been created: in order to market a program.

Exploding Shareware Myths

Although shareware has been around for years, myths about it still abound, most of them untrue. Below are some of the more common ones.

Myth Number 1: Shareware Programs Are Not Very Powerful

Nothing could be less true. In many cases, shareware programs are more powerful than their pricier commercial counterparts. And sales figures reflect that: For example, ProComm, a powerful communications program, was launched as shareware in the summer of 1985. Word-of-mouth commendations soon had sales skyrocketing—55,000 people paid the $50 registration fee and corporations began buying site licenses for it. It soon outsold many commercial communications programs, and eventually was launched as a commercial package called ProComm Plus. Earlier shareware versions are still in circulation, however.

Myth Number 2: Shareware Is Infected with Viruses

Again, not true. Online services, bulletin boards, disk vendors, and shareware authors rigorously test every piece of software to ensure it contains no viruses. You should take some basic antivirus precautions when obtaining shareware, of course, just as you should when buying commercial software. See Chapter 2 for help doing this.

Myth Number 3: Corporations Never Use Shareware

This is another fallacy. A surprising number of corporations recognize the benefits of shareware over commercial software, and so have standardized on shareware programs. For example, there are a substantial number of corporate site licenses for Automenu, a shareware menuing program, and for PC-Write, a shareware word processor.

Myth Number 4: Shareware Authors Are Unstable, Fly-by-Night Programmers

This is the last of the Big Four Myths. The only difference between shareware authors and other programmers is that they tend to value their independence more highly. Many of them, in fact, started off in large corporations before setting out on their own. Bob Wallace, author of the popular PC-Write shareware word processor, for example, was one of Microsoft's first employees, and was a programmer there for five years before setting out on his own. The author of the well-known PC-File database, Jim Button, was an employee of IBM before making the leap to full-time shareware authordom.

What to Expect from Shareware

Although shareware is available to try out for free, and though it usually costs a small fraction of what commercial programs do, you should expect nothing less from a shareware program than you get in a commercial product. That means trouble-free operation, solid technical support, and timely information about available upgrades.

Expect, however, down-home packaging, a lack of slick marketing materials, and a refreshing informality when dealing with shareware authors. When you call technical support, don't be surprised if the tech support person is actually the author of the program—many shareware shops are one-person operations.

Those are some of the reasons shareware is often available for much less than commercial software. The money doesn't go into fancy packaging, large marketing departments, or big advertising budgets. Funds generally go right into the pockets of the people who actually wrote the program. Indeed, shareware may be the ultimate in free-market Darwinism: Only the strong survive, since the thing that separates better-selling shareware programs from the less popular ones is usually the quality of the product, not a pretty package.

When calling tech support, you generally won't find toll-free 800 numbers; in most cases you'll call on your own nickel. So make sure before calling that you have a precise, solvable question, and that you have all the necessary information about the program and your system at hand. Shareware authors also sometimes have their own electronic bulletin boards, from which you can download their latest software and get technical support.

As with packaging, you'll find that shareware documentation tends to be less professional-looking than its commercial counterpart. Four-color art, typeset pages, fancy graphics, and sharp-eyed art direction cost money, and shareware authors economize where they can. Don't let that put you off, however; it has nothing to do with the quality of the program. Expect a (usually) refreshing writing style in shareware documentation, too, in stark contrast to the carefully sanitized language found in many commercial programs. Often, the documentation has been written by the shareware author, whose personality—eccentricities and all—tends to shine through.

Shareware upgrades tend to be less expensive than that of commercial programs. It's not uncommon to get free upgrades from the author. Even if the author decides to charge for the upgrade, you always have the option of first trying it out for free before deciding whether it's worth the price.

The Benefits of Shareware

Shareware offers a number of benefits besides simply letting you try out programs before you buy them. Their low price is a big one. Whereas commercial spreadsheets often sell for $500 and more, a shareware spreadsheet such as As-Easy-As carries a registration fee of only $50. Shareware authors will often give better deals to corporations on site licenses than will commercial software companies.

Since you'll only register for those programs you end up using regularly, you also get to try out far more software when using shareware than you do when testing commercial software. Test out two dozen commercial programs and you'll end up spending well in excess of $5,000—even if you don't like a single one of them. Try out the same number of shareware programs, and you'll have spent only your time.

Shareware authors also often pick up on specific needs quicker than do large software corporations. They have to, in order to survive. Since they're often one-person shops, they can get a product out on the street a lot faster, too. When Windows 3.0 first came out, for example, shareware authors were among the first to release programs improving on the justifiably maligned File Manager. The innovative COMMAND.COM replacement in Norton Utilities 6.0 and above, NDOS, has been available for years to shareware aficionados as 4DOS, from J.P. Software. The owner of Norton Utilities, Symantec, knowing a good thing when they saw it, licensed 4DOS from J.P. Software. They then tweaked it a little and turned it into NDOS. 4DOS is still available as shareware, incidentally.

Support is also a big factor. When you have trouble with a commercial program, you may spend a half an hour or more on the phone waiting for technical support—and while the voice that finally answers will usually be helpful, it also may be trying to hustle you off the phone to get to the next call. Call for technical support for a shareware program, and you'll probably end up with the program's author on the other end, who will not only answer your questions, but will also be interested in what kind of features you'd like to see in an upgrade—and may even put them in. And if you need a special printer driver, the author may write one for you.

The final benefit of using shareware is a subtle but still powerful one: Using shareware returns you to the earliest days of the PC, when programmers weren't faceless, when the best work was being done by individuals rather than by committees, when technical innovation was more important to companies than marketing niches and product positioning. Talk to any shareware author and you'll find that the pioneering spirit that existed back then still lives in them. Try out their software, come across an undiscovered gem that's never had a magazine writeup or gotten an inch of advertising space, and you'll experience some of the same fervor yourself.

Using Shareware: The Basics

When you first get an unregistered shareware program—from a bulletin board, say, or from a commercial disk vendor—you'll only have the disk or disks the program comes on. There will be no printed, bound documentation, no packaging touting the product's benefits, no keyboard templates or quick-help cheat sheets—nothing other than the files on disk to give you a sense of how or why to use the program.

Most shareware programs, though, will have certain standard kinds of files included with them. Learn the purpose of those files, and you'll find yourself learning the new shareware program with ease: often with more ease, in fact, than commercial programs that require you to wade through a sea of documentation.

The Makeup of a Typical Program

In general, you'll find four types of files on a shareware disk. The first type of file makes up the program itself: executable files and files related to them. You can tell an executable file by its *extension*, the three letters after the period in the file name. Executable files have the extension .EXE or .COM. The batch files that start up the program, if any, end with the extension .BAT.

A wide number of file types work in concert with executable files. Overlay files, to which .EXE or .COM programs refer when running certain operations, often have the extension .OVL. Files containing help information, which you get by pressing the help key in the program, more often than not end in .HLP. Files with the .PRN extension are printer drivers, though other extensions are also used.

The second type of file contains the program's documentation. These almost invariably end in a .DOC extension. Usually, the documentation file will be named after the program: The documentation for 4DOS, for example, is called 4DOS.DOC. Sometimes documentation will be named MANUAL.DOC. Usually, you'll need a word processor or text editor to view them on screen, although some programs have built-in software for viewing. Since they're plain ASCII files, any word processor or text editor should do. You can even print them, using DOS's print command or a word processor. (When you register the program, you'll usually get a set of printed, bound documentation, however.)

The third type of file is made up of the README files, often named READ.ME, README.1ST, README.TXT, README.DOC, or some variation on that theme. These are ASCII files; they can be read or printed out in the same way as .DOC files. (Usually, any shareware file ending in .DOC or .TXT is an ASCII file.) Generally, you should look at these READ-ME files before any others. They'll usually give details on how to use the program and provide information about the other files on the disk. They also often have late-breaking information that didn't make it into the documentation file. If there are any reported bugs, incompatibilities, or eccentricities in the program, this is often where you'll find reports about them. Sometimes, programs will also have a file called UPDATE.DOC, which contains information about changes in the most recent version of the program.

The final file type is made up of "housekeeping" files: files that let you know where and how to register, provide information to disk vendors, give details about the authors' other programs, and give information about the ASP. (Sometimes this information is found in the main documentation file.) The file asking you to register is often called, not surprisingly, REGISTER-.DOC. The one concerning disk vendors will usually be called (you guessed it) VENDOR.DOC. Other similar files usually end in a .DOC or .TXT extension.

How to Use a Typical Program

Let's say you've been trolling the bulletin boards, fishing for an interesting piece of shareware, or you get a disk with shareware on it from your local user group. You download it from the bulletin board or bring it home from the user group. You put the disk into your A drive and check it for viruses. Next, you copy it to a directory on your C drive, and now you're ready to explore. What do you do next?

Viewing the Files

First, check what kind of files you have. If you've gotten the program from a bulletin board, the odds are it's been *compressed*, shrunk down in size, so that it takes up less storage space on the board's hard disk. All the original files have been combined into this one compressed file, often called an *archive* file. Since this archive file is smaller than the original files, it also will take less time for you to download. There are a number of different compression formats, but by far the most popular is one called PKZIP. You can tell a program that's been "zipped" by its extension, .ZIP. Other popular compressed formats are .ZOO, .ARC, and .PAK.

To decompress a file in any of these formats, you'll need special software. All the popular decompression utilities are available as shareware (see

Chapter 4 for more information on how to find and use compression utilities). Sometimes, the shareware program will be *self-extracting:* that is, it will uncompress itself. Self-extracting shareware will end in an .EXE or .COM extension. To decompress a self-extracting file, just type the file name.

For example, let's say you've just downloaded a piece of shareware called Mindreader that claims it can read your mind, determine what you want to do at the keyboard, and enter DOS commands without you having to do any typing. The file name is MIND.EXE, and it's a compressed, self-extracting file.

After you download it, put the file in its own directory, which you might name \MINDREAD. Switch to that directory and type **MIND** at the DOS prompt. Files will automatically be extracted from it. Now, take a look at the files.

Six files make up our imaginary program: MINDREAD.EXE, MINDREAD.HLP, MINDREAD.DOC, README.1ST, REGISTER.DOC, and VENDOR.DOC. The first thing you should do is look at the README.1ST file. Use a word processor or text editor to do this. If you have DOS 5, you'll find that its text editor is ideal for this. If you have an earlier version of DOS and don't have a word processor or text editor, use DOS's TYPE command with the *pause switch*, /P. The TYPE command will display what's in the file on your screen. Without the pause switch, however, the entire file would go flashing by at once, and you'd be able to read only the last screen of text. The pause switch instructs DOS to let you see only one screen of text at a time, and to show you the next screen only when you hit a key. To use the TYPE command to view README.1ST, issue the following command:

```
TYPE /P README.1ST
```

The README.1ST file tells you that MINDREAD.EXE is the Mindreader program and that MINDREAD.HLP is the help file the program uses. It reports on the one bug that has been found so far: If you use the program while you're in a destructive state of mind, you could trash your hard disk. Other than that, it says, no problems have been discovered.

Printing the Documentation

Now you're ready to look at the manual. It's fairly lengthy, and you'd like it by your side when you run the program, so you want a printout. You can use your word processor to get one, of course. Or, if you prefer, you can use the DOS PRN (print) command. To print out the MANUAL.DOC file, issue the following DOS command:

```
COPY MANUAL.DOC PRN
```

The manual should come churning out of your printer.

Next, read the documentation. (You *do* read documentation, don't you?) It tells you that to run the program, you merely need to meditate for a moment, then type **MINDREAD** at the DOS prompt. The program will do the rest. You recall the warning in the README.1ST file about being in the proper state of mind before doing this, but you feel relatively cheery, and figure there's no danger of trashing your hard disk, so you try out the program. Magic! It actually works; it reads your mind and carries out your command—it loads a communications program so you can troll for more shareware.

You decide to register.

How and Why to Register Shareware

Registering your shareware program couldn't be simpler. The main documentation file often has information on how to register. Otherwise, there will be a file on the disk called REGISTER.DOC, or something similar. The file will contain registration information and a form with which you can register.

Print out the form, using a word processor or the same DOS command you used to print the manual. Then fill in the form and mail it with your registration fee to the shareware author. Within a few weeks you should receive a registered copy of the program in the mail. This should include bound documentation, if such documentation is available. If the shareware program included any nag screens requesting you to register, these should be gone from the registered version. Some registered versions also include features not found on the unregistered software.

You may be tempted to forgo paying the registration fee, even for a program you use daily. What, you might ask, is in it for you if you register?

Plenty! To begin with, you'll get support from the author. Are you having trouble with recalculations on your spreadsheet or getting your word processor to work with your oddball printer? If you register, you'll get help. Support policies vary from author to author, but ASP members are required to provide at least three months of tech support from the date you register. You can get this support by telephone, mail, or bulletin board. (Non-ASP members are free to set their own support policies, but these are often similar to ASP policies.)

Registration also gives you a chance to take part in the development of the software. When you call for support, as often as not you'll be talking to the program's author. If you offer suggestions on how to improve the program, they may well find their way into the next version.

When you register, you'll be notified of program updates, patches to the existing program, known bugs, and bug fixes. Newsletters about the program and other fact-filled missives may come your way as well. Sometimes, when you register, you'll get the next version or two of the program for free.

Whenever you register with an ASP author, you'll also have access to the ASP ombudsman. The ombudsman resolves any problems that arise between an ASP author and a shareware user. To contact the ombudsman, write to

ASP Ombudsman
545 Grover Road
Muskegon, MI 49442

or send a CompuServe Mail message to the ASP Ombudsman 70007,3536.

Finally, when you register, you're rewarding creative, independent people who have done top-notch work, and you're helping make sure they'll be able to do that work in the future. You'll not only get the satisfaction of helping them, but you'll be helping yourself as well. Authors who get enough registered users are able to write more programs—and will probably write others you like.

Where to Get Shareware

There may be thousands of shareware programs out there, but if you can't get your hands on them, they're not of much help to you. Luckily, it's exceptionally easy to find shareware. There are five main ways to get it: through user groups, from commercial disk vendors, through on-line services, from bulletin boards, and directly from the author.

Appendix C offers a comprehensive listing of vendors, on-line services, and bulletin boards. The following sections give an overview of these sources and the addresses of a few of the largest.

User Groups

The first place you should look for shareware is close to home, in your local user group. Most cities have at least one such group, and they can be found in less-populated areas as well. Fees for the groups vary, but usually run between $20 and $45 annually. With that fee you'll receive many other benefits, such as newsletters, discounts on hardware and software, and access to bulletin boards. Almost every user group also has a shareware library from which you can order shareware disks. Costs usually run from $3 to $6 per disk. Sometimes the disks will be made available at the beginning or end of user group meetings. It's not uncommon for a user group library to have several thousand different disks.

User groups are also excellent places to ferret out the good shareware from among the not-so-good. Attend any group meeting, and you'll soon find which are people's shareware favorites. User group newsletters often review shareware, too.

Note that you don't have to live near a user group to join it. Groups such as the Boston Computer Society—the largest user group in the world—boast members from all over the country. The Boston Computer Society has a particularly well-stocked and well-run shareware library, so you might want to join even if you live in the wilds of Montana.

Finding a user group is easy; simply contact

Association of PC User Groups
1730 M St. NW #700
Washington, D.C. 20036

The bulletin board number is (408) 439-9367. The association can also be contacted on MCI Mail with the ID number 379-0522. Most good-sized user groups are members.

Another good source is the Fog International Computer Users Group, which maintains a user-group list. Send a self-addressed, stamped envelope to

FOG International
P.O. Box 3474
Daly City, CA 94015
(415) 755-2000

Specify what you're interested in, and you'll be sent a list of user groups and (if you wish) bulletin boards near where you live.

A local computer retailer probably knows how to contact a user group as well. The store may be a member, and might even offer discounts to other members. In a pinch, you can also check the Yellow Pages.

Commercial Disk Vendors

The second place to find shareware is from commercial disk vendors. These are for-profit companies that sell unregistered versions of shareware. After you get the program, it's still your decision whether to register with the author. Disk prices generally range from $2 to $6.

Vendors can be small mom-and-pop operations (one such company in Florida is, in fact, called Mom and Pop's Software) or full-blown companies with a sizable staff and their own magazines. Some vendors have membership fees. Although you don't have to become a member in order to buy software from them, paying a membership fee means you'll pay less per disk. There may be other benefits as well, such as a magazine or newsletter subscription. For a $20 membership in PC-Sig, for example, you'll pay $4 instead of $6 per disk and get a yearlong subscription to *Shareware Magazine*. Write or call

PC-Sig
1030 D East Duane Ave.
Sunnyvale, CA 94086.
(800) 245-6717

You can fax them at (408) 730-2107. If you have a PC CD player, you'll be particularly interested in the PC-Sig Library on CD ROM. For $299 you get a CD with nearly 6,000 shareware and public-domain programs.

The newsletters themselves are often worth more than the price of membership. Nelson Ford, owner of the Public Software Library (PSL), publishes an especially useful and pithy newsletter for the PSL, and also has reviews of every program in his voluminous library available on disk. He also publishes a catalog for $19.95 of every disk he sells. The address is

Public Software Library
P.O. Box 35705
Houston, TX 77235
(800) 242-4775

Another disk vendor worthy of note is Public Brand Software, which has a sizable shareware and public-domain library and a free catalog. Public Brand operates a 24-hour toll-free number, for those times at 3 AM when you absolutely *have* to order that hard-disk optimizer you've been craving. Disks are $5 each, and all orders carry a $5 shipping charge. Write or call

Public Brand Software
P.O. Box 51315
Indianapolis, IN 46251
(800) 426-3475

Indianapolis-area callers, or those outside the United States, should dial (317) 856-7571.

In previous years, there was some friction between shareware authors and disk vendors since some commercial disk vendors had implied that shareware programs need not be registered. But those days are gone, and the ASP now provides a list of disk vendors that carry shareware programs.

On-line Services

Commercial on-line services, such as CompuServe and GEnie, are especially good sources of shareware. Almost every piece of top-notch shareware ends up on these services, and they may well be the single most comprehensive shareware source.

That's not to say there aren't some drawbacks to the services. They're often difficult to use, and they can be expensive as well—CompuServe, for example, charges $12 per hour of connect time. But you'll find it's well worth the cost. Not only will you find the largest shareware libraries in the world there, you'll also come across experts in almost any computer application you can name. You'll be hooked up to people around the globe; you can tap immense databases; and you'll be able to participate in forums on almost any special interest you can name. If you can afford it, by all means dial in.

CompuServe

CompuServe has a massive library, with thousands of programs, and scores—possibly hundreds—of applications added every month. The libraries on CompuServe can be found in the special-interest forums. These forums cover everything from astronomy to scuba diving, but among the most active are those forums devoted to computing. To get to a forum, you type **GO**, followed by the forum name. So, for example, if you were interested in system software and utilities, you'd type

```
GO IBMSYS
```

and press Enter at the CompuServe prompt, and you'd be switched to that forum. Then type

```
LIBRARY
```

and press Enter, and you'll be in the library, which has shareware, public domain, and text files for downloading.

Some of the larger shareware vendors, such as ButtonWare and Magee Enterprises, run their own forums on CompuServe. Of particular note is the shareware forum run by the ASP. To get to this forum, type either

```
GO ASPFORUM
```

or

```
GO SHAREWARE
```

at the prompt and press Enter. You may want to look first at a file named CATLOG.ZIP in the forum's library. This is a compressed file containing a list of programs written by ASP members.

Perhaps the best way to find a file is not through any one library, but by using CompuServe's searching mechanism, IBM File Finder. To access it, type

```
GO IBMFF
```

at the prompt and press Enter. After choosing the menu item for accessing File Finder, you'll be able to search for a file in a number of ways, including by keywords, by author name, and by file extension. See Figure 1.1 for the IBM File Finder search menu.

Figure 1.1
IBM File Finder's search menu

```
File Finder IBM
****************************************
Files are current as of: 03-Dec-91
****************************************
SEARCH BY:
 1 Keyword
 2 Submission Date
 3 Forum Name
 4 File Type
 5 File Extension
 6 File Name
 7 File Submitter (By User ID)

Enter choice !
```

Navigating through CompuServe can be difficult—it's not the most user-friendly of services. An excellent shareware program, Tapcis, will help you steer through the shoals, however, and will soon more than pay for itself (for more information about Tapcis, see Chapter 4). Also be forewarned that CompuServe is not cheap: You'll pay $12 per hour in connect charges. Write or call

CompuServe
5000 Arlington Centre Blvd.
Columbus, OH 43220
(614) 457-8600

You can call customer service at (800) 848-8990, or at (614) 457-8650 for Ohio residents and from outside the United States.

ZiffNet

Ziff-Davis's ZiffNet is another particularly good source of shareware programs. It's the home of PC/Connect, the on-line service of *PC/Computing;* PC MagNet, the on-line service of *PC Magazine;* and many other Ziff-Davis services. The ZiffNet library is stocked with hundreds of shareware and public domain utilities and programs. You can get them through the libraries of individual magazines, but a better way is to access the Software and Utility Library, shared by all the magazines. To do so, choose Software and Utility Library from the ZiffNet main menu. You'll then be greeted with the screen shown in Figure 1.2. When you choose Search the Library from that menu, you can then search the library in even more ways than CompuServe's IBM File Finder offers. Figure 1.3 shows the search screen.

Figure 1.2 The main menu for ZiffNet's Software Library

```
ZiffNet Library            SOFTLIB

 1 About the Library
 2 Instructions for Searching
 3 Search the Library
 4 Download a Utility
 5 Download the Latest Files
 6 NEW! Public Brand Software Forum
 7 Uploading Submissions
 8 Learn about Shareware and Freeware
 9 Leave a Comment

Enter choice !
```

ZiffNet, like CompuServe, costs $12 per hour. You can dial directly into ZiffNet, or get to the service from CompuServe by typing **GO ZIFFNET** or **GO ZNT**. By mail or phone it's

ZiffNet
10 Presidents Landing
Medford, MA 02155
(617) 393-3333

GEnie

GEnie, an on-line service run by GE Information Services, though not as large or as comprehensive as CompuServe, is still an excellent source of shareware, and it's cheaper as well. You pay a monthly fee of $4.95 for

Figure 1.3 The search menu for ZiffNet's Software Library

```
ZiffNet Library

SEARCH BY:

 1 Type of Utility
 2 Keyword
 3 PC Magazine Files
 4 PC/Computing Files
 5 PC Week Files
 6 File Name
 7 Date
 8 Author

Enter choice !
```

GEnie's basic services, and are then charged $6 per hour of connect time in non–prime time hours, or $18 per hour in prime time hours.

GEnie is organized into RoundTables, which are much like the forums on CompuServe. As on CompuServe, each one has its own library. On GEnie, you'll want to head over to the IBM RoundTable, which has probably the richest collection of shareware and public-domain programs on the service. The address and phone number are

GEnie
GE Information Services
Dept. 02B
401 North Washington St.
Rockville, MD 20850
(301) 340-4000

Call (800) 638-9636 for customer service.

Bulletin Boards

Electronic bulletin boards are probably the cheapest source of shareware you can find. There are thousands and thousands of these boards. You'll find at least one, and often several, near almost every hamlet and 'burg you can name.

All you need for getting onto these boards is a PC, a modem, a communication package, and a board's phone number. Bulletin boards generally have shareware libraries, as well as forums, conferences, electronic mail, message services, and far more. It's a more grass-roots, cheaper way to find shareware than any of the commercial services. In general, you only pay the cost of a phone call, although some of the larger bulletin boards have grown so large they've begun charging fees (albeit much smaller ones than the commercial services).

For a list of ASP-approved bulletin boards, turn to Appendix C. You can also write to

Association of Shareware Professionals
545 Grover Road
Muskegon, MI 49442

Directly from the Author

The final way to get shareware is directly from the author. To do this, you may have to send in a registration fee, although many authors will be willing to send you a version to try out before buying. They may also run bulletin boards from which you can download their programs. The most comprehensive list of shareware authors is maintained by the ASP. Write to the above address to get this list.

CHAPTER 2

Avoiding Viruses

What Is a Virus?

Symptoms of Infection

What to Do If You're Infected

Recovering from Infections

Reformatting Your Hard Disk

Practicing Safe Computing

VIRUSES ARE NO LONGER AN OCCASIONAL ODDITY OR A THEORETICAL nuisance—they've become an ever-present danger. Almost everyone knows someone who's been hit by them. I know of two major computer magazines and a metropolitan daily newspaper, as well as several acquaintances, who have been victimized.

Shareware has been the victim of guilt by association when it comes to viral attacks. Some people are leery of downloading files from bulletin boards, or using shareware at all, for fear of being attacked by an unwanted intruder. The truth is, most bulletin boards, on-line services, disk vendors, and shareware authors are meticulous about virus prevention, detection, and cure. They have to be, or they couldn't stay in business for long.

Still, the threat is real, and there are some basic precautions you should take when obtaining and using shareware (or any other software in fact, since even commercial, shrink-wrapped programs have been known to come with viruses attached). If you use common sense and practice safe computing, the odds are you'll never be infected.

What Is a Virus?

Viruses are nothing more than computer programs that have been designed to do damage rather than good. They're aptly named, since they bear a striking resemblance to biological viruses.

A biological virus needs a host in order to replicate itself. Once it invades a host—you, for example—it may lie dormant for years, undetected, until something triggers it or until you notice its symptoms. Or it may do its dirty work immediately.

Computer viruses operate in the same manner. In order to replicate themselves, they need a host to live in. Their hosts are the executable files on your computer (generally those ending in an .EXE or .COM extension). Viruses hide in these executable files, dormant, until the files are run. Then the virus springs to life; it searches out other executable files and attacks those as well.

A virus need not do damage to be classified a computer virus; it only needs to replicate itself in this manner. In fact, a virus called the Do-Nothing virus does no discernible harm at all. It simply lodges itself in executable files and then, as its name implies, doesn't do a thing.

But in the vast majority of cases, viruses do harm. The damage can be as innocuous as flashing phony messages on your screen, such as "I am hungry! Insert HAMBURGER into Drive A:" (one of the messages that the Joker virus sends across the screens of systems it infects). Or it can be as malicious as performing a low-level format of your hard drive, as is done by the Datacrime virus.

You get a virus by using infected software. Any new piece of software you put on your hard disk could harbor a virus, whether that software is downloaded from a bulletin board, bought at a store in shrink-wrap, or is pirated for you by a friend.

Viruses aren't the only type of destructive programs around; there are others as well, although they are not as common. For a description of these types of programs, see "Other Common Infections" below.

How a Virus Works

When an infected program enters your system, it can infect other files in a number of different ways, depending upon how it's been written. The virus can burrow itself into a .COM or .EXE file, becoming part of that executable file; or it can append itself to the executable file. Both generally happen so fast that there's no way for you to notice it occurring.

Some viruses will stay resident in your computer's memory as terminate-and-stay-resident programs (TSRs), making it easier for them to infect new programs. Others can alter the applications in which they live, and can even change a disk's boot sector so they can live there more easily.

But no matter how they work internally, viruses "piggyback" themselves onto other programs, then use those programs as launching pads to replicate themselves. They can then infect more programs, doing damage and trying to avoid detection along the way.

Viruses generally place messages, called *virus markers*, inside programs they've infected. They do this so that they don't keep reinfecting the same program time and time again, and can instead concentrate their efforts on uninfected files. Some of them only begin their destructive activity when they find no uninfected files.

Other Common Infections

Other kinds of destructive programs besides viruses can infect your PC: trojan horses, worms, and logic and time bombs. However, since viruses have gotten most of the publicity, all destructive programs are often referred to generically as viruses.

Trojan Horses are aptly named: They work just as the Trojan horse did in Greek mythology. The Trojan horse was a massive wooden horse left outside the walls of Troy. The Trojans hauled the horse in, assuming it to be a peace offering from their enemies, the Greeks. Hiding inside the horse were Greek soldiers, who slipped out of the horse after dark, opened the city's gates to the rest of the Greek army, and destroyed the city.

A trojan horse program attacks your PC in the same way. It appears to be a helpful application, but hidden inside it is a program doing damage invisibly.

You might be running what appears to be a game or graphics program, while actually a trojan horse is attacking your file allocation table (FAT).

Trojan horses don't replicate themselves, as viruses do. Instead, they do their damage when they're run disguised as applications.

Worms are designed to squirm through computer systems—and more commonly computer networks—and search out particular targets only. They act only on those targets. Sometimes worms gather information from networks, such as log-on names and passwords, and then send it back to the worm's creators, who then log into the system. Other times the worm may leave messages on the network or damage data. In general, worms are designed to wipe out all their traces so that no one knows a worm has been to visit. The most famous worm was one that infected the vast Internet network, bringing it to its knees when the worm replicated itself in an uncontrolled fashion.

Logic Bombs are programs that do their damage only when a certain set of circumstances exists; otherwise they remain innocuously in a computer system. Generally, logic bombs attack custom-written programs rather than off-the-shelf software. Cases of disgruntled former employees leaving destructive programs behind at their former workplaces often involve logic bombs. Logic bombs don't usually infect PCs since they're directed at specific, customized programs and a specific set of circumstances.

Time Bombs are similar to logic bombs, with a few important differences. They'll generally infect many different types of programs, not just one type. As their name implies, they're designed to go off at a specific time or date or after they've been run a specific number of times. When that time or date is reached, the program detonates and does its dirty work. The infamous Friday the 13th virus, which deletes whatever program it infects if that program is run on a Friday the 13th, is a time bomb. (The Friday the 13th time bomb is different from the Jerusalem virus, even though they do the same kind of damage.)

Common Viral Strains

Many different viral strains are in existence, and more are being written every day. The common, widespread ones are those most likely to infect your PC, however. A short listing of some of them follows.

The Jerusalem Virus may be perhaps the most well-known virus. This virus has many different strains, and goes by a number of different names, including the Israeli, Sunday, Black Hole, Russian, and PLO virus. It was first discovered in Israel, at Hebrew University, where it was designed to go off on Friday, May 13, 1988, the anniversary of the founding of Israel. Because of this, and because it was discovered in Israel, many people believe it was created by the PLO as an act of electronic terrorism.

It's been estimated that the Jerusalem virus is the cause of over half of all PC virus attacks. It has a number of different strains, all slightly different, but in general the virus attaches itself to .COM and .EXE files. Any infected program run on a Friday the 13th will be wiped off a hard disk.

The earliest variety had a bug that allowed it to keep reinfecting the same files, so it slowed the infected system down dramatically. Other variants destroy not just programs, but a hard disk's FAT. Another variety, the Century virus, has been designed to go off on January 1, 2000; it will zap your FAT on that date and write the words "Welcome to the 21st Century" on your screen. The Jerusalem virus will increase the size of .COM files by 1813 bytes, and the size of .EXE files by 1808 bytes.

The Columbus Day, October 13th, or Datacrime Virus gave viruses a great deal of publicity in October 1989. It was designed to go off on Columbus Day, and received a great deal of advance notice. Although not much actual damage was caused on that day, the virus is still floating around and presents a danger. Any program infected by this virus increases by 1,168 bytes. The program then slows, data is lost, and the hard disk is reformatted.

The Stoned or New Zealand Virus infects the boot sector of a hard disk. After every eight system bootups, it displays the message, "Your computer is now stoned. Legalize Marijuana." It can also cause data loss.

The Cascade, Falling Tears, or Falling Letters Virus infects .COM files, increasing their size by 1,704 bytes. Originally, it was a trojan horse that claimed it would turn off the NumLock key when a system was started, but in fact it made all the characters on a screen "fall" in a pile at the bottom of the screen. Later a hacker changed it to become a true virus that runs as a memory-resident program and infects .COM files, with the same results. Some strains increase .COM files by 1,701 bytes, and only attack systems with CGA or VGA monitors.

The Ping Pong Virus is a boot sector virus that activates randomly and makes a bouncing ball suddenly appear on the screen. To stop it, you have to reboot the system. Some strains only infect floppy disks; others attack hard disks as well.

The Pakistani Brain Virus was created at the Brain Computer Service store in Lahore, Pakistan. It infects the boot sector of a disk. One sign of infection is that the volume label of a disk is altered to read "(c) Brain." Originally it invaded only floppy disks, but a later variant attacks hard disks as well. One variety destroys the FAT on a hard disk.

Symptoms of Infection

Although there are many different types of viruses, the presence of some common symptoms on your PC should lead you to suspect that you've been infected. The existence of a symptom doesn't mean you've been infected; more often than not, something other than a virus is causing the problem. But if you experience any of the following behaviors, you should at least consider the possibility of a virus attack, and take action to detect the presence of a virus and then clean it up if you find one.

A Sluggish System may be the first sign of an attack. In particular, programs may take longer to load than they normally do. If you notice this happening, it may be because you've been hit with a virus that takes over the program's initial start-up procedures. During this extra start-up time, the virus is doing its dirty work.

Odd Disk Accesses are another danger sign. Your system may access several disks instead of just one, or it may access a disk more frequently or at odd times, so your hard disk light suddenly flashes on for no apparent reason. If you've been infected, you may notice that it takes a particularly long time to access a disk, even for a simple matter like storing a file.

Odd Error Messages that you've never noticed before are a warning sign as well. You should be especially suspicious if those error messages are not documented anywhere in the program you're running or in the DOS manual. Even normal error messages can spell danger: If a program suddenly starts flashing error messages when trying to complete an operation it used to perform flawlessly, it may be a sign of infection. Also beware if programs that were well-behaved before suddenly crash or behave oddly for no apparent reason.

A File's Sudden Disappearance or Appearance for no apparent reason should make you suspicious. Some viruses attack your PC by deleting files. Also watch out for directories that appear out of nowhere.

A Decrease in Available RAM could be because a virus has increased the size of your executable files, or is running as a TSR. If you notice a new TSR running when you're looking into memory (using DOS 5's MEM/CLASSIFY command or a program such as Quarterdeck's Manifest), you might have discovered a virus.

Executable Files Growing Larger for no apparent reason may be a sign that a virus has latched on. When a virus infects executable files, the virus commonly makes them larger by a certain number of bytes.

Your Hard Disk Suddenly Filling with Data indicates infection if there's no obvious explanation. It may mean that a virus has begun replicating, taking up more and more of your hard disk space.

If you notice any of these odd behaviors, suspect a virus and take immediate action.

What to Do If You're Infected

Let's assume the worst. You notice that your computer has been taking an unusually long time to load programs, and then see that the hard disk seems to fill up far faster than it should. You begin getting strange error messages, and your disk lights flash at odd times. You're pretty sure you have a virus. What to do?

Immediate Precautions to Take

First, turn off your PC at once. Take whatever floppy disks you've been using out of the drive, and note on their label that they may be infected with a virus. Then write-protect them: For 5 1/4-inch disks, place a tab over the notch at the disk's upper-right corner; for 3 1/2-inch disks, look for a small, black tab on the upper-left corner on the back of the disk and slide this tab to the up position, so that you uncover the small rectangular hole. If you have removable disk cartridges or streaming tape backups, remove them and label them as possibly being infected as well.

If you're connected to a network, call your network manager to make sure he or she knows of the potential virus attack and to ensure that you don't do any damage when you disconnect from the network. Then disconnect the network wires.

Write down all the symptoms that led you to believe you were infected by a virus. Pay particular note to unusual messages, files appearing or disappearing, increases in program sizes, and whether executable files changed size. This will help you identify the virus that may have infected you.

Now put a write-protected copy of your original DOS disk into your A drive, so that you can load DOS from the uninfected floppy disk, rather than from your infected hard disk. (Since you've write-protected the floppy disk, the virus can't attack it.) Boot up your PC with the write-protected DOS disk.

Using an Antiviral Program

Now you're ready to diagnose whether you've in fact been hit with a virus. You'll need a program designed to do this. There are a number of commercial programs available, but consider going the shareware route: Most major antiviral programs first appeared as shareware, and they're fast, time-tested, and efficient. Perhaps the most well-known is VIRUSCAN, from McAfee Associates. It's a program you should always have on hand to help you diagnose a virus attack.

Write-protect a disk with VIRUSCAN on it and place the disk in a drive. Then switch to that drive. If you want it to check your C drive for a virus, type

```
SCAN C:
```

If you have C and D drives, type

```
SCAN C: D:
```

The program will first check to see whether any viruses are running as TSRs, and then check your executable files for signs of infection. As it checks your files, it reports on its progress. Figure 2.1 shows VIRUSCAN checking a hard disk for a virus infection.

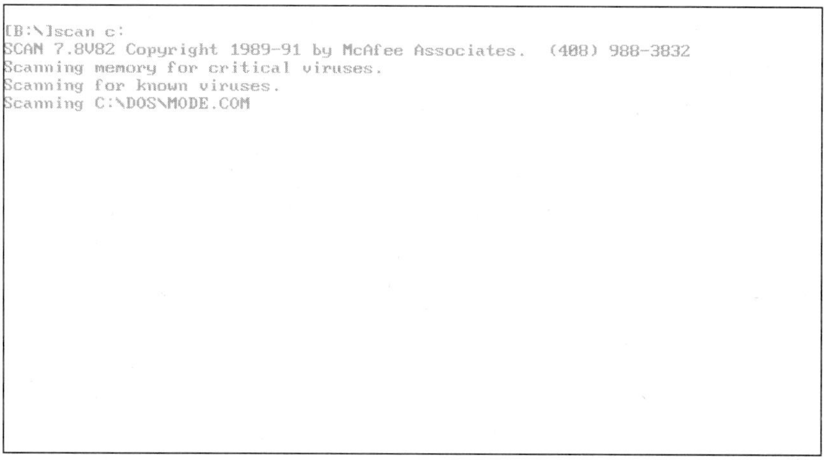

Figure 2.1 VIRUSCAN checking a hard disk for signs of infection

Note that the previous commands only check for the most common types of viruses that run as TSRs. For a more complete scan of TSR-type viruses, type

```
SCAN C: /M
```

Recovering from Infections

If VIRUSCAN reports that you've been infected, it allows you to delete the infected files. Let's say it finds that the program MINDREAD in the \MINDREAD directory has been infected with a virus. To eradicate the virus from it, you'd type

```
SCAN C:\MINDREAD\MINDREAD /D
```

Read on before you do this, however: VIRUSCAN would then delete the file infected with the virus, completely eradicating the file so that it cannot be recovered. Your file will be gone for good.

VIRUSCAN can't eradicate viruses that infect boot sectors and partition tables. To get rid of them, you'll have to use another McAfee program, CLEAN-UP. In general, CLEAN-UP may be better than VIRUSCAN in eradicating viruses, because CLEAN-UP will often be able to save your file when killing the virus. CLEAN-UP can kill viruses anywhere on your hard disk, not just those found in boot sectors and partition tables.

Another way to try to clear up a boot sector virus is by using the DOS SYS command. Put a write-protected DOS system disk in your A drive and type **SYS C:** at the prompt. This will overwrite infected programs with a new, uninfected copy. Be forewarned that this doesn't always work.

After you think you've rid yourself of all infected programs, run VIRUSCAN again, to make sure.

A word of warning about VIRUSCAN: Clever, malicious hackers have written and circulated bogus versions of the program. Disguised as antiviral software, these programs are actually trojan horses that do harm while users think they are disinfecting their computers. Versions 78 and 79 of VIRUSCAN were trojan horses, so if you see either of those versions floating around, avoid them.

For more information about VIRUSCAN, CLEAN-UP and other antiviral shareware programs, turn to Chapter 12.

Reformatting Your Hard Disk

At this point, you've eradicated all the known viruses from your system. You now have a decision to make: whether to reformat your hard disk. For absolute safety, you should take this step, even if you think all the viruses have been eliminated from your system. You don't want to take any chances, so do the safe thing and reformat.

Before reformatting, back up all your data files. Viruses don't infect them, so they're safe to keep. There are a lot of excellent shareware backup programs; turn to Chapter 11 for more information.

After you've copied your data files, read your DOS manual very carefully and reformat your disk. Then reinstall all your programs from the original software. It should now be safe to compute again.

Practicing Safe Computing

Of course, you'd rather not go through the detection and disinfection process—you'd rather that your PC wasn't infected in the first place. The good news is that if you practice safe computing, the odds are you'll never be hit with a virus. Even if you are, vigilance can ensure that the damage caused will be minimal.

The first and most often overlooked precaution is to make sure that other people don't use your computer. Even if they don't maliciously give your PC a virus, they may unintentionally run infected software on it. If you have a lock on your office door, use it. Some computers also have locks on them; when going home for the night, lock your PC and take the key with you. You can also install software on your hard disk that won't let anyone use your PC without the proper password. There are a number of shareware programs that do this, most notably PC-Vault (see Chapter 15).

Avoiding On-Line Dangers

In general, bulletin boards are safe, but you should still take some basic precautions. Remember that simply dialing into a bulletin board, browsing, reading, and leaving messages can't give you a virus. To get a virus you must download a program and then execute it.

For safe on-line computing, first check out the bulletin board itself. Find out how meticulous the system operator (sysop) is about screening new software, and whether the people who upload software are screened as well. The better-run boards will contact people who upload files by phone or mail, as a security measure. They'll also carefully check every new upload for viruses.

If the bulletin board has pirated software on it (commercial software illegally copied and distributed) then stay away. Clearly, the sysop is not a meticulous type, and downloading software from this board may lead to a virus infection. Consider that the hackers who uploaded the pirated software were able to beat the software's copy-protection schemes. They're probably capable of writing a nasty virus as well.

Even when you've found a bulletin board that appears to be reputable, take care. Don't download programs directly onto your hard disk. Instead, download them onto a blank, formatted floppy.

Before running a program, examine it. Does it promise more than its file size indicates? If it's a small .COM file, made up of only 512 bytes, and claims to be a relational database, suspect a virus and don't run it. Check for well-written documentation, including the author's name, address, and telephone number. If there's no documentation, or if it doesn't include names and addresses, don't take a chance by running the program.

Also look into the program code for any odd messages or suspicious comments. A number of shareware programs, including the superb List program, will let you do this. (For more about List, see Chapter 9.) Some virus writers can't resist the temptation of leaving nasty messages inside their programs.

Next, check the file size of your program against the file size in the documentation. If your documentation says the program is one size, but your disk says it's another, something might be amiss. You can also check for a program's file integrity: McAfee Associates' VALIDATE program can be used to tell whether a shareware program has been tampered with and therefore may contain a virus. (See Chapter 12 for more information about VALIDATE.)

Once you've given the program these checks, you can run it—but first only from the floppy. As you run it, look for any suspicious behavior. Watch out if files change size. Record the size of your COMMAND.COM file before running the program, and see if it changes size after the program is run. Examine other key files, such as CONFIG.SYS, as well.

If you have an old PC laying around unused, consider using it as your testing machine. Download to a floppy on that machine, rather than your main PC. After it seems secure on the floppy, test it out on that machine. If there are no signs of viruses after a while, you can safely use the software on your main computer.

If you don't have that option, after running the software from your floppy, consider waiting before putting it on your hard disk. Contact the shareware author and get an evaluation copy directly from the source, which will undoubtedly be virus-free.

If you do put the program on your hard disk, confine it to its own subdirectory. Some viruses have a hard time jumping across subdirectories, so if the new program does contain a virus, it may only damage data and files in its subdirectory. *Never* put the program in your root directory.

Avoiding Dangers from Floppy Disks

Bear in mind that the floppy disks you exchange with friends or co-workers may be infected. Indeed, some people believe that contaminated disks, not bulletin boards, are the primary vehicle for virus infections.

Whenever you're given a disk with a program on it, treat it as if it might have a virus. Subject it to the same scrutiny as you do files you download from bulletin boards, and follow the precautions outlined above. Be particularly wary of pirated software. Using such software is illegal, and you don't know how many hands it's passed through or how careful everyone along the way has been about watching out for viruses.

Never lend out your original program disks. If the person you're lending the disk to has an infected PC, your disk could become infected. Then, when you use it, you may infect your own computer. If you do lend out programs (and you should only do so if you are legally allowed to), hand out a copy only. And if you get the disk back, reformat it to kill any viruses.

If you're buying a new piece of software, and it's not in its original packaging or the shrink wrap is broken, bring it back to where you bought it. Some dealers allow buyers to return software even after it's been used, and you might have such a piece of software. A virus might have been placed on it, deliberately or accidentally. Also realize that even shrink wrap is no guarantee you're getting virus-free software—dealers can rewrap used software.

For shareware, register the program and run the copy you get from its author. There's no better way to guarantee virus-free shareware.

General Precautions for Avoiding Viruses

There are also a number of general precautions you can take to avoid infection. Write-protect COMMAND.COM and other executable files by changing their status to read-only, so that viruses can't attack them. To do this, you can use DOS's ATTRIB command. A simpler way is to use a good shareware hard disk manager. (For a selection of disk managers, turn to Chapter 8.)

Use write-protect tabs on the floppy disks you use to store data. This will prevent viruses from infecting them. Whenever you get a new, clean piece of software, make a backup disk immediately. Make sure to check executable files regularly for changes in size, too.

Back up your hard disk frequently. Although it won't prevent virus infections, it will at least ensure that you won't lose all your data if you're hit with a particularly nasty one.

You should also use some kind of virus prevention or detection software regularly. Prevention software is designed to stop viruses from infecting your PC, whereas detection software will immediately raise a flag if an intruder enters. There are a great many shareware products that do either of these.

Ross Greenberg's Flu_Shot+, for example, runs as a TSR and watches your system for signs of infection. If it notices a TSR start to run that you haven't told it about, it will warn you that a virus might be on the loose. It also automatically checks programs every time they run to see whether they've changed since you last ran them and warns you if they have.

McAfee's VSHIELD also runs as a TSR and scans for viruses as programs are loaded into memory. His VCOPY program replaces the DOS COPY command and scans for viruses as it copies programs to your disk. SENTRY, also from McAfee, monitors system areas prone to attack. (For more information about shareware antiviral software, see Chapter 12.)

So far you've seen the basics of using shareware and how to avoid virus infections. You're now ready for Part II—a look at the best shareware programs available in a variety of categories.

PART

2

The Programs

CHAPTER

3

Word Processors, Text Editors, and Add-ins

Word Processors

Text Editors

Outliners, Style Checkers, and Dictionaries

Add-ins for Commercial Word Processors

PEOPLE SPEND MORE TIME WRITING THAN AT ANY OTHER TASK ON A PC. So it's no surprise that the number and variety of shareware word processing and text editing programs is almost mind-boggling. While most shareware word processors tend to have fewer features than their commercial counterparts, several of them rival or exceed traditionally sold word processors. Windows compatibility, however, is another matter. As of this writing, several shareware text editors, but no major shareware word processors, have been written for Windows. Most, if not all, DOS-based programs, however, will run in a DOS window.

WordStar fans will exult in shareware word processors and text editors: Many programs use the one-time word processing giant's key combinations. Non-WordStar fans need not worry, however, since most programs also include alternate key combinations or easy-to-use menus.

Shareware text editors abound; there are far more shareware text editors than commercial ones, and they tend to be of a higher quality. There are also more shareware word processing utilities and add-ins than you can imagine—at least one is available for any task, no matter how small or narrow its appeal may be.

Listed below are a tiny fraction of the word processors, text editors, and related programs available as shareware. Spend some time on any bulletin board, and you'll find far more.

Word Processors

Word processors were among the first shareware programs ever written. Two of shareware's founding fathers created word processors: Quicksoft's Bob Wallace, who wrote PC-Write, and Jim Button, who created PC-Type. These venerable programs are still among the best shareware ever written.

The line between shareware word processors and text editors is small, but in general word processors concern themselves not only with entering words and moving them around, but also with how they look in print. They often include spell checkers, word counters, mail-merge features, the ability to create multiple windows, and other extras that have become commonplace in the commercial world.

Most shareware word processors make trade-offs between the size of the program and the power it offers. Some, like PC-Write, have become so large that they've spawned less-powerful, easier-to-use versions. Others, like Galaxy Lite, opt for fewer features so that they're still small enough to take along on a laptop. Below are the best you'll find.

Galaxy Lite

Galaxy Lite is an exceptionally easy-to-use word processor—which is quite a surprise, considering its depth and set of features.

For example, it lets you balance ease of use and power by letting you issue commands in several different ways. It features drop-down menus for those just learning the program, those who use word processors only occasionally, or those who simply like menus. Pressing F10 brings up the menu. A nice touch is easy mouse support: Click on the top of the screen and menus drop down. A scroll bar down the right-hand side lets you scroll through text using the mouse, à la Windows.

You can open two windows at once and easily switch between the two by going through the menu, clicking on the alternate screen with a mouse, or using the Alt-W key combination.

Galaxy Lite features a 50,000-word dictionary and macro writing facilities as well. It's a good program to take on the road, since the main executable file takes up only 74k.

A commercial version of the program, Galaxy Pro-Lite, costs $60 and has extra features, including more sophisticated printing and a larger dictionary.

Galaxy Lite
Registration fee: $
Starlite Software Co.
P.O. Box 370
Port Hadlock, WA 98339
(206) 437-0116; (800) 767-9611 (orders only)

New York Word

New York Word straddles the middle ground between word processors and text editors. When you first boot it up (type **WP**), you're greeted with a blank screen, which is a little disconcerting in a word processor. When you press Alt-M, though, a reassuring drop-down menu appears across the top of the screen. New York Word allows you to create footnotes, create and use macros, create and edit in multiple windows, and use different fonts. You can also create headers and footers, search for orphans and widows (single words left at the end of paragraphs or at the top of a page), do math calculations, create tables, and justify text. And if you just can't stand that blank screen, hit Alt-T and you'll get a simple ruler across the bottom of your screen.

For reasons not fully understood by the program's author, New York Word has become popular with lawyers. It's a fast and easy editor, there's no doubt about that, but beyond that, I can't understand it either. Go figure.

New York Word
Registration fee: $$
Marc Adler
Magma Systems
15 Bodwell Terrace
Millburn, New Jersey 07041

PC-Type

PC-Type is one of the granddaddies of shareware. Like PC-Write (see below), it's a powerful, full-featured word processor, with as many bells and whistles as its more expensive, commercial brethren. Jim Button, one of shareware's founding fathers, wrote this program, and it has withstood the test of time.

Like most other shareware word processors, PC-Type allows you to store files in ASCII format, so you can easily share text with other word processors and text editors. This means you can use PC-Type to edit files such as AUTOEXEC.BAT and CONFIG.SYS (although you'd be better off using a smaller text editor, as discussed later in this chapter). You also have the option of storing the file in PC-Type's own format.

The program takes up about 1.5 megabytes of hard disk space, which gives you some idea of how comprehensive it is. Name a feature—any feature—and the odds are that PC-Type has it. It covers all the word processing functions, both basic and high-end, that you'd find anywhere else. It performs word counts, has a 100,000-word dictionary for spell-checking, lets you draw lines and boxes, includes the ability to create and save macros, and lets you open multiple windows. Figure 3.1 shows three files open in PC-Type.

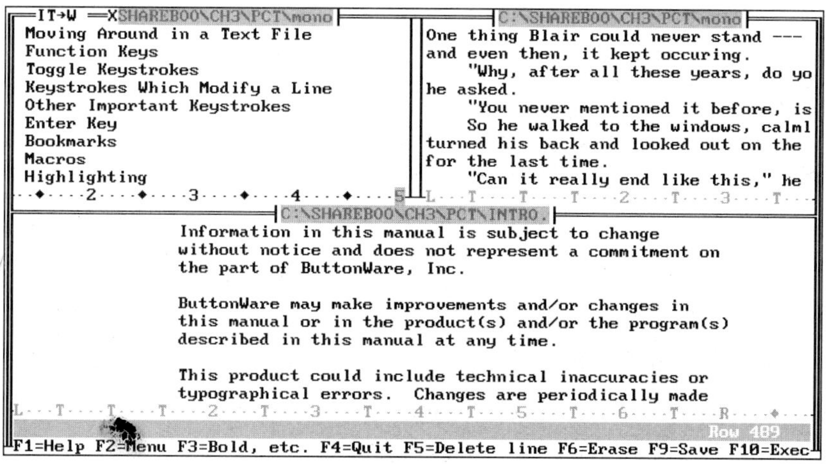

Figure 3.1
Working with multiple files in PC-Type

One of the things that separates many shareware word processing programs from commercial ones is graphics support. Shareware programs often fall short of their commercial counterparts here, but PC-Type doesn't scrimp. In addition to its ability to draw lines and boxes, it includes a facility for graphing data in bar and pie charts and in scatter diagrams. It also allows you to include and print graphics created with the GIF graphics file format.

Particularly nice is the program's ability to perform mail-merge tasks, which you can use to send out form letters and mass mailings. It also has a math calculator. And if all this isn't enough, there's a program included to help you with your Sunday crossword puzzles.

Another sign of the program's attention to detail: when you exit, it gives you vital information about the last file you edited, including its size and the number of words it contains.

Despite all this power, PC-Type remains easy to use. You can execute commands from the keyboard or go through the program's menus instead. As you work, a line across the bottom of the screen lists the uses of the major function keys. Context-sensitive help is easily reached by pressing the F1 key. Pressing F2 brings up the main menu, so you have all the power of the program at your fingertips.

Note that the developer, ButtonWare, although it still supports PC-Type, has gone commercial with its new products. It's concentrating on developing its PC-File database program further and will no longer be creating new products for the shareware market.

PC-Type
Registration fee: $$$
ButtonWare, Inc.
P.O. Box 96058
Bellevue, WA 98009
(206) 454-0479; (800) JBUTTON (orders only)

PC-Write

PC-Write is probably the best-known of the shareware word processors, and it may be the most powerful one as well. You'll find everything here you'd expect in a full-featured word processor: easy printer control, sophisticated editing functions, a spell checker, a powerful macro facility, the ability to create and work in multiple windows, and far more. You'll even find features that let you create tables of contents and indexes.

A great deal of thought has gone into stitching all of this together. Not only is the program well-integrated, but it has elegant touches you won't find elsewhere. For example, it lets you manage files without having to exit to DOS. And when you're editing a file, to change text from uppercase to lowercase, or vice versa, just hit the F8 key and the selected text will change immediately.

One particularly nice feature is that while you're printing one file, you can be working on another, something that few word processors of any stripe allow. Like most shareware word processors, it writes clean ASCII text so its output can easily be used with other programs.

The spell checker allows you to use a kind of shorthand in your text; you type only a few letters, and PC-Write fills in the rest. For example, let's say you use the phrase *in my humble opinion* a great deal. Let PC-Write know you want *IMHO* to be expanded to that phrase, and it will make the change automatically whenever it encounters *IMHO*.

PC-Write's Typewriter mode is also innovative; it lets you type directly to your printer, as if you were using a typewriter. You'll find this useful for solving the worst bugaboo of word processors: addressing envelopes.

A superb help system is always close at hand. You access it by pressing F1 twice. The top part of the screen shows the help options. As you scroll through the options, the bottom part of the screen shows the help text itself, which is pithy, to the point, and simple to follow. See Figure 3.2 for a typical help screen.

Figure 3.2
A sample PC-Write help screen

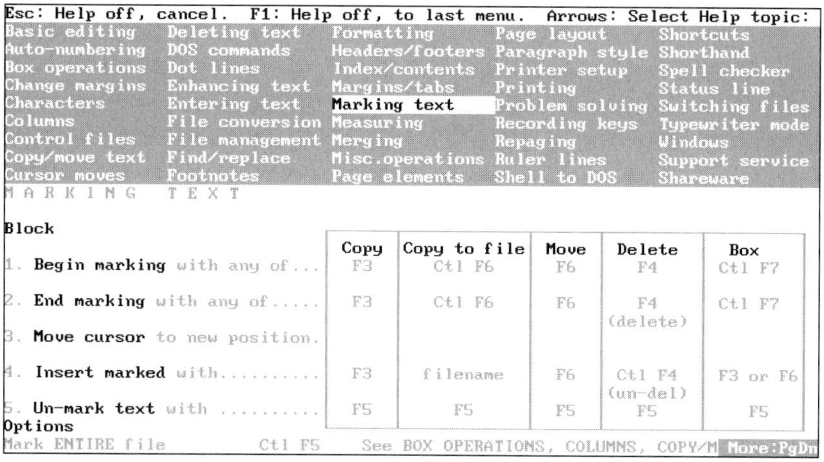

Normally when writing or editing in PC-Write, there will be a ruler near the top of the screen. Above that ruler is a menu listing function keys. The menu changes according to the function you're performing. This makes PC-Write easy to use without slowing you down as you learn it. Once you become more expert you can just press the function key without referring to the menu.

Some shareware word processors scrimp when it comes to printer support. They don't support a wide variety of printers, and even when they do they may not support all internal fonts. That's one place that PC-Write shines. It supports a dazzling array of printers, and it gives you access to their fonts as well.

Creating and working with windows is simplicity itself. If you're working in one window and want to create another, put your cursor where you want the new window to be and press F2. Figure 3.3 shows two windows open at once. To jump between windows, press F2 and then the Up Arrow key to move to the top window or the Down Arrow key to move to the bottom window. Moving text between windows is just as easy.

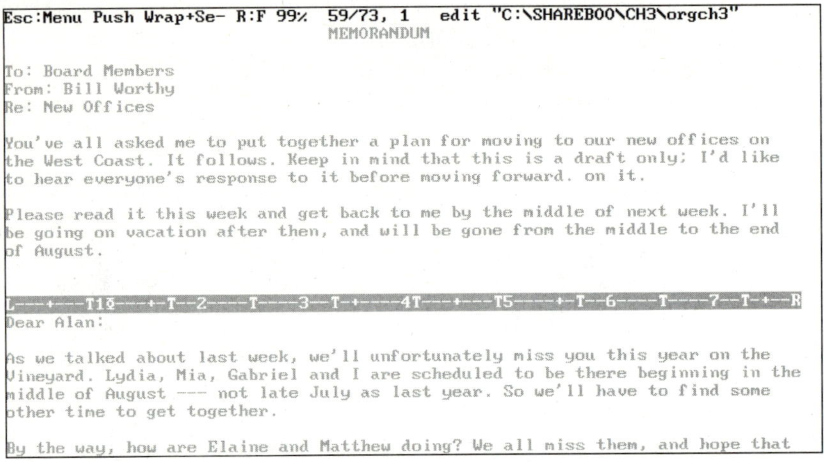

Figure 3.3
Two files active at once in PC-Write

PC-Write has drawing tools for drawing boxes around text. It can also create newspaper-style columns and perform mail-merge operations. In fact, there's little this program won't do.

PC-Write takes up about 460k of hard disk space (the main executable file takes up 262k of that). Quicksoft offers a year of telephone support with your registration, as well as a helpful newsletter.

PC-Write
Registration fee: $$$$
Quicksoft
219 First Ave. N, #224
Seattle, WA 98109
(206) 282-0452; (800) 888-8088 (orders only)

PC-Write Lite

Everything you always wanted in PC-Write, and less. PC-Write Lite is a slimmed-down version of Quicksoft's PC-Write. It's faster, easier to use, and takes up less disk space than its fuller-featured older sibling. Beginners in particular will like the smaller manual and easier-to-get-at formatting features. Writers will appreciate its extra speed, and laptop users will appreciate its smaller size (150k). Everyone will appreciate its smaller price.

Be warned, however, that with PC-Write Lite you give up the advanced features of PC-Write. You won't be able to do fancy formatting with it: There's no access to proportional fonts and you can't create multiple columns. It won't allow you to do mail merges, either. But for basic, straightforward word processing, this is a top choice.

PC-Write Lite
Registration fee: $$$
Quicksoft
219 First Ave. N, #224
Seattle, WA 98109
(206) 282-0452; (800) 888-8088 (orders only)

PC-Write Standard Level

PC-Write became a word-processing family when PC-Write Standard Level was introduced in the fall of 1991. Standard Level is an intriguing program, and you can expect commercial software to begin picking up on some of the concepts it introduces.

Generally, PC-Write Standard Level falls between PC-Write and PC-Write Lite in sophistication; it's more powerful than Lite, but still lacks some of PC-Write's advanced features, such as column support. It has pull-down menus, context-sensitive help, and a built-in conversion tool for translating WordPerfect files. The most interesting part of the product, however, is the level of customization it allows. By creating what it calls a *profile*, you define the features you want PC-Write to have, as well as the features you want left out. You further customize it by defining how those features will look and feel. You can, for example, edit the pull-down menus or create your own.

PC-Write Standard Level
Registration fee: $$$$
Quicksoft
219 First Ave. N, #224
Seattle, WA 98109
(206) 282-0452; (800) 888-8088 (orders only)

WordMaster

WordMaster is a slick, easy-to-run word processor that gives you many of the features of far more expensive programs at a low price.

Press F1, and a menu pops up at the top of your screen, allowing you to easily access WordMaster's many features. For those who become more familiar with the program, the same functions can be accessed via the keyboard.

WordMaster has the ability to open multiple files; record, save, and use macros; change text and font attributes; and control the look of your printed documents in a number of ways.

Of particular note are WordMaster's search and replace functions. Unlike many word processors—even of the expensive, commercial varieties—WordMaster will let you search within a defined block of text. One drawback: It doesn't have its own spell checker, even though that function is listed on its menus. For spell-checking, you'll have to install Turbo Lightning, from Borland International.

WordMaster
Registration fee: $
MasterWorks
P.O. Box 116
McLeary, WA 98557

Text Editors

There are more shareware text editors than you can shake a stick at. Even listing the best of them is beyond the scope of this book, so I've concentrated on reviewing only the best of the best.

Text editors have several things in common. They often imitate WordStar commands or have simple menus to follow. They concentrate more on moving words than on how those words will look on paper. They create pure ASCII text. They also tend to be inexpensive.

Programmers particularly favor text editors for their speed and ability to write ASCII text. A good text editor is invaluable for everyone else, as well, especially for editing and creating AUTOEXEC.BAT, CONFIG.SYS, and similar files.

Boxer

Forget everything you thought you knew about text editors—that they're bare-bones programs with only the most basic of editing commands. Boxer proves that all wrong. This remarkable program is fast like other text editors, simple like other text editors, and menu-driven like other text editors. It also includes hooks to compilers and so is useful as a programmer's editor. But there its similarities to other text editors end—because Boxer has many functions normally found only in full-blown word processors.

Boxer's commands are reached using a menu that drops down from the top of the screen (see Figure 3.4). To activate the menu, press F1. You'll find all the editing commands, file commands, and printing commands that you

You load the program by typing **Q**, followed by the file name you want to edit or create. In a flash, the program loads, complete with your file. The top of your screen gives you information about the file you're working on: its name and location, what line you're on, and where your cursor is on that line.

Press the Esc key, and a menu pops up at the top of your screen, from which you can easily access QEdit's many functions (see Figure 3.5). You can edit in multiple windows, create and use macros, search for text, and set margins. Almost any editing command you need is within easy reach. If you decide to forgo menus, you can use QEdit with keystrokes as well.

Figure 3.5

QEdit's main menu

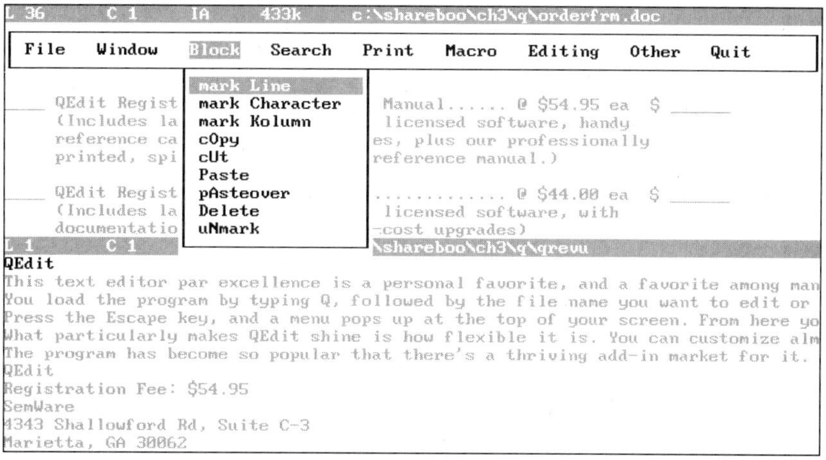

Flexibility is QEdit's strong suit. You can customize almost anything about the program with the companion QCONFIG.EXE program. You can customize the keyboard, defining which functions you want assigned to which keys. You can place the menu at the bottom rather than the top of the screen. You can even create your own help screens.

The program has become so popular that there's a thriving add-in market for it. You'll find many shareware programs that enhance QEdit's capabilities with mouse support, macros, and even WordPerfect 5.0 keystrokes. There's also a TSR version of QEdit available from its author.

QEdit
Registration fee: $$
SemWare
4343 Shallowford Road, Suite C-3
Marietta, GA 30062
(404) 641-9002

Ravitz Editor

Probably the most interesting thing about this text editor is its interface. You may find it confusing at first, but once you get the hang of it, you'll find it quicker than most menu-based programs. To execute commands, you type mnemonic commands at the command line (type **e** to edit a file, for example). To switch between the file and the command line, press the Esc key. Help is accessed by pressing F1, and F2 accesses a menu. The Ravitz Editor includes outlining functions, as well.

Ravitz Editor
Registration fee: $
Ravitz Software Inc.
P.O. Box 25068
Lexington, KY 40524

Tiny Word

A bare-bones text editor, Tiny Word has one big thing going for it: its small size. Taking up a minuscule 7k of disk space, this is an ideal text editor for your laptop. Don't expect anything fancy; nothing but basic features have been included to keep Tiny Word's size down to an absolute minimum. To print, you'll need a companion program, called (unsurprisingly) Tiny Print.

There are no menus to work from in Tiny Word, but those used to WordStar commands will find themselves on familiar ground. If you can't remember the WordStar commands, press F1 and you'll have a help file and editing commands close at hand.

Tiny Word & Tiny Print
Registration fee: $
Loys Software Development
1276 Crystal St.
Los Angeles, CA 90031

VDE

VDE straddles the line between text editing and full-blown word processing, although it doesn't come with the advanced features usually included in a word processor. It's small and fast, making it perfectly suited for writing and editing on a laptop. You can operate in command mode, entering commands directly from the keyboard, or elect to have a menu at the top of the screen for help. Press the Esc key to bring up the menu bar.

VDE has facilities for creating macros, for counting words in a file, for working in multiple windows, and for programming function keys. If you're looking for fast editing and a small program well suited for laptops, VDE is a solid choice.

VDE
Registration fee: Whatever you want to pay
Eric Meyer
401 12th Ave. SE, #139
Norman, OK 73071

WinEdit

WinEdit, a programmer's editor for Windows, can be used as a top-notch Windows text editor as well. It's fast and simple, it reads and creates ASCII text, and it's exceptionally easy to install: Simply copy two files—WINEDIT.EXE and WINEDIT.HLP—to a directory, add the program with the Windows Program Manager as you would any other Windows program, and you're ready to go. You'll find the usual pull-down menus across the top of the screen. An icon bar appears across the top of the screen as well, giving you access to common commands such as opening, creating, printing, and saving files, and cutting, pasting, and searching for text. Figure 3.6 shows how to search for text in WinEdit.

Another nice touch is that WinEdit lets you access all your Windows fonts, so you can create nice-looking output, a rarity for a text editor, and difficult even for many non-Windows word processors. It even lets you print headers and footers. And, of course, if you're a programmer, it gives you a variety of programmers' tools.

This program is superior in every way to Windows's Notepad. Though it doesn't approach the power of Word for Windows or Ami Pro, it's an excellent text editor. If you're looking for a solid Windows text editor, consider WinEdit.

WinEdit
Registration fee: $$
Wilson WindowWare, Inc.
2701 California Ave. SW, Suite 212
Seattle, WA 98116
(800) 762-8383

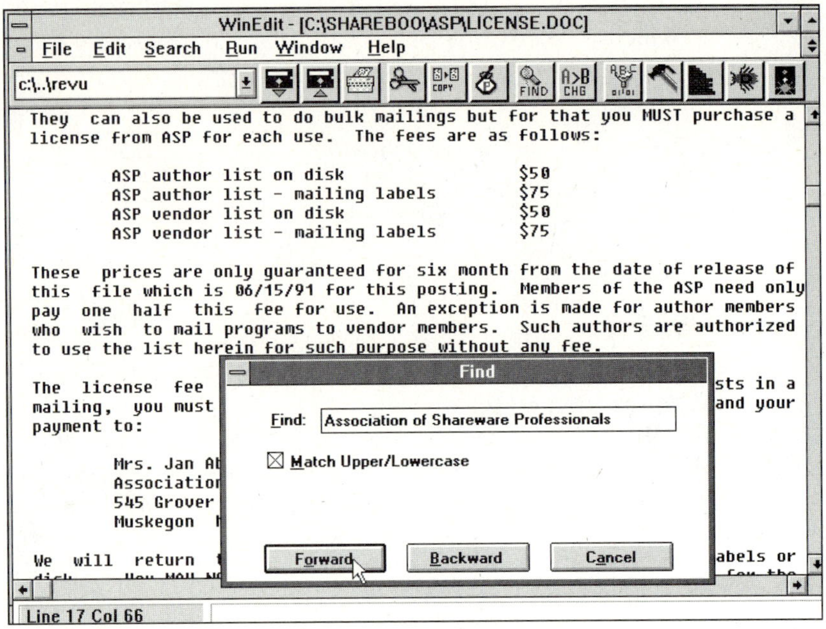

Figure 3.6

Searching for text in WinEdit

Outliners, Style Checkers, and Dictionaries

Entering and editing text using a word processor or text editor is often the easiest part of writing. The hardest part are those miscellaneous tasks: outlining your work before you begin, finding the exact word to express your thoughts, and making sure the document contains no spelling errors and is written in the best possible style. Below is a grab bag of programs to help you get through these tasks more easily.

Babble!

Ever wonder what Shakespeare would sound like if he had a Yiddish accent? Or how one of the President's speeches would sound scrambled and in Pig Latin? Now you'll know, with one of the strangest writing tools every created. Babble! takes samples of text, analyzes them, mixes them in various proportions, and then creates random babbles with them. It's like a sound-mixing studio, except you combine words rather than music.

To make the scrambled results even more entertaining, you can add special effects to the babble: various ethnic accents, Pig Latin (as shown in Figure 3.7), and more. Of course, not all text will sound different babbled than it did originally. As the program's documentation notes: "We tried it on legal boilerplate, but the stuff that came out sounded just like the stuff that went in!"

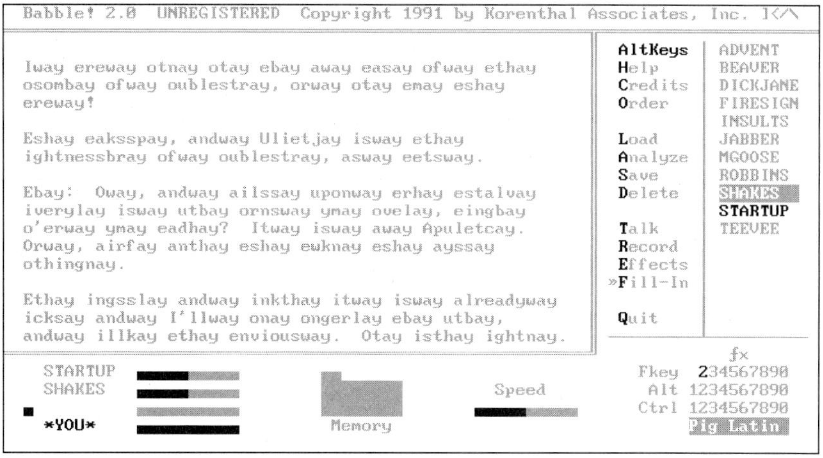

Figure 3.7
Shakespeare in Pig Latin

Babble!
Registration fee: $
Korenthal Associates, Inc.
230 West 13th St.
New York, NY 10011
(212) 242-1790; (800) KAPROGS (orders only)

Jorj

This dictionary functions as either a stand-alone program or a memory-resident one. When memory resident, however, it takes up 84k, so make sure you have room for it. It has definitions for 58,000 words (you'll find *heliotrope* here, but not *maculate*), and it's exceedingly simple to use. To make it memory-resident, type

```
Jorj *
```

To pop it up in the middle of an application, type Alt-J. Then enter the word you're looking for, and you'll get its definition.

Jorj goes beyond normal dictionaries, too. If you don't know how a word is spelled, spell it the way it sounds, and Jorj will look for it based on its pronunciation. You can also use it to create a list of words that have your given word in their definition. This is helpful for building lists from the dictionary. For example, type **vegetable**, and Jorj will list all the words with *vegetable* in their definition, in essence building a list of vegetables it finds. You can also browse through Jorj in the same way you would a printed dictionary.

Jorj
Registration fee: $
Jorj Software Co.
4354 Fletcher Road
Manchester, MI 48158

PC-Index

Don't even *think* of trying to compile an index by hand. It's one of the most frustrating, difficult, and time-consuming tasks you'll ever face. PC-Index makes the task easier. It will automatically create an index for you based on the words or phrases you want indexed—either ones you enter or those you have marked in a text file.

PC-Index
Registration fee: $$
Help Software
16706 Bradley Court
Belton, MO 64012
(816) 331-5809

PC-Outline

One of the simplest ways to get ideas down on paper is to write a clean, clear outline. But creating such an outline is not easy using most word processors and text editors.

PC-Outline has one reason for existence: to help you create outlines. And it does its job superbly. With it, you can enter thoughts and ideas randomly, later organizing them in outline fashion. You can hide and unhide levels of detail, so you can view either the most important or least important ideas at a time. You can easily print the outline or import it into your word processor. You can also have up to nine outlines on your screen at once. Add text editing features such as search and replace and block operations, and you have an outlining powerhouse. Figure 3.8 shows a typical outline created with the program.

PC-Outline can be accessed through menus or keystrokes, so it's quite flexible. Of particular importance is its ability to work as a memory-resident program, so you can always have your outlines close at hand.

PC-Outline
Registration fee: $$$
Brown Bag Software
2155 South Bascom Ave.
Campbell, CA 95008
(408) 559-4545

Figure 3.8
Creating an outline with PC-Outline

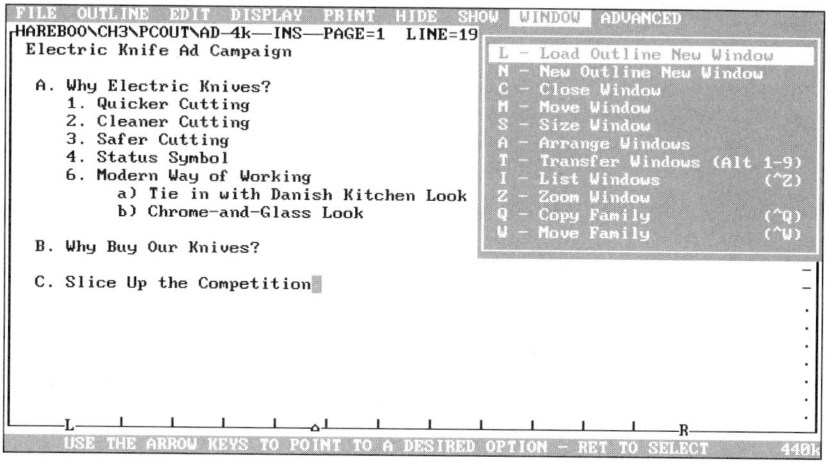

Readability Plus

Do you like numbers better than words? If so, this program may be for you. Readability Plus is completely different than any style checker you've ever seen. You feed it a piece of text, and it proceeds to do a thoroughgoing *mathematical* analysis of your writing.

The program creates four different indexes for analyzing your style, based on factors such as average sentence, word, and paragraph length, as shown in Figure 3.9. It also does what it calls a "mortar and bricks" analysis, checking what percentage of your words are in common usage (the mortar) and what percentage are more rare (the bricks), as shown in Figure 3.10.

If all this sounds rather dry, it's not—in fact, one of Readability Plus's greatest charms is its entertaining screens. It charts its findings about your writing in colorful detail, using countless screens filled with attractive charts and graphs. The program compares your results against ideal models of different kinds of writing, such as fiction, ad copy, general writing, and bureaucracy-speak.

The program originally was sold commercially for $129.95. When the parent company released a more powerful style checker, called Corporate Voice, it turned Readability Plus into shareware. Readability Plus is pretty, it claims to be scientific, and it's fun to use. But is it useful? Run it once. Then you be the judge.

Readability Plus
Registration fee: $
Scandinavian PC Systems
6 Nelson St.
Rockville, MD 20850
(301) 294-7450

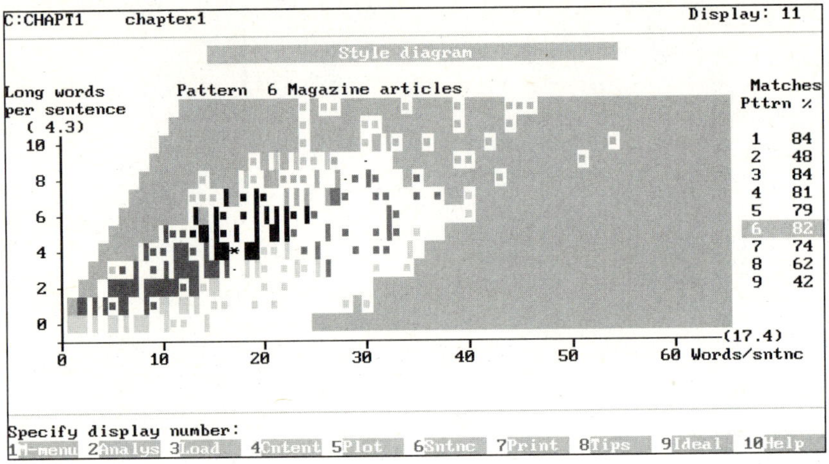

Figure 3.9
Readability Plus comparing a given writing style to any of nine ideal types

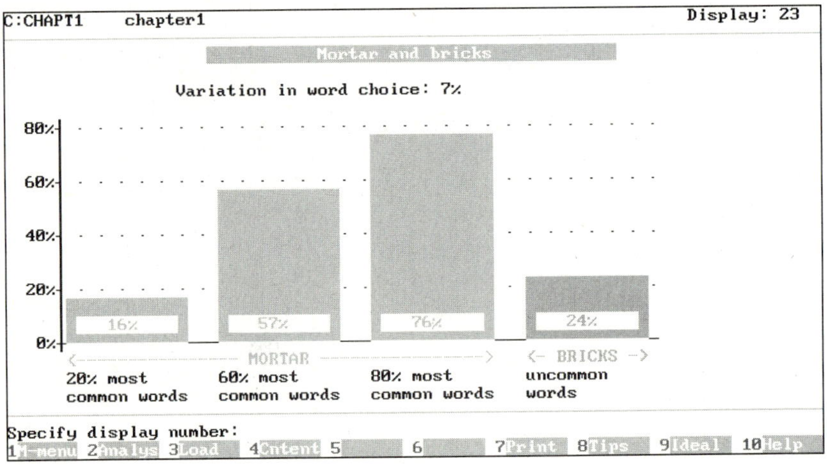

Figure 3.10
Readability Plus performing a "mortar and bricks" analysis of a writing sample

ShareSpell

Spelling errors are a bugaboo for many of us: The best-written report looks silly when you've spelled *accountability* incorrectly. ShareSpell solves this problem. It checks text files for incorrectly spelled words and makes suggestions you can use to correct them. One of this program's strengths is how easily it can be customized. For instance, you can add words to the dictionary or remove them. ShareSpell also lets you correct words manually if none of its suggestions is the word you want.

ShareSpell
Registration fee: $
Acropolis Software
P.O. Box 5037
Fair Oaks, CA 95628

Thesaur/Plus

How many times have you fumbled for the precise word you need to convey a shade of meaning, but come up empty-handed? With Thesaur/Plus, you'll search no more. This excellent thesaurus runs in memory-resident mode (taking up only 23k), so lists of synonyms are always at hand.

One of this program's best features is how easy it is to customize. You can change screen colors, assign a hot key to activate the program, and add and delete synonyms.

Thesaur/Plus
Registration fee: $
Derrick Burgess
23311 Schoolcraft St., #1
West Hills, CA 91307
(818) 347-2910

Add-ins for Commercial Word Processors

There are hundreds of shareware and freeware add-ins, macros, and improvements available for almost every word processor you can name. I've listed only a few here, to give a sample of the kind of variety you'll find both in shareware products and those available for free. On-line services such as CompuServe are brimming with these types of programs. Indeed, WordPerfect add-ins and macros alone have become a thriving cottage industry. There's also a great deal of variety to be found in Word for Windows add-ins and macros.

dtSearch

dtSearch is a text search-and-retrieval program for use with WordPerfect 5.0 and 5.1, WordStar, Microsoft Word, Word for Windows, MultiMate Advantage II, and ASCII files. It offers a great deal of flexibility in searching for text: You can search through an index or database you've created, for instance, or have it do a search of any document you specify.

You can do simple searches for individual words or phrases, or combine several of its search parameters with Boolean operators for more complex searches. Its real advantage, however, is its ability to use context when searching, so that you can search for words based on their relationship to other words. You could, for example, tell dtSearch to find every occurrence of the word *housing* when it is within 15 words of *mortgage*.

dtSearch
Registration fee: $$
DT Software, Inc.
2101 Crystal Plaza Arcade, Suite 231
Arlington, VA 22202

FAX.WPM

This is actually a macro with a single use: It creates cover sheets for fax transmissions and allows you to edit them. In addition to creating the cover sheet, it can also put in the recipient's firm name and fax number automatically. You can also use it to create a directory of fax numbers.

FAX.WPM
Registration fee: None
Available on CompuServe and other bulletin boards, often as WPFAX.ZIP.

MacroAid and WPTools

A collection of DOS utilities that adds power to WordPerfect macros, MacroAid works with macros for WordPerfect 5.0 and 5.1, PlanPerfect 5.0 and 5.1, DrawPerfect 1.0 and 1.1, ED 3.0, and Shell 3.0. Aimed at the hardcore macro creator, it's essentially a collection of tools to help users write more useful macros. The utilities are all run from the command line and do a variety of tasks, such as allow you to run self-modifying macros, convert macros to ASCII text or to WordPerfect files for easier editing, and compress macros so they load and run more quickly.

WPTools, a separate program from the same author, is a collection of utilities for WordPerfect 5.0 and 5.1 that permit you to do various useful things, such as extract comments from a 5.0 file and write them to standard output, search a directory for soft fonts, and convert all footnotes to endnotes and vice versa. The author also has several other WordPerfect add-ins.

MacroAid and WPTools
Registration fee: $
David Seidman
2737 Devonshire Place NW
Washington, DC 20008

WinWord Office Power Pack (WOPR)

This nifty little package of utilities for Word for Windows is a must for "WinWord" users. Whether you're a beginner or a power user writing programs in WordBasic, you'll find something here to suit your abilities. It's composed of 17 great utilities, many of which you'll soon find to be vital to your daily word processing.

Enveloper, for instance, solves perhaps the most common problem word processors encounter: printing envelopes. It works with Hewlett-Packard LaserJets, DeskJets, and compatible printers.

Dinger lets you easily insert any character from a font into your documents, and Killer allows you to delete files from within Word for Windows, a function that Microsoft inexplicably left out of the program. Word Counter does what it implies: It counts the number of words within a document or within a block of selected text. The Copy Library is a collection of routines in WordBasic.

Treasure Hunt alone may be worth the cost of the package. It's a collection of utilities that allow you to do such things as create hanging indents and bulleted lists or change the capitalization of a block of text.

There's one more benefit to using the WinWord Office Power Pack. It comes with possibly the most entertaining, off-the-wall, readable, and useful documentation in all of sharewaredom, courtesy of Woody Leonhard, president of the company that makes the package.

WinWord Office Power Pack
Registration fee: $$
Pinecliffe International (w10)
P.O. Drawer 7337
Coal Creek Canyon
Golden, CO 80403
(800) 659-4690

Xword

Most shareware text editors and word processors create ASCII text, so it's generally easy to edit files created by one word processor with another. That's not true of commercial programs; most of them have native file formats that can't be read by other programs. Although some of those programs allow you to save in ASCII format, you'll lose all your file formatting if you do so. Some commercial programs can't even save files in pure ASCII.

XWord solves this problem, converting files from one word processing format to another. Note that in some instances, some of the formatting will still be lost, but this is still far faster than retyping a whole file.

Xword
Registration fee: $
Ronald Gans
350 West 55th St.
New York, NY 10019
(212) 957-8361

CHAPTER

4

Communications and Compression Programs

General Communications Programs

Automating Access to On-Line Services

Bulletin Board Software

Miscellaneous Communications Utilities

Compression Programs

COMMUNICATIONS AND SHAREWARE HAVE ALWAYS GONE TOGETHER, and with good reason: Shareware has been at least partially responsible for the PC communications revolution. A large part of the reason that so many people go on line to computer bulletin boards and commercial services is to find the latest in shareware. Likewise, the communications revolution has fed the growth of shareware. As more people go on line, the audience for shareware grows, and so more shareware is written.

Because of this interdependent relationship, you'll find a shareware communications program for every possible need. In fact, you'll find more than one—often a dozen or more. For general communications, for instance, there are more shareware programs than you can imagine, and they rival (and often exceed) any commercial packages you'll find.

Shareware has really excelled in communications programs pointed at specific needs. Do you want to cut down the cost of using CompuServe or other on-line services? There are several programs available to help you. Would you like to automate access to bulletin boards, or set up one of your own? Shareware does the job again. And for those miscellaneous, oddball tasks such as sharing a single telephone line with a fax machine, a modem, and a telephone, you're sure to find a shareware package to your liking.

Compression programs are also intimately linked to shareware. These programs shrink a file down to a fraction of its original size, making downloads quicker and opening up valuable hard disk space. Without them, downloading and uploading files would be time-consuming chores, and bulletin board and on-line systems would have far less room to make shareware available to you. It's not surprising that compression programs began as shareware and public-domain software, and, in general, that's where they remain. As much as a good communications program, they're a vital part of any shareware toolkit.

General Communications Programs

Because of the intimate link between shareware and communications, there's always been a great number of general communications packages available. They range from the simple to the exceedingly complex, but most of them are fairly simple to use—once you get the hang of the vocabulary. ProComm, probably the best known of them, has done an especially good job of blending power and ease of use.

I've picked a half dozen or so of the best or most unique programs out there. You'll be able to get up to speed with all of them fairly quickly. While most offer the same basic features, they differ in the communications protocols they support, in their size and complexity, and in the kinds of features they include as accessories. None of them will steer you wrong.

BOYAN

BOYAN first became popular on college campuses, but the larger population of PC users has gradually begun to see the power and effectiveness of this communications program as well. It's one of the easiest of these packages to learn and use. If you run into trouble at any point, press Ctrl-Home, and context-sensitive help will pop up. The help system makes it easy to move from help screen to help screen. In fact, the program is so easy to use and configure, and the help screens so easy to reach and understand, you may never find yourself turning to the manual.

Like ProComm and other packages, the main communications tasks are done through a main dialing screen, which lists numbers you have entered. You get to the screen by pressing Alt-D. To do other tasks, you also use Alt key combinations, such as Alt-C for configuring (customizing) the software.

BOYAN includes a number of communication protocols, such as Xmodem, Ymodem, and ASCII. Its macro-writing language is also sound, and the program includes a Usage Log to track how you spend your time on line.

Perhaps the most innovative part of the program is its Directory File Manager, shown in Figure 4.1, which allows you to perform many tasks that you normally would have to use a hard disk manager for. Press Del to get to the File Manager. From here you can get a directory listing, change to other directories, and copy, rename, and view files, among other housekeeping chores.

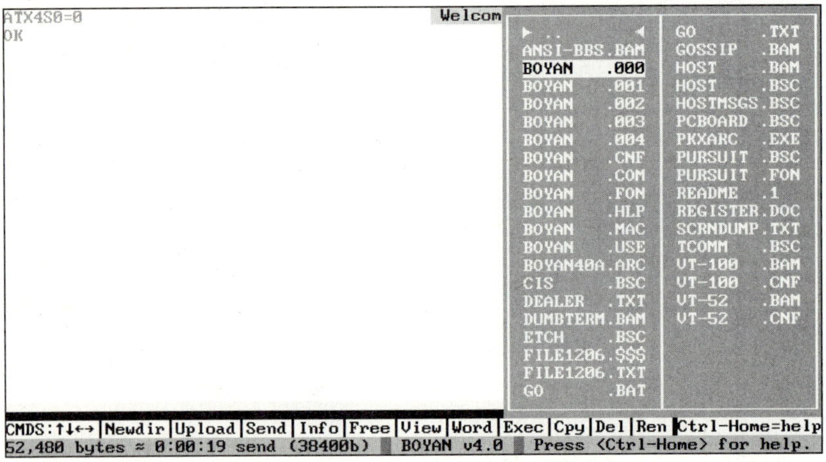

Figure 4.1
BOYAN's Directory File Manager

Better yet, when you highlight a file and press **I** (Information), BOYAN tells you the file size and how long it will take to upload that file at your current communications configuration. You can also send files directly from the

Directory File Manager, or tag several files for uploading, and then get information about the file size and upload time.

BOYAN
Registration fee: $$
Justin Boyan
BOYAN Communications
9458 Two Hills Ct.
Columbia, MD 21045

{COMMO}

An interesting little communications package, {COMMO} stresses small size, speed of execution, and flexibility instead of do-it-all communications. Configuring the program is simple; press Alt-G to bring up a self-explanatory configuration menu, fill it in, and you're ready to go.

As with other communications packages, Alt-D brings up the dialing directory. From there, you dial by moving a highlighted bar to the number you want to dial and pressing Enter. You can dial manually as well. {COMMO} also has a macro-writing facility and a host mode.

You can upload and download ASCII files with {COMMO}. It also includes the Xmodem and Xmodem-1k (old Ymodem) protocols for uploading and downloading files. For other types of file transfers, {COMMO} can be linked via built-in macros to external protocol drivers.

The program's executable file takes up not much more than 30k. It's an excellent tool for dialing into bulletin boards or online services for chatting, or for getting electronic mail through a service such as MCI Mail. If the bulletin board or online service also supports Xmodem, you'll get file transfers as well. And even if it doesn't, you can customize the program with a number of other file-transfer protocols.

{COMMO}
Registration fee: $
Fred P. Brucker
P.O. Box 9103
Santa Rosa, CA 95405
(707) 573-1065

ProComm 2.4.3

Possibly the most popular shareware communications package of all time, ProComm is one of the biggest success stories in shareware. Not long after this program was originally released in 1985, its sales skyrocketed. People recognized that the program was both powerful and easy to use—a unique combination, particularly rare in communications packages.

There's little the program doesn't include. You'll get many communications protocols, including Xmodem, Kermit, Telink, Ymodem, and CompuServe Quick-B. A number of terminal emulations are available. The dialing directory can contain 100 phone numbers and is very easy to set up. You can also create keyboard macros.

Additionally, ProComm has a powerful script-writing language for automating communications tasks. It's simple enough that you can write a script within minutes to automatically access a bulletin board or an on-line service, but it's sophisticated enough to encompass far more complex tasks.

Most of the work in ProComm is accomplished via the dialing directory. To bring this directory up, you press Alt-D. Adding phone numbers to the list is a snap. Type **R**, and ProComm will ask you which entry you want to revise. Pick an empty slot, and just follow the prompts.

Once you have numbers on the directory list, you type the number of the entry you want to dial, press Enter, and ProComm goes about its work. Figure 4.2 shows ProComm's dialing directory.

Figure 4.2
ProComm's dialing directory

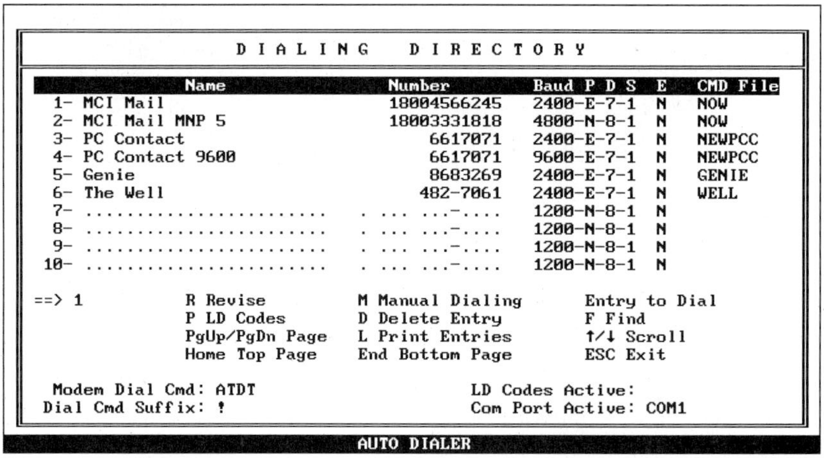

Customizing the program is simple; press Alt-S to bring up the menu shown in Figure 4.3, which allows you to change most of the program's options. Alt-Z changes its colors. Help is always near at hand via Alt-F10.

ProComm 2.4.3 was the last version of the program sold as shareware; all subsequent versions are commercially sold products, called ProComm Plus, a more powerful version. Even as commercial software, the program sells well: It makes regular appearances on software best-seller lists.

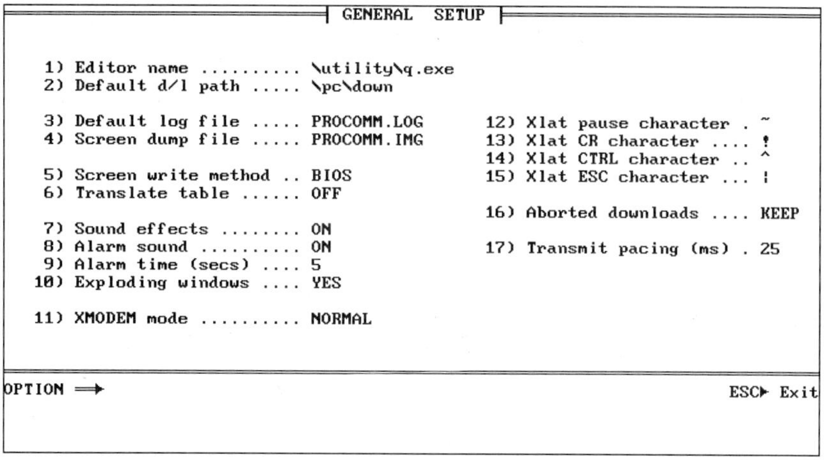

Figure 4.3
ProComm's general setup menu

The shareware versions, 2.4.3 and earlier, are still widely available. Don't confuse the shareware versions with the ProComm Plus Test Drive, however, which you may also see on bulletin boards. Test Drive is not a fully functioning version of the commercial package and lacks documentation; it's there only to give you a taste of the commercial package.

If you do PC communications regularly, you shouldn't be without ProComm. For a sophisticated package, choose the commercial version. For most communications needs, however, the shareware version is far more than adequate.

ProComm
Registration fee: $$
Datastorm Technologies
P.O. Box 1471
Columbia, MO 65205
(314) 474-8461

QModem

QModem is another communications powerhouse. It has all the features you'd expect in a high-end communications package: a variety of file-transfer protocols (Xmodem, Ymodem Batch, and Zmodem Batch among them), the ability to work with many different types of modems, and many terminal emulations. QModem also has a nice phone-log facility for tracking the calls you make and the calls made to you. An accompanying text editor allows you to write ASCII files, and QModem's QuickLearn scripting facility lets even beginners generate communications scripts quickly.

If you're familiar with ProComm, you're familiar to a certain extent with QModem, since they share a number of commands in common. Pressing Alt-D in QModem brings up the dialing directory, as it does in ProComm, and the QModem dialing directory looks and functions very much like ProComm's, as shown in Figure 4.4. In both programs, Alt-H hangs up a phone line and Alt-X will exit you from the program.

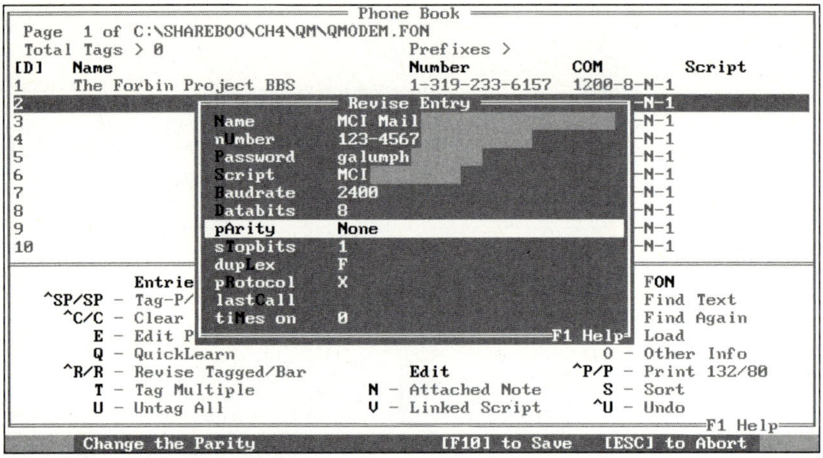

Figure 4.4
Adding a new entry to QModem's dialing directory

That's not to say these two programs are clones—far from it. QModem has an exceptional configuration facility, for example. And it has an especially powerful batch upload feature, and lets you create split screens easily. QModem also has a unique registration policy. It sells as commercial software for $99, but its "test drive" is available for free—no registration is ever required. The "test drive" is slightly less powerful than the commercial product. It will continue to be upgraded, but will always be less powerful than the commercial version.

QModem
Registration fee: Free
Mustang Software
P.O. Box 2264
Bakersfield, CA 93303
(805) 395-0223

Telemate

Telemate solves one of the biggest communications problems—it allows you to do other tasks while the program uploads or downloads files in the background. Normally, communications programs don't allow this kind of multitasking. Even multitasking programs such as DESQview and Windows have problems with communications in the background at times, particularly when using high-speed communications of 9,600 bps and faster. Telemate includes a multitasking kernel that lets you do other things within the program while background communications are going on. Note that you can't use other programs while this is happening—you can only use another part of the Telemate program (Telemate's text editor or its macro writing facility, for example).

There's more to Telemate than just background file transfers, however. It has a good number of file transfer protocols, can be completely mouse-driven, and has a unique View capability for looking at files stored on your system while you're on line. For the frivolous among us, Telemate's alarms can be configured to play snippets of music, such as the *William Tell* Overture.

Telemate
Registration fee: $$
Tsung Ju
10530 Keating Crescent
Windsor, Ontario
Canada N8R 1T5

Unicom

A sophisticated, fully featured communications package, Unicom is one of the few (perhaps the only) shareware communications programs written for Windows.

Like most well-written Windows programs, almost everything you need in Unicom is only a mouse click away. Across the top of the screen, just beneath the menus, are nearly two dozen icons, which you can click on to perform many communications tasks. You can click on icons to upload and download files, dial and hang up your modem, edit macros, set up file-transfer options, and much more.

There are also the usual menus across the top of the screen, from which you can get at all of the program's considerable power. Almost everything about Unicom can be customized, making it an even more powerful program.

Unicom has a full complement of file transfer protocols, including ZModem, ASCII, CompuServe B, Kermit, and Xmodem, and works at speeds between 300 and 19,200 bps. It also features powerful script-writing features, and the ability to capture screens from the Windows Clipboard.

One of Unicom's better features is its user-defined keys, which you can place along the bottom of the program's screen. You can define these keys to perform any function you want. They can launch other programs, download and upload files, execute DOS commands, split your screen in two for Chat mode with a remote user—their use is limited only by your imagination.

Unicom also makes use of Windows' graphics abilities. When uploading or downloading a file, for example, it displays a moving bar showing you the progress of the transfer as well as other vital statistics. Figure 4.5 illustrates a sample upload screen.

Figure 4.5
Uploading a file with Unicom

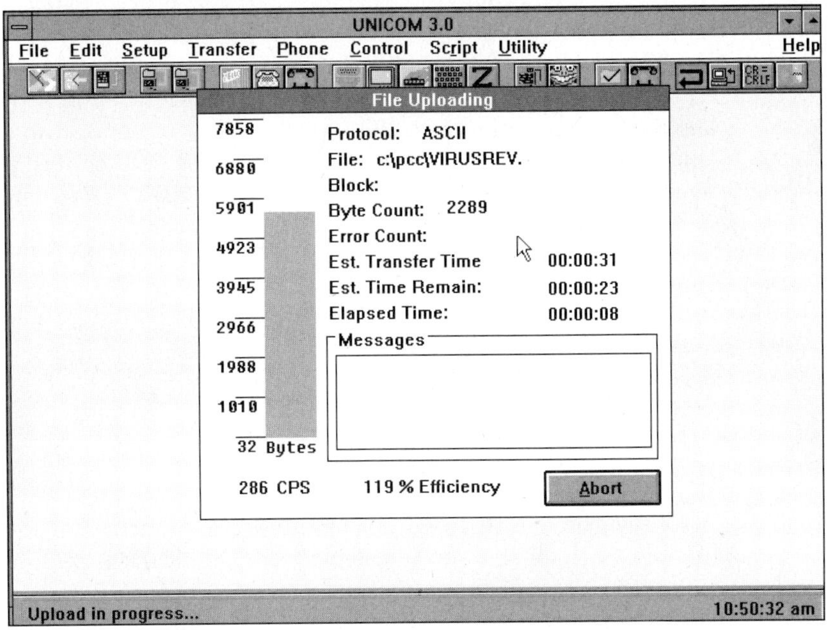

Unicom also includes several sample log-on scripts to popular on-line services such as CompuServe, so you can quickly and automatically log on to those systems. If you use Windows and are looking for a communications package, check out Unicom. One warning, though. Its "nag" screens asking you to register are intrusive.

Unicom
Registration fee: $$
Data Graphics
P.O. Box 58517
Renton, WA 98058
(206) 432-1201

Automating Access to On-Line Services

On-line services such as CompuServe, Prodigy, and GEnie are truly remarkable. They're repositories of vast amounts of information, sources from which you can download shareware and freeware, and a forum for like-minded people to chat and exchange information on line. More than any other communication medium, they've created a new "virtual" community—people can talk to and help one another, even though they may be located across the planet.

On-line services tend to be difficult to use, however, or else (in the case of Prodigy) extremely slow. Shareware programs, as usual, have jumped into the breach. A number of programs, notably Tapcis, can automate access to these services, making them more accessible and possibly saving you money in the bargain.

Autosig

Autosig is a program for automating access to CompuServe forums. In general, Tapcis (discussed in a moment) is easier to set up, although some people feel Autosig has a bit more flexibility once it's up and running. Tapcis is the more popular of the two programs.

Autosig lets you read and create messages off line and maintain an electronic address book, among other capabilities. In general, though, you'll need a bit of CompuServe know-how before attempting Autosig. On the bright side, it won't cost you anything.

Autosig
Registration fee: None
Available in Library 1 of the IBMCOM forum on CompuServe

eVa

Of the big three commercial on-line services, GEnie and CompuServe suffer from the same problem: They're both difficult to use. To help you to use GEnie more easily, there's eVa, written by the same person who wrote Proplus for Prodigy (see below). Although GEnie gives away its own software (Aladdin) for this purpose, eVa takes a different approach, which may be easier for some people to use.

The program is graphically oriented, supports a mouse, and features pull-down menus. It allows you to automate the process of sending messages by letting you compose them off line with its text editor and by downloading messages so you can read them off line. eVa also includes a fast navigation tool, a macro creation facility, and more.

eVa
Registration fee: $
Philippe Rabergeau
Gateway Software, Inc.
61 East 8th St., Suite 128
New York, NY 10003
(212) 505-6203

Proplus

Prodigy, IBM and Sears' on-line service, is incredibly easy to use, but exceedingly slow, and at times tiresome to use as well. It's graphically oriented. This means that as you move from screen to screen, you have to wait while its graphics are downloaded onto your PC from Prodigy and your screen repaints. Prodigy receives income from advertisers who flash messages across your screen as you navigate the system, and therefore its modus operandi is unlikely to change.

Proplus will give you the on-line tools that Prodigy forgot to include, making your life on line more palatable, as well as navigation and messaging tools. It allows you to create messages off line and then upload them, and its message editor includes a spell checker with a 60,000-word dictionary. It can also download messages so you can read them off line.

The program allows you to create keyboard macros for use both on and off line. The ability to create keyboard macros for on-line use is especially helpful, because it will allow you to navigate through Prodigy quickly and easily. Proplus won't change Prodigy's basic look and feel, but it will make using the service less painful.

Proplus
Registration fee: $
Gateway Software
Philippe Rabergeau
61 East 8th St., Suite 128
New York, NY 10003
(212) 505-6203

Robin!

Another program to automate access to Prodigy, Robin!, like Proplus, lets you upload and download messages. It takes a slightly different approach, however, especially in uploading. Instead of using a built-in text editor, you create an ASCII file with your external text editor or word processor, and then use Robin! to upload the message.

Robin! also lets you use keyboard macros (which it calls scripts) to make it easier to navigate through Prodigy. Here again, however, you'll have to use a text editor or word processor to create a script describing your on-line actions, and then use Robin!'s script compiler to let that script run. Robin! also comes with a number of prewritten scripts.

Robin!
Registration fee: $
McQuay Technologies
8045 Antoine, Suite 291
Houston, TX 77088

Tapcis

CompuServe is the main highway of on-line services, and Tapcis is the best vehicle you can get to make the drive as fast and smooth as possible.

You'll use Tapcis mainly to get at the various forums on CompuServe. Although CompuServe is made up of far more than just these forums, they're one of the main attractions of the service, covering everything from scuba diving to WordPerfect support. There are two primary reasons for getting onto these forums: to exchange notes and information with people who have the same interests as you and to download text files and shareware. Tapcis excels in helping you do both.

CompuServe is famous for its user-unfriendly interface, and navigating through it is often a painful process. With Tapcis, you may never have to face the dreaded ! prompt again, and you'll save money in the process. You set up Tapcis to work with whichever forum(s) you're interested in. The program will dial CompuServe for you and do the job you've asked it to do. You can have it automatically download every message in the forum, download certain messages only, or send you the header information of every message or selected messages. You can then select (by typing an **R** by their names) those files you want downloaded, as shown in Figure 4.6. Tapcis then goes back on line to download the messages you chose.

The program will also create catalogs of every downloadable file in the forums you're interested in. You can then pick files from the catalog and instruct the program to download them.

That's only the surface of what the program can do. It will also keep track of your time on line and thus how much you can expect to be billed, allow you quick access to CompuServe Mail, and create an address book of people to whom you send electronic mail via CompuServe, among other useful services.

When used properly, the program can cut your CompuServe bill tremendously. Normally, you read and compose messages on line when using

CompuServe. With Tapcis, you read and compose messages off line. The only time you're actually on line is when you're uploading or downloading messages or headers. The savings can be enormous.

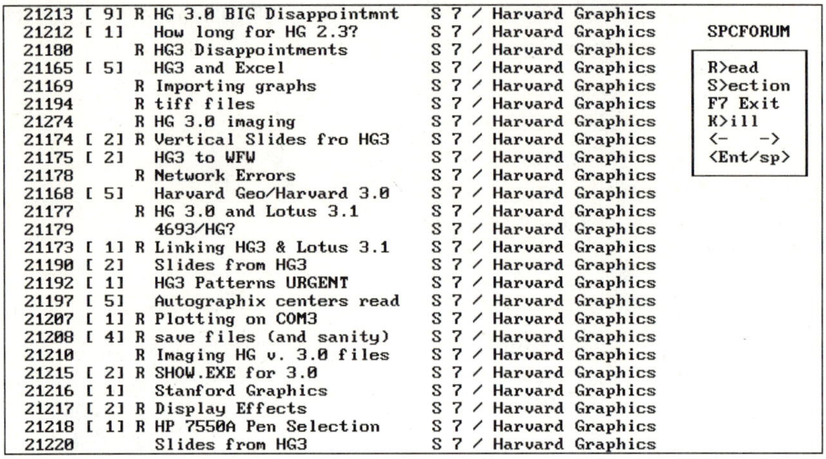

Figure 4.6 Marking selected messages for downloading with Tapcis

Some people will use these savings to get more out of CompuServe than before. Before Tapcis, they might have visited three forums regularly; with Tapcis, they can visit 12 for the same on-line cost.

Tapcis has its own forum on CompuServe (type **GO TAPCIS** to get there), where you'll find the latest version of the program, in addition to many add-ins that make the program even more useful and powerful. If you regularly use CompuServe, you shouldn't be without this program.

Tapcis
Registration fee: $$$
Support Group, Inc.
Lake Technology Park
P.O. Box 130
McHenry, MD 21541
(800) USA-GROUP; (301) 387-4500

Bulletin Board Software

Will you ever set up a bulletin board system? Maybe not—but then again, you might surprise yourself. Running a bulletin board is not just a job for hackers. Both large corporations and small businesses, for example, are finding that bulletin boards are useful business tools.

For a large corporation, setting up a bulletin board can make sense as a way to keep in touch when branch offices are separated geographically or when employees are on the road. Small businesses can use it to maintain closer relations with their customers, because it's an ideal way to handle customer service, ordering, technical assistance, and even marketing. Although setting up and running a bulletin board takes a lot of work, it's not rocket science, and the software you'll find below can make it even easier.

Even if you don't run a bulletin board, you'll find software here that will make your time spent on bulletin boards far more efficient. These programs will do for bulletin boards what Tapcis does for CompuServe (see the preceding section).

RBBS

An exceedingly popular and powerful bulletin board system, RBBS (for Remote Bulletin Board System) has grown over the years to become one of the bulletin board industry's standards. It has powerful messaging, uploading and downloading features, as well as a great deal of built-in security, so that unauthorized callers can't wreak havoc on your system.

RBBS is unique not only for its power, but for its means of distribution: It's given away for free. Simply download it from a bulletin board. Or, if you prefer, send a nominal fee to the PC Capital Users Group, and you'll get the complete system sent to you. (In fact, the group says that no profit is allowed to be made in distributing RBBS. They will accept donations, but they prefer them to be in the form of service, equipment, shareware, or improvements to the program.)

RBBS
Registration fee: None
Capital PC Users Group Software Exchange
P.O. Box 1785
West Bethesda, MD 20875.

Robocomm

Do you want to make your time spent on bulletin boards more efficient and productive? If so, you need Robocomm, a tool for automating much of your bulletin-board activity.

Robocomm lets you create what it calls *agendas*. The agendas lay out exactly what you want to do on line. Robocomm can upload and download your messages. It can also download and upload files, scan downloaded files for viruses, let you run DOS programs while you're on line, and far more.

Note that although Robocomm will download messages for you, it won't enable you to read and respond to those messages. For that you'll need Deluxe/2, a separate shareware off-line mail reader.

Robocomm will save you tremendous amounts of time, and money as well. As a starter, you'll spend less on telephone bills. You'll also save on access fees when you dial into those bulletin boards that charge fees—particularly the new breed of "super" bulletin boards, with massive collections of files and information.

Robocomm works only with PCBoard bulletin boards, so before registering, make sure the systems you dial into are PCBoards. It will let you log on to many of these boards, and set up separate agendas for each. Figure 4.7 shows how a new bulletin board is added to Robocomm.

Robocomm
Registration fee: $$
Parsons Consulting
P.O. Box 67D07
Los Angeles, CA 90067

Deluxe/2
Registration fee: $20
Sparkware
P.O. Box 605
Cordova, TN 38018

Figure 4.7
Adding a new listing to Robocomm

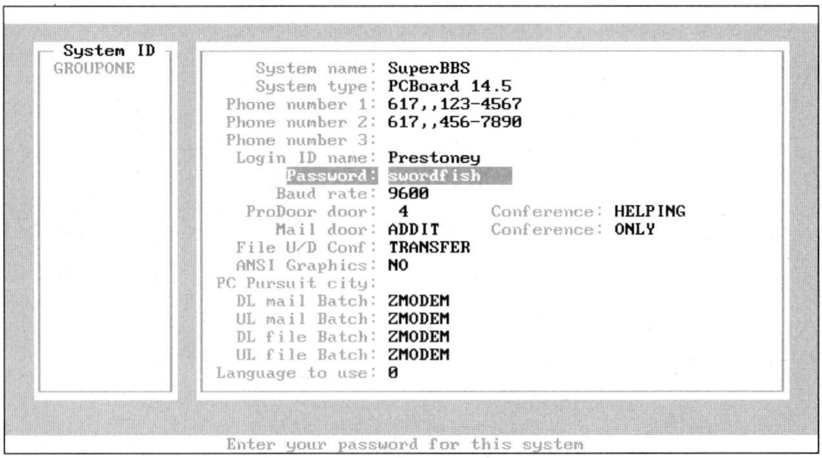

Wildcat!

This is a full-featured bulletin board that's still easy to set up (at least by the standards of bulletin boards). There are numerous Wildcat! boards already in existence, so if you set one up, you'll find yourself in good company.

Wildcat! includes the ability to let people download with a wide variety of protocols, such as Xmodem, Ymodem Batch, Zmodem Batch, and Kermit. Its messaging system includes carbon copying and providing return receipts. Wildcat! supports transmission rates of up to 19,200 bps.

The unregistered shareware version supports only one phone line, and it doesn't include many of the higher-end features, but it will give you a taste of the real thing.

Wildcat!
Registration fee: $$$$
Mustang Software
P.O. Box 2264
Bakersfield, CA 93303
(805) 395-0223; (800) 999-9619 (orders only)

Miscellaneous Communications Utilities

There's a whole group of shareware communications programs that can't be categorized. They tend to perform only one task, but perform it well, and very often there's no commercial counterpart for them. Below is just a sampling of what you'll find on bulletin boards, on-line services, and from disk vendors.

Backmail

One of the more unique and innovative communications programs you'll ever find, Backmail is an electronic mail program that functions in the background while you carry on your normal work on your PC. It can eliminate frustrating games of phone tag and save you time and phone expenses.

To send a message with Backmail, you pop up the program by hitting a hot key. Then you compose your message and send it. (You can also send files.) Backmail will dial the modem and send the message or file from the background, while you continue whatever you were doing.

Message recipients must also have Backmail working on their PCs. When Backmail makes a connection, it will send the message or file you've sent, again working in the background. The recipient can then respond or forward messages to other people.

A commercial version of the program is also available with more features, including a script-writing language and the ability to *load high* (in the unused "space" between 640k and 1 megabyte in RAM) under DOS 5.

Backmail
Registration fee: $$
Alethic Software
52 Parkhill Road
Halifax, Nova Scotia
Canada B3P 1R5
(902) 423-9860

Elsewhere

Elsewhere is a unique piece of shareware that, in essence, lets you be two places at once. Using Elsewhere, you can dial into a distant PC, as long as both are equipped with modems. You then control that distant PC from your own keyboard. With it, you can also transfer files between the computers.

There are myriad uses for such software, most notably dialing into your PC at work from your PC at home. Do you have a printing job that's going to take several hours, but don't want to stay late at the office to get it done? Not to worry! Load Elsewhere on your work PC, drive home, load Elsewhere on your home PC, dial into work, and then tell your PC at work to begin printing. Now you can sit at home while the printer back in your office churns away. (You'll have to pay for phone charges, though.)

File transfer between two PCs is also very useful. If you're working at home on a deadline and suddenly realize you've left important files back at the office, you can dial your work PC and ask that the files be transferred to you at home. You can also schedule file transfers to occur on a regular basis—without having to be there to handle them.

Elsewhere can also be used for those involved in technical support. When others are having trouble, instead of having them describe the symptoms to you over the telephone, you can dial into their PC. Then you can watch their screen on your own PC as they work.

Elsewhere
Registration fee: $$
Interlink Technologies
Kevin Kiley
80 Grove St.
Waldwick, NJ 07463

PCFDial

Do you live on the telephone? Are your fingers tired of punching buttons? If so, you need PCFDial. Taking up a mere 7k as a TSR, the program dials any phone number displayed on your computer screen and logs every call you make in a history file. It will also pop up at user-defined intervals while you're on the phone, reminding you how long you've been talking. Nice bonuses include a pop-up listing of the time of day for every area code in the country, which you can sort by state or area code.

PCFDial
Registration fee: $
Barn Owl Software
P.O. Box 74
O'Fallon, IL 62269
(618) 632-7345

QuickTalk

QuickTalk is a small, TSR communications program with one main purpose: It will enter ASCII text directly into your applications program from an on-line system, bulletin board, or electronic mail system. When you're in your word processor, for instance, you can pop up QuickTalk over the program, have it dial a phone number, and then have it enter ASCII text into the word processing program. A commercial version is also available that allows you to perform background transfers of binary files.

QuickTalk
Registration fee: $$
SilverSoft Inc.
1301 Geranium St. NW
Washington, DC 20012
(202) 291-8212

Remote Control

Pity your poor telephone line. It's forced to perform triple and quadruple duty—handling voice calls, modem communications, incoming and outgoing faxes, and telephone answering machines. To solve the problem, you may be forced to buy an additional phone line, or even two.

Remote Control will save you the extra expense. It's a software-based telephone line switcher, enabling you to select which device receives the call, so that you don't need an extra phone line. Note the use of the word *select:* Remote Control usually won't perform the job automatically, as do hardware-based line switchers. You have to tell it which device is to receive the call.

If you have distinctive ring service from your phone company, on the other hand, Remote Control can work automatically. Distinctive ring service lets you have three phone numbers on one line; each number has a different tone. Remote Control can use those tones to automatically switch the call to the proper device.

You can also use the program with a pager. Set it up so that whenever you have a message on your answering machine, it instructs your modem to dial your pager.

Remote Control
Registration fee: $
Charles Eglinton
Electronic Technologies
3985 South Rochester Road, Suite H
Rochester, MI 48307-5135
(313) 656-0630; (800) 325-7379 (orders only)

Compression Programs

Without compression software, shareware would not be nearly as popular as it is today. Compression programs shrink the size of files, so that you can download software to your system faster. They also allow bulletin board operators to store more programs for you to peruse and download and let disk vendors squeeze more shareware programs onto individual disks. Compression software is also used to decompress the files after they've been compressed so that you can use them. If you download shareware from bulletin boards, for instance, you'll need PKZIP, which is virtually a compression software standard.

The usefulness of compression software goes well beyond shareware, however. If you have files you use only occasionally, you can use compression software to shrink them down, freeing up more of your hard disk space. Then when you want to use the file, decompress it again. Some compression programs will even shrink the size of executable files (those ending in .EXE or .COM) and let you run them in their shrunken form.

Everyone should have at least one compression utility handy. The following programs are the best ones available.

ARC and ARCE

ARC was released back in 1985, and was the dominant compression program until PKZIP came along. ARCE is a faster version of ARC.

ARC, like PKZIP (discussed in a moment), can be used to compress and extract files and to create self-extracting files. ARC tends to compress and extract files faster than PKZIP does, but it's not nearly as efficient—its compressed files are larger than PKZIP's. Like PKZIP, ARC is command-line driven and not easy to use for complex work.

If you spend much time downloading files, you'll need ARC. While most files are in the ZIP format, there are still a good number of files that use ARC instead.

ARC
Registration fee: $$
System Enhancements Associates, Inc.
21 New St.
Wayne, NJ 07470

ARCE
Registration fee: None
Vernon D. Buerg
139 White Oak Circle
Petaluma, CA 94952

ArcMaster

It's difficult enough to learn the syntax of one file-compression program, but when you work with more than one, it becomes almost impossible. ArcMaster makes using file-compression programs easier, by serving as an easy-to-use front end to many of them. It also allows you to convert files compressed with one program into the compressed files of another. It works with all the major file-compression programs, with the exception of the ZOO format.

ArcMaster is menu-driven and simple to use. All your work is done in a split-screen display. The program has some nice extra features: It will allow you to search for files, give you a report on your memory usage, password-protect your PC, and give you access to the antiviral VIRUSCAN program. You can also launch other programs from within ArcMaster.

ArcMaster features an excellent help system, so you'll spend as little time as possible with the manual.

ArcMaster
Registration fee: $
New-Ware
8050 Camino Kiosco
San Diego, CA 92122
(619) 455-6225

LHA

LHA is another file-compression program. By default it creates files with .LZH extensions. This program comes from Japan, and has become something of a standard over there, according to the program's author. You won't find many LZH files on bulletin boards in the U.S., however. LHA excels in creating self-extracting files, which it does with speed and efficiency.

Earlier versions of this program were called LHARC, and even the most recent version of the program is sometimes called by that name.

LHA
Registration fee: None
Available on many bulletin boards, CompuServe, and GEnie

PAK

PAK has been around since 1988, and has gained only modest popularity on bulletin boards. Still, you may see a file with a .PAK extension every once in a while, and if you want to decompress it, you'll need PAK. PAK will also decompress files created by PKZIP and ARC, and so is worth a look at for this reason.

PAK
Registration fee: $
NoGate Consulting
P.O. Box 88115
Grand Rapids, MI 49518
(616) 455-6270

PKLITE

Another solid offering from "zipmeister" Phil Katz, who wrote the PKZIP programs, PKLITE presents an interesting variation on the theme of file compression: It compresses executable files, and then lets them run in compressed form. This can save you substantial amounts of hard disk space. You can save up to 70 percent of disk space on some files (70-percent compression), although on a dozen files I tested, the average amount of compression was 35 percent.

Note that you can't use PKLITE on Windows or OS/2 programs, or any programs that use overlays.

PKLITE
Registration fee: $$
PKware, Inc.
7545 North Port Washington Road
Glendale, WI 53217
(414) 352-3670

PKZIP

Quite simply the best compression program you'll ever find, PKZIP was released in 1989, and almost overnight overwhelmingly became the compression utility of choice among bulletin board operators and on-line aficionados. In fact, it became so popular that it's become the standard for storing compressed files on bulletin board systems. Some bulletin boards, in fact, only have files stored in the ZIP format.

Therefore, if you plan to download any software, you'll need this utility. It can be found on any bulletin board or on-line service you can name. The file you'll find on bulletin boards is *self-extracting*, which means that the file you download is composed of compressed files that can decompress themselves. If the file you download is PKZ101.EXE, for example, you would type **PKZ101** at the DOS prompt, and the files that make up PKZIP would automatically decompress.

What's known as PKZIP are in fact several different programs. PKZIP can compress files individually or combine a group of files into a master archive file.

PKZIP is useful not just on bulletin boards, but to give you extra hard disk space as well. If there are files or programs you don't regularly use, zip them, and you'll save a vast amount of hard disk space. How much space you save will vary, but figure on getting about 65- to 70-percent compression on ASCII files—that is, they will be 30 to 35 percent of their original size. Binary program files will achieve around 50-percent compression.

The syntax for using PKZIP is rather complex. As a simple example, if you were going to zip a single file named MYFILE and call the new file MYFILE.ZIP, you would issue the following command:

```
PKZIP MYFILE.ZIP MYFILE
```

PKUNZIP takes care of the extraction work on files that have been zipped with PKZIP. If you want to unzip a file named MYFILE.ZIP, you would issue the command

```
PKUNZIP MYFILE
```

and the files would be extracted.

PKSFX is used to create self-extracting files, such as the PKZ101.EXE file mentioned above. To create a self-extracting file, you first need to create a zipped file. After the file has been zipped, you turn it into a self-extracting file. To create a self-extracting file from MYFILE.ZIP, you would type

```
ZIP2EXE MYFILE.ZIP
```

and a file called MYFILE.EXE would be created. The MYFILE.ZIP file would still remain.

There are far more handy jobs you can use PKZIP for. PKZIP is command-line driven, so it's not the easiest of programs to use, and there's quite a complicated syntax for its commands. For the basics of extracting files and creating zipped and self-extracting files, though, it won't take you too long to get up to speed.

> **PKZIP**
> Registration fee: $$
> PKware, Inc.
> 7545 North Port Washington Road
> Glendale, WI 53217
> (414) 352-3670

PKZMenu

PKZIP's one drawback is that it can be difficult to use. Although you'll be able to accomplish simple tasks with it without difficulty, once you try to do anything fancy, you'll often find yourself at a loss. That's where PKZMenu comes in, with a menu interface to help you work with the PKZIP family of programs, as shown in Figure 4.8.

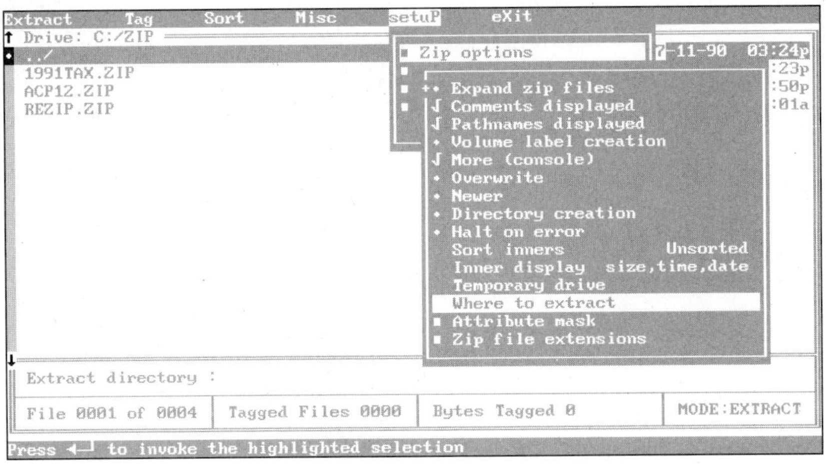

Figure 4.8
Setup options for PKZMenu

The main part of the screen is made up of a listing of files in a directory—the files on which you'll act. At the top of the screen is a pull-down menu that lets you access any of PKZIP's many features. There are also keyboard shortcuts for performing many tasks.

PKZMenu
Registration fee: $$
PKware, Inc.
7545 North Port Washington Road
Glendale, WI 53217
(414) 352-3670

Shez

Shez allows you to convert files among the different file compression formats, so you can, for example, turn an .LZH file (created with LHA) into a .ZIP file created with PKZIP. This menu-driven program works with ZIP, ARC, LZH, ZOO, PAK, and ARJ compression file formats. Figure 4.9 shows Shez's file-conversion menu.

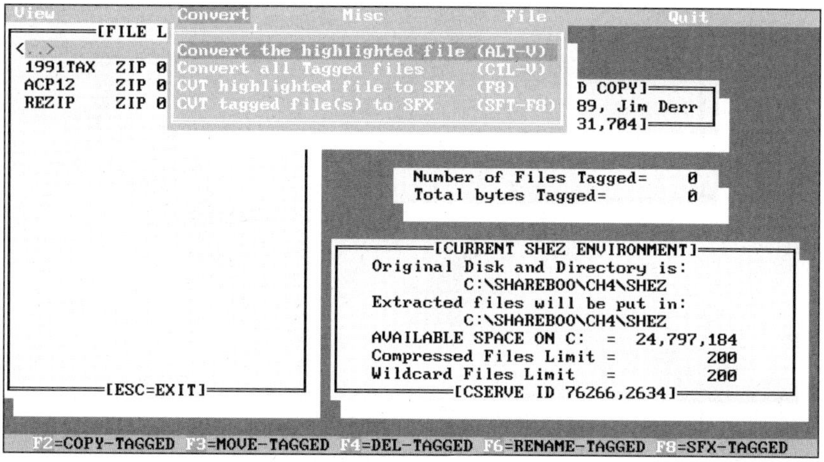

Figure 4.9 Shez's file-conversion menu

Shez also lets you use any of the different formats to compress and extract files and to create self-extracting files. It will also let you peek inside compressed archives to see file contents. Shez can be used with a mouse, and it supports the antiviral VIRUSCAN program from McAfee Associates. Best of all, it's menu-driven, so that you can use the power of many different compression programs without memorizing their complex and eccentric syntaxes.

Be aware that Shez is only a shell program that lets you use compression programs more easily. To use it, you'll also have to have the original compression programs.

Shez
Registration fee: $
California Software Design
James Derr
P.O. Box 15248
Santa Rosa, CA 95402

Zip Manager

Zip Manager is a Windows program that makes working with compression utilities, especially the PKZIP family, a snap. It's easier to set up and use than some other programs—everything you need is only a mouse click or two away. Setup is just a simple matter of filling in dialog boxes and clicking on radio buttons, as shown in Figure 4.10.

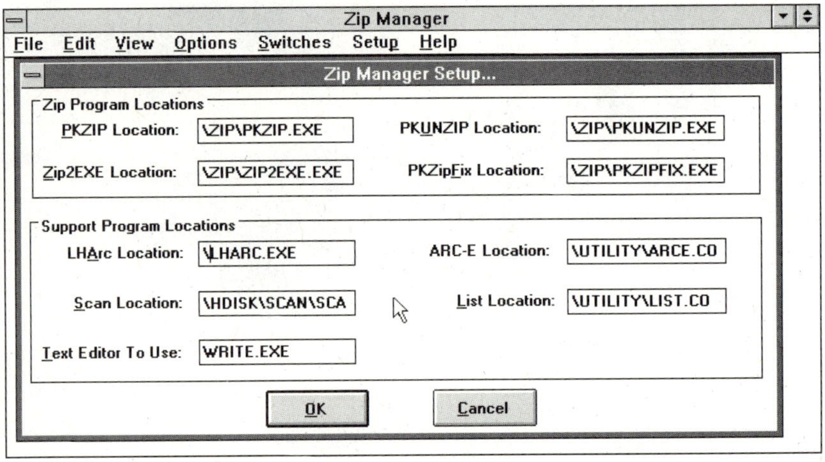

Figure 4.10 Configuring Zip Manager

Zip Manager works with PKZIP, ARCE, ARC, and LHA, although its primary purpose is to make using PKZIP easier. It also works with the antiviral VIRUSCAN program and the superb file viewer List. You can also have it launch your favorite text editor.

Zip Manager is essentially a shell. To make it fully functional, you'll have to get the various compression utilities and programs it supports.

The program has only one drawback: It won't convert files among the various compression formats.

Zip Manager
Registration fee: $
Moon Valley Software, Inc.
107 East Paradise Lane
Phoenix, AZ 85022
(602) 375-9502

ZOO

ZOO is more popular with UNIX users than it is in the PC world, but occasionally you'll find a file on a bulletin board with a .ZOO extension. In order to use that file, you'll need to first decompress it with ZOO. ZOO has some interesting features. For example, you can list and delete individual files from an archived file with a .ZOO extension. ZOO is available for free on many bulletin boards.

ZOO
Registration fee: None
Available on many bulletin boards

CHAPTER

5

Spreadsheets

Spreadsheets

Lotus 1-2-3 Templates, Add-ins, and Utilities

LOTUS DEVELOPMENT CORPORATION'S 1-2-3 SPREADSHEET WAS THE application that helped launched the PC revolution in corporate America. Thousands upon thousands of PCs were bought just to run that software.

Spreadsheets can be used for something as simple as toting up a row of numbers or as complex as sophisticated scientific and statistical calculations. It's particularly useful for budgeting and for performing "what-if" calculations—for example, figuring out how much of a house you can afford today, and then how much of a house you can afford if the interest rate drops 1 percent and you get an 8 percent raise.

You'll find a wealth of shareware spreadsheets, and you'll find even more variety among templates and add-ins to be used with Lotus 1-2-3. Commercial spreadsheets are big-ticket items, often costing $500 or more, but you'll find shareware alternatives for $100 and less, and often under $50. You don't need 1-2-3 to calculate that kind of savings.

Spreadsheets

Possibly because Lotus 1-2-3 has always had such a lock on the market, and because of the increasing popularity of other commercial programs, such as Borland's Quattro Pro and Microsoft's Excel, there has never been a large number of shareware spreadsheets floating about. And, although spreadsheet technology doesn't advance at a very rapid rate, shareware authors have often been a step behind their commercial counterparts.

That's not to say that you won't find top-notch shareware spreadsheets available, because you will. Perhaps dedicated spreadsheet jockeys may want to stay with the big, well-known commercial names, but everyone else would do well to take a close look at shareware alternatives. Many of them offer far more power than the average user (and some advanced users) will ever need. Some products carve out a unique niche, such as InstaCalc, which runs as a TSR so you always have your spreadsheet only a key combination away. Still others stress simplicity over power and ease of use over bells and whistles. All of them have registration fees that are a tiny percentage of the $500 price tags usually attached to their commercial brethren.

As-Easy-As and Alite

One of the most popular shareware spreadsheets, As-Easy-As will surprise you with the amount of power hidden not far beneath the program's surface. Unless you need the extraordinary power of 1-2-3 or Quattro Pro, or Excel's unique abilities in creating charts and working with graphics, As-Easy-As should serve you well.

As-Easy-As includes all the basic mathematical spreadsheet calculations you would expect, and it can create spreadsheets of 8,192 rows by 256 columns. It can also import and export dBASE III and IV files, record macros, handle ten different types of graphs, solve equations, and more. It creates graphics when used with EGA and Hercules monochrome graphics cards, as well as on CGA cards. It can also import Lotus .WKS and .WK1 worksheets.

You can use As-Easy-As to link spreadsheets and to export graphics files in PIC format to be used with desktop publishing and word processing programs. It includes database functions and a built-in word processing module.

Type **ASEASY** to launch the program. There are a number of handy switches available when you do so. To set up the program to use EGA mode, for example, you would type **ASEASY /E**. If you wanted to launch the program and have the spreadsheet SALES.WKS in the C:\SALES subdirectory loaded immediately, you would type

```
ASEASY /AUTO=C:\SALES\SALES.WKS
```

and that spreadsheet would be loaded when the program started up.

The basic As-Easy-As screen is full of information. Along the top is a list of the uses of the function keys. At the bottom you'll find the name of the file you're working on, the time, the amount of memory available, and the working mode you're in. In the middle of the screen, taking up most of the real estate, is the spreadsheet itself.

To perform most functions, press **/** (the slash key) to get a pull-down menu like the one shown in Figure 5.1. You can configure the program to show your menu vertically on the left or right side of the screen, or horizontally across the top in the familiar 1-2-3 pattern. Typing **!** (an exclamation point) toggles the menu between horizontal and vertical orientation, and typing **.** (a period) switches the vertical menu from side to side on the screen.

There's a surprising number of chart types you can create with the program. You can choose from X-Y, Line, Bar, Stacked Bar, Area, Hi Lo, Pie, and several others. Just follow the Graphics menu and you'll soon be creating them with ease. Figure 5.2 is a sample of what As-Easy-As can do with charts.

If you're new to spreadsheets, you might find As-Easy-As to be somewhat rough going at first. The documentation generally assumes that you're familiar with spreadsheets. If you're not, it can be a bit confusing. If you know the basics of using a spreadsheet, however, you'll soon be creating formulas with ease.

There's little this top-selling spreadsheet can't do. It features graphing options not often found in other shareware spreadsheets, such as the ability to create radar and delta graphs. Its data management and database functions are solid, its printing abilities substantial, and it has a good number of macro commands. In fact, it's become so popular that there are even foreign-language versions of the spreadsheet.

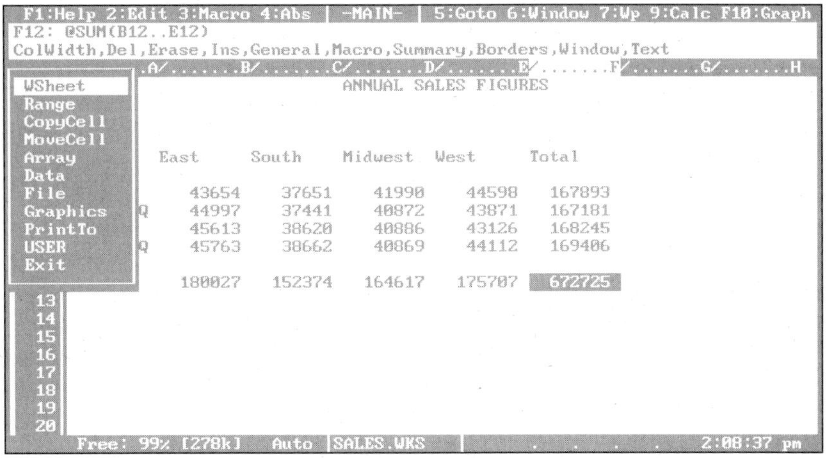

Figure 5.1
As-Easy-As with the main menu in its default position

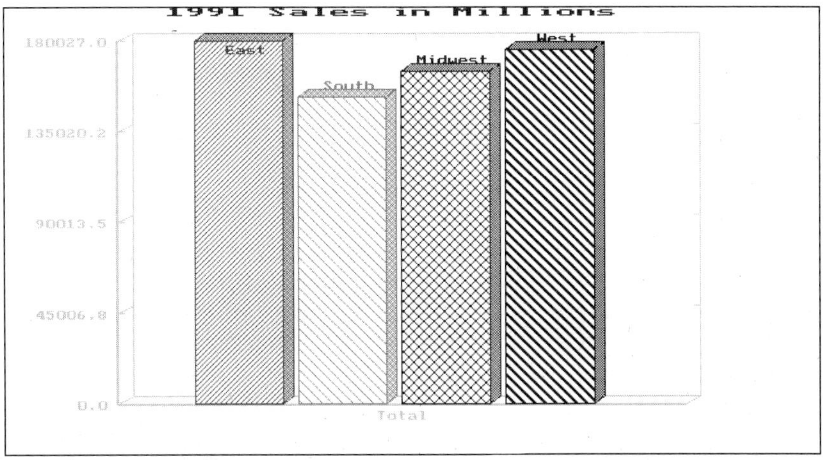

Figure 5.2
A bar chart built with As-Easy-As

As with 1-2-3, you'll find a number of add-ins to use with As-Easy-As, many available from Trius, the program's creators. Some will handle printing, allowing you to print your spreadsheets sideways (called *landscape* orientation). Still others let you create full three-dimensional charts. And there are also many add-in templates that can help you with tasks such as deciding whether to lease or purchase an item or choosing among different types of life insurance. When you register As-Easy-As, you'll get several of these add-ins for free.

Alite

This is essentially As-Easy-As on a diet. Its prime virtue is that it can be run in less memory, and so should be considered if you need to take a spreadsheet along on a laptop as you travel.

Alite can't create spreadsheets as large as those of its heftier older brother; its maximum is 2,048 rows by 128 columns, instead of 8,192 rows by 256 columns. It creates five chart types (X-Y, Line, Bar, Stacked Bar, and Pie) instead of ten, and it has been similarly slimmed down everywhere else, too. But it's a solid, straightforward spreadsheet that looks and feels precisely like As-Easy-As. For those who don't need all of As-Easy-As's substantial power, Alite is a good bet.

Note that although As-Easy-As add-ins will work with Alite, none are included with the registered version.

As-Easy-As
Registration fee: $$
Alite
Registration fee: $
Trius, Inc.
231 Sutton St., Suite 2D-3
North Andover, MA 01845
(508) 794-9377

ExpressCalc

ExpressCalc is a simple, straightforward spreadsheet that can handle most of the basic calculation chores you'll have. Two of its features make it stand out.

First, it has the ability to link ExpressCalc spreadsheets to databases. If you use File Express (made by the same company that makes ExpressCalc) or PC-File from ButtonWare, ExpressCalc can get data from them, put it into the spreadsheet, and perform calculations on that data.

ExpressCalc's second noteworthy feature is how customizable it is. Through the use of a profile file (an ASCII file that has the extension .PRO), just about every aspect of the program can be customized. You control not just colors and screen display, but the format of the numbers and text you type into cells, the display of formulas in cells, and printing commands, to mention just a few.

Be aware that ExpressCalc is a somewhat bare-bones program and doesn't have some of the bells and whistles of other shareware spreadsheets.

ExpressCalc
Registration fee: $$
Expressware
P.O. Box 230
Redmond, WA 98073
(206) 788-0932

EZ-Spreadsheet

A serviceable, no-frills spreadsheet, EZ-Spreadsheet's primary virtue is its relative ease of use. Pressing / (the slash key) brings up a menu, as it does in other spreadsheets; unlike some others, however, the menu reads as if it's been written in English. When you access certain commands from the menu, advice or warnings are given. EZ-Spreadsheet also includes several sample worksheets to help you devise your own.

Heed a word of warning, however: With the unregistered version, you'll have to wait while numerous nag screens load before you can actually use the spreadsheet, and the printing feature is not enabled until you register.

EZ-Spreadsheet
Registration fee: $$
EZX Publishing
P.O. Box 58177
Webster, TX 77598
(713) 280-9900; (800) 873-2799, ext. EZS23 (orders only)

FreeCalc

FreeCalc is perhaps the easiest shareware spreadsheet to use. Even if you know nothing about spreadsheets, it should take you only a short amount of time to put together your first worksheet with it.

FreeCalc is easy to use because it breaks most of the conventions followed by other shareware spreadsheets. You won't find the ubiquitous / (slash) command here to bring up a menu. Instead, there's always a menu on display at the bottom of your screen, which keeps all of the spreadsheet's power within easy reach.

It breaks another convention, too. You don't type formulas directly into the spreadsheet, as with most spreadsheets. Instead, you're prompted to fill out a series of screens (one is shown in Figure 5.3). The information from those screens then goes into building the formulas. This makes it easy for users who don't know the proper formula syntax to begin building fairly sophisticated spreadsheets very quickly.

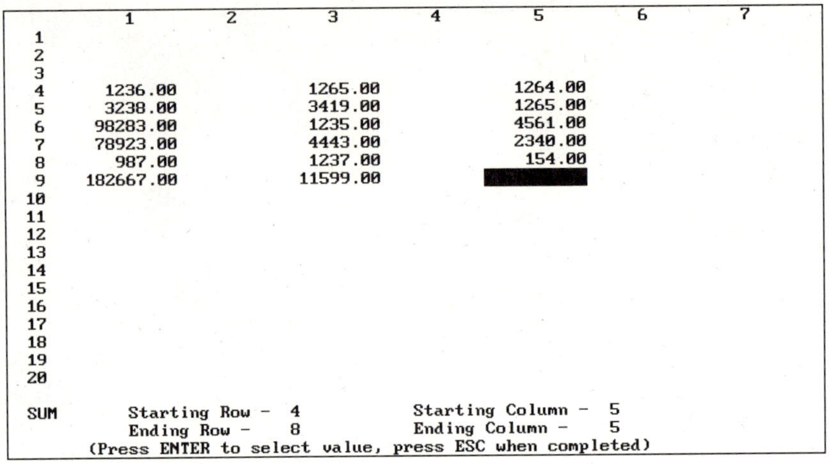

Figure 5.3
Creating a formula with FreeCalc

It also uses an uncommon naming convention for its cells. Instead of using a letter for each row and a number for each column, it uses numbers for both rows and columns. The top left cell of a FreeCalc spreadsheet is called Row 1, Column 1 instead of the standard A1.

FreeCalc also has a word processing mode and supports math coprocessor chips.

Spreadsheet jockeys may be put off by FreeCalc's unusual structure, and especially by having to go through a menu to create a formula in a cell. But if you're a novice or someone who doesn't use spreadsheets very often, FreeCalc may be your best bet.

FreeCalc
Registration fee: $$
Stilwell Software Products
16403 North 43rd Dr.
Glendale, AZ 85306
(602) 820-4952

InstaCalc

How would you like to have your spreadsheet a keystroke away, no matter where you were: at the DOS prompt; in your word processing program, communications package, or database; and even when on-line? Better yet, how would you like to exchange data between your current application and a pop-up spreadsheet with a few keystrokes?

Impossible? No. That's what you get with InstaCalc, a remarkable pop-up spreadsheet. Load the program, then press Alt-I (or another combination you define), and InstaCalc pops up, ready to do your bidding.

You'll find InstaCalc to be a fully featured spreadsheet. Though not quite as powerful as As-Easy-As, it's generally easier to use. Although it has fewer functions, the functions it has are generally easier to reach.

Load InstaCalc by typing **INSTA /P** at the command line (leave off the /P switch if you want it to run as a non-TSR). You can also tell InstaCalc how much memory to allocate for your data. If you wanted it to allocate 80k for your data, for example, you'd type **INSTA /P80000**. By default it allocates 40k. If you want to take it out of memory after it's loaded, type **INSTA /U** at the DOS prompt.

InstaCalc's main screen has a row across the bottom of the screen listing the uses of function keys. To activate the menu with which you'll do most of your work, press **/** (the slash key) and a drop-down menu will appear at the top of your screen, as shown in Figure 5.4. The bulk of the screen is taken up by the spreadsheet.

Figure 5.4
InstaCalc's main menu and several submenus

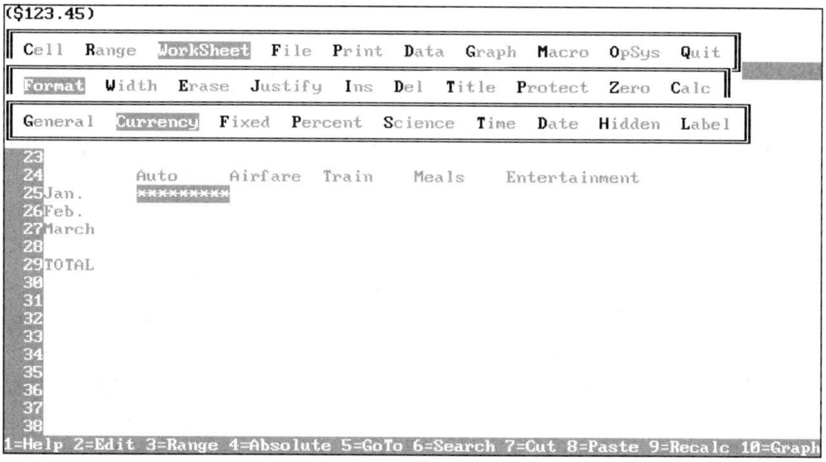

InstaCalc's help features are noteworthy. The screens are context-sensitive, so the help you're getting is always applicable to the problem you're facing. And they're hypertext-like, making it easy to maneuver through them and obtain related information.

The program lets you easily create charts and graphs. With most spreadsheets, creating graphs is a frustrating, time-consuming chore. With InstaCalc, however, simple menus guide you through every step of the process (as Figure 5.5 shows) so that creating attractive graphs is a snap.

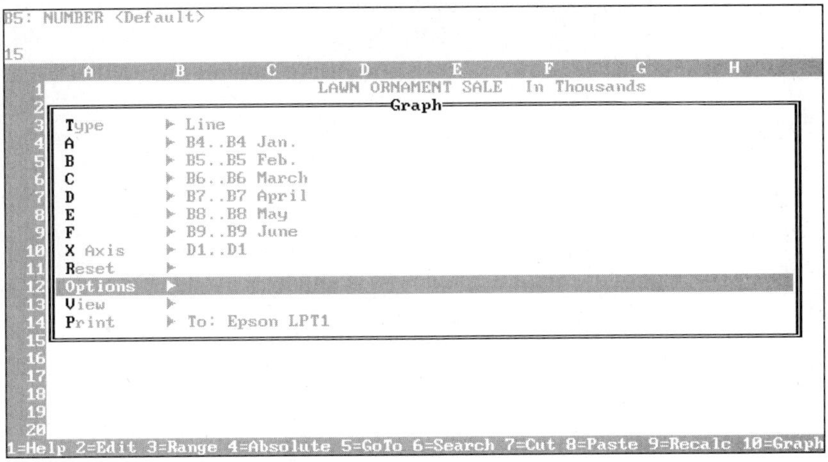

Figure 5.5
Filling out an InstaCalc chart menu

Possibly the program's most unique feature is its ability to cut and paste data between itself and an underlying application. Let's say you're in your word processing program, writing a memo about sales figures for the past year. You'd like a set of figures about the year placed at a certain point in the memo, and you'd like to import them from a spreadsheet you've created in InstaCalc.

To do so, simply move your cursor to the point in the memo where you want the data inserted, and press Alt-I to bring up InstaCalc. When you're in InstaCalc, press F8. Move your cursor to the upper-left corner of the data you want to move, press **.** (a period), move your cursor to highlight the data, and then press Enter. InstaCalc will ask you what kind of line ending—either a carriage return, down arrow, or right arrow—you want for the data, and then automatically place the data in the memo you were writing in your word processor. Figure 5.6 shows data that will be pasted to another application.

You can also bring data into InstaCalc in a similar manner. For example, if you have data in a database that you'd like in an InstaCalc spreadsheet, press Alt-I when you're in your database to bring up InstaCalc, move to the point where you want data placed, and press F8. You'll be put back in your database. Move your cursor to the data, press **.** (a period), highlight the data, and then press Enter. The highlighted data from your database will be put into your spreadsheet.

Much of the program, including its colors, can be easily customized using a separate setup program, which you run before loading InstaCalc.

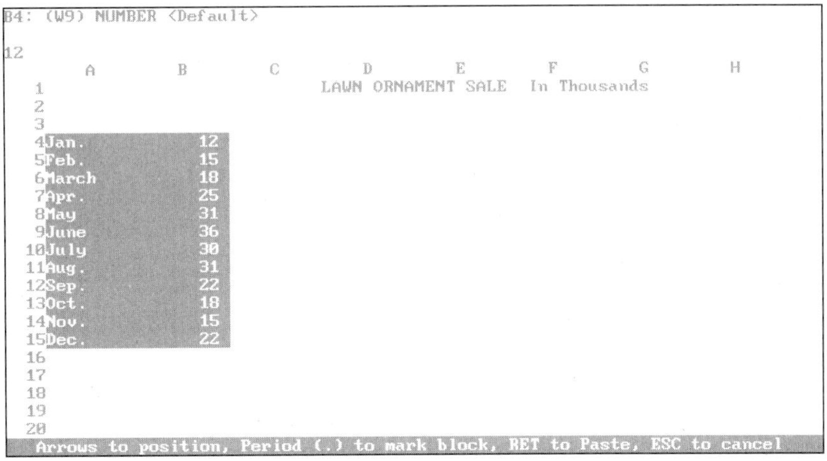

Figure 5.6
Marking data to be pasted to an underlying application

One final note: You may also find versions of a shareware spreadsheet called ProQube Light from FormalSoft, the company that wrote InstaCalc. That spreadsheet is no longer supported by FormalSoft, since a spreadsheet called ProQube is available commercially from another firm.

InstaCalc
Registration fee: $$
FormalSoft
P.O. Box 1913
Sandy, UT 84091
(801) 565-0971

PC-Calc+

Another of ButtonWare's popular line of shareware products, PC-Calc+ is noteworthy for how easy it is to use. As with many other shareware spreadsheets, pressing **/** (the slash key) brings a menu to the screen. Its main menu is shown in Figure 5.7. PC-Calc+'s vertical, drop-down menu can be placed at various points on the screen by moving it with the arrow keys. (The way the menu works and moves will be familiar to users of other ButtonWare products.) To make things faster for experienced users, you can bypass the menus in some instances by using keystrokes.

Also making the program easy to use is its excellent context-sensitive help. Press F1 at any point for a help screen, which can then be repositioned anywhere you want in the same manner as the menu bar. Figure 5.8 shows a sample help screen. To get general help at any point, press F2.

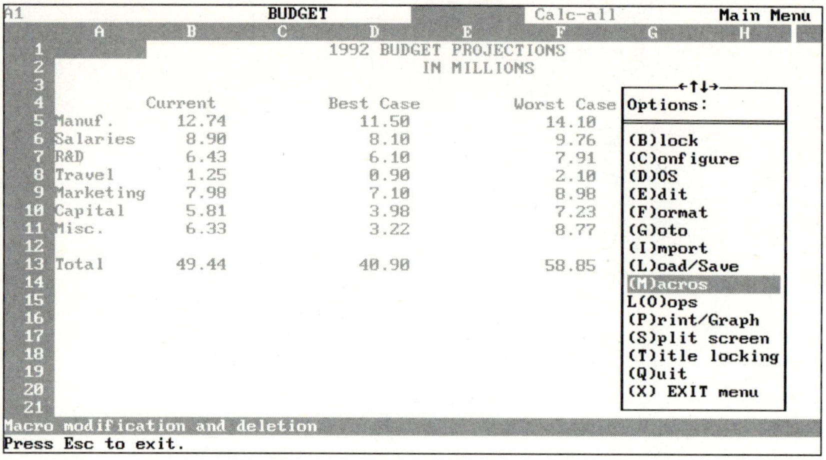

Figure 5.7
PC-Calc+'s main menu

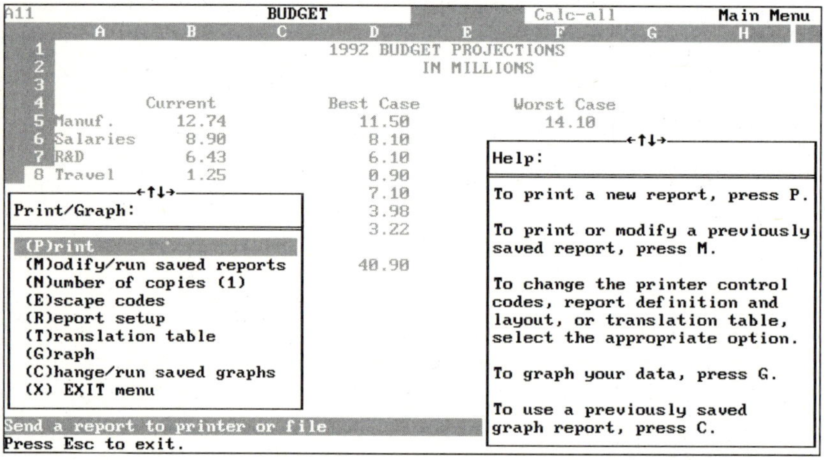

Figure 5.8
One of PC-Calc+'s context-sensitive help screens

The third thing that makes PC-Calc+ one of the easier spreadsheets to use is its excellent documentation. A brief, helpful tutorial, followed by a comprehensive command listing, brings the power of this spreadsheet to novices as well as advanced users.

That's not to say that PC-Calc+ has sacrificed power in its zeal for simplicity—far from it. The program features trigonometric capabilities;

supports 8087, 80287, and 80387 math chips; and includes a wide variety of statistical functions and nice formatting features.

Its ability to create graphs easily is particularly unique and impressive. Choose (P)rint/Graph from the main menu, and then (G)raph from the sub-menu. You'll be guided to define the area of the screen you want to graph and to answer a few simple questions. You're then sent into the program's chart-making module, and your chart is created for you automatically.

Even better is that once you're in the chart-making module, it's simple to change the type of chart you want. If you think your information is better expressed in a pie chart rather than a bar chart, just tell the program to make a pie chart instead, and the data you've already defined will be put into pie form, as shown in Figure 5.9. You can also customize many features of the chart at this point.

Figure 5.9
A pie chart created in PC-Calc+'s chart-making module

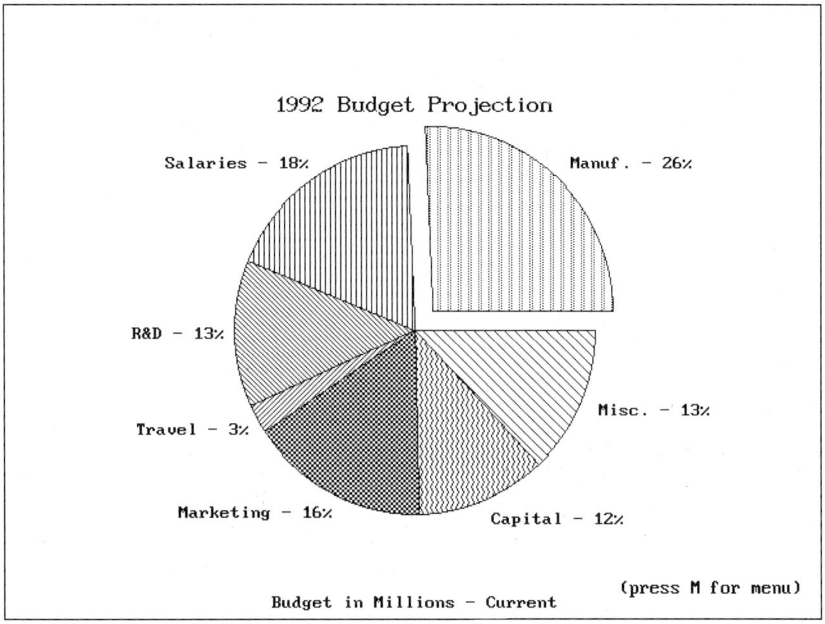

You'll find the program is very flexible when you start it. You can have it load a spreadsheet of your choosing when you load the program. You can also tell it to run a macro automatically on startup. If you have an EGA or higher-grade monitor, you can have 35 to 50 lines per screen displayed rather than the default of 25.

To run the program and have it automatically load your BUDGET spreadsheet, for example, you would type **PCC BUDGET**. To have it display

43 lines on an EGA monitor, or 50 lines on a VGA monitor, you would add the parameter **/E=H**. To have it run macro D upon loading, add the parameter **/M=D**. To do all this in one line, the proper syntax would be

```
PCC BUDGET /E=H /M=D
```

You can also set these parameters as defaults. While some shareware spreadsheets offer more power than PC-Calc+, few of them blend sophisticated capabilities with ease of use quite so seamlessly.

PC-Calc+
Registration fee: $$$
ButtonWare, Inc.
P.O. Box 96058
Bellevue, WA 98009
(206) 454-0479; (800) JBUTTON (orders only)

Power Sheets

As its name implies, Power Sheets is a powerful spreadsheet, with far more capabilities and horsepower than the average user will ever need. If you're a high-end spreadsheet maven, or if you just like to know that all that power is waiting for you to unleash it, you'll find this spreadsheet to your liking.

Power Sheets is a three-dimensional spreadsheet—your data is contained in many layers of rows and columns. (Power Sheets calls each layer of data a *page.*) In essence, when you use Power Sheets, you're using a "data cube," since you can use each layer of data in the spreadsheet.

You'll find an extremely rich library of functions built into Power Sheets, including trigonometric and Boolean functions. It also includes a programming language so that experts can write self-contained applications with the program. Power Sheets comes with a number of such programs already built in.

Even though it has an enormous amount of power, it's still not that difficult to use (although it might not be the right spreadsheet for those who are leery of numbers). Because of its 3-D nature and its numerous functions, it can be confusing. Dedicated number crunchers, though, will be pleased at what they find.

Power Sheets
Registration fee: $
Al Baker
3936 Sunset Lane
Northbrook, IL 60062
(708) 480-9505

Lotus 1-2-3 Templates, Add-ins, and Utilities

Pick a financial or numerical problem, any problem. Chances are, there's a 1-2-3 template, add-in, or utility out there to solve it for you. There are thousands of such templates and add-ins available. If you work in an office, someone down the hall from you has a library of them, you can be sure. There are also many shareware and public domain templates and utilities. The following is just a small sampling of some of the more useful ones.

Lotus Worksheets and Macros

You can get a disk that contains many Lotus templates for a wide variety of needs from the disk vendor PC-SIG: macros and programs that do such things as financial analysis, creating mailing labels, preparing data for import into 1-2-3, and creating menu macros. Note that the fee to PC-SIG is *not* a registration fee; it's only the cost of the disk with the programs on it. If you decide you like any of the templates on it, you should register with the author of the template (registration information will be included with the disk).

Lotus Worksheets and Macros
Disk fee: $
PC-SIG
1030D East Duane Ave.
Sunnyvale, CA 94086
(408) 730-9291

Rat

No, perhaps Rat is not the best choice of names for a program, but that doesn't mean this utility isn't useful. It's a programmable mouse driver for 1-2-3 (and other programs) that includes a menu interface for 1-2-3. You can also create your own menus with Rat and change the ones already written, making 1-2-3 even easier to use.

Rat
Registration fee: $
Ronnie D. Tanner
10509 Woodland Dr.
Greenville, TX 75401

Scientific and Engineering Tool for Lotus 1-2-3

A menu-driven template for those who use 1-2-3 for scientific and engineering applications, this tool can be used for operations as simple as basic arithmetic or as complex as sophisticated statistical analysis and equation solving.

Scientific and Engineering Tool for Lotus 1-2-3
Registration fee: $
K.I.T.A.L. Software
P.O. Box 748
Karmiel 20100
ISRAEL

Success

This is a set of useful templates for small-business owners and others. It includes templates for creating travel expense reports, purchase orders, invoices, and purchase requisitions, as well as a weekly calender. Especially useful is a template that figures out the price of a home you can afford, along with the amount of the loan you'll need for the home and the size of the down payment.

Also included are eight images in PIC format, which you can use to jazz up presentation spreadsheets. The images include a variety of arrows, a picture of a computer, star bursts, and a dollar sign. Better still, these templates and PIC files are free.

Success
Registration fee: None
Available on CompuServe in the LOTUSA forum, under the file name of SUCCES.ARC.

Templates of Doom

Are you tired of dull manuals, tiresome tutorials, and run-of-the mill books, but still want to learn how to use a spreadsheet? If so, Templates of Doom is for you. Templates of Doom is a funny, fast-paced tutorial, disguised as an adventure game; its opening screen is shown in Figure 5.10. It has you solve a series of 25 increasingly difficult puzzles in a race against the clock. You'll come across exotic locales and even stranger characters, and your only weapons are your intelligence and your growing knowledge of spreadsheets.

Templates of Doom works with 1-2-3, with "work-alikes" such as Quattro Pro and VP Planner, and with Microsoft Excel. You go into the game a beginner and come out with a basic understanding of the use and design of spreadsheets—and you've had a lot of fun in the process.

Templates of Doom
Registration fee: $$
Solar Systems Software
8105 Shelter Creek
San Bruno, CA 94066
(415) 952-2375

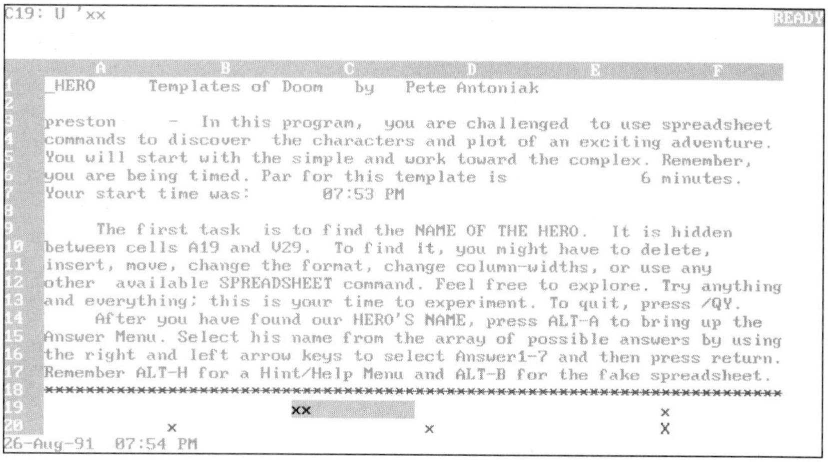

Figure 5.10
The start of the Templates of Doom quest

Total Investor

If you're lucky enough to have amassed a financial portfolio, this template will track and analyze it for you. It provides a complete statement of your current account, reports on your capital gains, and lets you sort the securities in your portfolio in a number of different ways. It will also chart the value of your portfolio over time, so you can see its worth on a graph.

The most powerful part of the template has to do with the way in which it analyzes your portfolio, helping you make decisions about what to buy and sell. It uses a variety of financial and statistical functions and formulas to give you a good look at your finances.

Total Investor
Registration fee: $$
Hughes Financial Services
P.O. Box 1244
Nashua, N.H. 03061

The Whiterock Alternative

Lotus 1-2-3 is an enormously powerful spreadsheet, but it's never been accused of being easy to use. There's a kind of macho ethic associated with the spreadsheet that can be summed up in the saying "No pain, no gain." The idea seems to be that you have to suffer if you want to build a spreadsheet.

If you use The Whiterock Alternative, however, you'll get much gain with little pain. It's a menu interface for 1-2-3, designed to make the notoriously difficult spreadsheet easy to use. Press Alt-M and you'll get its main menu.

The Whiterock Alternative offers more than just a menuing shell. It also includes powerful worksheets specifically designed for the menuing front end. You pay one fee for the shell, which comes with a variety of spreadsheets and utilities, and then another fee for each of the additional spreadsheets you use. The basic program includes a loan analyzer, a mailing-list database, a checkbook ledger (shown in Figure 5.11), a library of useful macros, and a worksheet to help you keep track of hours spent on particular tasks, to help you in job-costing.

The Whiterock Alternative
Registration fee: $
Whiterock Alternative
P.O. Box 45458
Seattle, WA 98145

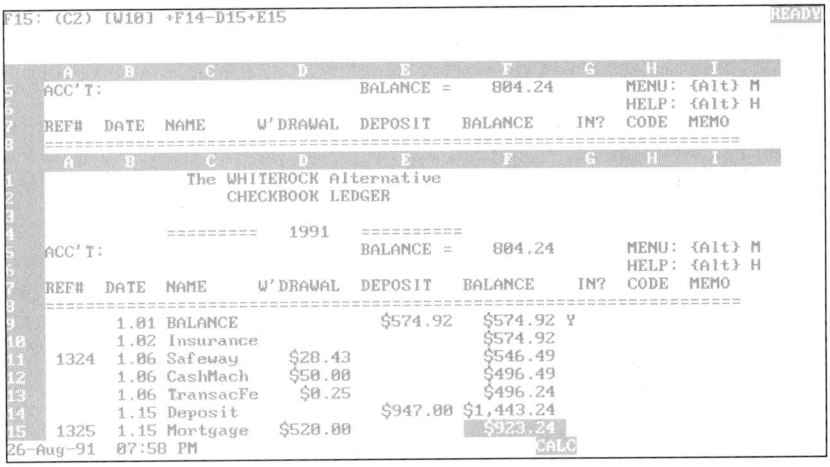

Figure 5.11
The Whiterock Alternative's checkbook ledger for 1-2-3

CHAPTER

6

Databases and Database Utilities

Databases
dBASE Utilities
Miscellaneous Databases

DATABASES, PERHAPS BECAUSE THEY ARE AMONG THE MOST POWERful of PC applications, may also be one of the most misunderstood. Many people are intimidated by the confusing terminology the programs often use. And it's true that databases can be quite complex applications.

But databases need not be difficult to use. Although they can be used by programmers to write complete applications, they can also be useful even if you have very little computer experience, to allow you to assemble a Rolodex of telephone numbers or create a catalog of your record collection.

In general, databases are simply a way to allow you to give order to information: they're electronic filing systems. If you have a database containing the names of members of a PC users group, for example, and you want to send out a mass mailing to all the members, you could use a database to create a letter individually addressed to each member, and then to print out mailing labels to send the letters. Some databases have a module for writing the letter itself; others require you to use a word processor for that. You also could use a database to keep track of your checks or your expenses.

Most shareware databases are used for these kinds of applications, rather than for programming. PC-File, ButtonWare's well-known shareware database, is a particularly good choice. That's not to say, however, that shareware databases can't be used for programming: a number of them can. WAMPUM in particular stands out as a top choice.

In addition to databases, you'll find a great many shareware database utilities, especially for the ever-popular dBASE. The second part of this chapter looks at those utilities, which let you do everything from easily finding and deleting duplicate records from a database to helping database programmers more easily create dBASE screens.

Finally, there are the unclassifiable database programs—hundreds of them. You'll find pop-up databases, databases for tracking graphics, and far more. I've listed some of these programs at the chapter's end.

Databases

There are a surprising number of feature-rich shareware databases available. Some are flat-file databases, in which all the information is stored in a single file. Others are more complex relational databases, which allow different database files to have links between them.

Although shareware databases often lack the programming prowess of their commercial brethren, they usually have one big advantage: they're easier to use. Simple-to-follow menus are generally the rule. You should be able to create your first database file in surprisingly little time. And, as with most other shareware, these databases tend to be priced well below the costs of commercial databases. For these reasons, if you've been scared away from databases in the past, shareware should give you an excuse to jump in and try one. You'll be surprised at how easy databases are to use.

FastFile

This is a particularly good database program if you need to take one on the road. The executable file is relatively small (it takes up only 97k), so you can easily fit it, along with other applications, on a single floppy. Since FastFile keeps its data in memory when loaded, rather than on disk, it tends to be fast, too, and to use little battery life on laptops.

A basic, no-frills, menu-driven program, FastFile comes with eight prebuilt databases for tasks such as keeping track of your checks, tracking invoices, keeping tabs on clients, and helping teachers keep track of students' grades. You can get four additional application files at a modest cost. It can also be used to create mailing labels.

FastFile
Registration fee: $
R.D. (Monte) Benham
312 West Tucannon
Kennewick, WA 99336
(509) 783-3829

File Express

A very easy but powerful flat-file database, File Express is organized simply and logically, so that even those new to databases can set up a new database quickly and easily. But it has enough raw power and bells and whistles to keep even experienced users happy.

You do almost everything in File Express using simple-to-follow menus and by responding to prompts. The main menu, seen in Figure 6.1, sets the tone for File Express—it's clean-looking, self-explanatory, and written in simple English.

To open an existing database, move your cursor to 1 - Open a Database, or type the number **1**, and press Enter, and you'll be greeted with a screen that lists all the existing databases. When you choose one of those databases, the database will load. You'll then be sent back to the main menu, where you can do work on the database.

If you instead want to create a new database, again move your cursor to 1 - Open a Database, or type the number **1,** and press Enter. The screen listing existing databases will appear. Instead of choosing an existing database, type in the name of the database you want to create, and press Enter. You'll be greeted with a screen that will help you define your database. Name each of the fields, define its type and length, and you've defined your database. Figure 6.2 shows an example of database definition with File Express.

Figure 6.1
File Express's main menu

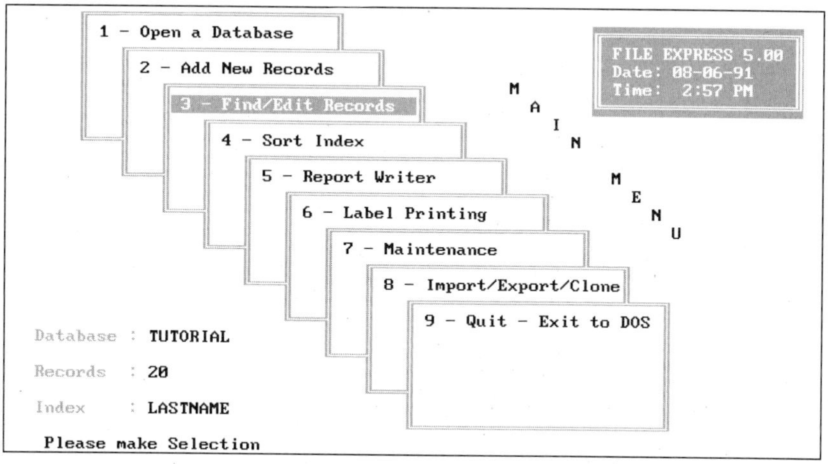

Figure 6.2
Defining the fields in a new database with File Express

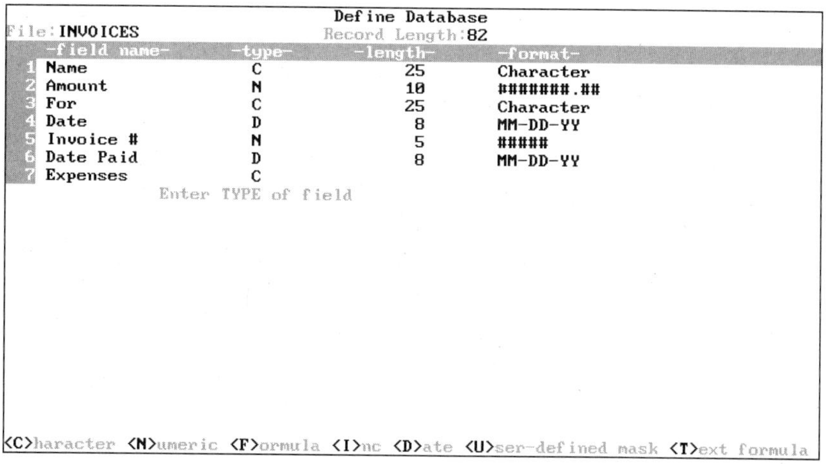

After you've defined your database, it's time to add new records. From the main menu, choose 2 - Add New Records. Fill out the record, and press F10. You've just added a record, as illustrated in Figure 6.3.

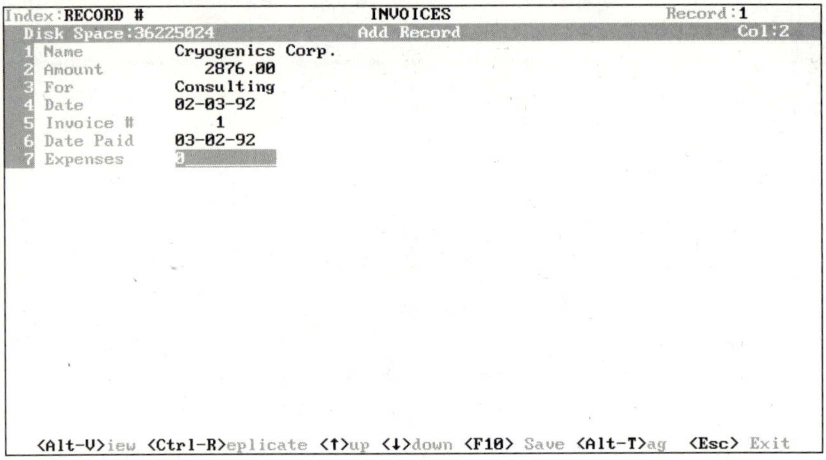

Figure 6.3 Adding a new record to a File Express database

Searching for a record in a database is similarly easy. Choose 3 - Find/Edit Records from the main menu, and use the Find menu to choose the kind of search you want to perform. You can perform a fast, simple search by using the Quick Scan mode. For more complex searches, choose Find/Edit a Record from the Find menu. You'll then be presented with a screen that allows you to use operators such as > (greater than) and < (less than). You can also combine several search criteria. See Figure 6.4 for a sample of how to use this search method.

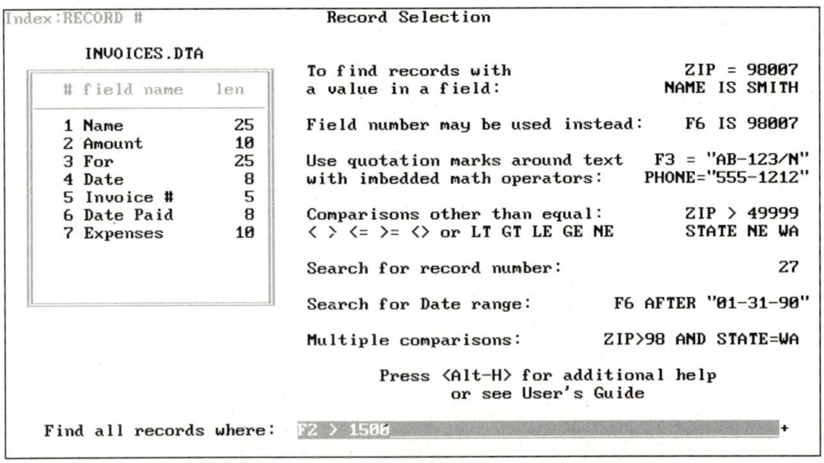

Figure 6.4 Searching for a record with File Express's > operator

Just about everything else in File Express works similarly to creating databases and records and searching for records. Making everything simpler as well are easy-to-read, context-sensitive help screens.

The program hasn't sacrificed power in order to be easy to use, though. You'll find keyboard macros and macro keys, a powerful report generator, and the ability to create mailing labels and import and export databases. It's also easy to customize.

File Express
Registration fee: $$$
Expressware
P.O. Box 1800
Duvall, WA 98019
(800) 753-3453

Information Please!

This is a simple, free-form database. Instead of defining fields, you type in your information using the program's text editor. Then you define *key words* to attach to each record. Later, you can search the database using those key words to pull up the record you want. This program wouldn't be useful for things such as creating an electronic Rolodex or keeping track of your checks, but would be your best bet to organize more free-form information, such as notes about an ongoing project.

A unique aspect of the program is that you can tie each record to a graphic file in PCX format, so your database can include pictures. The program ships with a database of common DOS problems and their solutions, which in itself is a good value.

Information Please!
Registration fee: $$
TexaSoft
P.O. Box 1169
Cedar Hill, TX 75104
(214) 291-2115

Instant Recall

Though this shareware program is no longer supported by its authors, versions of it are still floating around on bulletin boards and are available through disk vendors. (It has been replaced by a more powerful, commercial version of the package, called Memory Mate, from Broderbund Software.)

Instant Recall is a TSR, so it's easy to get at your data—it's always only a keystroke away. This is a free-form database, so you won't define fields or key words with it. The program is best suited for jotting down ideas, notes, and other information that's not easily categorized. When you search for a word, it searches every word in the database, not just key words.

Instant Recall
Registration fee: None
Instant Recall is available from disk vendors such as the Public Software Library.

PC-File

This is a relational database almost everyone will love. It accomplishes the seemingly impossible: It's easy enough for rank beginners to use, and powerful enough for database mavens as well. All in all, it's a remarkable combination of power and ease.

Beginners will appreciate its menu-driven format. After you've loaded the program, you should be able to create your first database in less than 10 minutes, and be ready to start adding records. Experienced users will revel in its advanced features. Its files are dBASE-compatible; it offers LAN support, password protection, and a macro language; and it has powerful, sophisticated searching features, including Boolean logic and the ability to search for data in a memo field. It lets you sort up to ten fields at once. Experienced users can bypass some of the menu screens and use the keyboard instead.

What can you do with PC-File? Almost anything you want. It can create mailing labels, perform mail-merge tasks, generate reports, and create and print a variety of graphics from your database. It even has a phone dialer, so that you can have your modem dial your telephone and keep track of your phone calls for you.

When you load PC-File, you're asked whether you want to load an existing database or create a new one. If you tell it to load an existing one, you'll be greeted with the program's Master menu (shown in Figure 6.5). This is the main menu, from which you'll do most of your work. By using function keys or scrolling to a menu item, you'll be able to search the database, add new records, create graphics or reports, write letters, and perform a variety of housekeeping chores with a number of utilities.

To search for data, press F2, or scroll to the Find a record item on the Master menu. After two search menus, in which you define how you want to search for data, you're presented with a screen in which you enter the data to search for. PC-File does the rest. Figure 6.6 shows a typical search screen.

You use the other functions in PC-File in a similar manner. To create charts based on your data, pick F4 from the Master menu and fill out a series of forms. You'll soon have a chart created simply and easily.

Figure 6.5
PC-File's master menu

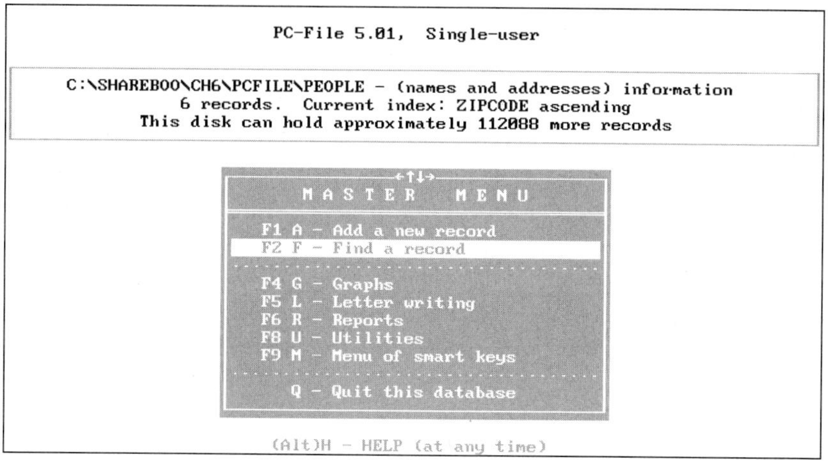

Figure 6.6
Searching through a PC-File database for a last name

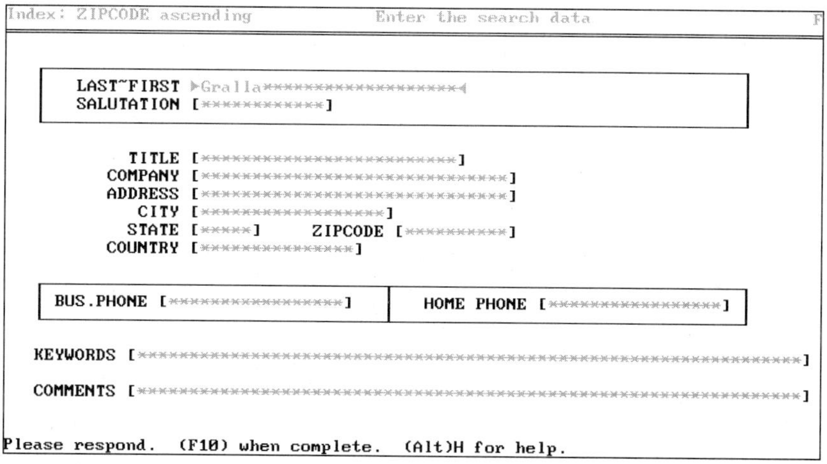

One especially noteworthy feature is the built-in text editor. If you want to create a mass mailing with some databases, you'll have to figure out ways to link your database and word processor. This is not necessary with PC-File. It has a module for letter writing and performing mail-merge operations, so it can all be done in a single step. See Figure 6.7 for an example of how to create a mass-mailing document using PC-File.

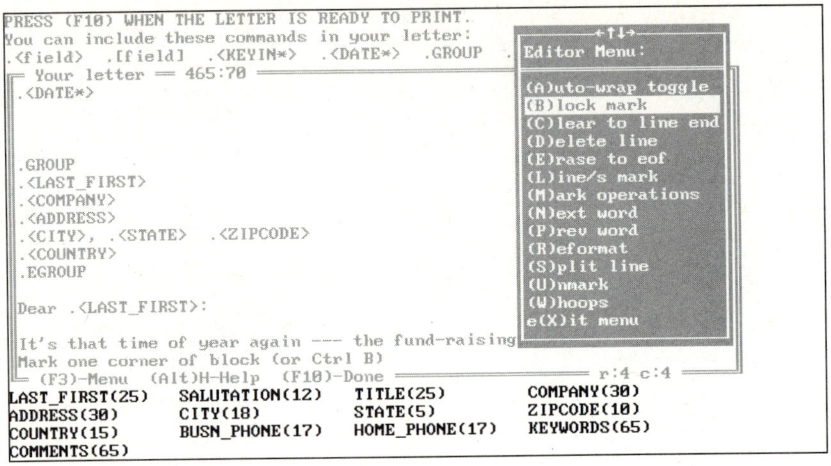

Figure 6.7 Using PC-File's letter-writing module to compose a form letter

Creating a new database from scratch is similarly easy. Decide what fields you want in each record; provide information about each field, such as its length and the type of field it will be (numeric, date, or text); and you have a database.

This brief description doesn't even begin to hint at the power and flexibility of PC-File. Its sorting and indexing capabilities are prodigious, it can export graphs in PostScript format, its ability to import and export data is outstanding, it's easily configured, and it has solid macro support. The built-in, context-sensitive help is well-designed. You can even use a mouse to drive the program.

Be aware that although ButtonWare will continue to support shareware versions of PC-File, versions 6.0 and above, including the Windows version, are not shareware and are only available commercially. The last shareware version was version 5.0.

PC-File
Registration fee: $$$$
ButtonWare
ButtonWare, Inc.
P.O. Box 96058
Bellevue, WA 98009
(206) 454-0479; (800) 528-8866 (orders)

ProFile

ProFile falls into the medium range for ease of use for shareware databases, but it's definitely near the top when it comes to power. In particular, its searching and indexing capabilities are worthy of note, allowing for exceptional sophistication and flexibility. Its mathematical functions are solid as well, and it can create more databases and records than you'll ever need to use: over two *billion* records per database. It features drop-down menus and context-sensitive help, so it's not as difficult as you might think to get at all this data.

When you first load ProFile, you're presented with a list of all your existing databases and asked to choose among them. If you'd rather create a new database, type in the name you want it to have. If you'd prefer not to create a new database or load an existing one, press Esc; you'll be brought into ProFile's main menu, shown in Figure 6.8. (When you load an existing database, you'll also be brought to this main menu.) This is the command center for the entire program.

Figure 6.8
ProFile's main menu

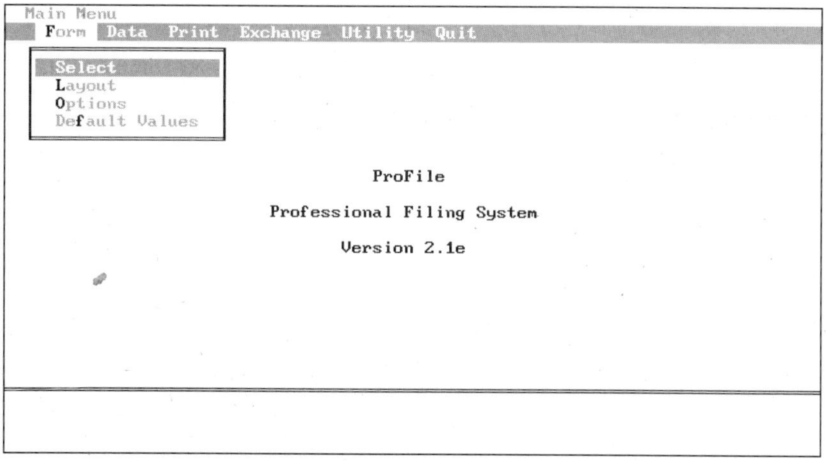

If you reach the main menu and then decide you want to create a new database, pick Select. Create a new database by typing in its name. At this point, you can either design the new database from scratch or model it after one that already exists. To model it after one that exists, type the name of the model, and press Enter.

If you're going to create a database from scratch, you'll be presented with a primarily blank screen, where you can create your new database structure. Move your cursor to the point where you want a field, type in the field's name followed by a colon (:), and type underline characters (_) to represent the length of the field. Do this for all the fields, and then press F10.

Now you're ready to define each field a little further. At the bottom of your screen will be a form to fill out about each field you've created. Here you'll define all the field's characteristics—for example, whether the field should be character-based, number-based, or based on some other characteristic. You'll also define rules about entering data into each field. For example, you can force certain fields to be filled in all the time and others to be entered in upper- or lowercase letters, to be indexed or not, and so forth. You can even define a help screen to accompany each field. See Figure 6.9 for an example of how to create the form for a new database.

Figure 6.9
Creating the form for a new ProFile database

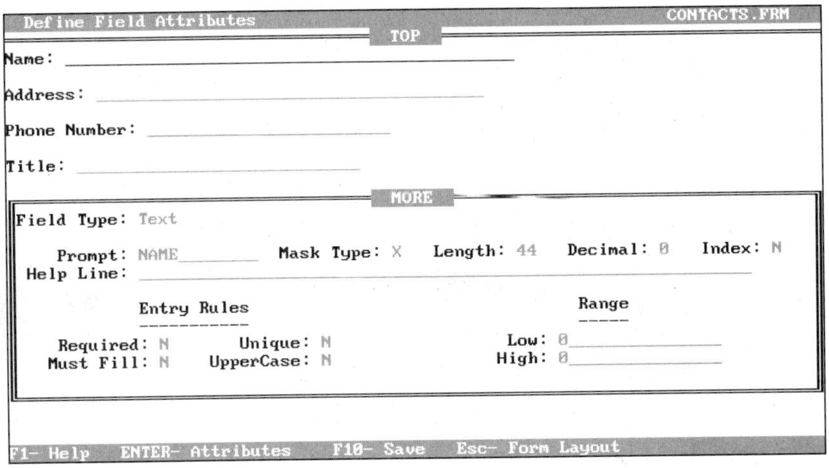

Once the database has been created, you add records by choosing Data and then Add from the main menu. Then simply fill out the form you've created, as shown in Figure 6.10. Everything else in the program is similarly menu-driven.

One of the program's more interesting features is its superb mathematical operations. If you define one of the fields in the database as a calculated field, you can perform sophisticated mathematical calculations upon it. You can perform simple math, such as addition, subtraction, multiplication, and division; but you can also do more complicated operations, such as squares and square roots, sines and cosines, arc tangents, and logarithms.

For safety's sake, ProFile backs up your files automatically. It has a dialing function, so you can use your modem to dial any telephone number in your database. And its ability to create sophisticated reports—with detailed data and an attractive look as well—is top-notch.

ProFile
Registration fee: $$
National Software Design
12505 Fostoria Way
Darnestown, MD 20878
(301) 921-4283

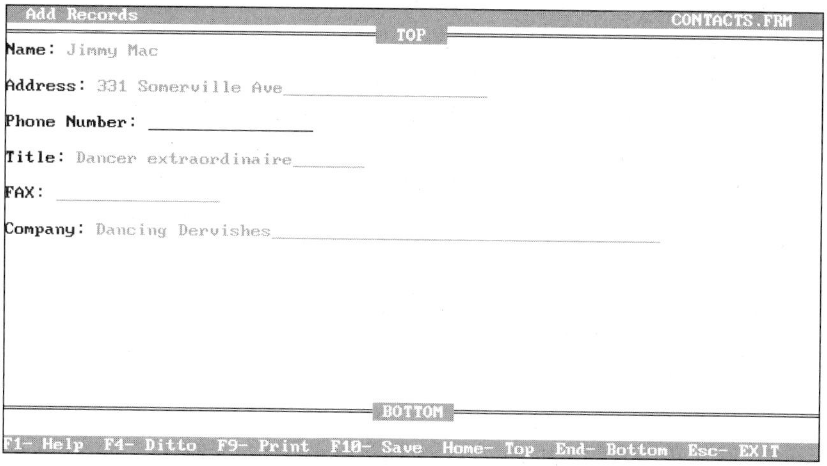

Figure 6.10 Adding a record to a ProFile database

WAMPUM

An exceptionally powerful and complex relational database, WAMPUM is actually two programs in one. One program is a database manager, which functions pretty typically. The other part is a programming tool—you can use WAMPUM to create full-blown applications.

WAMPUM (which stands for Ward's Automatic Menu Package Using Microcomputers) writes dBASE-compatible files, so that importing and exporting data from other database programs is easy. It has powerful reporting features, the ability to create labels, and a text-editing module for writing mail-merge form letters.

Most of your work will be done in WAMPUM's main menu, shown in Figure 6.11. Scroll to the item you want or press the associated letter's key, and you'll generally meet with a submenu. Figure 6.12 shows the submenu that lets you choose an existing database file to load.

Although learning WAMPUM for the first time isn't particularly easy, once you know your way around a little, performing most database functions is fairly straightforward. To alter an existing database, for example, you would first load a database, then choose the option labeled "B - BUILD new file" from the main menu and put an asterisk in place of a file name when a submenu comes up. You can then alter the form of your database.

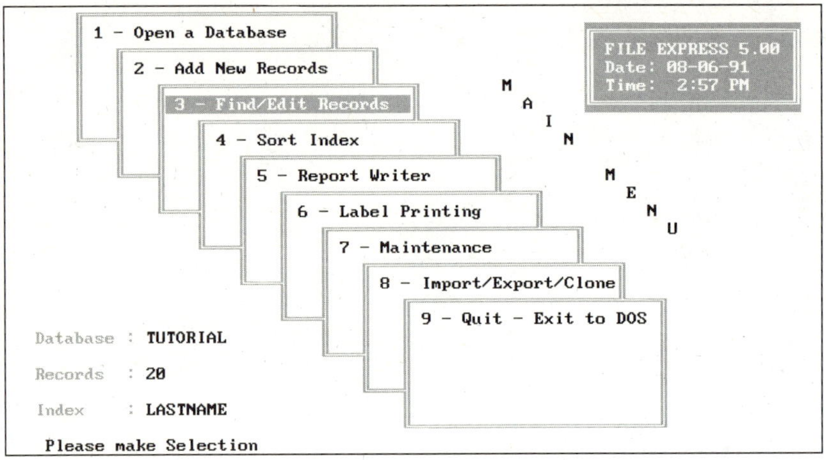

Figure 6.11
WAMPUM's main menu

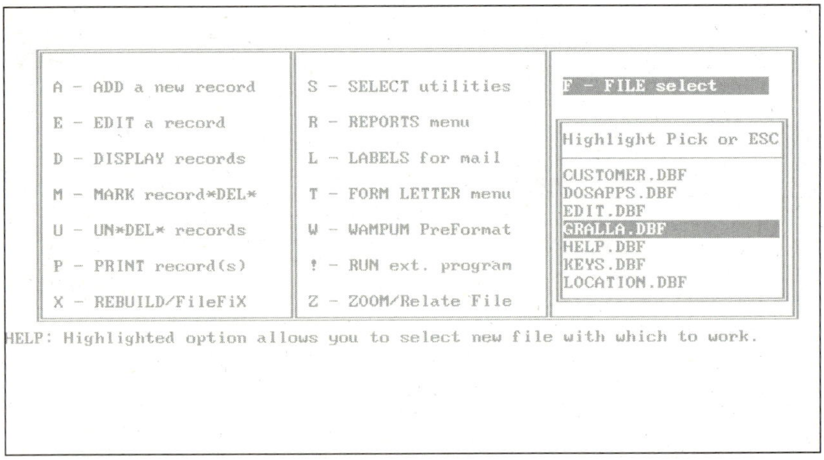

Figure 6.12
Choosing a database from WAMPUM's main menu

The program is quite configurable, offers many useful utilities, and is an exceptional value for the power it has. It can also be loaded as a TSR, taking up only 20k of memory, so that your database files are always easily accessible. You can use PCX files as fields, too, to create a database of images. And it has a built-in phone dialer and network support.

WAMPUM
Registration fee: $$
Ward Mundy
4160 Club Dr.
Atlanta, GA 30319

dBASE Utilities

There's no doubt about it—dBASE is *the* de facto database standard. That program has spawned a sizable subindustry of add-ins and utilities, both in the commercial and shareware worlds. The following is just a small sample of shareware utilities that work with dBASE. Note that many of these utilities will work not just with dBASE itself, but also with dBASE-compatible files, which many databases, shareware and otherwise, are able to create.

Data Master

Data Master is a superb program for helping you work with dBASE databases. It's menu-driven, and you'll probably find it easier to use than dBASE itself. One of its more interesting features converts Lotus 1-2-3 worksheets into dBASE files and changes dBASE files into Lotus 1-2-3 worksheets. You can also look at 1-2-3 worksheets and do some simple editing on them.

But this program's emphasis is on working with dBASE files, not spreadsheets. Data Master lets you create new databases, edit existing ones, add and copy records, change the structure of your database, look for and delete duplicate records, and perform sophisticated queries and create reports, as well as many other functions. Since it's menu-driven, it's easy to use. To perform many database functions, for example, you would choose USE from the main menu, press Enter, and then choose the function you want to perform from the submenu shown in Figure 6.13.

There's a wealth of features here. Do you need to perform mathematical calculations? Press F6, and up pops a calculator. It also has a basic word processor for creating and editing files. With it, you can create a form letter, use Data Master to perform a mail-merge, and then print out the letter and mailing labels. Data Master also offers LAN support.

Data Master
Registration fee: $
RKS Software, Inc.
3820 North Dittmar Road
Arlington, VA 22207

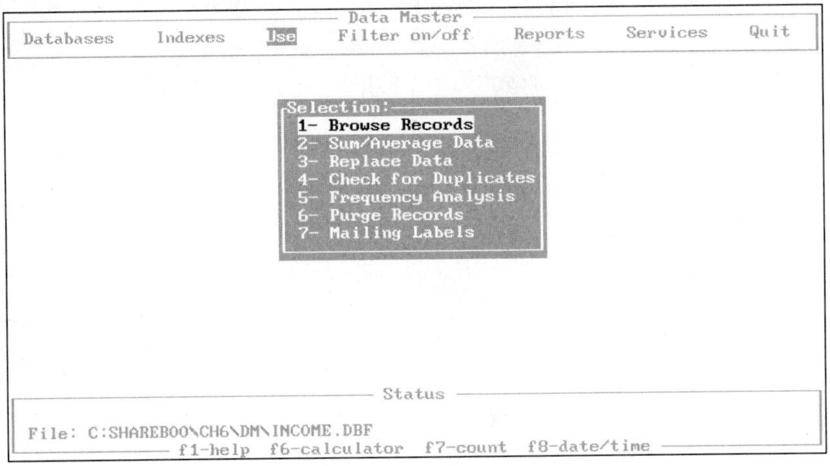

Figure 6.13 Data Master's main menu, with the Use submenu displayed

dbClean

dbClean will search out duplicate files on your database and, if you so desire, will delete them as well. Doing this will save disk space and make your database work more quickly, since there'll be less information to sift through. Use the Turbo mode, and the program will automatically find duplicate records and delete them without your intervention. For safer, but slower operation, use the Batch or Interactive mode.

dbClean
Registration fee: $
Practical Programs
1013 East Diamond Blvd., Suite 141
Anchorage, AK 99515

DBSCAN

A useful little utility, DBSCAN lets you browse through the contents of a dBASE file without ever actually having to load dBASE. You use it directly from the DOS prompt by typing **DBSCAN**. Note that, although you can browse through a database, you can't change or add records, create reports, or do any kind of database housekeeping. The registration fee includes full source code so that it can be incorporated into your own database application.

DBSCAN
Registration fee: $$
Softshop
P.O. Box 353
Sandown, NH 03873
(603) 887-4887

DBSCREEN

This is a handy utility for those who create dBASE applications. With it, you can create your screens by "painting" in Edit mode in a full screen display, rather than by having to enter rows and numbers in a format file. This Painting mode lets you directly create the form of your database. The same author has a number of other dBASE utilities that do things such as change tabs into spaces, encrypt files so that only you can access them, and decrypt them to allow anyone to use them.

DBSCREEN
Registration fee: $
Michael Speyer
1406 NE 154th St.
Seattle, WA 98155
(206) 365-7248

dBSearch

This is a program that lets you manage dBASE files without having to use—or even know—dBASE. Featuring pull-down menus, it allows you to browse, sort, and search for records; print records and mailing labels; and more. It will find use among people who have been given or inherited a dBASE file, but who don't quite know what to do with it.

dBSearch
Registration fee: $
Dave Wallen
Reliable Programming
P.O. Box 530950
San Jose, CA 95153

PopDBF

PopDBF is a TSR that lets you get at dBASE-compatible database files instantly. Load the program, and then whenever you want to get at database information—even when you're in another program—press Alt-Backspace, and up comes PopDBF.

PopDBF will do more than just allow you to view the files. You'll also be able to delete files and records, print records, search for strings anywhere in the database, append and edit records, and more.

Although it's quite an easy program to use, context-sensitive help is available by pressing Alt-F1, and general help by pressing F1. A companion program, PopAid, will allow you to create a database structure if you want. You can then add files to the database using PopDBF.

PopDBF
Registration fee: $; $$ for both PopDBF and PopAid
Bowen Software
P.O. Box 2134
East Peoria, IL 61611
(309) 699-0950

Miscellaneous Databases

Do you have a number of images in PCX format on your PC, and need a way to keep track of them? Need instant access to a database, even when you're in another program? These are just two of the problems that miscellaneous databases can solve for you. The databases listed below are usually designed for a single task, and so tend not to be as broadly applicable as general-purpose databases.

There are hundreds of these programs out there; the following is just a small sampling of what's available. They'll give you a taste of what you can find if you spend enough time on bulletin boards or browsing through disk vendors' catalogs.

dLITE

Full-featured database programs like dBASE and PC-File have one problem in common—their records are not always within easy reach from external applications. To get at them, you have to exit the application you're in, load the database, and do a search. Then, information in hand, you'll have to exit the database and reload your previous program. Not a pretty process.

dLITE has an answer for the problem—it runs in the background as a TSR, waiting to do your bidding. When you need to get at your database, press Alt-1, and dLITE pops up over your current application. You then have access to your data.

Once dLITE pops up, you can do a number of things with your database. You can add, edit, delete, and undelete records. You can create mailing labels, lists, and reports. You can also use some handy utilities, to create and rebuild indexes, for instance.

What's especially useful about dLITE is that it enables you to paste a record from the database to your underlying application. To do so, first load dLITE as a TSR, then run your application. Press Alt-1, choose PASTE from the dLITE menu, and press Enter. You'll be prompted to search for a record, which will then appear on your screen when found, as shown in Figure 6.14. Type **Y** to answer the question "PASTE this record?", and the record will be pasted to your underlying application.

Figure 6.14
Pasting data to an underlying application with dLITE

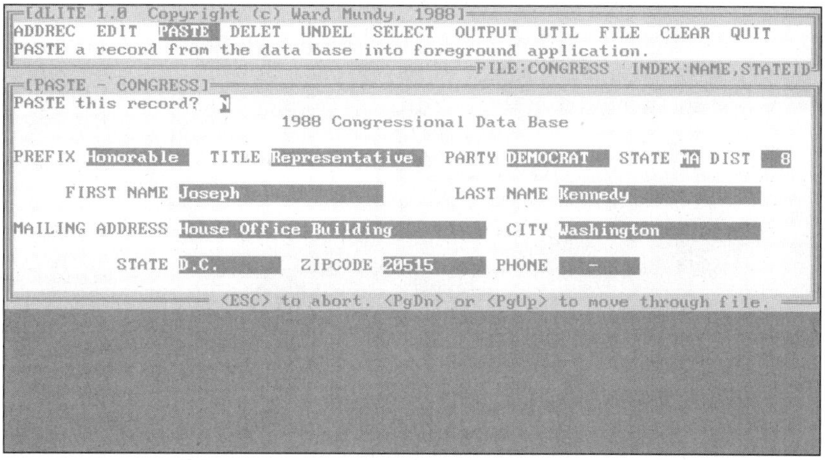

dLITE comes with two sample databases: a listing of every member of Congress and an index to *PC Magazine*.

dLITE
Registration fee: $
Ward Mundy
4160 Club Dr.
Atlanta, GA 30319

Find-X

A cataloging system more than a general-purpose database, Find-X is ideal for creating a database of your music, video, or software library, or of your home inventory for insurance purposes. You assign a number to each item you're keeping track of, and give the record a date and a descriptive identification. You can then use fairly sophisticated search criteria to find whatever item you're looking for.

Find-X
Registration fee: $
John Forester
Custom Cycle Fitments
726 Madrone Ave.
Sunnyvale, CA 94086
(408) 734-9426

Image Access

Image Access is a unique database whose purpose is to keep track of pictures and images instead of raw data. You set up a database as you would any other, put in the records, including a description of the image you're tracking, and then associate that record with an image file. You can then search through the database as you normally would. When you find a record you want to view, you'll first see the text part of the record. If you then want to see the image itself, press F10, and the image will appear on screen.

The images have to be in TIF, PCX, or MSP format to be accessed by the program. These are common graphics formats, often produced by scanners and paint packages. Many clip art images are also available in these formats.

There are a number of uses to which this database might be put. Desktop publishers can use it to inventory their image library. Realtors can use it to keep a photo database of houses. As an added plus, the images can be printed out, along with the notes accompanying them, on HP LaserJets, Epson LQ 24-pin printers, or the IBM ProPrinter X24 printer.

Image Access
Registration fee: $$
Wierenga Software
P.O. Box 595
Muskegon, MI 49443

Treebase

This is one of the odder, and more interesting, databases you'll ever find. Throw away any ideas you have about what a database is before trying this program.

Treebase operates from a visual tree display, as shown in Figure 6.15. It's set up in a hierarchical manner, much like the subdirectories on a hard disk: There's a root with various branches and subbranches coming off from it. Each item on the tree is a record; Treebase can hold 32,767 records of any length per database. Records can be free-form text only.

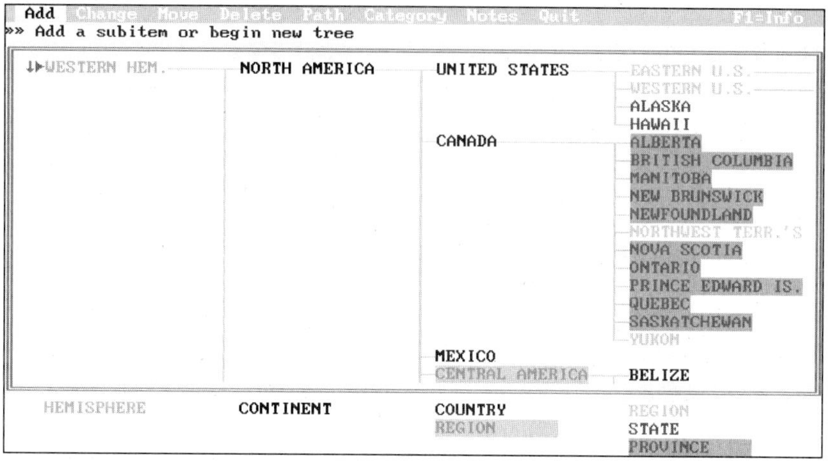

Figure 6.15
Treebase's tree structure

You wouldn't use this database for purposes such as tracking invoices or creating a Rolodex of contacts. Instead, you'd use it for creating a genealogy chart, or for similar purposes.

Treebase
Registration fee: $
TB Software
P.O. Box 19495
Johnston, RI 02919

CHAPTER

7

Finance and Business Programs

Business and Accounting Programs

Personal Finance Programs

THE PERSONAL COMPUTER HAS AFFECTED BUSINESS AND FINANCE MORE than it has any other aspect of daily life. Walk into any business and you'll most likely find a drastically different way of working than ten years ago, all due to the PC. Not only have businesses been affected; more and more people are using the power of the PC to manage their personal finances as well.

Although much of this change has come about because of spreadsheets and databases, business and finance programs have made their mark as well. Most companies' finances are computerized, and these days, those records are often stored on personal computers, rather than mainframes and minicomputers.

There's an enormous amount of finance and business shareware available, both for companies and for individuals. On the business end, most of the software is aimed at small and home-based businesses. In addition to the many general accounting programs available, you'll find a lot of shareware aimed at specific niches—real estate investment, for example—so that by using shareware, you can easily computerize virtually every aspect of any small business.

The same holds true for personal finances. There are numerous checkbook-management programs, home-accounting programs, tax programs, and a variety of miscellaneous financial aids. With them, you can easily bring the power of the PC to bear on your money, no matter how much or how little you have.

Business and Accounting Programs

If you run a small business, you know how easily you can become bogged down in day-to-day financial minutiae. If you're not careful, you can spend more time writing checks and invoices and balancing your accounts than you do in getting new work and finishing up the old.

Accounting programs will help, and there are a great many available as shareware. Medlin Accounting is a particularly solid, popular program. With it, you can spend more time making money than keeping track of it.

There's far more to shareware business software than accounting programs, however. You'll find a program for virtually every need. There are single-use programs that will do such things as manage a dentist's office or help you run a daycare center. There are far too many of these packages to fit in this book; spend some time perusing bulletin boards or the catalogs of disk vendors and you'll find hundreds of them.

What is included here are some general-purpose business programs—software that will help you manage your time, save on shipping costs, or create business forms. All of these programs can help you run your business more effectively. And some of them, such as the time-management program

TickleX, can help you even if you don't own a business. The following is just a sampling of what's available—investigate shareware sources for others. You'll find more than I can possibly list here.

Checkmate Plus

This software is difficult to categorize. Checkmate Plus is powerful enough to handle the accounting needs of small businesses—especially small, home-based ones—and yet simple enough that you could use it to manage your personal checkbook.

The program will create sophisticated reports about your finances (including income statements and balance sheets); balance your checkbook; write the checks that you pay on a regular basis, such as your mortgage; and print those and other checks. And you don't need to be a CPA, or even have a background in finance, to use it.

The drop-down menus across the top of the screen make it simple to access even the program's most complex functions. To create reports, for example, you move your cursor to the Report option on the main menu and then choose from a variety of submenu items until you locate the report you want to create. Fill in these forms, and you'll have a printed report.

Its reporting capabilities are also unique in another way. Checkmate Plus can create line graphs and two- and three-dimensional bar graphs based on your reports to show such things as your expenses versus your income over time, your income or expenses by month, and a number of other financial factors. Figure 7.1 is a graph showing the activity in a checking account over a year's time. Having your finances graphically displayed often makes a far more effective statement than just listing numbers on a page.

Checkmate Plus includes financial tools for calculating loan payments and interest earned. It also lets you set a financial goal and tells you how much you must save each year in order to reach that goal. This is a top program that small or home-based businesses, and anyone else who needs help with a checkbook, should take a close look at.

Checkmate Plus
Registration fee: $$
Custom Technologies
P.O. Box 62118
Colorado Springs, CO 80962
(800) 541-6234; (719) 260-0486

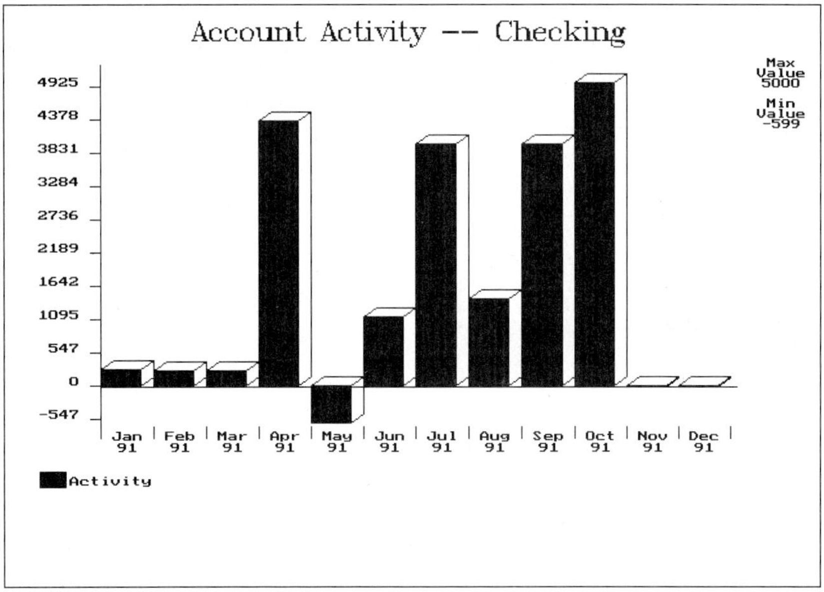

Figure 7.1
A Checkmate Plus graph showing checking account activity

Contact Plus

Do you earn your living by the contacts you make? If you're a salesperson, a real-estate or insurance agent, an attorney, or someone in a similar occupation, you do, and you need Contact Plus.

Contact Plus is a contact-management program. At its simplest level it tracks the names, phone numbers, and addresses of clients, and does so exceptionally well, using an excellent phone-and-address log, as shown in Figure 7.2.

But Contact Plus does far more than that. It also lets you list the best time to contact someone and the name of his or her receptionist, and will store information about the last 30 phone calls you made to that person, including the time, date, duration of the call, and your notes about it. You can also customize the program by defining your own fields in the contact database for whatever use you wish.

Since Contact Plus is a database, you can search all the fields. If, for example, you remember talking to someone about Blue Meanie Cigars, but don't remember who it was, you can search for the words "Blue Meanie Cigars" and up will pop information about the call.

Contact Plus also makes it easy for you to send follow-up letters after phone calls by letting you create template files with the client's name and address already entered.

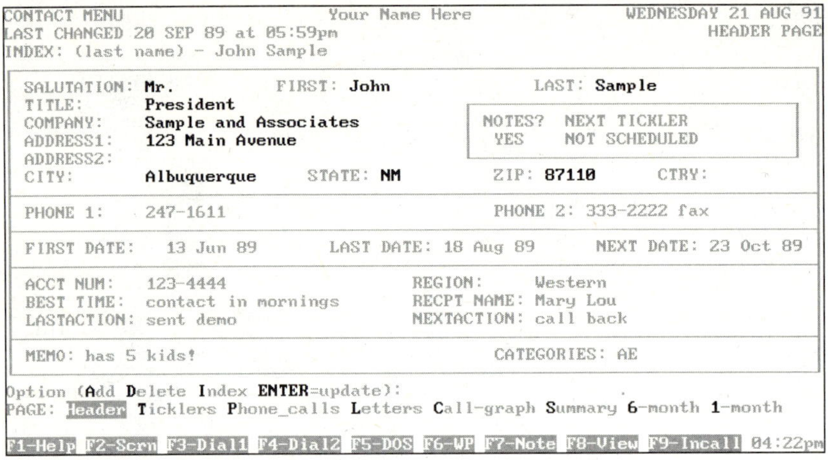

Figure 7.2
A phonebook listing from Contact Plus

The program logs all the calls you make, includes an autodialer so your modem can dial your telephone, and lets you do mail merges for mass mailings. One extremely helpful feature allows you to create "ticklers"—reminders to take some action concerning a client, such as sending a card on her birthday. It includes sophisticated reporting features so you can examine virtually any aspect of how you make contacts. It prints envelopes, too. In fact, it does just about everything you need if you make your living by your contacts.

Contact Plus
Registration fee: $$
Contact Plus Corporation
P.O. Box 3992
Albuquerque, NM 87190
(505) 881-3223

Fast Invoice Writer and Fast Statement Writer

The names say it all: These programs write invoices and statements for you, and fast. They're simple fill-in-the-blank systems; they'll calculate state and city taxes, percentage discounts, and shipping charges; and they can print on envelopes. Both programs are so easy to use, there's no documentation included—or necessary.

Fast Invoice Writer and Fast Statement Writer
Registration fees: $$ for Fast Invoice Writer;
$ for Fast Statement Writer
H&P Software
218 Newman Ave.
Pueblo, CO 81005
(719) 561-0810

FormGen

Sometimes in business the simplest things can become the most annoying. Take forms, for example. Perhaps you need an invoice form. Try creating it with your word processor. Go ahead, try—it will teach you the true meaning of frustration. And spending $500 on a desktop publishing program is not only overkill, but the program won't necessarily provide exactly what you need.

FormGen will. It will let you easily create any business or home form you can think of, including price lists and maps. It's exceedingly simple to use and powerful as well. A number of add-ins available from the author make it even more helpful, including collections of prebuilt home and business forms and a companion program to help make filling in forms easier.

FormGen
Registration fee: $
FormGen Corp.
13 Holland Drive
Bolton
Ontario Canada
L7E 1G4
(800) 263-2390 (in U.S.); (416) 857-4141

Hours/Expense/Miles Program

Whether you're in business for yourself or you work for someone else, keeping track of your billable expenses is never a pleasant chore. This program will help change that. It keeps track of your expenses, the miles you drive, and the number of hours spent working for each of your clients. Since the program is a database, you can create reports on any item you wish. If you want to know, for example, how much expense money a particular client still owes you, you'll be able to find out with a few keystrokes.

Hours/Expense/Miles Program
Registration fee: $
Contact Plus Corporation
P.O. Box 3992
Albuquerque, NM 87190
(505) 881-3223

Medlin Accounting

This accounting program for small businesses is really a series of five modules, rather than a single, integrated program. You'll find modules for a double-entry general ledger, accounts receivable, payroll writing, accounts payable, and invoice writing. And although the program handles finances in a sophisticated way, it's surprisingly simple to use.

This separation of modules might seem odd, but is in fact quite economical. You may, for example, need a general ledger but no other part of the program. In that case, you only pay for the ledger part of it—each module is individually and inexpensively priced. There is, however, a downside to this—if you need to use the results of one module in others, you'll have to enter the figures manually. With the exception of the General Ledger and Accounts Payable, the modules are not integrated.

The most important part of the program is the General Ledger. It includes a prewritten Chart of Accounts, which establishes accounting codes. You can use the codes as is, add to them, delete from them, or start from scratch and completely rewrite them.

Once you've set up the Chart of Accounts, you're ready to enter transactions. Provide a description of each transaction, a check number, date, account number from the chart, and the dollar amount of the transaction. Figure 7.3 shows a number of such entries.

You can create many different kinds of reports based on the transactions, and you can print them to the screen, to your printer, or to a disk.

The Accounts Payable module will track your accounts payable and will also write checks for you. The menus for this module are very much like those for the General Ledger; you make entries in much the same way as you do in the General Ledger. Also as with the General Ledger, you can create a variety of reports and have them sent to a disk, screen, or printer.

In fact, each of Medlin's modules looks and feels very much the same as the others, so that when you've learned one, you've essentially learned them all. A nice extra is that in any module a calculator pops up when you press the F10 key.

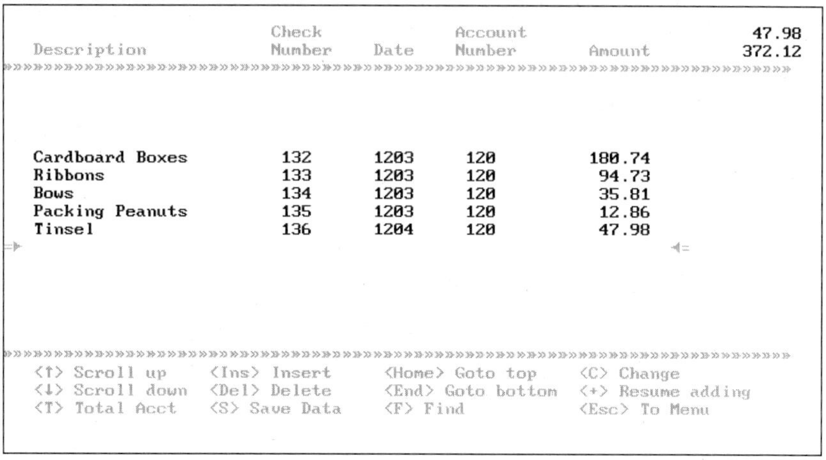

Figure 7.3 Transaction screen from Medlin Accounting's General Ledger module

Medlin Accounting
Registration fee: $
Jerry Medlin
1461 Sproul Ave.
Napa, CA 94559
(707) 255-4475

Pony Express

Pony Express won't speed the delivery of your mail or packages, but it will let you know the most economical and efficient way to get them to their destinations. It will be especially helpful to the small business that doesn't have its own mailing facilities.

Pony Express will figure out shipping rates for you, based on package weight, the origin and destination zip codes, and any additional factors (such as optional insurance) that affect the cost. But the program does even more. It also calculates the estimated time of your package's arrival, based on the zip codes and the service you've chosen. This is more than a convenience—it can also save you a great deal of money. You might find, for example, that your package will arrive the same day whether you use an expensive or an inexpensive mail option—and so you'll choose the cheaper option. Pony Express calculates United Parcel Service as well as U.S. Mail, so you'll be able to compare the two to get the best possible price. Figure 7.4 shows a comparison of the prices and shipping times for sending a 25-pound package from Cambridge, Massachusetts, to Spring Valley, New York.

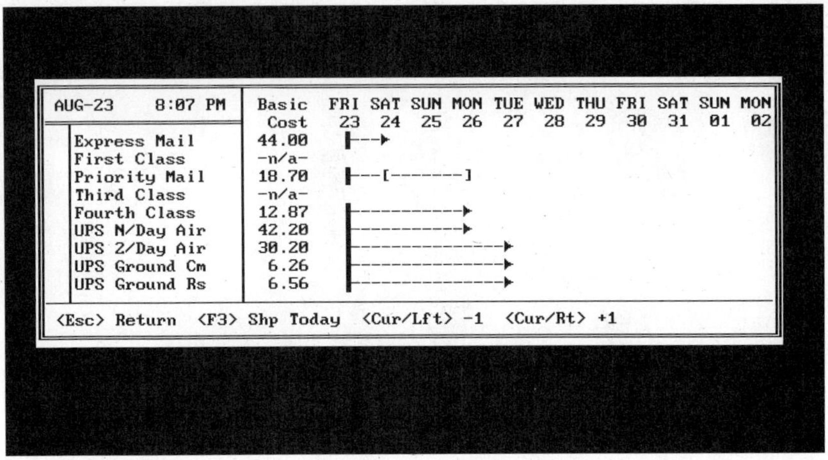

Figure 7.4
A comparison of shipping charges and arrival times

Pony Express can be run as a TSR, so it can be popped up at any time, and it's exceptionally easy to use. If you do more than just a minimal amount of mailing, it's a must-have package.

Pony Express
Registration fee: $$$
Melisco Marketing, Inc.
9719 Ensley Lane
Leawood, KS 66206
(913) 642-5005; (800) 642-5045 (for orders)

Que Accounting

This powerful accounting program is more for the high-end user than the novice. Accountants will appreciate its ability to handle several companies and different departments within companies. It also has password protection; each company or department can have a distinct password, for greater security. It features a notepad for creating and editing notes and memos, budget analysis reports, and an on-line accounting primer.

Que Accounting
Registration fee: $$
Que Accounting, Suite 180
1450 West Chester Pike
West Chester, PA 19832
(215) 344-7628

TickleX

Are you having a hard time keeping your business appointments straight? Have you ever completely forgotten to do certain important tasks that need to be done? If so, you need TickleX.

TickleX is an all-in-one scheduling program that organizes your calendar, schedule, and to-do lists. It will issue "ticklers" to remind you to do certain tasks. It can also tally the hours you've worked on various projects, the expenses incurred on those projects, and the income generated by them. It integrates all these figures and also can handle simple project-management chores.

TickleX uses its calendar as its organizing scheme. Fill in your appointments or schedules, tell the program whether you want to be reminded of them ahead of time, and if so, how far ahead, and you're ready to go. Figure 7.5 shows a typical day's listing.

Figure 7.5
A day's schedule in TickleX

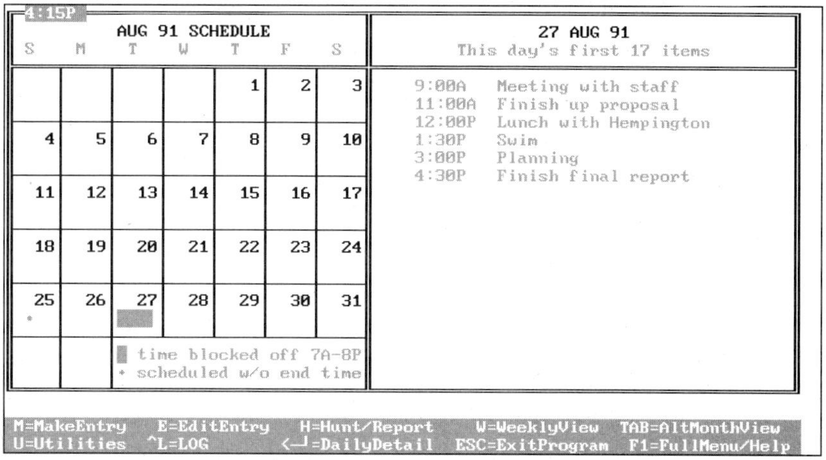

TickleX can work as a resident program, but it's more useful as a TSR. When you're in the middle of another task and you make an appointment, you just need to pop up the program and type in the appointment. Although you can find many uses for the program, it will be especially useful for the self-employed and others involved in many projects at once.

TickleX
Registration fee: $$
Integra Computing
P.O. Box 72063
Marietta, GA 30007
(404) 973-3586

Personal Finance Programs

You don't need to run a business in order to use your PC to help you manage your money. There are a great many shareware financial packages that will do everything from manage your household checkbook to help you make investments and do your taxes.

You don't need to be a financial whiz to use these programs, and you don't need to have a lot of money either. Most of them are quite simple to use and are aimed at handling any kind of finance, small or large.

Checkbook programs are particularly popular and useful. WinCheck, for Windows users, is particularly noteworthy, although I've included some top-notch DOS-based ones as well.

In addition to the sampling of personal finance shareware given here, you'll find another category out there: templates for 1-2-3 and other spreadsheets to help you manage your finances. There are hundreds of these floating about. A few are included in Chapter 5, but many more are available.

AM-TAX

Even if you use your computer for no other financial help, you should use it for one chore: helping you prepare your taxes. Putting together a yearly return is one of the most confounding, time-consuming, and frustrating chores you'll ever attempt. AM-TAX will make it less so.

If you're familiar with completing tax forms, you already know how to use AM-TAX. You simply fill out a tax form on screen, as shown in Figure 7.6. The program does all the calculations for you, so you won't need a calculator nearby to get the work done.

When you're filling out the 1040 and need to fill out a related form or schedule, all you do is press F6 at the place on the 1040 where information from that form or schedule should go, and the related form appears. For example, on the 1990 Form 1040, income from a business or a business loss is reported on line 12. To arrive at that number, you need to fill out Schedule C. With AM-TAX, when you get to line 12, you'd press F6, and Schedule C would pop up. Then when you'd filled out Schedule C, the "bottom line" of that form would automatically be placed on line 12 of the 1040 form in AM-TAX.

Figure 7.6 Working with AM-TAX

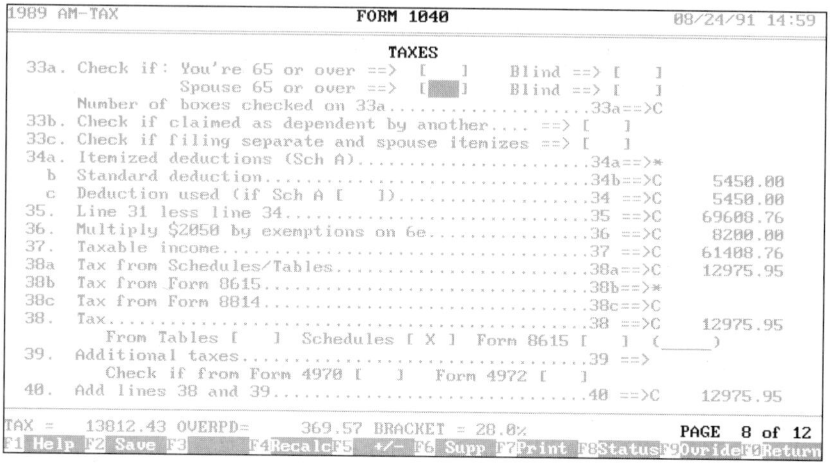

The program is especially useful for creating "what-if" tax scenarios. Should you itemize or take the standard deduction? Instead of spending hours frantically hitting calculator keys, you just fill in a few blanks, and AM-TAX does the work for you. What would be the tax break if you bought a house? Again, with AM-TAX, that will be easy to determine.

AM-TAX is in fact a family of tax programs, not a single one. The basic (Personal-1) AM-TAX program includes 26 forms, schedules, and worksheets, and can print out IRS-approved tax forms on dot-matrix printers. Those schedules include the 1040 and Schedules A through SE, as well as a number of supporting forms.

The slightly more expensive Personal-2 program includes everything that the Personal-1 does, and adds extra schedules and forms, for a total of 44. It includes Schedules 1, 2, and 3, Form 1040A, and a number of others. It can also print out the 1040 and 1040A on HP-compatible laser printers, although a T cartridge is required for this.

The AM-TAX Professional version has a tax organizer and can print client-instruction letters and invoices. There is also an Electronic Filing version that allows you to electronically transmit certain tax returns to the IRS.

Be aware that although AM-TAX will give you help in calculating your taxes, it won't provide any financial advice. For that, you'll still need to see an accountant.

AM-TAX
Registration fee: $$ for Personal-1 or Personal-2 version;
$$$ for Professional version
AM Software
P.O. Box 25010
Kansas City, MO 64119

Capital Gainz

This investment-tracking program is designed for the small investor, particularly those who invest in mutual funds and dividend reinvestment plans. If you're familiar with financial jargon (and if you're an investor, you almost certainly are), you'll find this program quite easy to use.

You'll find especially helpful the program's ability to figure out your actual total return on an investment over a period of time. Also advantageous is a "what-if" analysis that allows you to determine whether to make a particular sale. It will retrieve information to fill out Schedule D of the federal tax form and has a number of other niceties. If you're an investor, it's worth a look. If not, you can always dream...

Capital Gainz
Registration fee: $$
Dave Cohen
DBLinx
1117 Manchester Dr.
Cary, NC 27511
(919) 469-5196

ExpressCheck

Do you have a hard time balancing your checkbook? Would you like to see a report detailing exactly where your money goes every month? How about having regularly recurring checks, such as your rent payment, written for you every month?

If you answered yes to those questions, then a checkbook-management program, such as ExpressCheck, is probably for you. These programs bring the power of the computer to bear on one of the more annoying little tasks in life.

ExpressCheck lets you write checks, flag checks with budget codes to make it easier to track your expenses later, create reports of your checkbook and expense activity, and more. It has searching abilities so you can easily track down individual checks and expenses. Most of its forms for writing checks, deposits, or withdrawals resemble checks, so you'll be on familiar ground when using ExpressCheck.

ExpressCheck
Registration fee: $
David Berdan
Expressware Corporation
P.O. Box 1800
Duvall, WA 98019
(206) 788-0932; (800) 753-3453 (for orders)

FastBucks

No, this program won't, as the name implies, make you some quick bucks. But it's likely to save you money and at least help you manage what you already have more easily. FastBucks is an all-purpose personal money manager, and it does its job superbly. While it's primarily for managing personal accounts, those with a home-based or other small business would also do well to consider using it.

A simple, menu-driven program, FastBucks divides its work into four sections: an account manager, a budgeting modeler, a financial calculator, and a report writer. When the program is loaded, the screen is divided into five sections—one for each function and a fifth section of utilities to help you use the program. Figure 7.7 shows FastBucks' opening screen.

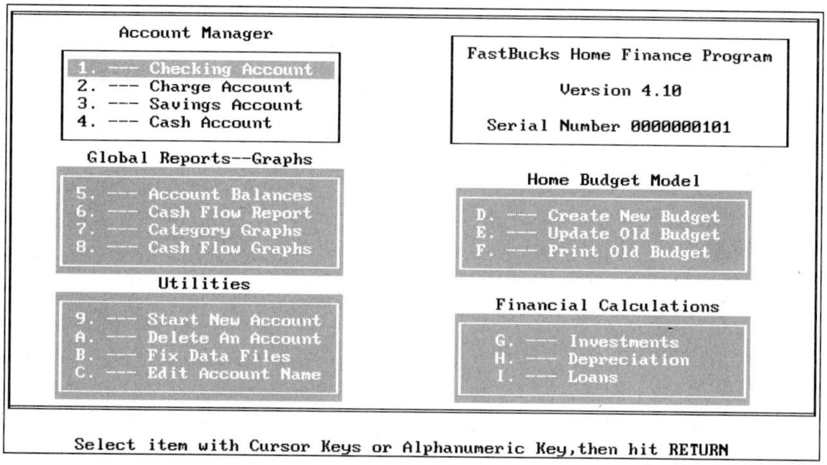

Figure 7.7 FastBucks' opening screen

The Account Manager can handle checking and savings accounts, as well as charge and cash accounts. It can do far more than merely keep track of and reconcile your checks. You can create reports on your account in any number of ways. Do you need to see which checks are still outstanding?

FastBucks will show you. How about a list of all your ATM transactions? Again, it's on the menu. Want a list of all your tax-deductible contributions? FastBucks will create that for you as well. You can even graph your account activity. See Figure 7.8 for the screen listing all you can do with FastBucks' Account Manager.

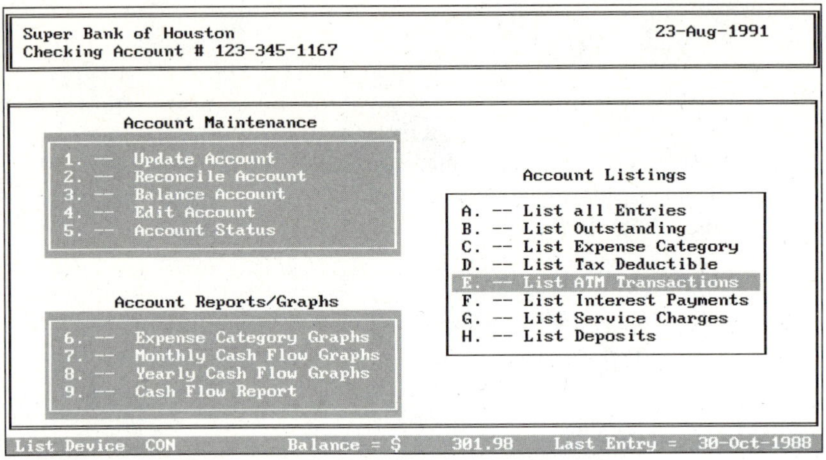

Figure 7.8
FastBucks' Account Manager screen

The Budgeting module will be especially helpful to people who closely plan their finances—or want to start. You can create a weekly, biweekly, semimonthly, or monthly budget. FastBucks walks you through how much income you have and then helps you figure out how much your monthly expenses are. It will then calculate how much you can *really* afford to spend on each budget category and also create a graph so you can easily see where your money is going.

The Financial Calculations module is helpful for anyone planning to take out a loan, make an investment, or depreciate property. It will calculate the future value of a one-time investment or the future value of a regularly recurring investment, such as contributions made to a savings account. It will also let you plan backwards: you can define the amount of money you want saved by a certain date, and then have the program tell you what kind of investment you'll have to make to meet that goal. The Depreciation Calculator is similarly sophisticated, and the Loan Calculator will be a godsend to anyone considering taking out a loan of any kind.

The Reporting module lets you look at your finances from a number of different points of view. You can look at your account balances, at your cash flow, and at different categories of income and expenses. It will create not just number-based reports, but will also graph your finances, as shown in Figure 7.9.

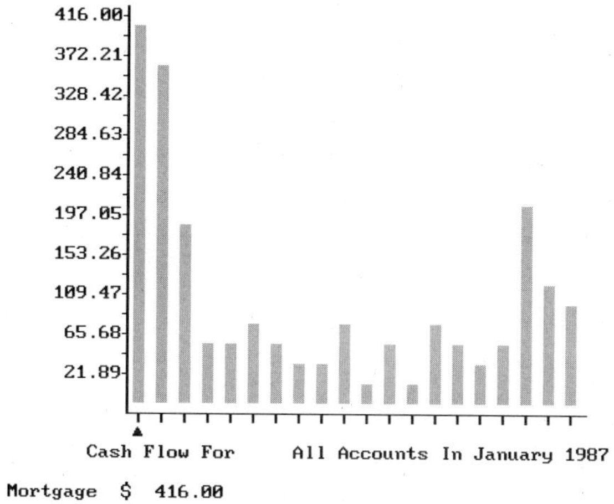

Figure 7.9
A graph showing cash flow on a monthly basis

If you want to bring the power of your computer to bear on your personal finances, FastBucks deserves a close look.

FastBucks
Registration fee: $$
Dennis C. Lozen
Software Expressions
P.O. Box 301002
Houston, TX 77230
(713) 541-3063

Point and Shoot Home Manager

Ah, the joys of running a home: bills to pay, valuables to document, maintenance to take care of, a car to keep in tip-top shape, records and miscellaneous information to track. Sometimes it makes you long for the days when you owned little more than the clothes on your back.

But you don't really have to return to poverty to find some peace. Point and Shoot Home Manager is here to ease your burden. An all-in-one program for managing every aspect of your home, it's really a series of interrelated databases.

The databases are accessed via the main menu. To enter a record in the Home Maintenance database, for example, you choose the Homework item from the menu and press Enter. Then fill out the details of the maintenance you did, as shown in Figure 7.10.

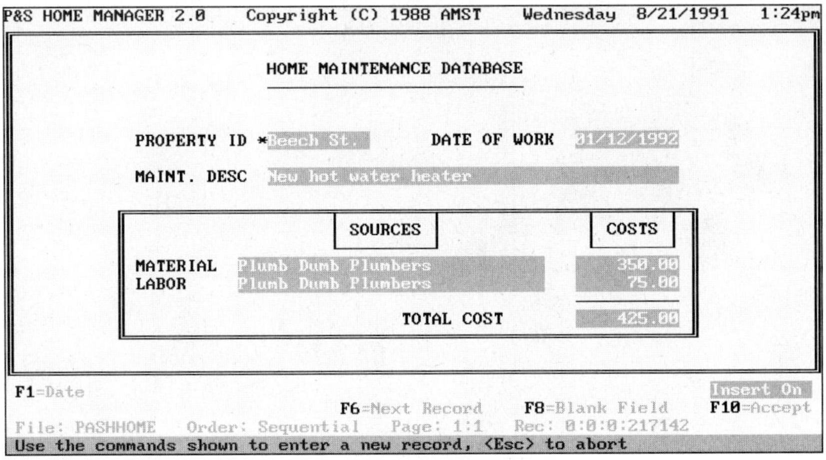

Figure 7.10
Entering a record in the maintenance database

Once you've entered records in the database, you can perform a number of functions on those records. You can search for a given record—to find out, for example, how much you paid the chimney sweep to clean your chimney three years ago. Even more useful are the reporting features, which would allow you to calculate, for example, how much you've paid for electrical work over the last five years.

The program also includes a database for tracking all your valuables so you have a complete list of them in case you need to file an insurance claim. And it has another database designed to let you track where you keep all your valuable records. If you think you don't need it, just try locating the warranty agreement for your refrigerator or the documentation for your VCR.

You'll find the Financial Calculator of particular help. If you're considering taking out a loan and want to know how much you'll have to pay every month, it will calculate that for you. Better still, it will calculate, based on your finances, how large a loan you can afford. It will also calculate how much money you'll have in your savings account if you follow a particular savings plan, how much you must save every month to reach a particular financial goal, and other similar questions.

Point and Shoot Home Manager also includes a simple text editor for writing short letters and notes, an accounting/general ledger module, a phonebook for keeping track of names and addresses, a calculator, a calendar, and the ability to print labels for mail-merge operations.

Point and Shoot Home Manager
Registration fee: $$
Applied Micro Systems Technology
P.O. Box 1596, Welch Avenue Station
Ames, IA 50010

Ultra-Check

Ultra-Check is a simple, straightforward, easy-to-use checkbook management program. With it, you'll be able to keep track of your outgoing and incoming expenses, balance your checkbook with ease, assign expenses and income to categories so you'll know where your money is going, and create reports to get a better handle on your finances.

It automates much of your checking activity. You can preassign categories to certain checks you write regularly, such as your phone bill. You can even tell the program the amounts to fill in for checks whose amounts never vary, such as mortgage or rent checks. And it will print your checks as well.

The program's main screen is a check ledger, as seen in Figure 7.11. The top part of the screen is the ledger itself. The bottom-left part of the screen lists the function keys available, and the bottom-right shows details of the ledger entry on which the cursor is currently resting.

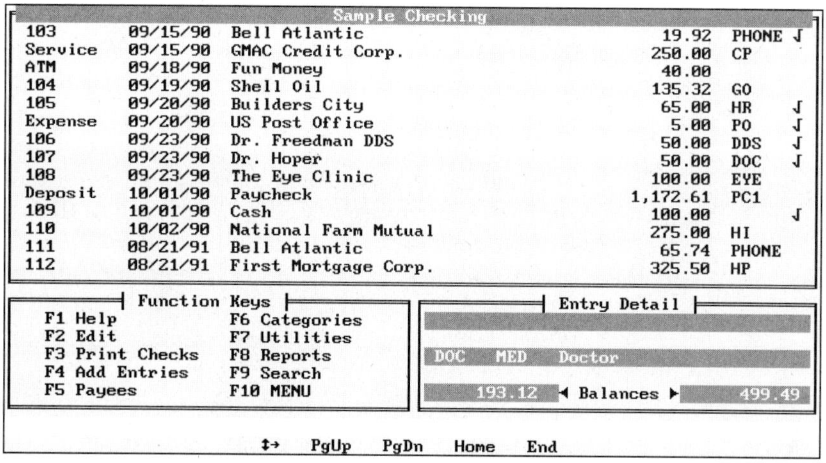

Figure 7.11
Ultra-Check's main screen

To write a new check, press the F4 key and fill in a form asking for details about the check. To create reports, press F8 and follow the instructions.

Ultra-Check is more than just a check-writing program; it is truly a complete personal financial manager. And for such a powerful program, it's surprisingly easy to use. Although Ultra-Check won't actually make check-writing a pleasure, it will make it easier, allowing you to get a grip on your finances.

Ultra-Check
Registration fee: $$
Jon Kolstad
P.O. Box 372
Washougal, WA
(206) 835-8769; (800) 874-9702 (for orders)

WinCheck

Don't be fooled by this program's name—WinCheck does far more than let you keep track of your checking account. It's a complete Windows-based personal finance manager, sophisticated enough to track personal finances, but simple enough that you don't need an M.B.A. to master it.

Both its power and ease of use are due in large part to its being written for Windows. Windows' graphical approach is surprisingly well-suited to a personal finance manager. Icons, scroll and menu bars, fill-in-the-blank checks, control bars, and other Windows tricks make this program not only simple, but a pleasure as well.

You'll find just about everything here you need to manage your checkbook. There are tools to track checks and incoming and outgoing cash, and to manage multiple savings accounts and credit cards, as well as multiple checking accounts. Not only does the program track your accounts, but you can use it to write checks and print them out on a laser or dot-matrix printer.

WinCheck's main screen is a check register that details all your checking transactions, as shown in Figure 7.12. The main area of the screen resembles a check register. Double-click on any check listing, and you'll get information about the check or deposit. The top of the screen has icons and pull-down menus for all the program's features.

Lending this program much of its power are its sorting and reporting abilities. As you write checks and record deposits, you key each transaction to a category you've set up. For example, tag all your food purchases to a subgroup called groceries and later you'll be able to create reports that let you know how much you spend over a given time for food. If you have more than one source of income, key the money you make over and above your regular salary to your Moonlighting account—you'll know instantly how lucrative that activity is.

To create reports, you can choose from 20 prewritten report types, as shown in Figure 7.13. You can also easily create new custom reports.

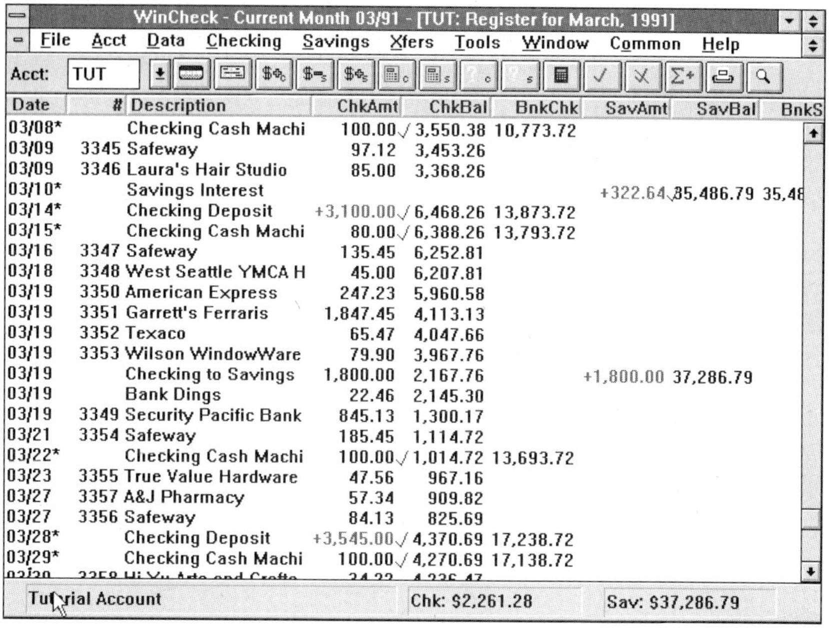

Figure 7.12
WinCheck's main screen, showing the check register

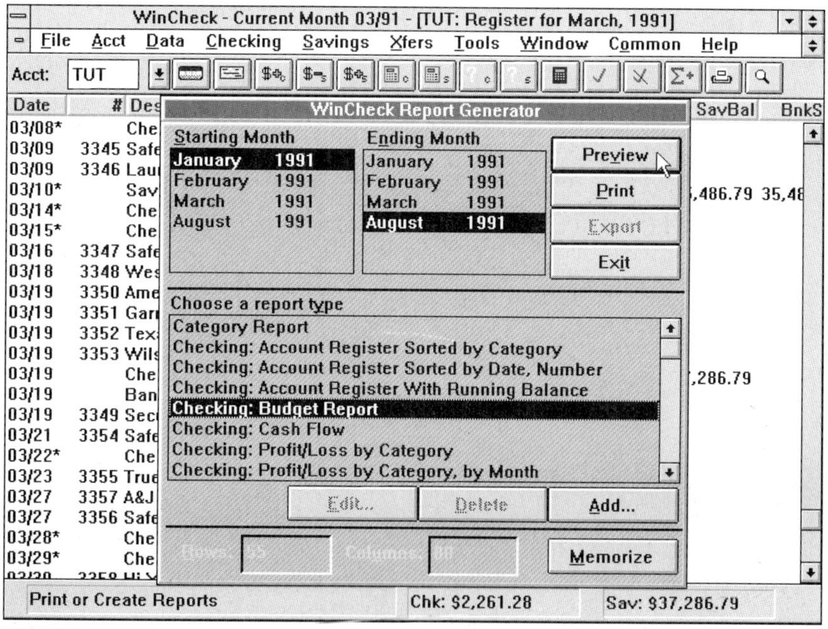

Figure 7.13
Choosing a report form in WinCheck

Equally powerful is WinCheck's budgeting feature. You can use the program to set budgets for yourself within a variety of categories, to track how well you keep to those budgets, and to create budget reports.

WinCheck lets you set up templates for checks you write regularly, such as rent or mortgage. It can also import data from the popular Quicken money manager. It has a calculator, the ability to search through check entries for information, and far more. If you use Windows and are looking for a personal finance manager, look no further than WinCheck.

WinCheck
Registration fee: $$
Wilson WindowWare
2701 California Ave. SW, Suite 212
Seattle, WA 98116
(206) 937-9335; (800) 762-8383 (for orders)

CHAPTER

8

DOS Shells and Menu Programs

DOS Shells

Menu Programs

NO ONE HAS EVER ACCUSED THE PC OF BEING EASY TO USE. THE PROBlem is twofold. First, DOS is somewhat arcane—full of strange commands that can be difficult to remember. At times it even seems willfully structured to be as difficult to use as possible. The simple act of moving a group of files from one subdirectory to another can take innumerable keystrokes and cause untold frustration.

The second problem is that in order to run different programs, you have to remember the subdirectories they're in and the names of the executable files that start them. Each program also has a variety of command-line switches for running in a certain configuration, which you can recall only if you have a photographic memory. Some programs may require you to add terminal switches, such as \Mono or \V100T, to your commands. If you have half a dozen or more programs you run regularly and a similar amount you run less frequently, you'll often find yourself fumbling at the keyboard just to find the right keystrokes to get them running.

That's where DOS shells and menu programs come in. While these two types of programs serve different apparent purposes, they have one thing in common: They'll make your life at the keyboard far easier than it is today.

DOS shells shield you from the unfriendly DOS prompt. They'll let you see your disk and file structure at a glance, in a tree-like listing of all your directories and subdirectories. They'll give you access to DOS commands—even the most complex—with a few easy keystrokes, or through a menu. Some let you point at a program file with your cursor and run it. They even include commands that DOS forgot.

There are a great many shareware DOS shells, probably more than you'll find in the commercial world. With this much variety, you'll undoubtedly find one to your liking. You'll even find the old-time, commercial stalwart XTree now available as shareware, although a higher-end version of the program is only available commercially.

Menu programs shield you from the DOS prompt as well, but for a different reason. Instead of giving you access to DOS commands, they give you single-keystroke access to all your applications. With these programs you'll press a single key, and the software of your choice will run.

As with DOS shells, the variety of shareware menu programs is dazzling—there's far more available in shareware than there is commercially. Menu programs can be as simple as PCMENU, which stresses letting you set up simple menus within minutes. Or they can be as complex as Hard Disk Menu (HDM IV), which has so many sophisticated features that using it could be compared to putting your PC on automatic pilot.

DOS Shells

Most shareware DOS shells perform the same basic functions. They'll show you your hard disk's directory structure in tree form. They'll let you manage your directories and the files in them with a few keystrokes. They'll give you easy access to DOS commands.

Where they differ is in their ease of use, and in the extras they throw in—and you'll find a lot of extras. Some, like Hard Disk Director, include a menuing system. Others, like StupenDOS, will let you run compression programs, making those notoriously difficult programs easy to use. Still others, like XTree, stress ease of use and a solid, all-around set of features.

I've included only a sampling of the top shareware DOS shells; spend just a little time on a bulletin board, and you'll find many others. When choosing one, look beyond the basics, and find the one whose extra features fit in best with the way you compute.

Hard Disk Director

This program bills itself as more than just a simple DOS shell. It promises to manage not only your files and directories, but your programs as well, with its menu system. While this might sound like a "throw-in-the-kitchen-sink" approach, it works surprisingly well.

Hard Disk Director performs all the normal DOS shell functions for copying, moving, deleting, and renaming files and directories. You can even move entire subdirectories, with all the files in them, to a new directory. It also has a number of utilities built in, including ones that tell you what percent of your hard disk is full and how many disks you'll need to back up given directories.

There's a nifty command-line directory changer that lets you quickly jump to a specific directory. If you wanted to change to the \WKSHEET subdirectory, for example, and didn't want to type the full name, you could type **DL WK** at the command line. You would then be placed in the first directory listing that began with the letters WK.

When you load Hard Disk Director, it will display all the directories on your disk in tree form. The top of the screen lists function key commands. Figure 8.1 illustrates a typical tree display on the Hard Disk Director's opening screen.

Hard Disk Director is actually a set of four programs, not one. The DOS shell is named DL.EXE. A streamlined version of the program, DB.EXE, helps you manage individual directories rather than an entire disk. When you're in a directory in which you want to do work, type **DB**, and the program loads. You'll get a listing of every file in the directory. You'll be able to perform the functions on the files just as if you were using the more complex Director.

Figure 8.1
A tree display on Hard Disk Director's main screen

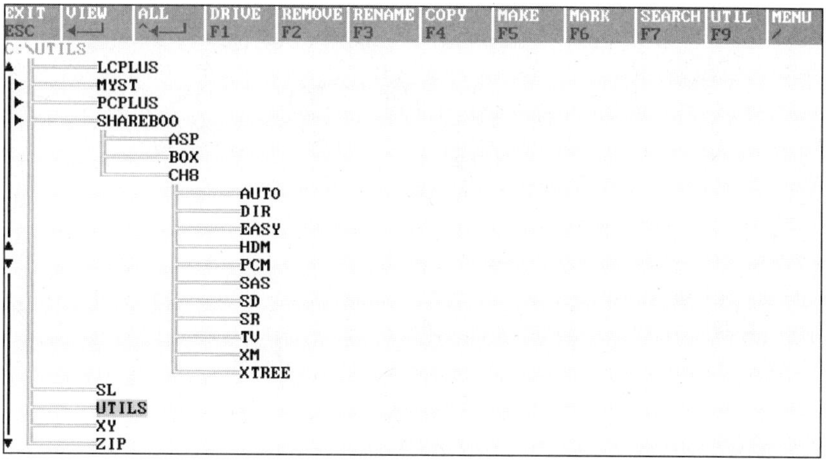

The DA.EXE file lets you work on all the files on your disk without a tree listing. Type **DA** and it will list all the files on your disk, in a sort order you specify.

The DM.EXE file is a menu program. Although not as sophisticated or powerful as other shareware menuing programs, it's serviceable and helpful. It will also let you park the heads on your hard disk.

There's also a fifth file, but it's not truly a separate program. DCONFIG.EXE lets you configure the Hard Disk Directory in many different ways, to best suit your own preferences.

Hard Disk Director
Registration fee: $
Helpware
1537 Fourth St.
San Rafael, CA 94901
(415) 453-9779

Still River Shell

If you're looking for an extremely easy-to-use, intuitive DOS shell, the Still River Shell may well fit the bill. Its screen layout is clean and simple to follow, its menu clear, and its overall construction logical.

That's not to say the program is dull or simplistic. The Still River Shell does everything you'd expect from a DOS shell, and more. In addition to the usual file and directory features, there are excellent file- and text-finding tools. You can also define 40 keys to perform any function you'd like.

When you first load Still River Shell, you'll be presented with a screen divided into two main sections, with a menu running across the bottom (see Figure 8.2). The left section of the screen shows the files in the current subdirectory, and the right gives information about the disk. It also gives you vital statistics about the current directory, including information about the number of files, subdirectories, and bytes contained within it. To execute a command from the bottom menu line, either move your cursor to the command desired and press Enter, or type the first letter of the menu entry.

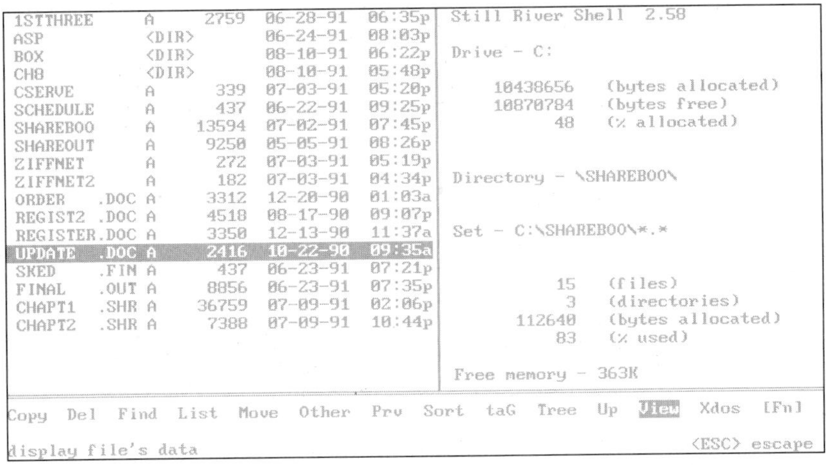

Figure 8.2
Still River Shell's opening screen

Of particular note are the program's searching abilities. If you want to find a given file, choose Find from the menu, and type the name of the file you want to find. Wildcards, such as *, are allowed. Still River Shell will speedily search out the file or files you're looking for and list them on screen, complete with the subdirectory in which they can be found. You can then perform a number of operations on the files, such as copying, deleting, moving, and viewing them. You can also write the list of files to an ASCII file.

Searching for text within a file is done in the same way. Making this search tool particularly powerful is its ability to limit the scope of a search: You can search a certain directory, the entire disk, or certain files only. For example, if you wanted to find every file with a *.DOC extension in the \SHARE subdirectory which contained the word *shareware,* you would type

```
\SHARE\*.DOC SHAREWARE
```

on the search command line. Still River Shell would then list every file in that directory with a *.DOC extension that contained the word *shareware.*

Still River Shell
Registration fee: $$
Bill White
P.O. Box 57
Still River, MA 01467
(508) 456-3699

StupenDOS

StupenDOS is an excellent DOS shell, with extra punch: It makes it easier to use the notoriously difficult-to-master compression program PKZIP.

StupenDOS does everything you expect from a DOS shell: It will let you easily manipulate files and directories in any number of ways and allows you to view and edit files and run programs. It also has a nice file-find feature.

When you start StupenDOS, the left side of the screen will show you either a directory listing or a tree listing of your entire disk, as you choose. The right side shows information about your entire hard disk. The top part of the screen has a pull-down menu, and the bottom lists function key shortcuts for common commands. To use the pull-down menu, press an arrow key, and the menu will drop down. Figure 8.3 shows StupenDOS's main screen.

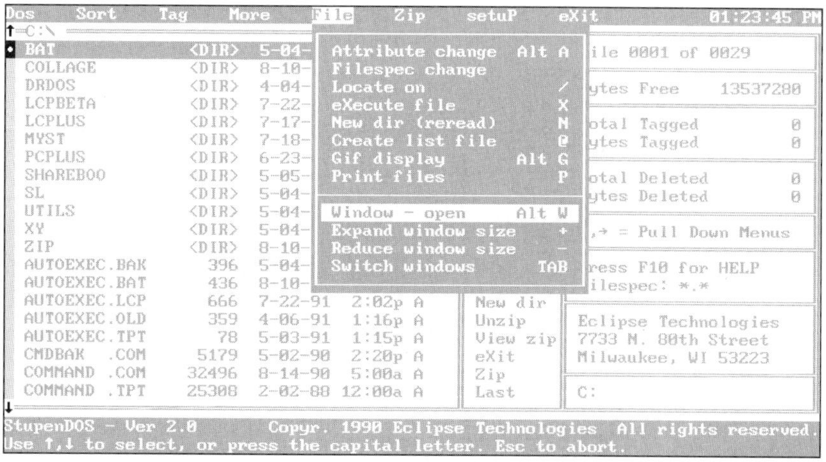

Figure 8.3 StupenDOS's main screen with the File submenu pulled down

From this main screen you can use all of StupenDOS's functions. One of the program's nicer touches is that you can split the file and directory display on the left part of the screen into two windows, and then work independently in each window, as shown in Figure 8.4. You can also size each window however you would like.

Figure 8.4
Working with two windows open in StupenDOS

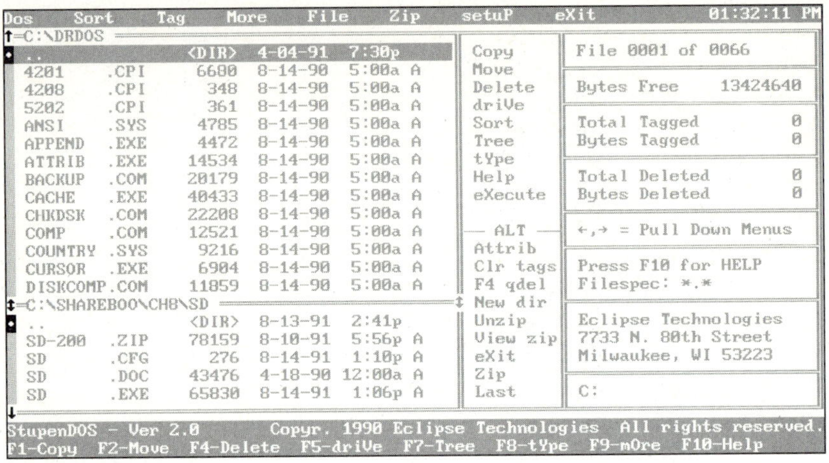

What really sets this shell apart, though, is its integration with the PKZIP family of compression programs. Using key combinations or the drop-down menu, you can zip, unzip, and view a zipped file by simply pointing at it. There's a kind of synergy at work between StupenDOS and PKZIP that gives each of them even more power than usual when they're used in concert. With StupenDOS's ability to quickly navigate a hard disk, you can see at a glance which files you want to archive, and then quickly zip them using the program's access to PKZIP, for example. If you come across files you zipped some time ago while looking through your hard disk, and you've forgotten what they contain, you can use the Zip file viewer to see what files are contained in each zipped file. You can then delete them, unzip them, or leave them as is.

StupenDOS is a solid, helpful DOS shell. If you need a DOS shell and use PKZIP regularly, you probably couldn't come up with a better choice.

StupenDOS
Registration fee: $
Douglas Hay
Eclipse Technologies
7733 North 80th St.
Milwaukee, WI 53223

Swiss Army Shell

As you might guess from this program's name, there's a lot packed into this program; it aspires to be the Swiss army knife of DOS shells. You'll be able to use it to manage your disk, subdirectories, and files with ease. Like many other DOS shells, it shows a tree structure of your hard disk on the left side of the screen, and on the right shows a listing of files in the current subdirectory. Across the top of the screen is a menu of the commands available to you.

There are a few extras thrown in as well. Like StupenDOS, it can act as a nice front end to the PKZIP compression program, so that you don't have to remember that program's often arcane commands. You can configure it to work with your word processor or text editor, too, so you can edit files. The Swiss Army Shell's low registration fee makes it a particularly good choice for those on a budget.

Swiss Army Shell
Registration fee: $
Steven C. Lee
304 Pierson Dr.
Trussville, AL 35173
(205) 655-3926

Treeview

An excellent, simple-to-use DOS shell, Treeview gives you instant access to the most common DOS commands. Add this to its ability to give you a tree-like view of your hard disk, and you'll find that Treeview is an excellent all-around disk manager and DOS shell.

Treeview will either give you a tree listing of your entire hard disk or a listing of individual directories. Navigating is simple: Use the pull-down menus across the top of the screen or keyboard shortcuts. Figure 8.5 shows a tree listing with the Options menu selected.

Macro commands, the ability to split the screen into multiple directories, and the ability to run external programs from within Treeview's menus are just a few of the program's more useful features.

Treeview
Registration fee: $$
Magee Enterprises, Inc.
P.O. BOX 1587
Norcross, GA 30091
(404) 446-6611; (800) 662-4330 (orders)

XTree

Once their programs gain a devoted following, some shareware authors opt to release commercial versions, while still supporting their original shareware programs. More rarely, a company goes in the opposite direction after a number of years of commercial success.

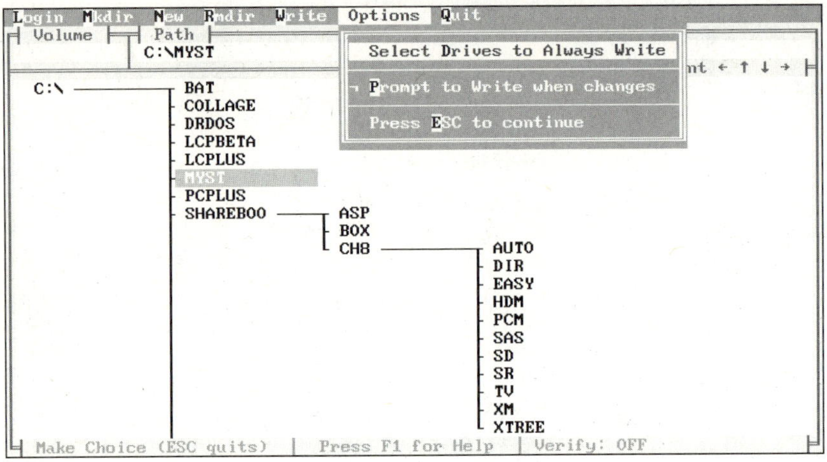

Figure 8.5
Treeview's directory tree listing

XTree, from XTree Company, has chosen to go that route. After a number of years of being one of the leading commercial DOS shells, the program is now available as shareware. (The company still sells two commercial versions, called XTree Gold and XTree Easy.)

A look at the shareware version shows why the program has been such a commercial success. XTree is one of the smartest, easiest, most logically organized DOS shells you'll find.

You get single-keystroke access to many DOS commands, such as those for deleting, copying, and renaming files, and for making, removing, and changing the names of directories. Better yet, you can perform those commands on groups of files or entire directories at a time. You get sophisticated directory listings and file statistics as well.

There's also much here that DOS doesn't have. XTree allows you to see every file on your disk in one long display, and lets you sort them according to a number of different attributes. It allows you to modify the names of disk volumes without forcing you to reformat your hard disk. And it lets you move files, either individually or in groups, from one directory to another in one simple operation. You can also launch applications from directly within XTree, making it your complete operating environment.

XTree's first screen is its command center: a tree view of all the directories and subdirectories on your hard disk. The screen is split; the top half shows your disk structure, and the bottom half shows the files in the current directory. As you move your cursor through the directories on the top half of the screen, the bottom half of the screen shows the file listing for that directory. Figure 8.6 shows this main screen.

Figure 8.6

XTree's main screen

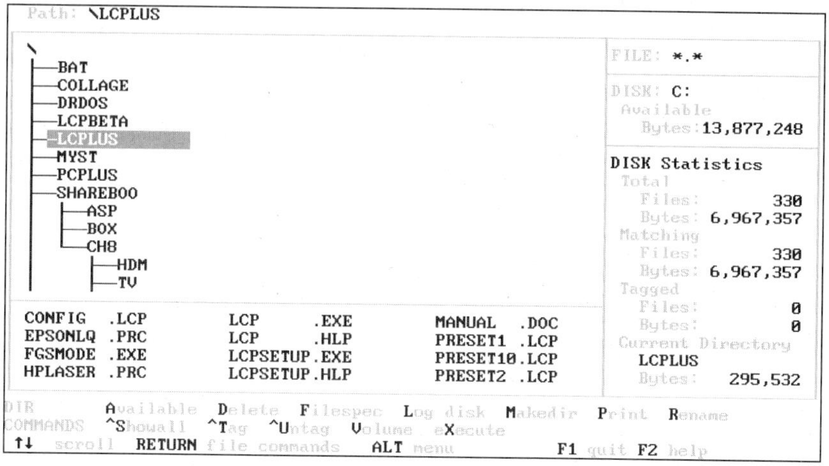

It's in this main screen that you'll spend most of your time. Notice that, in addition to information about the current subdirectory, you're also given similar information about your entire hard disk. At the bottom of the screen is a listing of operations available to you. Press the Alt key for even more commands.

To move your cursor from the tree listing at the top of the screen to the file listing at the bottom, press Enter. Once you're in the file listing, if you press Enter again, the tree listing will disappear, and the file listing will take up the entire screen. To get from this screen back to the main screen, press Enter again. As you move your cursor from the directory listing at the top of the screen to the file listing at the bottom of the screen, the command menu will change, since the commands available for file and directories are different.

One of the program's most useful features is its ability to let you view files without having to start the program that created those files. Move your cursor to the file, press **V**, and a file viewer will show you the contents of the file. A listing across the top will show you the commands available while you're in the viewer. The viewer is particularly helpful when you're pruning old files from your hard disk. You can view files you think you don't want, and if you truly don't want them, you can delete them from within XTree.

Working with files is exceptionally easy. To delete a file, put your cursor on it and press **D** for delete. To move a file, press **M**. Most commands are similarly easy to execute.

One of the program's most powerful—and most dangerous—features is its ability to perform operations on groups of files. To do this, you first tag a group of files, one by one, by pressing **T** as your cursor rests on each file in turn. To tag an entire directory, press Ctrl-T when your cursor is in the file window, and the whole directory will be tagged. Then, when you want to perform an operation, such as moving the files, you can do it en masse.

The usefulness of tagging files is obvious, but it's dangerous as well, because you can easily delete a group of files with a few keystrokes. Be warned, also, that if you press Ctrl-T when your cursor is in the directory window, rather than the file window, you'll tag every file on your *disk*, not just in a single directory. If you then tell XTree to delete that group of files, you'll just have erased every single file on your disk.

XTree is one of the most powerful disk managers you'll ever come across. Its commercial older brother, XTree Gold, has even more power. Registered users of XTree can upgrade to it at a moderate cost.

XTree
Registration fee: $
Executive Systems XTree Company
4330 Santa Fe Road
San Luis Obispo, CA 93401
(805) 541-0604

Menu Programs

Among the myths of the computing world are these: Programs that actually make your computer easier to use are only for wimps, and menus are for novices and only get in the way of power users.

In fact, although it's true that menus help novices and intermediate users, they also give power users more power. Everyone enjoys saving keystrokes and getting instant access to all their programs. And many menu programs allow you to do far more than just run your programs. They'll log the amount of time you spend in different applications. They'll prevent unauthorized people from running your software. They'll do certain tasks for you on a regularly scheduled basis, such as backing up your hard disk, while you're elsewhere.

And they'll do even more. Some, such as Menu Commando, come with DOS shells. Others, like Automenu, include a built-in text editor and screen blanker (sometimes called a screen saver). And still others, like PowerMenu, include a slew of helpful utilities, such as a TSR map.

There are many more shareware menu programs than are available commercially, so you can be picky about the one you use. When choosing one, balance how easy it is to use against the extra features it offers.

Automenu

A very powerful but difficult-to-master program, Automenu is still worthwhile if you have the time and energy to devote to learning the sometimes complex manner in which it sets up menus.

It's one of the most powerful menu programs you can find. It can accept user input when running a menu item; can execute menu selections on a timed, unattended basis; and can remove itself from memory when a menu item is run. It also allows for the creation of as many menus as you wish and includes a screen saver and built-in text editor.

It comes already configured with several menu items on its main screen, but you can customize those as you wish. See Figure 8.7 for Automenu's main screen, which has been customized by deleting some menu items and adding others.

Figure 8.7 Automenu's main menu, after being customized

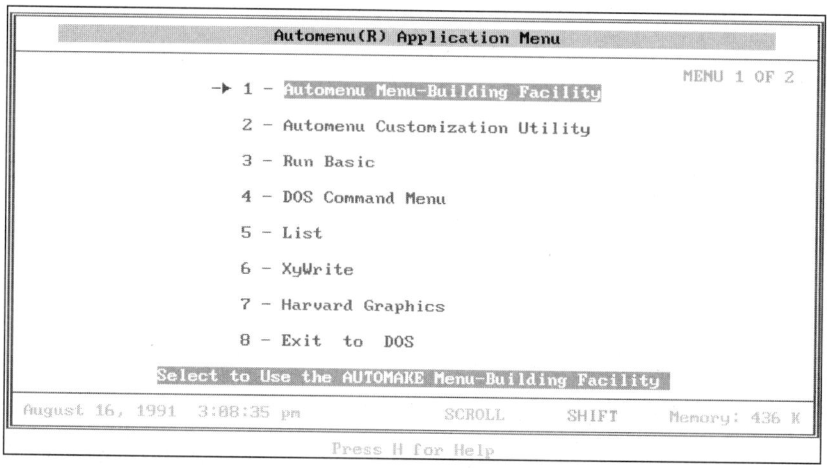

Automenu uses what it calls its Menu Definition Language to enable you to create new menu items. You create a Menu Definition File with the program's Automake editor (called the Menu-Building Facility on the main screen). Automake can be run in either novice, intermediate, or advanced mode. In essence, when building a new menu item in Automenu, you're creating a sophisticated type of batch file.

You don't have to know the Menu Definition Language if you want to create simple menus, however. To do that, just fill out forms that include information such as a file's name, path, and executable file, and the program will turn up as a menu item.

This program isn't for those who want to set up quick, simple menus, but if you need to do some complex menu work, Automenu is worth a look.

Automenu
Registration fee: $$
Magee Enterprises
P.O. Box 1587
Norcross, GA 30091
(404) 446-6611; (800) 662-4330 (orders)

Hard Disk Menu (HDM IV)

A menu program with something for everyone, Hard Disk Menu (HDM IV) can do just about everything you would expect, and then some. You can create as many menus and menu items as you're ever likely to need; you can control everything with a mouse; you can have HDM IV run programs for you at a given date and time, when you're not at the keyboard; you can run batch files as menu items; and you can have password protection. HDM IV also allows up to ten macros to be run with any menu file. HDM IV will log the amount of time spent on different programs. It can even dial your telephone.

Getting at all this power is not particularly difficult, either. Drop-down menus appear across the top of your screen when you press F10; from here it's easy to control virtually everything about the program. Once you get familiar with HDM IV, you'll probably use shortcut keys instead of the menu structure.

Each menu in HDM IV has ten entries. Any of these entries can be a program, a batch file, or a submenu. Figure 8.8 shows an example of HDM IV's main menu.

To add an entry to the main menu, press Enter, and then fill out two simple forms detailing the item you want to add to the menu, as shown in Figure 8.9. Alternatively, you could press F10 and use the drop-down menus.

Rather than filling out the forms, you could type directly on what HDM IV calls a Menu Action Line, using HDM IV's command language and DOS commands to speed things up.

Although HDM IV is a sophisticated, complex program, you need not be a pro to use it. With its pull-down menus and generous help system, you'll be able to write menus quickly. If you are a pro, however, you'll find plenty of depth to the program. Using menus, submenus, macros, batch files, timed execution of programs, the ability to pass keystrokes to other programs, and other features, you can adapt this program to be a complex, automated command center for your PC. It also has extensive security features.

Figure 8.8
HDM IV's main menu

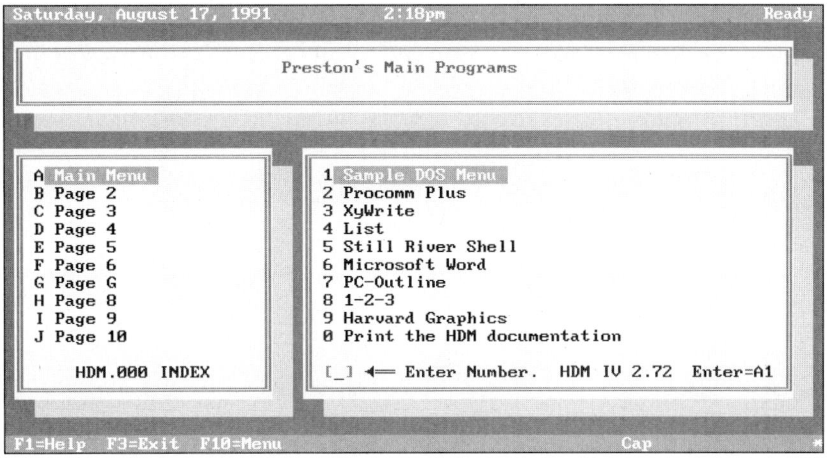

Figure 8.9
Filling out the form to add a new menu entry

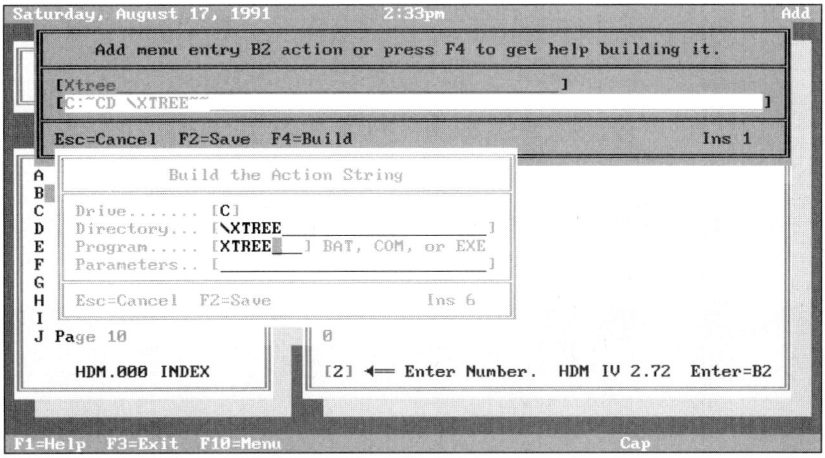

Hard Disk Menu
Registration fee: $$
Jim Hass, President
MicroFox Co.
P.O. Box 447
Richfield, OH 44286

Menu Commando II

A powerful menu program, Menu Commando II will surprise you with how easy it is to use. It allows you to set up far more menus than you'll ever need. You can create 26 entries in the main menu (shown in Figure 8.10), and each of those entries can be a submenu, which can also have up to 26 entries. And *that* menu can have up to 26 entries, and so on, ad infinitum (or until you run out of hard-disk space). Drop-down menus give quick access to all the program's features.

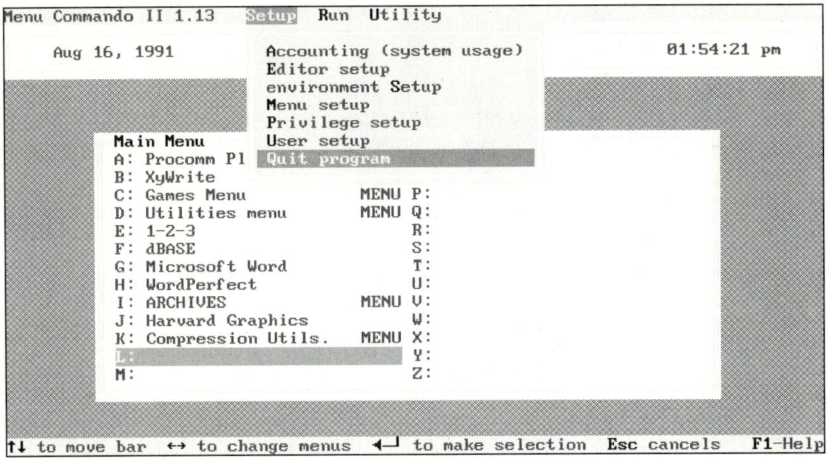

Figure 8.10 Menu Commando II's main menu

A great deal of attention has been paid to making this program as easy to use as possible. For example, if you use a great many submenus nested within one another, Menu Commando II has a simple way to help you keep track of all of them. In the screen in which you set up your menus, you'll be presented with a tree display, so you can quickly see the structure of all your menus and submenus.

Setting up your menus to run programs is a snap as well. From the main menu, choose Setup, then Menu Setup, and press Enter. You'll be presented with a split screen. On the left side will be a listing, in a tree display, of all the menus and submenus you've set up. (If you're just starting the program, and haven't set up any, the only listing will be for the main menu.) On the right side is a listing of all items on the menu you've highlighted. To move from one part of the screen to the other, press the Tab key.

To add a menu item, tab over to the right side of the screen, highlight a blank menu item, and press F7. Tell the program whether you want to put a submenu or a program in that slot, and then you'll be presented with a form to fill in. If you're adding a program, the form will be a long one, and will ask you for information such as the program name, its path, and the file which will execute it; whether it should include a password; and a number of other items, as shown in Figure 8.11.

Figure 8.11
Filling in the form for adding a new program to the menu

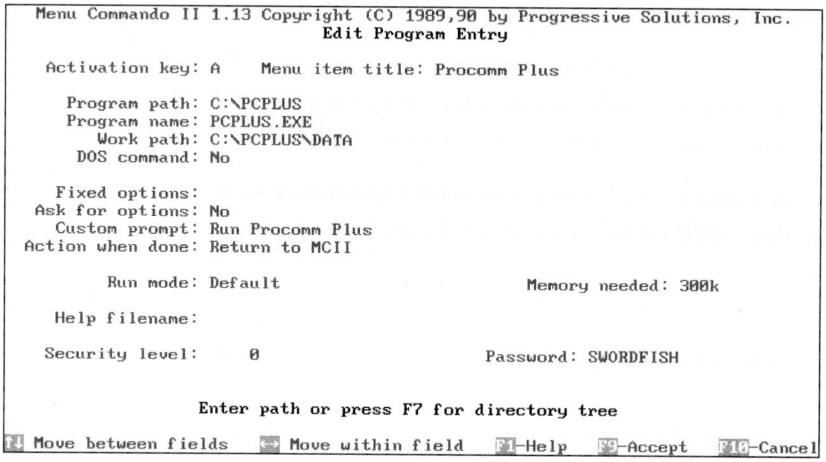

Even here, much attention has been paid to making the program easy to use. Should you forget the path for the program you want to add, Menu Commando will show you a tree structure of your hard disk so that you can choose the proper directory, as shown in Figure 8.12. And if you forget the name of the program's executable file, it will present you with a list of files in the directory. After filling out the form, you're done; you can then run the program from the menu.

Menu Commando enables the use of passwords, which can be assigned not just to restrict access to individual programs, but to entire menus as well. It includes a screen saver, a built-in text editor, a limited DOS shell, a file locator, a superb security system, and a number of helpful utilities. It will also track how much time was spent running each of the programs listed on your menus for you.

Menu Commando II
Registration fee: $$
Progressive Solutions, Inc.
P.O. Box 276125
San Antonio, TX 78227
(512) 670-1061

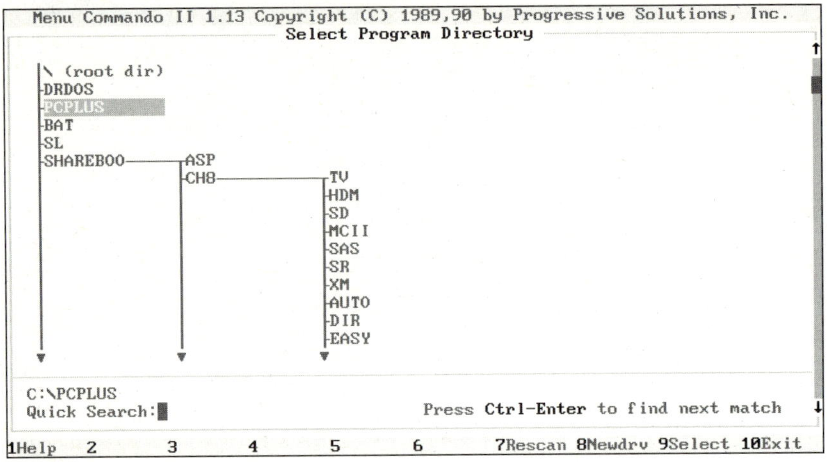

Figure 8.12 Menu Commando's directory tree display

PCMENU

This may be the easiest menu program you'll ever find. If you want to create simple menus, you'll only need to skim the documentation and spend 10 or 15 minutes at the keyboard to have completed menus, ready to run.

When you first load PCMENU, you'll be presented with a blank menu in the middle of the screen, flanked on either side by a calendar, as shown in Figure 8.13. The calendar to the left shows the current month; to the right is the next month. The top of the screen tells you the current date and time, and at bottom is the listing of your current directory.

You can create two separate menus with PCMENU, each with ten menu items on it. To get from one menu to the other, press the Right and Left Arrow keys.

To create a new menu item, press the Alt key and the function key you want associated with the menu item. For example, to have the first menu item run the XyWrite word processor, you would press Alt-F1 and fill in the on-screen form that appears, as shown in Figure 8.14.

You'll first have to name the menu listing; call it whatever you like. Next, you'll be asked for the path to the directory where you want your data files stored. Note that this is *not* necessarily the same as the path for the executable program itself—it's just where you want your data files stored. On the next line fill in the command that loads the program. Be sure to include the path where the program can be found.

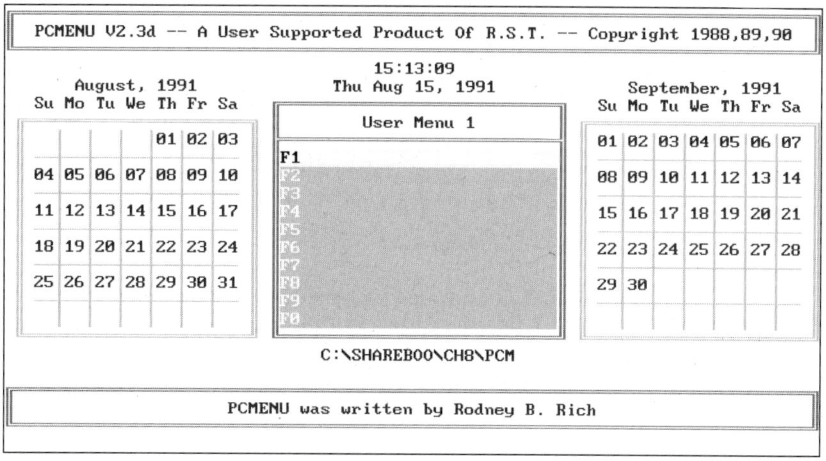

Figure 8.13
PCMENU's opening screen

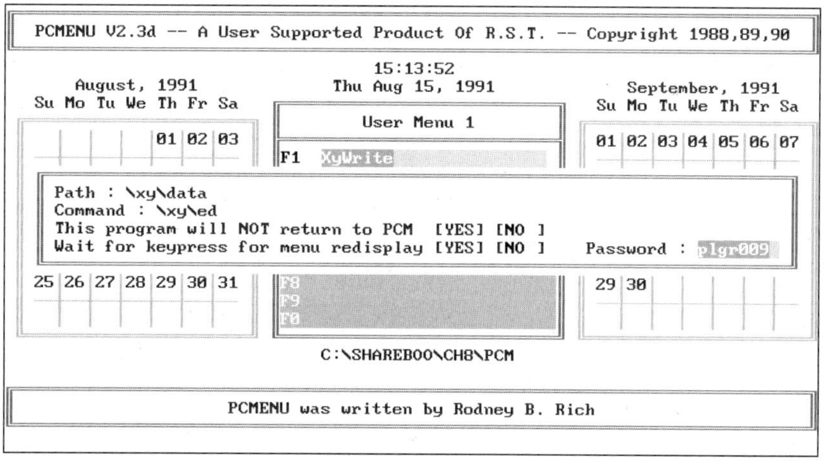

Figure 8.14
Creating a new menu listing in PCMenu

The next two lines include options that make this program not only simple to use, but extremely useful as well. The first option asks whether you should be returned to PCMENU after the menu item runs, or whether you should exit PCMENU after running the menu item. The next item is a particularly helpful one: You can either set it to return automatically to PCMENU after exiting the program item, or, instead, set it up so that a keystroke is required to return you to PCMENU. You'll find this second option helpful when you're running a DOS command or other program that displays data on the screen and then immediately quits, such as the DOS CHKDSK command. If this option didn't force you to press a key before returning to PCMENU, CHKDSK would flash its information on the screen too fast for you to read. Using this option, you can view the data on the screen, press a key, and then return to PCMENU. The last item allows you to attach passwords to your programs, so that programs can only be run by you or by people to whom you've given your password. Each program can have a different password.

After you've filled in each item, your menu listing will be complete. You can run any item by scrolling to it and pressing Enter, or by pressing its function key. See Figure 8.15 for a complete menu.

Figure 8.15
A complete menu created with PCMENU

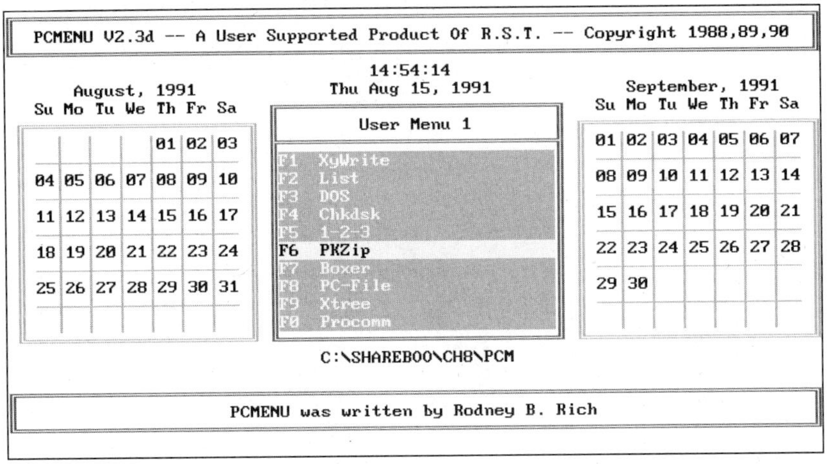

PCMENU is more than just a menu program; it also allows you easy access to DOS commands. It has a simple DOS shell built in (see Figure 8.16), which you access by pressing the PgDn key.

PCMENU
Registration fee: $
Rodney B. Rich
2661-A Garfield
Tyndall AFB, FL 32403

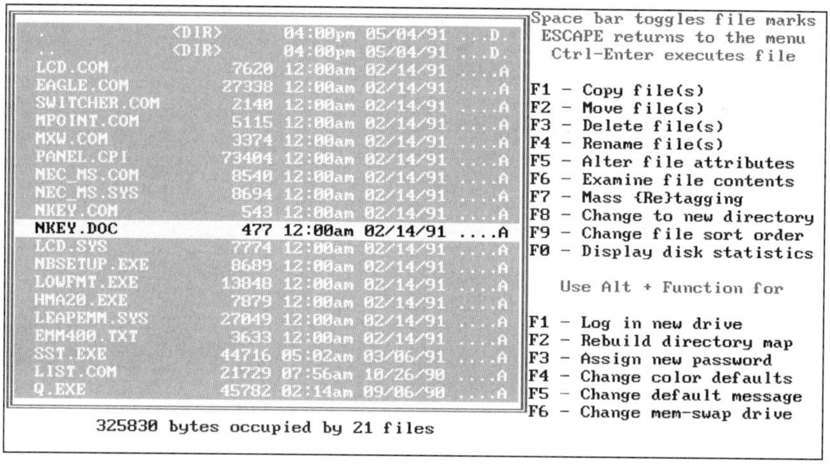

Figure 8.16
PCMENU's simple but useful DOS shell

PowerMenu

A simple-to-use menu program, PowerMenu doesn't come with all the bells and whistles of other menu programs, but it has some useful utilities you won't find anywhere else.

When you first run PowerMenu, it looks through your hard disk and installs many of the programs it finds there onto its menu. Thus when you first begin to use it, you'll find some of your programs are ready to run. As with other menuing programs, items on a menu can either be programs or submenus. See Figure 8.17 to see how PowerMenu handles two levels of menus.

To add a new menu item, press the Insert key, and up will pop a form to fill in. You'll enter information such as the program name, its subdirectory, the command to execute it, whether it has a password, and whether there are optional parameters it should use, as shown in Figure 8.18.

Most of the program operates in a similarly straightforward manner. Of special note are a number of utilities not generally found in menu programs. You'll find, for example, a simple, useful DOS shell, called Disk Manager. There are also utilities to report the amount of free RAM, whether your printer is on line or not, and the number of serial ports you have. There's also a memory map which reports on what TSRs are running, how much memory they're using, and what addresses they occupy, as shown in Figure 8.19.

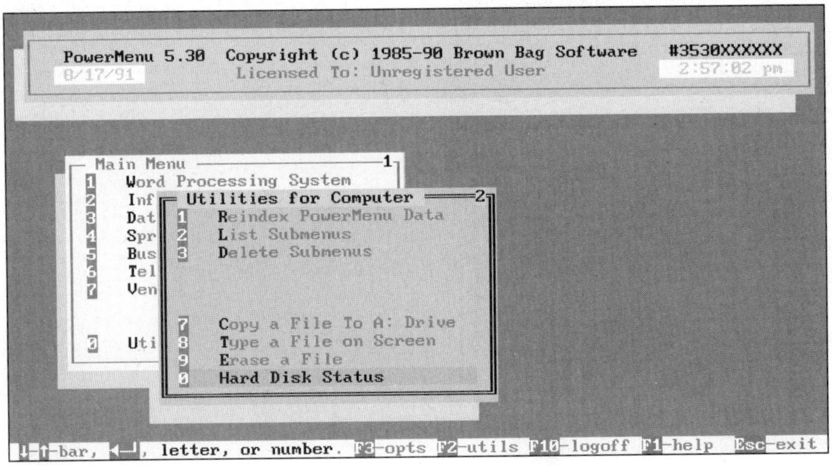

Figure 8.17
PowerMenu's main menu and a submenu

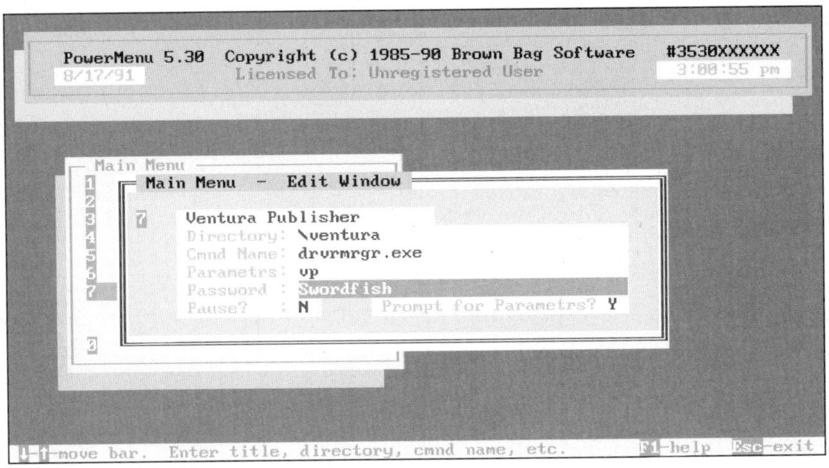

Figure 8.18
Adding a new menu item in PowerMenu

PowerMenu
Registration fee: $$$
Brown Bag Software
2155 South Bascom Ave.
Campbell, CA 95008
(408) 559-4545

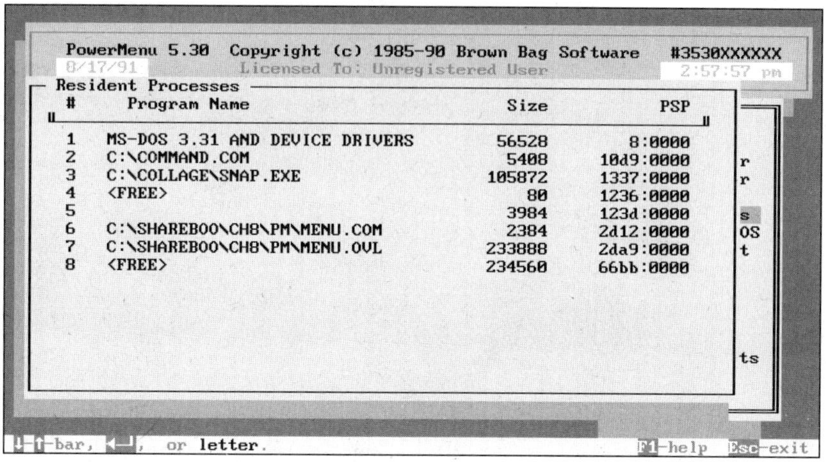

Figure 8.19
PowerMenu utility for complete reports on TSRs

QuikMenu

Most menu programs are functional, but not particularly pretty to look at. QuikMenu is different. Not only does it give you instant access to all your programs, it does so in an eye-pleasing manner.

Although the program does not run under Windows, its design owes a lot to that program. Easy-to-change colors, nice-looking fonts, radio buttons, scroll bars, sculpted 3-D menu items, and exploding screens all make QuikMenu a pleasure to look at as well as to use. Figure 8.20 shows QuikMenu's approach to menus.

QuikMenu hasn't sacrificed utility in the name of beauty, though. It has what you would expect in a solid menu program. You can create many levels of submenus, include passwords for greater security, log the amount of time you spend working with each program on the menu, and drop down to DOS when you want to. It also has mouse support.

When you first load it, QuikMenu will automatically create menu buttons for programs it finds. There's a text viewer and other helpful utilities as well.

QuikMenu
Registration fee: $
OSCS
354 NE Greenwood, Suite 205
Bend, OR 97701
(503) 389-5489

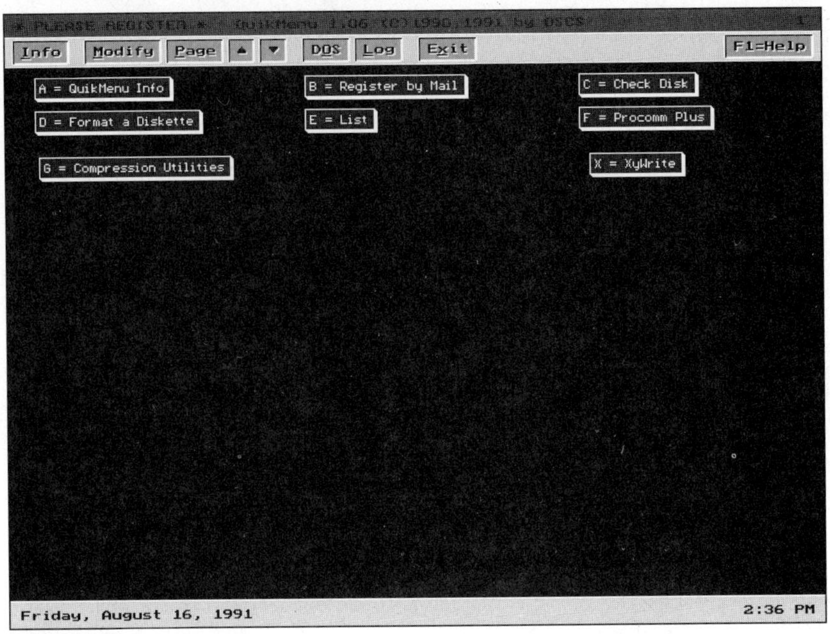

Figure 8.20
A graphic menu from QuikMenu

XMenu

This is a straightforward program that offers few power features, but makes up for it in simplicity. It offers simple password protection, a log of the amount of time spent on different menu items, and the ability to create submenus. If you want to spend the least amount of time possible setting up menus and don't care for high-end features, it deserves a look.

XMenu
Registration fee: $
Gary Wood
5401 Lakeview Road
North Little Rock, AR 72116

CHAPTER

9

General Utilities

File Utilities

Command-Line Utilities

Batch and Start-up Utilities

Miscellaneous Utilities

MENTION SHAREWARE TO MANY PEOPLE, AND THE FIRST WORD THAT will come to their minds is *utilities*. They assume that shareware programs are all one-trick ponies that can do only one utility-related task, but do it well.

It's easy to see where this misconception comes from. There are, in fact, thousands upon thousands of shareware utilities available, and many more are written every day. This is an area in which shareware tends to be superior to commercial products: Often, the function a shareware utility performs today will be found in a commercial product tomorrow. For example, the functions of DOS 5's DOSKEY program have been available for many years in shareware such as Anarkey and CED.

The commercial utilities available, such as Norton Utilities and PC Tools, tend to be utility *collections*. Although they're quite useful, in some cases outperforming their shareware counterparts, they also tend to be sizable programs with far larger pricetags than shareware utilities, many of which are free.

Shareware utilities, in contrast, tend to be inexpensive, small, and geared to a single specific task. There's a shareware utility for every problem imaginable, and then some. Do you need to find a file on your hard disk, and only know its name? Use SST. Would you like to make life at the command line more manageable? Get 4DOS. Do you want to pump up your batch file power? Find STACKEY. Have you ever wanted to take a look into your PC's memory and see what TSRs are there? Look for PMAP. You'll find a shareware solution for just about any problem at the keyboard.

I've divided the general utilities that follow into four categories: file utilities, command-line utilities, batch and start-up utilities, and miscellaneous utilities. File utilities are those which help you use and manage files. Command-line utilities let you master the DOS prompt. Batch and start-up utilities give you extra batch commands and let you boot up your PC with more flexibility. And miscellaneous utilities are, well, miscellaneous, doing everything from converting between graphics formats to helping you out of system lockups.

These programs are only a taste of the utilities that are available. Spend some time on a bulletin board or with a disk vendor's catalog, and you won't believe what else you'll find.

File Utilities

DOS has never been very kind when you're working with files. It lacks even the elemental tools for viewing, copying, deleting, and searching for files, among other tasks.

This is where shareware comes in. There are hundreds, perhaps thousands, of utilities for doing such jobs. The best known is probably List Plus, which may be the best all-around file viewer you'll find. But there are many others that will do other jobs equally well. What follows is a sampling of the best.

CLEANUP

Your hard disk is littered with little "mistake" files of zero, one, and two bytes. To get rid of them all could take you hours. It won't take long, however, if you use CLEANUP. This little program finds files of zero, one, and two bytes, and then erases them if you want them zapped.

In the process, you'll recover more disk space than you might think. Every file, no matter its size, takes up a minimum of two clusters, which usually means 2048 bytes. With earlier versions of DOS, these tiny files can take up eight clusters. The files won't appear to occupy that much space, because they only show the amount of data they contain, not what DOS allocates for them.

Be careful when erasing these tiny files. Some programs use zero-byte files for a variety of purposes, such as copy protection.

CLEANUP
Registration fee: None
Don Phillip Gibson
910 East 11th St.
Winfield, KS 67156
(316) 221-0605

FGREP

There are a lot of shareware programs that search for files based on their names, and they're certainly useful. When you're searching for a file, however, you often don't recall its name; instead, you remember what was in it. When that happens, file-searching utilities won't help you a bit.

FGREP will, however. This program, which resembles the similarly named UNIX utility, will search through files for text and then report back to you on the results. It's exceptionally flexible, and can do a great many types of searches. You can, for example, search in one file for every occurrence of a particular string of text. Or you can search in a given directory for every file that contains the string, or search a group of directories.

For example, if you wanted to find every file that had to do with salary projections for 1993, you would search for "1993 salary." FGREP would then look for every occurrence of those words in your files, no matter what type of file they were in, and report on what it found.

FGREP
Registration fee: None
Christopher J. Dunford
The Cove Software Group
P.O. Box 1072
Columbia, MD 21044
(301) 992-9371

List Plus

Possibly the most popular shareware program of all time, List Plus is one utility that absolutely everyone who puts finger to keyboard needs as part of his or her computing toolkit. List Plus allows you to do a great number of computing tasks—it's a file viewer, a directory lister, a DOS shell, a phone dialer, and far more.

On its simplest level, though, List Plus is a file viewer. If you want to view the contents of a file, but don't want to wait until your word processor or text editor loads, you would use List Plus. Let's say you wanted to view a file called MANUAL.DOC. On the command line, you would type **LIST MANUAL.DOC**, and you would be viewing the contents of the file in a flash. You scroll through the file by using the PgUp, PgDn, and arrow keys.

List Plus will also filter out "junk characters," to make it easier to view the file; will list the file in hexadecimal format if you so desire; and will display the file in either 25- or 43-line mode if you have an EGA or VGA monitor. The program will also let you view files that have been compressed and are in ARC, LZH, PAK, or ZIP format, as well as self-extracting files with a .COM or .EXE extension. (To do that, however, you'll also need another program written by List Plus's author, called File View.) Aside from these viewing capabilities, List Plus can also search for text within files, and has many other helpful viewing features.

If all List Plus did was allow you to view files, it would be well worth the cost. But the file viewer is just the beginning of what this remarkable utility can do.

For starters, List Plus will display all the files within a subdirectory. Type **LIST** on the command line, and you'll get a display like the one shown in Figure 9.1. You can set it to display from one to six columns of files, and you can toggle among the type of displays at will.

Across the bottom of the screen are the commands available. You can view files (the program calls this command List), copy, delete, rename, edit, move, sort, tag, and untag files. You can also view compressed files and change your path. To use any of these functions, type the first letter of the function. To move a file, for example, you would point at a file with the moving bar, type **M**, and then tell the program where to move the file.

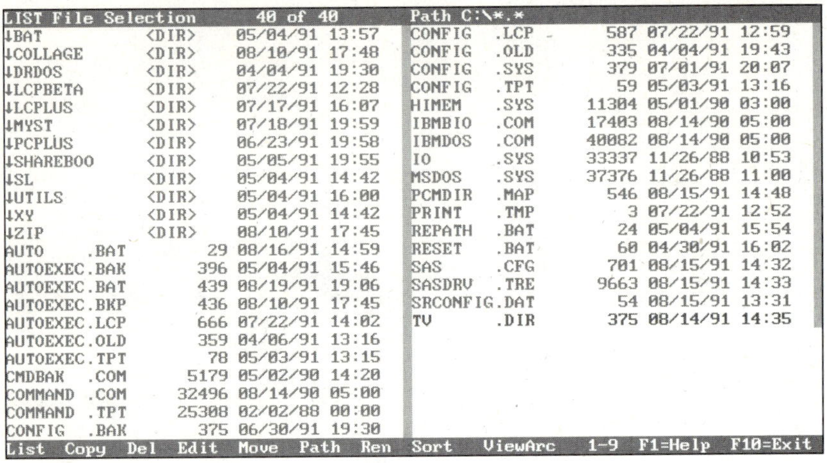

Figure 9.1
A two-column directory display in List Plus

If you'd rather have information about your hard disk (such as files used and capacity available) listed at the bottom of your screen, instead of a list of commands, press F2. To toggle it back to the command listing, press F2 again.

To use List Plus to edit files, you'll have to do a little bit of work. List Plus doesn't come with a text editor. You'll have to create a batch file called EDIT.BAT, which will contain the commands for loading your text editor. If, for example, your text editor or word processor is found in the \TEXTED subdirectory, and needs the command EDIT to load it, the EDIT.BAT file would contain the line \TEXTED\EDIT. Make sure to put the EDIT.BAT file on a path listed in your AUTOEXEC.BAT file. Then, when you type **E** while you're in List Plus's file display, you'll load your text editor.

You can also run programs from List Plus. Highlight them and type **I**, and the program or batch file will run. It will even dial your phone for you using your modem. While you're viewing a file, simply press Ctrl-T, and then follow the instructions for dialing the telephone. (It's not a communications program, however; you can't upload or download files. You can only talk on the telephone after it's been dialed.) When you're done, pressing Ctrl-H hangs up the phone.

There's even more to List Plus, and the best way to get acquainted with it is to go out and use it. One final note: The program's author, Vernon Buerg, gives shareware an interesting twist. He merely *suggests*, instead of requiring, payment for his program. Any amount is acceptable, though he suggests $20 as the right figure.

List Plus
Registration fee: $
Vernon Buerg
139 White Oak Circle
Petaluma, CA 94952

PCOPY

DOS's COPY command is often more trouble than it's worth. How many times, for example, have you copied a file, only to find that the new file you've just created has written over a file with the same name? And that's just the beginning. COPY's limitations are legion. There must be a better way!

Luckily for you, there is: PCOPY. If you try to copy a file, and the name of the new file name already exists, PCOPY will warn you, and ask if you want to rename the file, stop the copying operation, or overwrite the old file.

That's just one of this handy utility's many features. If you try to copy a file to a directory that doesn't exist, PCOPY will warn you and then create the new directory if you so choose. There are also far more options for copying files, including copying only files that have been updated since the last copy. PCOPY will also move files between drives and directories by copying the file to a new drive or directory, and then erasing the original from the old drive or directory. It allows for the use of the wildcards * and ?, and many other options.

PCOPY can be used either directly from the command line or through the menu shown in Figure 9.2. This menu brings all the program's many options and switches within easy reach.

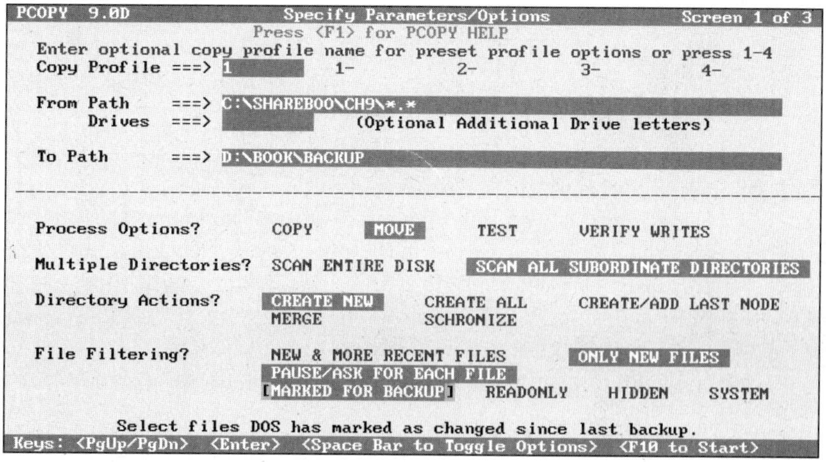

Figure 9.2
PCOPY's menu-driven mode

There are a great many uses for PCOPY. For example, it's good for making backups. Because it will copy files between drives, and can be set to copy only files that have been updated since the last copy, it's ideal for quick and easy disk backups.

PCOPY
Registration fee: $
Patri-Soft
P.O. Box 8263
San Bernardino, CA 92412
(714) 352-2820

PDELETE

PDELETE does for DOS's DELETE command what PCOPY does for the COPY command—it's safer, it's smarter, and it's far more powerful. Do you want to delete only those files updated before or after a certain date? It's no problem with PDELETE. It will also delete files based on the status of their archive bits, which makes customized mass deletions far easier. It will delete hidden, system, and read-only files, and can do away with entire directories at a time. And in a pinch, it has an emergency feature that lets you stop the deletion while it's in process.

PCOPY and PDELETE combined make a powerful set of file-management programs. They'll let you keep your hard disk in backed-up, fighting trim.

PDELETE
Registration fee: $
Patri-Soft
P.O. Box 8263
San Bernardino, CA 92412
(714) 352-2820

Professional Master Key

An extremely powerful set of utilities, Professional Master Key performs many disk and file operations, much like the Norton Utilities or PC Tools. It can be used even by novices to do things such as restoring deleted files, but it can also be used by experts to peer deeply into disks and systems and perform powerful file and disk functions. In fact, with these programs you can manipulate individual sectors on a disk.

Each of the individual programs can be run from the command line, or they can instead be accessed from the program's main menu, shown in

Figure 9.3. To run one of the programs, move your cursor to the name of the function you want to run, and press Enter.

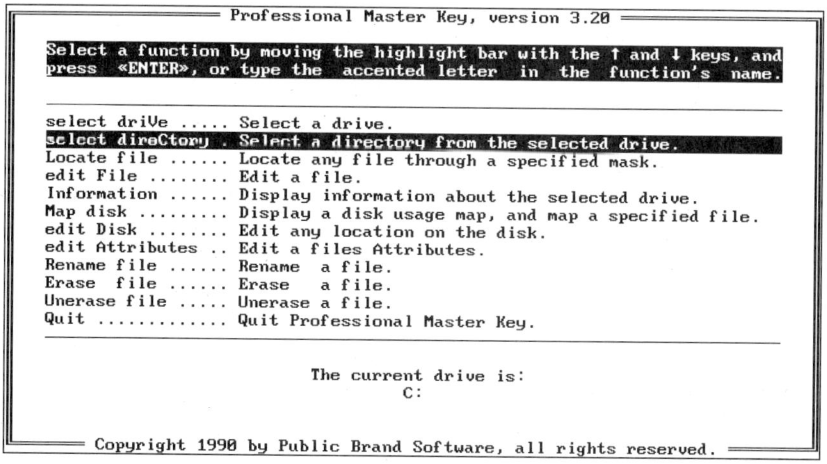

Figure 9.3
Professional Master Key's main menu

Most people will find the file and disk utilities of greatest use. You'll especially want to note Professional Master Key's Unerase utility. You may have deleted files by accident in the past, only to spend hours re-creating them—if it was possible at all. With Professional Master Key, those days are gone: You'll be able to restore files that you've deleted. (Note, however, that if you've written files to disk since you deleted the file, you may not be able to recover it.)

The program will also let you delete any file on your disk, even if it's a hidden, system, or read-only file. It has a file finder that lets you search for files on your disk. It allows you to rename individual files and even entire directories. You can call up a map of your hard disk, showing used sectors, bad sectors, and what percentage of the disk is unused. And you can get information about your hard disk or a floppy, as shown in Figure 9.4. The program also has a text editor for editing small text files.

Some of its more powerful utilities should only be used by those familiar with the intricacies of hard disks. For example, it will let you change the contents of any sector on your disk, including the boot sector and File Allocation Table (FAT). It will let you completely wipe out all traces of a file with the use of its Zero File Utility; it will also let you erase every bit of data on your hard disk by wiping it clean. And it has a utility that will help you restore your hard disk should you accidentally format it.

Figure 9.4
Professional Master Key's report on disk information

```
Professional Master Key, version 3.20

Information On Drive C:

Disk capacity information...
     190  Megabytes total disk capacity possible.
      26  Megabytes disk capacity available (13% free).

Disk logical dimensions...
     512  Bytes in each sector.
  391166  Sectors existing on the entire disk.
  390752  Data Sectors possible for file usage on the disk.
       8  Data Sectors exist in each Data Cluster.
   48844  Data Clusters possible for file usage on the disk.
       1  Reserved Sector(s) at the beginning of the disk.
       2  FAT copies available, each using 191 sectors.
     512  Files allowed in the Root Directory.

        Start of all FAT sectors:      sector    1
        Start of the Root Directory:   sector  383
        Start of all Data Sectors:     sector  415

Copyright 1990 by Public Brand Software, all rights reserved.
```

Although many of the program's utilities are clearly aimed at the power user, there are some utilities, such as Unerase, that even beginners shouldn't be without.

Professional Master Key
Registration fee: $
Public Brand Software
P.O. Box 51315
Indianapolis, IN 46251
(317) 856-7571; (800) 426-3475 (orders)

QDups

This program helps you rid your disk of duplicate files—you'd be surprised how many you'll find. On two of my hard disks, from 5 to 10 percent of my total disk space was taken up with duplicate files, such as HIMEM.SYS, which a number of programs install without asking.

To run the program, type **QDUPS** and press Enter. The program will search through your hard disk for duplicate file names. It then displays a listing of every duplicate file it finds, including the time and date each file was last used, its size, the type of file it is, and what directory it is in. A typical listing is shown in Figure 9.5.

On the left part of the screen, QDups also displays the size of your disk, the percent of disk space you have free, the total number of duplicate files, the total number of bytes in those files, and the percentage of disk space taken up by those duplicate files.

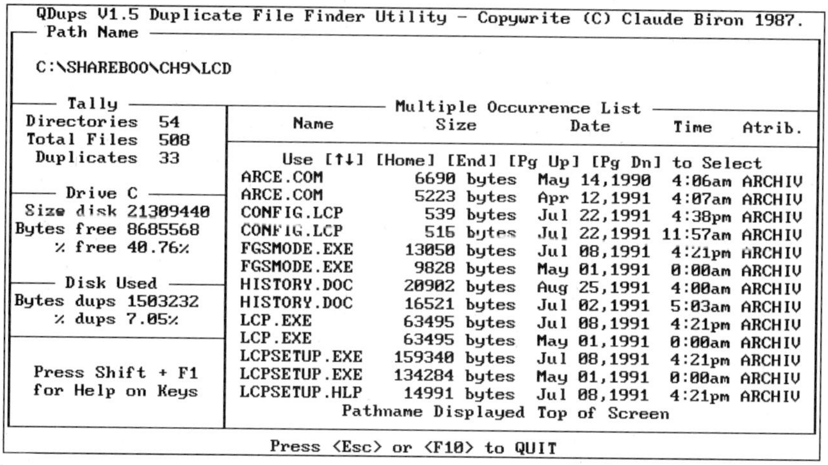

Figure 9.5
The results of a search done by QDups

At this point, QDups doesn't actually examine the files to see if they're exact duplicates; it only lists files with exactly the same names. You might have different files with the same name, for example, READ.ME files from different programs. Before deleting any files, however, you can have QDups compare them, to see if they are actually identical, or are different files. To do so, press F3, highlight one file and press Enter; then do the same for the other file. QDups will tell you if the files are identical. If they are, you can delete one by pressing Ctrl-D when the file is highlighted.

QDups
Registration fee: $
Claude Biron
103 West 23rd Ave.
Vancouver, British Columbia
Canada V5Y 2H1

Rock Utilities

This collection of over two dozen utilities will help you through almost any file- or disk-related problem you can name. For example, you'll find a utility that will move files from one directory to another. There's a replacement for DOS's DIR command that will do things such as automatically list the contents of compressed files. One utility will let you turn off the Caps Lock, Num Lock, Scroll Lock, and Ins keys without touching them. Another controls your keyboard speed.

Particularly powerful is a utility that will delete a directory and all the files within it. The utilities also include a text-search utility, which will search through files for a given piece of text. There's also one that will erase all traces of a file from your disk so that the file can never be undeleted, even with the most powerful undelete utilities.

You can run the utilities from the command line, or, even easier, you can access them via a shell called the Rock Initiator, shown in Figure 9.6.

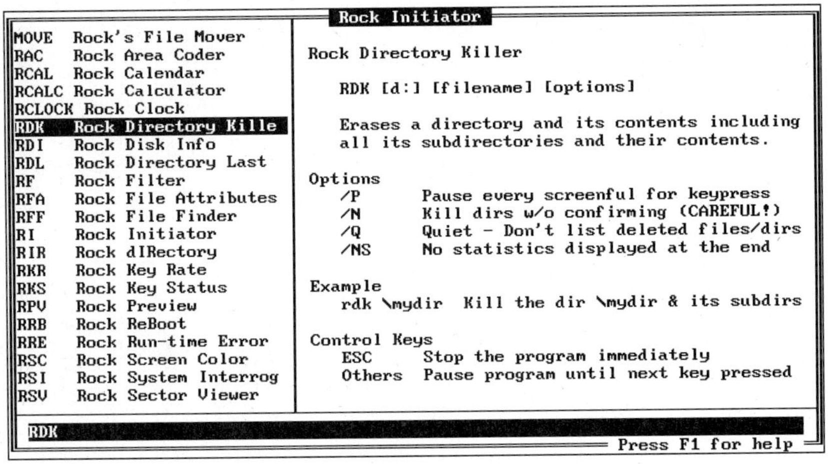

Figure 9.6
The Rock Initiator menu shell

The program isn't limited to the usual file and directory utilities, though. There's a calculator to help you do basic arithmetic functions, a utility to look up the area code and time zone for cities, and a word counter that counts the number of words, characters, or lines in a file or group of files.

Considering these utilities' low price and their breadth, this is one of the better deals you'll find.

Rock Utilities
Registration fee: $
Rob Argy
Rock Systems
101 North Main St., Suite 150-125
Ann Arbor, MI 48104
(313) 971-9123

Supersonic Search Tool (SST)

Don't even bother to count all the shareware file-finding utilities available; the numbers will make your head spin. But the Supersonic Search Tool (SST) is the best one you'll find. Even if you already have a file-searcher, you should take a look at SST—it's to other search utilities what the Concorde is to a biplane. It's blazingly fast, extremely flexible, and will do far more than just search for files.

How fast is it? It took just over six seconds to find the 21 PCX files out of 3,943 files in 156 subdirectories on my hard disk. How flexible is it? Your searches can be remarkably sophisticated. You can tell it to search only for files with certain extensions, you can tell it to search only through certain directories, you can search by file size and the last time a file was modified. You can even exclude certain file types from the search so that it won't, for example, bother to look at executable files.

The program will also search through archive files created with popular compression programs, so that if there's a file hidden in a compressed archive, you'll be able to find it. It will display duplicate file names, and delete any files you wish it to during the search. So it's a great tool for cleaning your hard disk of those annoying backup files that many programs create.

SST is run from the command line, and there are a great many switches available to do all the searches. Because of this, at times the program can be confusing to use. Consider the example the program's author gives to show the power and sophistication of the program:

```
SST cde:*.bak "[0-9]" -gt1024 -lt2048 -s12-10-89 -b12-20-89 -v
```

This command would delete each file with a .BAK extension on drives C, D, and E that has a number somewhere in the file name (such as PROG01.BAK). It would only delete those files, however, if they were from 1,025 to 2,047 bytes in length and were last modified between the dates of 12-10-89 and 12-19-89.

Of course, you probably won't be doing such complex searches. For simpler searches, it's an easy program to use. For example, to search for the file WHERE.AMI, you would type

```
SST WHERE.AMI
```

on the command line, and press Enter. To search for every file with the extension .TIF in the directory \ART, and all the subdirectories contained in \ART, you would type

```
SST *.TIF \ART
```

If you have a hard disk and ever forget where you've put a file, you need SST.

Supersonic Search Tool
Registration fee: $
Keith Ledbetter
4240 Ketcham Dr.
Chesterfield, VA 23832
(804) 674-0780

Trash-It

There's no escaping it: You're going to delete important files, not be able to recover them, and spend hours trying to re-create them, if you can re-create them at all. You can have a utility that can undelete files and still not be safe. Even the best and most sophisticated of them can't recover files that have been overwritten by a newer file.

You'll never have that problem with Trash-It. With Trash-It, when you delete a file, it isn't really deleted from your disk. Instead, it's moved to a \TRASH subdirectory. If you find out you need the file, you'll only need to go to that subdirectory and get it.

If you're not careful, however, your hard disk could easily fill up with Trash-It files. So make sure to clear out the \TRASH subdirectory regularly. When you delete a file from that subdirectory, it is, in fact, deleted from your hard disk. To make the cleaning easier, Trash-It users get several utilities when they register. These utilities will automatically delete files from the \TRASH subdirectory when they've been there a user-specified number of days. They can also compress the files in the subdirectory using the PKZIP compression utility.

Trash-It
Registration fee: $
RSE Incorporated
1157 57th Dr. SE
Auburn, WA 98002
(206) 939-4105

Command-Line Utilities

The bare C prompt: What could be more disconcerting or difficult to use? There's a fair amount of power buried in DOS, but getting at it at times seems impossible when all you have is C> on an otherwise blank screen.

These utilities will make your command-line life easier. Some, like CED, will allow you to edit your command line. Although DOS 5's DOSKEY finally gave that power to DOS, the utilities below, such as CED, still pack more punch than DOSKEY does.

Other utilities, such as Anarkey, simplify your life at the keyboard by reducing the number of keystrokes you have to type to get anything done. And then there's 4DOS, a complete replacement for COMMAND.COM, which contains numerous commands that DOS forgot. You'll find other command-line utilities here as well. Use them, and that bare C prompt may not seem so inscrutable after all.

AI

How good is your typing? For most of us the answer is "Not very." You've probably made numerous mistakes at the command line, typing DUR, when you meant to type DIR, for example. AI takes care of those errors. It corrects your typing errors by learning from your mistakes. Every time you type something at the command line and get an error message back from DOS, AI asks for the command's proper spelling. The next time you make that spelling mistake, it warns you that you've made a typing error and suggests the proper command. Press Enter, and the command is executed.

AI also has a command-line editor that can recall past commands and lets you edit at the C prompt. You can also attach macros to the function keys (F1 through F10).

AI
Registration fee: $
AAron Computer
P.O. Box 4708
Mesa, AZ 85211

Anarkey

Don't be fooled by this program's name—it's the farthest thing from anarchy you may ever find. Its sole reason for existence is to save keystrokes, and so bring order to your life at the keyboard. It does this exceedingly well.

On the simplest level, Anarkey is a command-line editor, letting you save and edit DOS commands. In that respect, it's similar to DOS 5's DOSKEY utility. But it does far more than DOSKEY, and is superior in other respects as well.

It will complete file names, program names, and directory names at the command line for you. For example, if you wanted to change to the directory \WKSHTS, you would type **CD\W** at the command line, and then press the Tab key. If \WKSHTS was the only directory beginning with W, your command line would now read CD\WKSHTS. If other directories begin with W, repeatedly pressing the Tab key will bring each to the command line in turn. In a similar manner, you can bring file or program names to the command line.

Anarkey also allows you to quickly change and edit your *environment variables*—the elements of your path statement. Type **PATH** on the command line, press the F9 key, and your path statement will appear on screen. You can now edit it, store it, and your new PATH variable will be in effect.

Perhaps its most powerful feature is its use of what it calls *AKAs*. Similar to some programs' macros, these allow you to assign a single word or character to represent a command. When you type that word or letter on the command line and press Enter, Anarkey will execute the original command. For example, if you wanted to load your word processor with a single keystroke, you could define the string \EDITOR\EDITOR.EXE as the letter E. Then every subsequent time you typed an **E** and pressed Enter on the command line, the string \EDITOR\EDITOR.EXE would be executed.

What makes AKAs even more powerful is that they can take the place not just of a single command, but of a whole string of them. When you add to it the ability to use the powerful DOS batch-file parameters %1 through %9, you end up with more than just a keystroke saver. In essence, Anarkey can act as a powerful batch-file creator.

Anarkey has many other features as well, including the ability to execute multiple commands from the command line, eliminating the need to type a command, press Enter, then wait for the next prompt from DOS.

Anarkey
Registration fee: $
Moderne Software
P.O. Box 3638
Santa Clara, CA 95055

CED

There are many shareware command-line editors available, but this one is the best. CED allows you to easily edit the command line, scroll back through previously issued commands, and execute or edit them, and lets you create what it calls *synonyms*, which are essentially the same thing as Anarkey's AKAs—a string of commands executed with a couple of keystrokes. In fact, CED was the first utility that offered such a feature.

DOS 5's DOSKEY has similar capabilities to CED, but it's not as powerful. CED, for example, can purposely ignore certain commands, such as FORMAT, when you tell it to, something that DOSKEY can't do. For those who haven't yet gotten DOS 5, this is a must-have utility. And even if you have DOS 5, it's worth a look.

CED
Registration fee: None
Christopher J. Dunford
The Cove Software Group
P.O. Box 1072
Columbia, MD 21044
(301) 992-9371

EXECUTE

This nifty little program won't change your life at the keyboard, but it will certainly make it easier. EXECUTE allows you to execute multiple commands from the command line at once. These can be DOS commands solely, or you can launch full-blown applications. Type **EXECUTE**, followed by the commands you want (separated by semicolons), and they'll be run in the order you type them. The DOSKEY utility in DOS 5 performs a similar task, but it's not as powerful as EXECUTE. EXECUTE, for example, can delay running some programs by seconds, minutes, or even hours.

EXECUTE
Registration fee: $
MAH Software Services
29 Beech Court
Babbitt, MN 55706
(218) 827-2787

4DOS

Pick a command-line problem. Any problem. The chances are that 4DOS, a remarkable replacement for, or addition to, COMMAND.COM, can solve it. This program contains the commands and tools that DOS—even the much-touted DOS 5—forgot. In fact, the program is so innovative that Symantec licensed it from its shareware author, tweaked it, and now markets it as NDOS, a replacement for COMMAND.COM. NDOS is available as part of Symantec's Norton Utilities, in Version 6 and above. You can still get 4DOS as shareware, however.

What does 4DOS do? Just about everything. It enhances standard DOS commands and adds many powerful commands of its own. It has sophisticated batch commands for writing batch files. It has a command-line editor, and an *alias* function (like the AKAs in Anarkey) so that you can define a lengthy set of commands to be executed with a few keystrokes. It lets you write descriptions of your files and directories; when you issue a directory command, you'll see the descriptions in addition to the normal directory listing. It also has an excellent on-line help system, and even more features.

4DOS can either be used as a replacement for COMMAND.COM, or can be loaded on top of it. If you're going to use it instead of COMMAND.COM (which is the best way to run the program), you would add the following line to your CONFIG.SYS file and make sure that your 4DOS files are in your root directory:

```
SHELL=C:\4DOS.COM /P
```

When you load 4DOS, you can use a variety of switches to control such things as the environment size, the size of the alias list, and swapping to memory, among others.

Once 4DOS is loaded, you can press the F1 key if you need help. You'll get an on-screen listing of 4DOS and DOS commands and functions. Move your cursor to the one you want, press Enter, and you'll get information about the command.

4DOS enhances many basic DOS commands such as DELETE and COPY. For example, with the DELETE command, you can erase files with several different extensions by issuing a single command, instead of having to enter several commands, as you would have to do with DOS. You can have 4DOS require you to confirm the deletion by typing **Y** when prompted. And you can perform any of these functions in your current directory or, instead, across your entire hard disk. Thus, for example, if you wanted to delete every file with the extensions .BAK, .TMP, and .PRN on your hard disk, and you wanted 4DOS to prompt you for confirmation before deleting each file, you would issue the following command:

```
GLOBAL DELETE /P *.BAK *.TMP *.PRN
```

4DOS adds many other commands that DOS lacks. It has a MOVE command, so that you can move files among directories. There's an EXCEPT function, which allows you to perform operations on every file but those you've excluded from the operation. It will allow you to issue multiple commands from a single line. In short, there are dozens of 4DOS commands not found in DOS.

4DOS lets you create remarkable batch files because of the power of its batch language. Commands include beeping the PC's speaker at a certain tone and for a certain amount of time, executing nested batch files, accepting user input from the keyboard, drawing boxes and lines in colors, positioning the cursor at a certain part of the screen and displaying text, and far more. Batch-file jockeys will have a field day, and even those who write simple batch files will benefit.

There is even more to 4DOS, including commands that are specifically geared to work with DOS 5. The only way to find out about this remarkable product is to try it for yourself.

4DOS
Registration fee: $$
JP Software, Inc.
P.O. Box 1470
East Arlington, MA 02174
(617) 646-3975; (800) 368-8777 (orders)

LCD

One of computing's most annoying tasks is the simple act of changing directories. If you have enough of them on a hard disk, it's difficult to remember their names. You'll waste time typing **CD \SALSRPT**, **CD \SALESRPT**, then **CD \SALRPT**, when the subdirectory was called \SALERPRT.

LCD (Let's Change Directory) has the answer for you. Type **LCD S**, and if the \SALERPRT subdirectory is the only one on your hard disk beginning with S, you'll be switched directly to it. If others exist, a window will pop up with every directory beginning with that letter, as shown in Figure 9.7. Move your cursor to the right one, press Enter, and you're there.

Figure 9.7
A pop-up listing of every directory on disk beginning with S

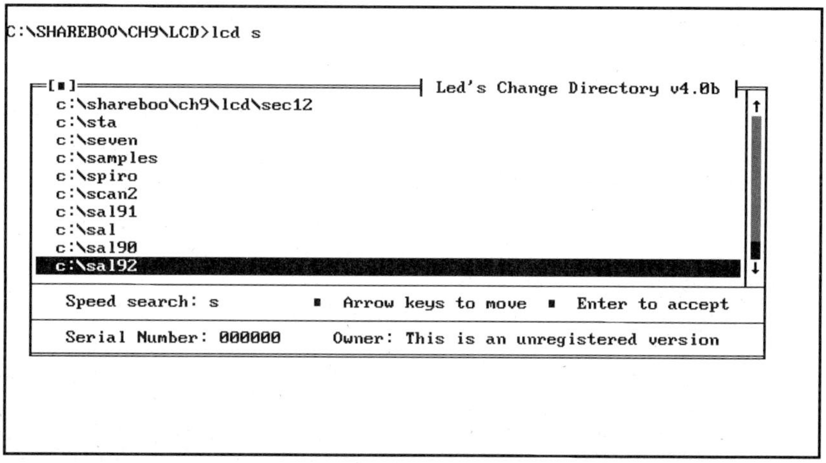

One note: When you use LCD for the first time, you'll type **LCD /SCAN**, which will create a database of your subdirectories. After this, you'll have to rescan your hard disk after creating or deleting a directory in order to keep LCD's database of your subdirectories up to date.

If you have DOS 5, however, you won't have to scan, as long as you use LCD along with the DOSKEY command. To do this, put the following lines in your AUTOEXEC.BAT file:

```
DOSKEY CD=lcd $1
DOSKEY MD=lcd md $1
DOSKEY RD=lcd rd $1
```

This way, you can use the familiar DOS CD command instead of the LCD command, but LCD will be working the entire time. And you'll never have to rescan your hard disk.

LCD
Registration fee: $
Keith Ledbetter
4240 Ketcham Dr.
Chesterfield, VA 23832
(804) 674-0780

Batch and Start-up Utilities

Batch-file jockeys take heart; there's more to life than DOS's sometimes-anemic batch commands. In fact, there's a whole world of powerful batch commands out there. Shareware programs such as STACKEY will give you batch-file power you thought might never exist. You'll find dozens of commands and functions you wish DOS had.

I've also listed here several start-up utilities that will let you reboot your PC with a different start-up configuration whenever you want. You'll be able to run one configuration for Windows, another for DESQview, and another for running on a network, for example. If you have a complicated setup, you'll soon find them invaluable.

BOOT.SYS

If your hardware or software setup is at all complicated, you most likely have multiple AUTOEXEC.BAT and CONFIG.SYS files on your hard disk, all with different names. One might load network drivers and a RAM disk, another Windows but no network drivers, and a third TSRs and a CD-ROM driver. To use these different configurations, you have to copy and rename files, reboot, and in general cause untoward mayhem every time you want to use a new set of start-up instructions. And whenever you want to add a new one... Perhaps it's best not even to talk about it.

BOOT.SYS solves the problem for you. It allows you to easily run different start-up setups from your AUTOEXEC.BAT and CONFIG.SYS files—all without having to copy and rename files. Using BOOT.SYS, you create a menu. Every time you start up, you then choose which CONFIG.SYS and AUTOEXEC.BAT configuration you want to run from the menu. The program allows for nested menus, so your start-up choices can be as complicated as you like. A companion program, BOOT.EDIT, lets you edit individual lines "on the fly," while booting up your CONFIG.SYS file.

BOOT.SYS
Registration fee: $$
Public Software Library
P.O. Box 35705
Houston, TX 77235
(713) 524-6394; (800) 242-4775 (orders)
For general information, contact:
Hans Salvisberg
Bellevuestrasse 18
CH-3095, Berne
Switzerland

Eissinger Utilities

This rich set of utilities will help you build powerful batch files. Even if you're not a batch-file jockey, however, you'll probably find something here to your liking. In addition to creating batch files, it will report to you on your hardware configuration, the amount of memory you have installed, drive information, and other hardware tidbits, as well as providing information about your DOS environment. It also "pumps up" DOS commands such as TYPE and ECHO.

Where these utilities really shine, however, is in creating versatile batch files. They will let you, within batch files, control the placement of the cursor on your screen, change your screen and border colors, and allow a batch file to act on a user's input. The utilities will also allow batch files to generate tones from the PC speaker, and let you clear specified portions of the screen. There are also a number of UNIX-like utilities that can be added to the batch-file programmer's toolbox.

Eissinger Utilities
Registration fee: $
Michael A. Eissinger
346 East Cedar
Hanford, CA 93230
(209) 582-5830

REBOOT

REBOOT is aimed at the same problem as BOOT.SYS—how to simplify your life when you have multiple start-up configurations, and therefore multiple AUTOEXEC.BAT and CONFIG.SYS files.

REBOOT takes a slightly different approach to the problem than does BOOT.SYS. You create a set of two files for each start-up configuration: one .SYS file and one .BAT file. If, for example, you had specific .BAT and .SYS files that started up Windows, you could call them WIN.BAT and WIN.SYS. For a DESQview start-up, you would have files called DESQ.BAT and DESQ.SYS. You might have a number of other start-up configurations as well.

When you wanted to restart your system with a specific configuration, you would type **REBOOT**. A menu of all your start-up configurations would then appear, as seen in Figure 9.8. Move your cursor to the configuration you wanted to use, press Enter, and you'd start up with the configuration you pointed to.

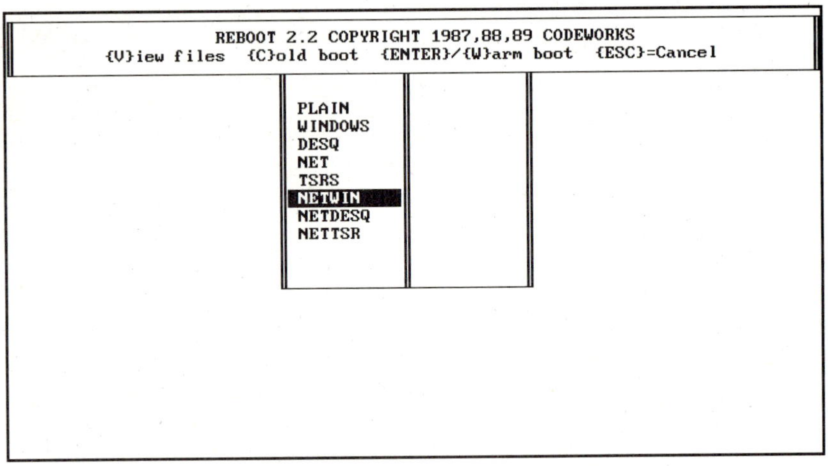

Figure 9.8
REBOOT's menu of start-up configurations

REBOOT
Registration fee: None
Codeworks
45321 North 7th St. East, Suite 59
Lancaster, CA 93535

STACKEY and BATUTIL

These superb batch-file enhancers are a must-have for everyone who wants to get more power out of their batch files. The two come packaged together, and they allow batch files to do far more than simply play back keystrokes.

STACKEY can be used to send keystrokes first to your keyboard buffer, and from there into your batch files or programs. For example, you could use it to create a batch file that would run a spreadsheet, load a certain file and perform a procedure or set of procedures on that file, print out the results, and then exit the program.

And STACKEY does even more. You can use its utilities to perform a wide variety of chores, such as rebooting your PC, changing colors, and sending a file to the printer.

BATUTIL, its companion program, pumps up batch files by adding color and sound, and by allowing them to pause and wait for user input. When combined, these two programs add substantial power to your batch files. Be aware, however, that these are not simple programs, and will require some learning time.

STACKEY and BATUTIL
Registration fee: $$ for both programs
For orders:
Support Group, Inc.
Lake Technology Park
P.O. Box 130
McHenry, MD 21541
(301) 387-4500; (800) 872-4768
For support and questions, contact:
Ctrlalt Associates
260 South Lake Ave., Suite 133
Pasadena, CA 91101

Miscellaneous Utilities

Not all utilities can be easily categorized. That's one of their great allures: They tend to do very specific jobs, and to do those quite well.

Below is a short listing of just a few of these uncategorizable utilities. Notable is Graphic Workshop, an unbeatable utility for anyone who works with graphics files.

Graphic Workshop

If you work with graphics on the PC, good luck to you. Nowhere is the computer's Tower of Babel more evident—or confusing. There are innumerable file formats, and they rarely work with one another. You may have scanned in an image with a hand scanner and created a .TIF file, only to find your graphics program won't accept .TIF files. Or you may have used a paint program to create a .PCX file, and then found out your word processor only handles .TIF files. The list goes on and on, but in general, trying to take a graphics file from one program and use it with another will usually get you the traditional New England response to a request for directions: "You can't get there from here."

With Graphic Workshop, you *will* get there from here, however. This unique program converts files from one graphics format to another. All the popular formats are included. It will handle PostScript (EPS), PCX, TIF, WordPerfect (WPG), GIF, BMP, and many file formats. You can even convert a MacPaint file to a PC file and vice versa.

Converting files is exceptionally easy. Load the program by typing **GWS**. Then switch to the directory in which you have graphics files you want to convert. Graphic Workshop's main screen will list all the graphics files in that directory. Move your cursor to the file you want converted, and press F2. A menu will appear, showing you all the graphics formats to which you can convert the file, as shown in Figure 9.9. Move your cursor to the file format desired, press Enter, and the job is done.

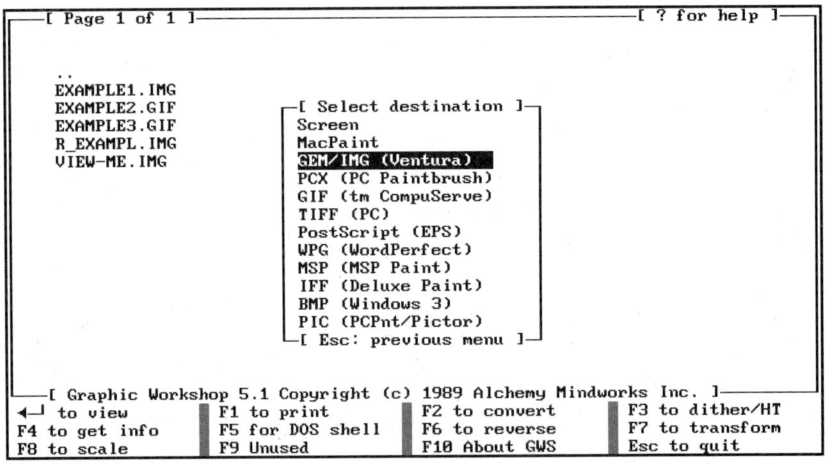

Figure 9.9
Graphic Workshop's conversion menu

The program will do more than convert files, however. It will let you manipulate them as well. With it, you can rotate and flip images, dither colored images so they become black and white, reverse monochrome images so that black becomes white and vice versa, and scale images. Graphic Workshop will also let you print the files.

The program also may have the oddest registration policy in all of sharewaredom. Instead of paying a traditional registration fee, the program's author urges you to buy a copy of the book *Coven: A Novel*, by Steven William Rimmer. If you send comments about the book, or a photocopy of its cover, you'll be a registered user. Alternately, you can pay the registration fee.

Graphic Workshop
Registration fee: $$ (or $3.95 for the Rimmer book)
Alchemy Mindworks Inc.
P.O. Box 500
Beeton, Ontario
Canada L0G 1A0

Last Resort

You've lived through it more times than you'd like to admit: Your system locks up, and you've lost every bit of work since the last time you saved a file. When was the last time you saved a file? Oh, about four hours ago. If you have a RAM disk the problem is even worse, because all your work may have been in the RAM disk, and so was never actually saved onto your hard disk.

Last Resort is designed to save you at these times. When your system locks up and you have Last Resort loaded, hit a key combination, and you'll be able to copy files from your RAM disk to your hard disk or to floppies. It will also help get your keyboard unlocked; you should be able to exit without rebooting. Last Resort won't work every time, but if it works just once, it's paid for itself many times over.

Last Resort
Registration fee: $
Dr. Masaaki Sawada & Associates
Lady Davis Institute for Medical Research
Sir M. B. Davis Jewish General Hospital
3755 Chemin Cote Ste-Catherine
Montreal, Quebec
Canada H3T 1E2

PMAP

Ever wonder what TSRs you have loaded, and how much memory each takes up? Now you can have an answer, with PMAP (Program Map). PMAP will look through your PC's memory and report back to you on what's in use. (DOS 5 will also do that for you, but PMAP reports back in far greater detail.) As Figure 9.10 shows, PAMP lets you know far more than just the program name and memory consumed. It also tells you where in memory those programs reside, gives you the memory manager you're using, summarizes expanded and extended memory use, and more.

Figure 9.10
PMAP's report on the state of a PC's memory

```
C:\SHAREBOO\CH9\PMAP>pmap
pmap 2.10 Copyright (C) 1986-1991 by The Cove Software Group/C.J.Dunford

Addr  Program   Parent    Parameters          Han Blks  Size   Vectors
----  --------  --------  ---------------     --- ----  ------ --------
10D9  command   command  C:\ /P /E:512         0   2     5408 2E
1237  4dos      4dos                           1   3     3440 22 23 24 2F
1312  snap      4dos                           0   2   105888 05 08 10 13 15 21
                                                                25 26
Other allocated blocks                             1    56528
Total conventional free memory                     1   471504
Largest conventional free block                        471504
Next program will load at 2CEE

Extended memory summary:

  INT 15 ext mem available              0
  XMS driver not present

Expanded memory manager no present

C:\SHAREBOO\CH9\PMAP>
```

PMAP
Registration fee: None
Christopher J. Dunford
The Cove Software Group
P.O. Box 1072
Columbia, Maryland 21044
(301) 992-9371

Popsicle

You're in your database or word processor, you need to run a DOS command, you're not multitasking, and your program won't let you shell to DOS. What to do? You'll have to quit your program, run the DOS command, and then reload your program, right? Wrong—if you have Popsicle. This small TSR will pop up over your program (unless the program is graphics-based) and allow you to run a DOS command (though not all of them), and then disappear until the next time it's needed.

Popsicle
Registration fee: $
J. Douglas Haacke
1825 Clark Ave.
Billings, MT 59102

CHAPTER

10

Windows Utilities

Program Manager Replacements

Task Manager and File Manager Replacements

Icon and Wallpaper Utilities

Graphics Utilities

Miscellaneous Utilities

WHEN WINDOWS 3.0 WAS RELEASED, IT DIDN'T JUST SHAKE UP THE world of commercial software—significant reverberations were felt in the shareware world as well. Over and above its standardized graphic interface, multitasking and live links between programs had suddenly become realities, rather than mere pipe dreams.

After all the initial hoopla, however, it soon became apparent that although Windows was a far richer environment than DOS, it also had its problems. For years, shareware authors have been finding things that DOS can't do, or doesn't do well, and remedying the situation; soon the same thing happened with Windows. First a trickle, and then a flood of shareware has become available—which makes Windows an even more rewarding operating environment in which to work.

In general, most Windows shareware programs are utilities. Relatively little application shareware (databases, spreadsheets, word processors) has been written for Windows. In this book, the few such programs that are available are covered in the chapter corresponding to the software category they fall under. For example, you'll find the excellent Windows checkbook manager WinCheck in Chapter 7, "Finance and Business Programs."

Shareware authors were among the first to pick up on one of Windows 3.0's most obvious flaws, a File Manager that was not especially useful or elegant. The METZ Desktop Navigator, for example, greatly improves on it.

Shareware authors have also tried to improve the entire way that Windows operates, and so have written many replacements for the Program Manager. There has been a flood of icon managers and individual icons, as well. And you'll find a dizzying number of utilities that do everything from managing your graphics files to reporting on free memory to making better use of the mouse.

This chapter is divided into five sections. There's one on replacements for, or improvements to, the Program Manager. Another section covers replacements for, or improvements to, the File Manager and Task Manager. A third section covers icon and wallpaper utilities. There's a fourth section on graphics utilities, and a fifth on miscellaneous utilities.

An entire book could be written on shareware utilities for Windows. It's one of the most vital and exciting parts of the shareware scene today. Use what's here as a starting point and venture out on your own—you won't believe what awaits you.

Program Manager Replacements

One of the best things about Windows is that if you don't like the way it works, you can easily change it. The heart of Windows is its Program Manager, and shareware authors have been working overtime finding ways to improve on it.

There are those who use Windows because of its multitasking ability, but hate to click on those cute little icons to run programs. Others would do away with the keyboard as much as possible, and "iconize" everything in sight. Luckily, there's room for both viewpoints, because there are programs that will let you work either way. Launcher, for example, lets you run programs using a menu instead of icons. Aporia, on the other hand, lets you turn everything imaginable into an icon.

Each of the following replacements for the Program Manager doesn't just change the Program Manager, but the entire way that Windows works. Choose your favorite, based on your personality and your way of working.

Aporia

Do you like working with icons? I mean do you *really* love them? If you do, then Aporia is the program for you. It's Windows heaven for the icon-crazy.

What it does, essentially, is turn everything you can imagine into an icon on your desktop. These icons aren't the same Windows icons you're familiar with; rather, they're depictions of the type of program or function the icon represents. So an icon for a Program Manager group will be represented by a desktop, for example, and an application program will be represented by a hammer, to show that it's a tool.

Aporia takes all of your Program Manager groups, and turns each into an icon (which the program calls Desk Tools). Double-click on the icon representing a group, and a labeled icon representing each program in that group will spring to your screen. To run a program, double-click on its icon, as you normally would in Windows.

In addition to these icons, down the right side of your screen, Aporia places a number of icons for common functions and tools, such as getting a tree listing of your hard disk, getting help, and copying, hiding, and deleting files. Figure 10.1 shows an Aporia desktop filled with icons.

Aporia does more, however, than merely fill your screen with icons. It lets you perform commands by moving icons around the desktop. For example, you can delete files by dragging their icons over to the Trash tool. (This is similar to the Macintosh Trash can.) When you move a file to the Trash tool, it's not really deleted. Although it will vanish from the subdirectory where it resided, a copy will be maintained in a \TRASH subdirectory. When you want to clean out that subdirectory, there are tools to allow you to do so.

Aporia also lets you drag an icon for a data file over to an icon for a program, so that the program will automatically run that data file.

Aporia's icons can be changed and customized. You can even use your familiar Windows icons, by using an Aporia conversion tool to convert ICO files to the AIF format and extension that Aporia assigns to its icons.

Aporia can be run as your Windows shell instead of the Program Manager. To do so, call up your SYSTEM.INI file, and change the line

```
SHELL=PROGMAN.EXE
```

to

```
SHELL=APORIA.EXE
```

Or you can run Aporia as you do any other Windows application.

Figure 10.1
Icons on an Aporia desktop

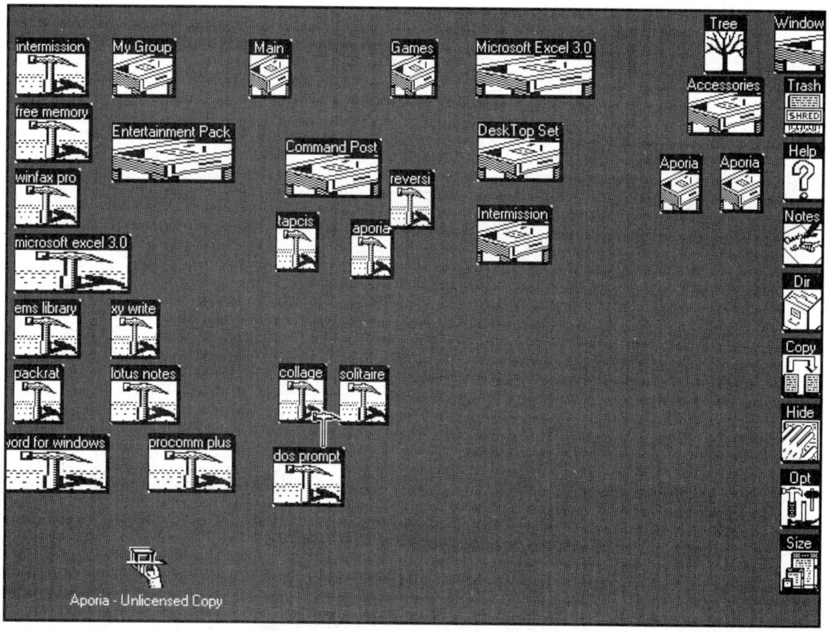

When using the program, you should take some care: it can quickly clutter your screen with confusing icons. But for icon lovers of the world, Aporia is a reason to exult.

Aporia
Registration fee: $$
NewTools
P.O. Box 3269, Church St. Station
New York, NY 10008

Command Post

Command Post is a more flexible, more fully featured Windows front-end than the Program Manager. It lets you more easily tailor Windows to the way you want to work than does Program Manager, and provides a number of tools that Windows lacks.

When you load Command Post, the top of your screen will be filled with the program's menus, which are easily and thoroughly customizable. Below that, you'll see a list of all the drives on your system. One of the drives will be highlighted; that's your current drive. To the right of the drive list will be your current directory, and beneath it a list of all the files in your current directory will be displayed. Figure 10.2 shows Command Post's main screen with the main menu popped up.

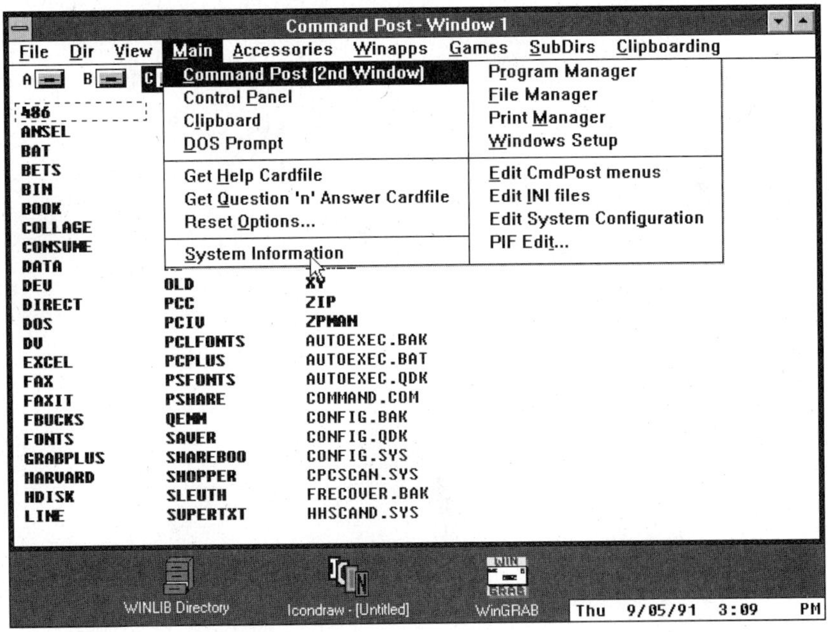

Figure 10.2
Command Post's main screen with the main menu displayed

The menu items across the top of the screen give you far more options than does the Program Manager. You can perform many file functions from the File submenu, such as copying, renaming, moving, deleting, and browsing through files. The Dir submenu can similarly perform directory functions such as renaming, deleting, and creating directories. The View submenu lets you arrange your windows in numerous ways and allows you to change your Windows *wallpaper* (screen backgrounds).

The Main submenu gives you access to many of Windows' resources, such as the Program Manager, File Manager, Control Panel, and Clipboard. It also lets you edit WIN.INI and other INI-format files, and change your system configuration. And it lets you edit and create your own Command Post menus so that you can configure Command Post any way you wish.

Other submenus let you access the Windows Clipboard quickly, launch applications, run games, and switch to specified subdirectories instantly.

Even the system menu box in the upper-left corner of the screen is different from the plain Windows menu box. It includes all the standard items, but adds an entirely new column that lists the names of all the programs that are running. To switch to one of the programs, you just double-click on its name. Command Post also displays, in the lower-right portion of the screen, a digital clock listing the date and time.

You can open several main Command Post Windows at once, and also use several of the program's facilities simultaneously, such as its directory tree listing and file viewer, as seen in Figure 10.3.

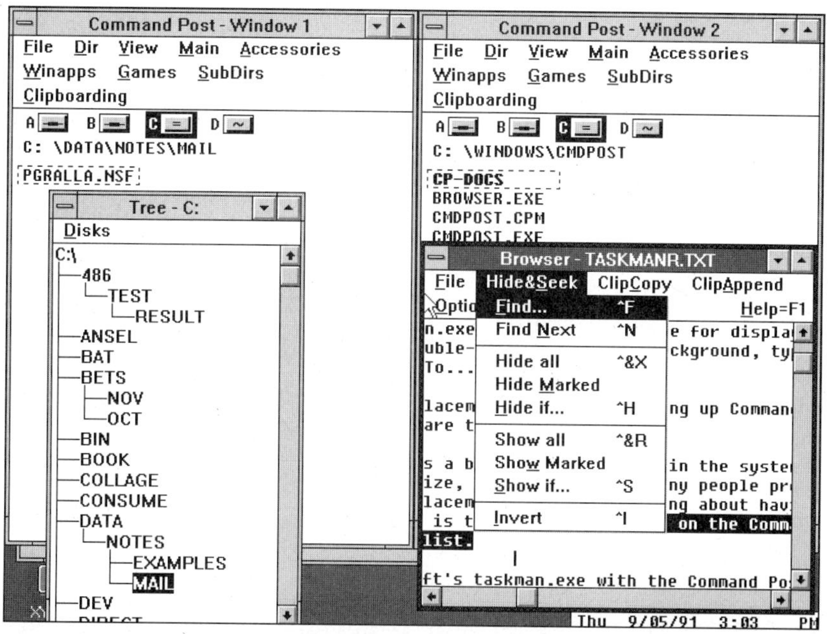

Figure 10.3 Two windows, a file directory, and a file browser open in Command Post

If you want to create your own menus, the Command Post Menu Language will let you do it. The language will be familiar to users of the same company's WinBatch shareware, because the syntax and many of the commands are the same.

Command Post
Registration fee: $$
Wilson WindowWare
2701 California Ave. SW, Suite 212
Seattle, WA 98116
(206) 937-9335; (800) 762-8383

Launch

Windows' icons are undoubtedly cute, but are they really useful? Does it make sense to have to search around your desktop until you find the right one, and then double-click on it? And although the icons are pretty, each one that you display uses memory and eats away at precious system resources.

For those who like Windows, but think icons are overrated, there's Launch. Instead of loading programs from icons, Launch lets you run them directly from the desktop. To load Launch, just click anywhere on the empty desktop with your left mouse button, or press Ctrl-Alt-L, and the Launch menu will pop up. (These defaults can be changed easily if you wish.) You configure your Launch menu to list all the programs you run. All you need to do is highlight the program you want to run, let go of the left mouse button, and your program will run.

Editing or creating a new menu item is easy. Run Configure Launch from the Launch menu, and click on Menu. To create a new Menu item on the Launch menu, click on New Item, and fill in the dialog box. To edit an existing item, highlight the menu item, click on Edit, and fill in the dialog box, as shown in Figure 10.4. You can also create submenus, and then new menu items under those submenus.

If you want fast access to your programs and have become annoyed with icons, or don't like the way they chew into your system resources, Launch is a sound bet.

Launch
Registration fee: $$
Summit Research, Inc.
3321 Lauren Way
Lewisville, TX 75028

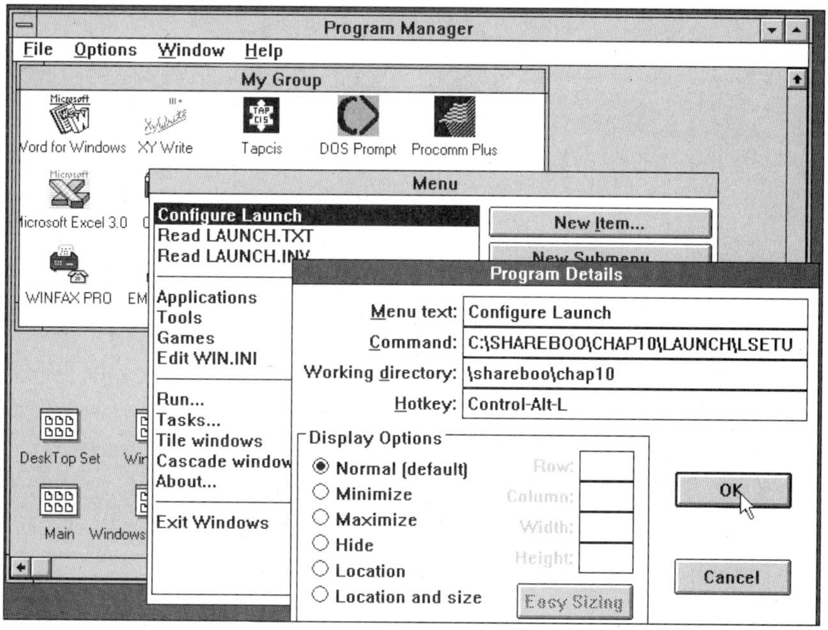

Figure 10.4
Editing a Launch menu item

Sloop Manager

Sloop Manager is an interesting replacement for the Program Manager. It will perform all of the Program Manager's functions, and adds a host of its own. With it, you'll be able to perform certain tasks, such as adding items to a group, simply by dragging icons—something the Windows 3.0 Program Manager doesn't allow. It also permits the creation of groups within groups (although Sloop Manager calls them folders rather than groups).

You can run Sloop Manager as a separate Windows application, but if you're going to use it to any extent, you'd be much better off using it as a Windows shell, replacing the Program Manager. To do that, change the line SHELL=PROGMAN.EXE to read

```
SHELL=SLOOPMAN.EXE
```

in your SYSTEM.INI file.

With Sloop Manager you'll be able to create 200 folders, each of which can hold 200 items. Items don't have to be programs—they can be data files as well.

The ability to create folders within folders is one of the reasons you might want this program. Why would you want to have folders within folders? Because that often better reflects the way you actually work. You might have a folder named Corporate Stuff, for example. Within that folder, you could then have folders for each of the types of work you do: budgeting, planning, managing, and the like. Within each of those folders, you would have the data files and programs that you normally use for that task. Figure 10.5 depicts Sloop Manager managing folders within folders.

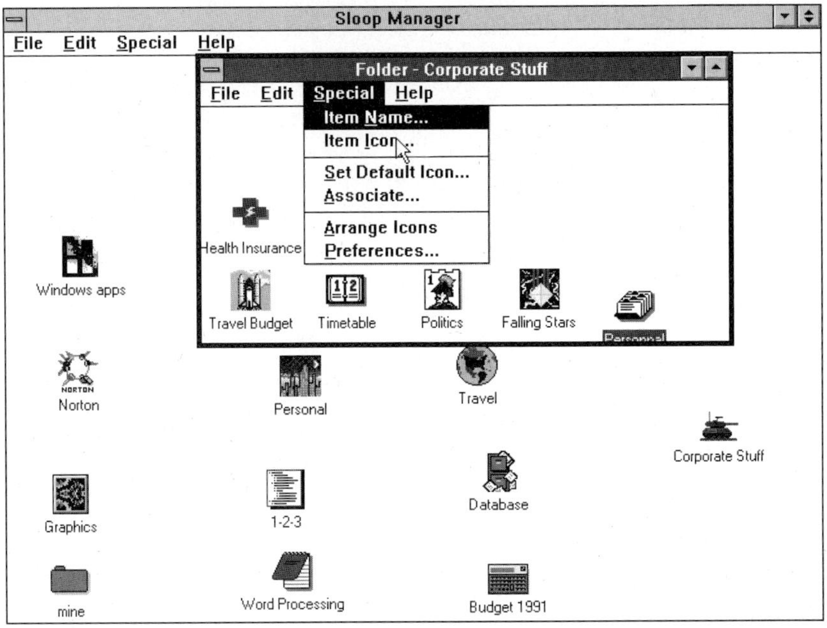

Figure 10.5 Sloop Manager's folders within folders

Sloop Manager has a lot of other extras as well. Its Run command stores the last 12 commands you've executed, and you can browse through them and reissue any you'd like. It also features password protection.

Sloop Manager
Registration fee: $
Sloop Software
6457 Mesedge Lane
Colorado Springs, CO 80919
(719) 260-0433

Task Manager and File Manager Replacements

Some of the best shareware programs to come out soon after Windows 3.0 was released were improvements on the program's File Manager. There have been many more since. METZ Software, in particular, seems to have made a cottage industry out of this. Not only do they have a replacement for the File Manager, but they have one for the Task Manager as well.

All of the following programs are better in one way or another than the Windows 3.0 File Manager. Use any of them; you can't lose.

METZ Desktop Navigator

The METZ Desktop Navigator is a solid alternative to the Windows 3.0 File Manager. With it, you'll be able to perform all the file and directory functions you would expect—copying, deleting, moving, creating, and renaming, to name just a few. You'll get many more as well.

When you load the program, you'll get a tree listing of your hard disk, as shown in Figure 10.6. As with virtually all Windows programs, pull-down menus across the top of the screen let you access the program's functions.

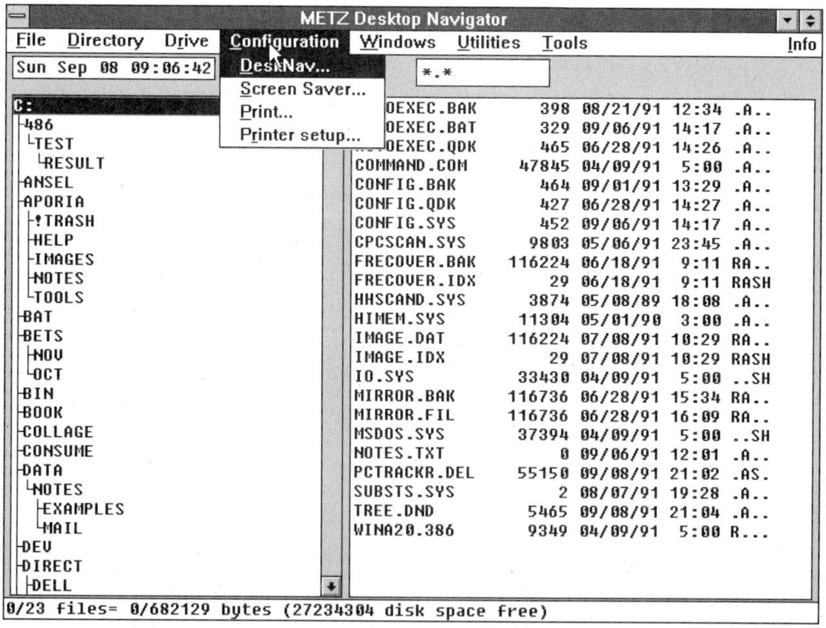

Figure 10.6 METZ Desktop Navigator's tree listing of a hard disk, with the Configuration menu pulled down

With METZ Desktop Navigator, you can move an entire directory tree to another drive or subdirectory. But it will do more than just manipulate files and directories. You can, for example, use it to run a digital clock, so that you always know the time and date, and there's a utility that tells you the largest block of conventional memory that is free. You can also use the program to run a customizable screen blanker. Other utilities include a file finder and a program that password-protects your system so that only you can use it.

METZ Desktop Navigator
Registration fee: $
METZ Software
P.O. Box 6042
Bellevue, WA 98008
(206) 641-4525; (800) 447-1712 (orders)

METZ Task Manager

Windows' Task Manager is a somewhat useful tool, but the METZ Task Manager is a powerful one. The METZ Task Manager runs in place of the familiar Windows Task Manager, and gives it far more functions.

Click on the background portion of your screen, or press Ctrl-Esc, and the METZ Task Manager pops up, ready to do your bidding. It lets you customize your Windows screen layout in a number of different ways and allows you to configure your system by choosing your default printer, checking on system status, and running a screen saver, among other options. But its best feature is that you can use it to quickly launch your favorite applications. Instead of moving your cursor to an icon and double-clicking, you can customize the METZ Task Manager so that your applications can be launched directly from the Task Manager, as shown in Figure 10.7.

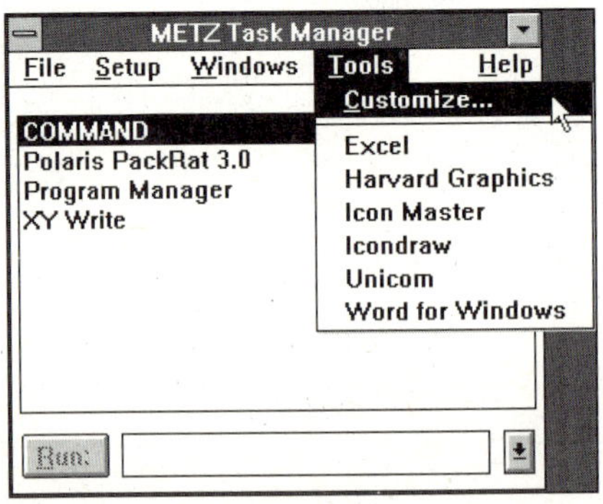

Figure 10.7 METZ Task Manager with customized applications ready to run

METZ Task Manager
Registration fee: $
METZ Software
P.O. Box 6042
Bellevue, WA 98008
(206) 641-4525; (800) 447-1712 (orders)

WinNAV

Navigating through your hard disk with Windows 3.0 has always been a chore. Its File Manager has been maligned time and time again, and justifiably so. It's awkward, it's difficult to use, and it lacks many necessary tools.

WinNAV repairs this omission, giving you a wide variety of navigational, directory- and file-management, and viewing tools that the File Manager lacks. In fact, you can use WinNAV to replace not only the File Manager, but the Program Manager as well. It can be configured to easily launch any Windows or DOS program you have on disk. And you can create pop-up menus and dialog boxes, as well as assign function keys to perform certain tasks.

What you'll probably use it for most, however, is as a hard-disk manager, much as you might use a program such as Xtree with DOS. When you launch WinNAV, it displays a directory listing of your hard disk. On the left side is the current directory, along with its subdirectories, and on the right side is the list of files in the current subdirectory, as shown in Figure 10.8.

Across the top of the screen are eight pull-down menus, many of which can be customized. From the File menu, for example, you can do common file-related tasks such as copying, deleting, and renaming files. But you can also do more. You can compress files using any one of the popular compression formats, including ZIP, ARC, PAK, ZOO, LZH, and many others. You can also delete, rename, and create directories from here.

From the View menu, you'll not only be able to look at files in the usual way: You can also look into compressed archives of files created in the ARC, ZIP, and LZH formats.

The Action menu is one of the most helpful menus. From here you can open data files and run the applications that created them simply by clicking on the data file. You can also just run the programs. The Action menu's Launch submenu is especially powerful. You can use it to create a menu of programs that can be launched directly from WinNAV, without having to go through the Program Manager.

There's far more power in this program than this brief description can possibly give. If you're unhappy with the File Manager or Program Manager or are just looking for a better way to work with Windows, check out WinNAV.

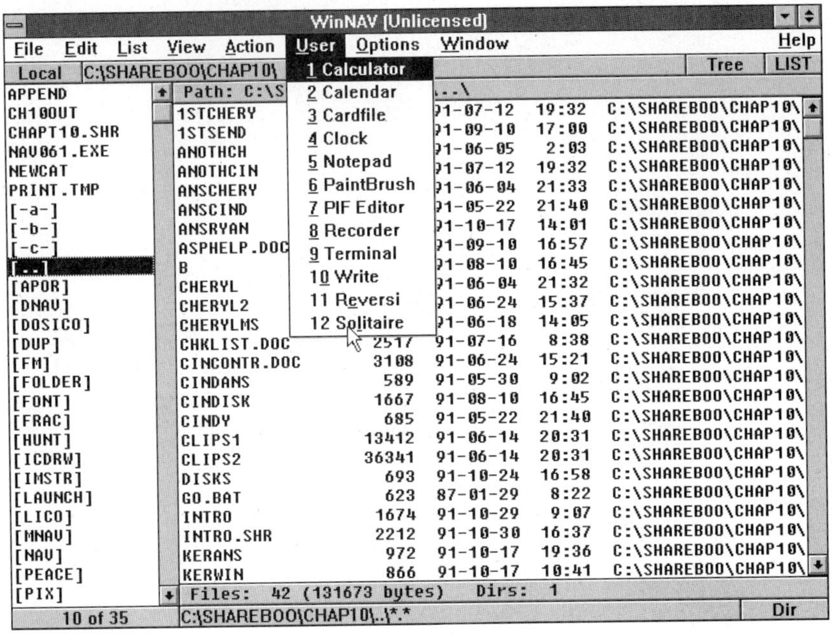

Figure 10.8
WinNAV's main screen with a customizable menu for launching other applications selected

WinNAV
Registration fee: $$
Richard S. Patterson
FlashPoint Development
P.O. Box 270492
Houston, TX 77277
(713) 726-1892

Icon and Wallpaper Utilities

What would Windows be without icons? More time and effort have gone into creating and using them than you can imagine—in both the commercial and shareware worlds. Dial into a bulletin board or an on-line service such as CompuServe and you'll find thousands of new icons you can download and use with your programs. The same holds true for Windows wallpaper (screen backgrounds).

Windows, however, doesn't provide much in the way of icon management. Icons occur in a number of different formats. Some are embedded in programs, whereas you may have others collected in a single-file library. Still others may be in individual files with a .ICO extension. Because of that, you'll need an icon manager, such as IconMaster, to keep track of them all. And if you *really* like icons, you need an icon creator (Icondraw, for example), so that you can make some of your own.

Note that I haven't included any individual icons, wallpaper, or icon and wallpaper libraries. However, these are readily available from any disk vendor or on-line service. (See Appendix C for a full listing of sources.)

DOSICON

You've gone to all the trouble of amassing a nice icon collection, and you've attached icons to all your DOS programs, so that when they're in program groups, they're colorful and pleasing to the eye. But then the trouble begins. Whenever you run a DOS program, and then minimize it, that ugly, gray DOS box appears on your desktop instead of the colorful icon. And there's nothing you can do about it.

Actually, there *is* something you can do about it, with DOSICON. Using it, a DOS program opened and then minimized will appear on the desktop as an icon, not as the DOS box.

DOSICON
Registration fee: $
Kok Hong Soh
1504 North Rogers Road, Apt. 1106
Olathe, KS 66062

DUPICON

If you have an icon library of any size, odds are you have duplicates. You'd like to keep your hard disk as clean as possible, but it's hard to know when you have doubles, and it's a lot of work tracking down individual icons, comparing them, and then deleting them.

DUPICON will do that work for you. It doesn't run from Windows; instead, it's a simple DOS program. The best way to run it is to keep all your icons in a single directory. Then switch to that directory and type **DUPICON**. The program will ask if you want to preview the duplicate icons, or have them deleted automatically. It then checks for duplicate icons, and either previews or deletes them, depending on what you've told it to do.

DUPICON
Registration fee: None
Keith Ledbetter
4240 Ketcham Dr.
Chesterfield, VA 23832
(804) 674-0780

Icondraw

Are you one of those people who can't get enough icons? Do you *know* you could create the ultimate icon, if you only had the chance? Well, here's your chance. It's Icondraw, and it will let budding Dalís and Matisses take their best shot at icon drawing. With it, you'll be able to create 16-color, 32-by-32-pixel icons.

Icondraw gives you a variety of tools to do this. There are tools for free-hand drawing; for creating boxes, filled rectangles, and solid and hollow ellipses; and for drawing lines. Figure 10.9 shows an icon created with Icondraw. Several sample icons, including the one in the figure, are included with the program.

Figure 10.9 A cool, refreshing icon created with Icondraw

Icondraw
Registration fee: $
Philip B. Eskelin, Jr.
10007 NE 125th Lane, #4
Kirkland, WA 98034

IconMaster

There's no way around it—managing icons is messy work. They're scattered across your disk, in different subdirectories and programs and in different file formats. You might have an icon associated with one program that you'd like to use for another. Or you might have an icon that's attached to an .EXE file that you'd like to change—perhaps turn its background from blue to yellow. You might have one collection of icons that's simply a gathering of individual .ICO files, and another that's put together into an EXE library. You'd like to know exactly what icons you have on disk, and you'd like to be able to use them and edit them in any way you wish.

Unfortunately, Windows offers no easy way to do it. There's simply no capable icon tool shipped with Windows. But you can get IconMaster. It will manage every aspect of your icons, truly living up to its name. With it, you'll have complete icon mastery.

The first thing IconMaster will do is let you see what icons you have on disk. Open the program, and scroll through your subdirectories. You'll be able to view every icon on disk, whether the icon is in ICO format, or in a file with an .EXE or .DLL extension. If you have an icon collection with an .EXE extension, you'll be able to view that entire collection. Your screen will display all the icons, as seen in Figure 10.10. If there are more icons than can fit in one screen, you can scroll through your collection.

Figure 10.10
Looking into an EXE icon library using IconMaster

You'll not only be able to look in .EXE files that are icon collections, but in any .EXE file that contains an icon. So you can look inside any Windows program and view its icons using IconMaster.

Viewing the icons is just the most basic part of this program. The more powerful part is how you can use it to control them. You can extract icons from any file with an .EXE extension and use that icon in another program; for example, if you have a Windows program with a particularly nice icon, and would like to use that icon with another program, you can do it, even if the icon is contained in the program's .EXE file. Just use IconMaster to look inside the .EXE file, highlight the icon when it shows on screen, and copy it, giving it a name with an .ICO extension. Now you can use the icon with any program, just as you can any normal .ICO file.

You can also edit icons with IconMaster. Let's say you have an icon collection with an .EXE extension. View the icons in the file with IconMaster, click on the icon you want to edit, and click on Edit from the Icon menu. You'll then be able to edit the icon, as seen in Figure 10.11.

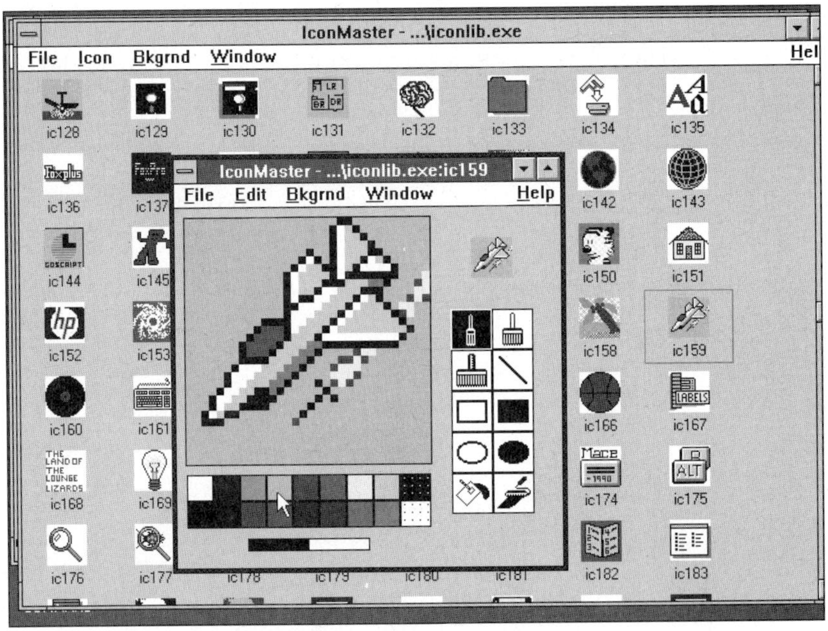

Figure 10.11
Using IconMaster to edit icons

IconMaster has other features as well. You can create new icons from scratch, sort icons into subdirectories, capture screen images and turn them into icons, and more.

IconMaster
Registration fee: $
Phillip Kaufman
19987 Moran Lane
Saratoga, CA 95040

LISTICO

This program does for icons what the file-viewing program List Plus does for text files. With LISTICO you will be able to view all your icon files with ease. You can also use it to launch any one of four icon-drawing and editing programs, including Icondraw.

One of the program's more interesting features is that it can be run either from Windows or from DOS. To run it from DOS, switch to the directory in which you store your icons, type **LISTICO** and press Enter, and you'll see, on screen, all the icons in the directory and their names. You can also view an individual icon by following the LISTICO command with the icon name. To view an icon named BIGPIC.ICO, for example, you'd type

```
LISTICO BIGPIC.ICO
```

Once you're in the program, you can launch any one of four icon editors, and then edit your icon files or create new ones. (The icon editors aren't included with the program, and must be obtained separately.)

To run the program in Windows instead of DOS, type **WIN LICO**. Change to the various directories in which you store your icons, and you'll be able to view them easily, as shown in Figure 10.12.

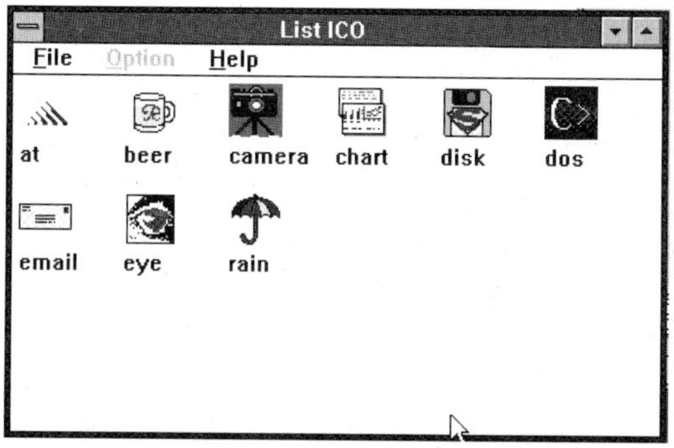

Figure 10.12
LISTICO's listing of icons in a subdirectory

LISTICO
Registration fee: $
Philippe Rabergeau
Gateway Software, Inc.
61 East 8th St., Suite 128
New York, NY 10003
(212) 505-6203

ZiPaper

If you regularly use wallpaper as a Windows background, you know how easily you get bored with any one pattern. You'll want to use new wallpaper in Windows far more often than you repaper your living room.

There are a couple of problems with that, however. First is disk space. Wallpaper files (which have a .BMP extension) accumulate quickly, eating up hard disk space. And the point of wallpaper is that you'd like to be surprised—you want to be greeted by something new each time you run Windows.

ZiPaper will solve both problems for you. If you use PKZIP to compress all your .BMP files into a single .ZIP file (which saves a great deal of disk space), ZiPaper will automatically extract a different .BMP file from the .ZIP file every time you run Windows.

The first step in running ZiPaper is to zip all your wallpaper files into one archive file. Then, before you run Windows, run ZiPaper from the DOS prompt. Now load Windows. In the Control Panel, click on Desktop. You'll find a box labeled "Wallpaper." Click inside it, on the File box. If there's a file there, delete it, type **WALLPAPER.BMP**, and you're ready to go. This will set Windows to load the File WALLPAPER.BMP (the file name ZiPaper uses for its wallpaper file) every time Windows loads. Note that you won't have to go through the Control Panel step every time you run Windows; you'll just have to do it the first time. From that point on, ZiPaper will run correctly.

ZiPaper
Registration fee: $
Daniel Thomas
2301 North Huron Circle
Placentia, CA 92670
(714) 524-5625

Graphics Utilities

For the first time, Windows has made the PC truly a graphics machine. Not only does the operating environment operate graphically, but many Windows programs and tools make it easy to create graphics.

But there are many drawbacks. Graphics files come in many different formats, and they're often not easy to manipulate. That's where a utility like

WinGIF, and the others listed here, comes in—helping you manipulate and manage graphics files.

I've also included Fonter in this section, which is a utility to help manage fonts. Some might not consider fonts to be graphics, but managing them presents many of the same difficulties as does managing graphics files.

Fonter

Icons aren't the only things that Windows mavens accumulate—they tend to gather fonts as well. You may have only a dozen fonts or so on your system, or you may have 30, 40, or even more. If you have programs that scale and handle fonts, such as Adobe Type Manager (ATM) or Bitstream's FaceLift, you probably have many, indeed.

The point is, you don't really know what fonts you have, do you? Wouldn't it be nice to know what fonts you have, be able to view them, and keep a list of them handy? Fonter will do all that for you, and more.

Fonter lets you view, on screen, fonts from 6 to 36 points, in regular roman, bold, italic, and bold italic, as seen in Figure 10.13. You can view the entire character set of any individual font, too, and then cut and paste between that font and another Windows application. You can also zoom in and out on individual characters.

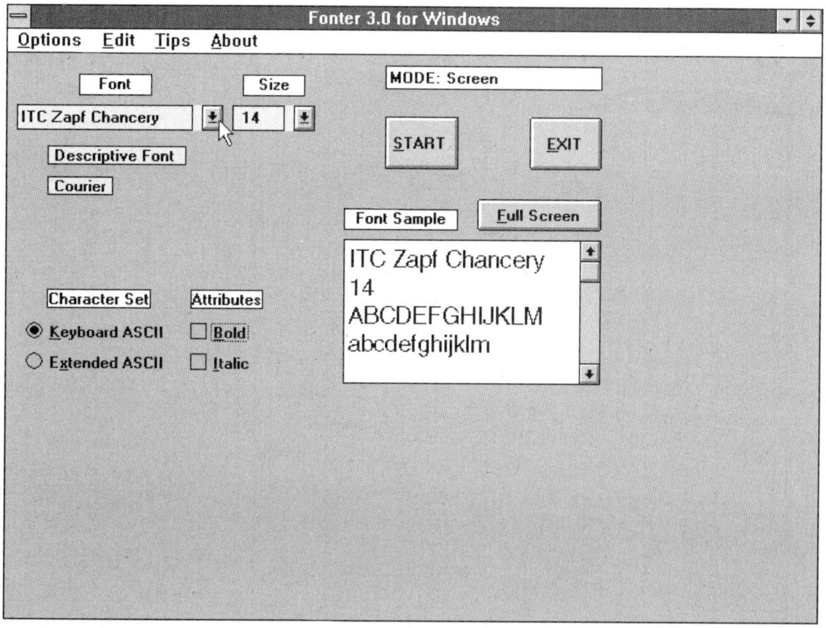

Figure 10.13
Viewing a font sample with Fonter

With Fonter, you'll also be able to print a sheet showing keyboard characters or the ANSI character set of a font. The sheet will show you the character, the ANSI code for the character, and the keyboard combination needed to produce the character. This is particularly useful when you have a symbol or dingbat font and want to know how to produce each of the characters in the font.

It will also print a sheet listing all of your fonts and a set of pages showing the character set for each font, so that you can have a complete font catalog of everything on your system.

Be aware that Fonter doesn't always work with the SuperPrint font-scaling program. And when you print your fonts out, it will take a *long* time. But it's worth it to know and see everything you have on your system.

One final note: To run Fonter, you'll need to have Microsoft's Visual Basic program, or a run-time version of it. You can get the run-time file from many disk vendors, or you can download it from CompuServe. You can find it in the PCContact forum with the file name VBRUN.EXE or something similar.

Fonter
Registration fee: $
George Campbell
1472 Sixth St.
Los Osos, CA 93402

Fractint for Windows

Not long ago, Microsoft launched what I thought was one of the better computer-related ad campaigns I've seen. Big, bold type across the top of magazine pages announced something like, "Now You Can Use the Incredible Power of Windows...To Goof Off!"

It was selling Microsoft's Entertainment Pack, a group of Windows games. But I think of that campaign every time I run Fractint. It generates colorful *fractals*—irregular shapes produced by mathematic equations. This program has mere dozens of formulas for fractals, but the number of fractals you can actually generate is infinite. That's because you can change many aspects of each formula. Run this program and be prepared for hours of unproductive goofing off.

Fractint for Windows
Registration fee: None
The Stone Soup Group
Available in CompuServe's WINADV forum under WINFRAC.ZIP. It's also available from many on-line services, bulletin boards, and user groups.

PixFolio

This is a Windows graphics program with a twist. It doesn't just allow you to view and edit graphics files—more importantly, it enables you to create catalogs of your images so that you can find them with ease.

Anyone with a substantial number of images on disk knows just how important having this kind of catalog can be. Graphics files can litter your disk with different extensions and different names; you might have created them in one program but wish to use them in another. PixFolio solves that problem for you.

PixFolio lets you view and manipulate graphics files in seven different formats: IFF, PCX, TIF, TGA, GIF, BMP, and RLE. It will allow you to convert files from one kind of graphics format to another; to crop, copy, resize and paste images; to manipulate the image's palette; and to perform other graphics-related tasks.

Other programs do these same things, but PixFolio also lets you create catalogs of images. You choose the images you want cataloged, issue the Catalog command, and follow the program's prompts. Figure 10.14 shows an image being cataloged.

Figure 10.14 Cataloging an image with PixFolio

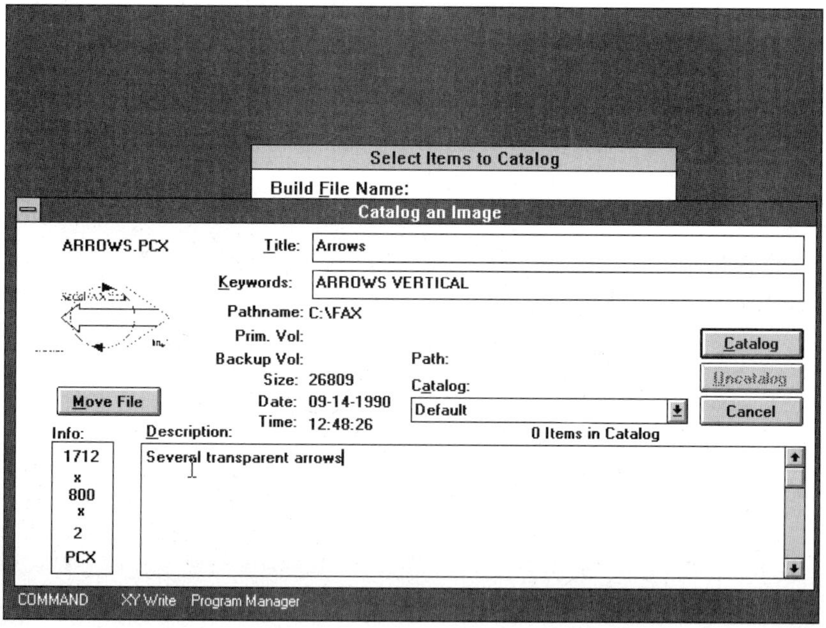

You can create many different catalogs of images, and can then easily browse through the catalogs. You can also print them out, so that you have paper copies of the catalogs. Once you find the image you want, you can call it to your screen and use PixFolio's image-manipulation tools on it.

PixFolio
Registration fee: $
Allen C. Kempe
298 West Audubon Dr.
Shepherdsville, KY 40165

SnapShot

There are times you'd like to capture one of your screens in Windows, or possibly just a portion of it. You might need the capture for documentation, or you might want to use the screen, or a portion of your screen, with another program.

SnapShot will do that for you. Load it, and then use the right-hand mouse button as you would the button on a camera. Move your cursor to an object you want to capture, press the button, and you'll capture the image. To view the image, maximize SnapShot, and you'll see it. You can even capture individual icons, as seen in Figure 10.15.

Figure 10.15
An icon captured with SnapShot

When you capture images, they're also placed on the Windows Clipboard. From there they can be made available to other Windows applications.

SnapShot
Registration fee: $
Lucas Systems
c/o Beacon Hill Software
P.O. Box 8494
Boston, MA 02114

WinGIF

Windows finally brings the promise of graphics to everyman. But there's just one problem. Everyman doesn't have the rich set of graphics tools needed to handle them—until WinGIF, that is. This program will allow you to do a number of tasks, making it easier to work with graphics in the Windows environment.

The first thing it will do is allow you to view graphics files in the GIF, PCX, BMP, and RLE formats. This is a boon, since you may have no way to view those graphics files, or you may have to use a different program to view each one. Now you'll need only one.

File viewing is only the first step. WinGIF also gives you a set of tools for manipulating those images. You'll be able to resize, crop, rotate, and invert them. WinGIF will also let you create a mirror image of the image. You'll be able to dither the image in a number of different ways, and change the color palette, brightness, and contrast. In short, you'll be given full control over how the image looks. Figure 10.16 shows the menu for changing the palette of a BMP-format image.

You'll also be able to take images in GIF and PCX formats and turn them into .BMP files, the files that Windows uses as wallpaper. This means that any .PCX or .GIF file you see can be turned into Windows wallpaper. The program also enables you to create a slide show on your computer screen, using graphics files. If you use graphics at all with Windows, WinGIF is a must-have piece of shareware.

WinGIF
Registration fee: $
SuperSet Software Corporation
P.O. Box 50476
Provo, UT 84605

Figure 10.16
Controlling the palette of a BMP image with WinGIF

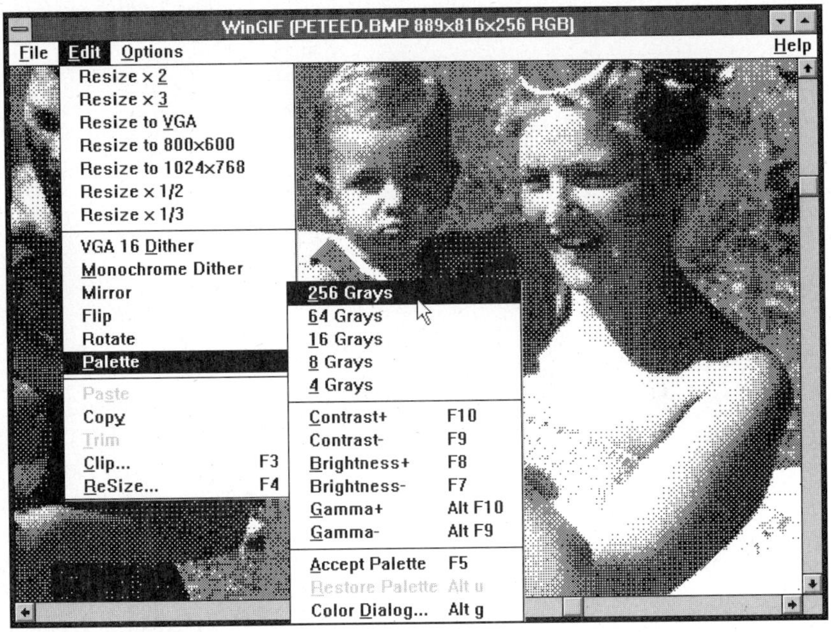

Miscellaneous Utilities

Think of any difficulty you have with Windows. Now think about this: There's a shareware utility that will solve it. Want to bring true batch-file power to Windows? Get WinBatch. Would you like to use *all* the buttons on your mouse, not just the left one? Buy Whiskers. Would you like to know how much memory you have available? Look for FreeMem. The list could go on, but you get the idea.

I've included below some of the more interesting utilities available. Spend time browsing through shareware sources for more; you'll find a utility for whatever ails you.

FreeMem

We've all gotten it at one time or another: the dreaded "Out of Memory" message. Once 3Mb or 4Mb of RAM seemed limitless, but Windows is a memory hog. Before you know it, you have to close applications just to keep Windows running.

FreeMem won't give your PC more memory, but it will let you know how much you're actually using in Windows. In fact, it's generally not just

RAM you need to worry about in Windows, it's system resources—portions of memory that Windows reserves for certain tasks.

Some programs drain these resources quite quickly. When you run FreeMem, it discreetly displays the amount of resources used by the system, in the corner of your screen. You can double-click on the display, and it will give you a more complete rundown of your use of system and memory resources, as seen in Figure 10.17. When you notice resources getting low, you know it's time to close down some programs.

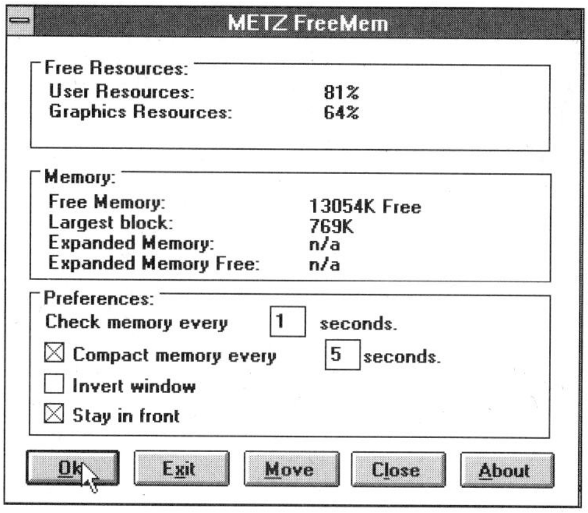

Figure 10.17 FreeMem's expanded display, detailing memory and system resources

FreeMem
Registration fee: None
METZ Software
P.O. Box 6042
Bellevue, WA 98008
(206) 641-4525; (800) 447-1712 (orders)

Hunter

There are many file-finding utilities in DOS that will search for file names, and for text within files. Because of that, when you're in Windows and need to find a file, or a text string within a group of files, you'll often find yourself running a DOS window to get at the DOS prompt.

Hunter does for Windows what utilities such as SST and FGREP do for DOS. It allows you to search for specific files or groups of files (those ending in the extension .PCX, for example) on your disk. You can tell the program to stop when it finds the first file, or to provide a full report of every file it finds instead. It will also search for hidden and system files if you tell it to. It has similarly flexible capabilities when searching for text.

Hunter
Registration fee: None
Hunter can be found on various on-line services, such as CompuServe.

Mouse Cursor Changer

Are you tired of the same old cursor on your desktop? Looking for something new? Well, here's something for you. The inelegantly named Mouse Cursor Changer will change your mouse cursor to any one of 25 shapes. You'll find skinny cursors, huge cursors, cursors in the shape of hands, left-handed cursors, and many more.

You run the program from within Windows, choose your cursor from any of the 25 choices, then exit Windows and run a batch file, which will change the cursor for you. The next time you run Windows, you'll have the new cursor on your screen. If you want to return to your original cursor style, you run a separate batch file after exiting to DOS.

Mouse Cursor Changer
Registration fee: None
Farpoint Software
2501 Afton Court
League City, TX 77573

Screen Peace

This was one of the first screen savers for Windows, and is still one of the best. For the uninitiated, screen savers are Windows programs that will, after a predetermined amount of time, blank the screen and then put a moving image up on it. (The most famous of screen savers is probably the one found in the Macintosh world—an aquarium filled with swimming tropical fish.)

The idea behind screen savers is that if the same image is left for too long on the screen, the image can be "burned into" the screen, so that a ghost of the image will be left on screen forever.

Whether that's true is open to debate. Many people say that modern VGA monitors won't let that happen. Whether it happens or not, however, screen savers are just plain fun, and this is a great one. It features many options. You determine how long a period of inactivity must pass before the screen saver goes to work. And you'll find not just one animated image, but a collection of several. There are screen savers with blocks filling up the screen, falling snowflakes, a kaleidoscope, sticks, and more. You can even change the options on each module—for example, the number of snowflakes that appear at once on the screen, and how fast they fall. The program will also randomly change your Windows wallpaper if you so choose.

What's also nice about this program is that many other people have written animated modules for it, so you can easily add to your screen saver collection.

Screen Peace isn't quite as universally available as shareware as it once was; a commercial version of Screen Peace called Intermission has been released.

Screen Peace
Registration fee: None
Screen Peace is still available on some bulletin boards, and from disk vendors such as the Public Software Library.

Whiskers

Have you ever wished that your right mouse button could perform some kind of function in Windows? Although a rare program or two makes use of that button, in general, the mouse's right button is less useful than your appendix.

Whiskers lets you make use of the right button. When the program is loaded, you can program the mouse's right button to function as do different keystrokes, such as Enter, PgUp, PgDn, Del, any of the function keys, and others. You can also have it switch you to the Task Manager or have it cycle through your applications.

You can define functions for the right button in its normal state and with the Shift key, the Ctrl key, and both keys depressed. If you have a three-button mouse, you can similarly program the middle button. The programming is as easy as clicking on a few buttons, as shown in Figure 10.18.

If any of your programs already use the right or middle mouse button, you can tell Whiskers to go to sleep when you're in that application.

A commercial version of Whiskers, called Whiskers Professional, is also available with many added capabilities.

Whiskers
Registration fee: $
Numbers & Co.
Route 1, Box 59A
Oroville, WA 98844
(509) 476-2216

Figure 10.18
Programming the mouse with Whiskers

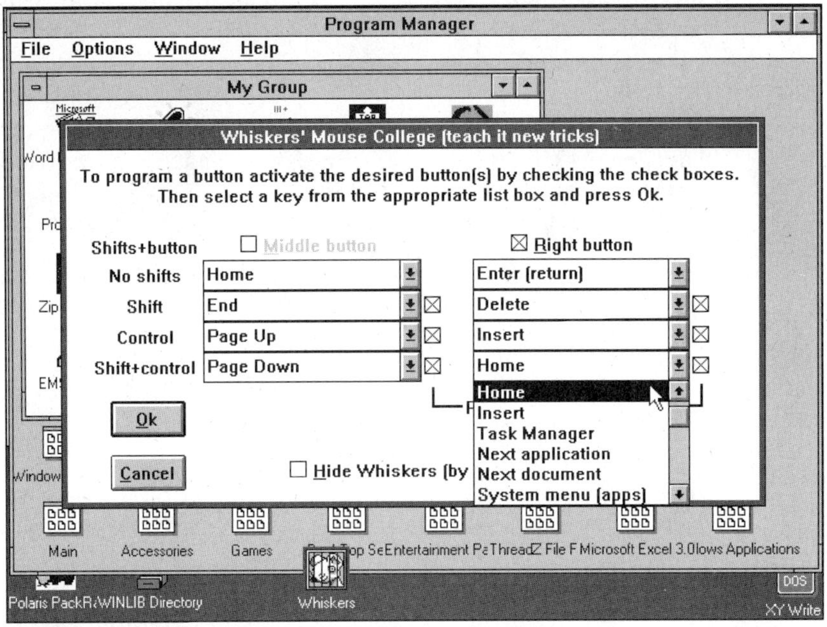

WinBatch

Windows can do many things, but it's missing one very basic function that DOS users have gotten used to—the ability to write batch files. If you've grown used to automating your computing life with batch files, switching over to Windows can be a great leap, and a frustrating one.

WinBatch gives you that batch file power when you're in Windows. It offers the types of commands you're used to in DOS. But it also goes beyond DOS's batch language, bringing the considerable power of Windows to every batch writer's toolkit.

Using it, you can perform basic operations such as automatically running Windows programs; copying, moving, deleting, and renaming files; reading and writing text files; copying text to and from the Windows Clipboard; and scrolling file and directory lists.

But that's just the beginning. The true power of this program lies beyond those simple techniques. It lets you create windows and dialog boxes, allowing you to position and manipulate them on the screen. With it, you can create dialog boxes that accept user input and then branch to a specific operation based on the input. You can make your windows zoom to full screen, shrink to a partial screen, or shrink all the way down to an icon. It will let you send keystrokes to Windows programs from a batch file, as if you were typing them while you were at the keyboard. It will perform string and arithmetic operations. And it has a companion program, WinMacro, that lets you create macros and then place those macros on the control menus of Windows programs.

Even though the WinBatch language is powerful and complex, writing simple Windows batch files with it is not very difficult. You simply use a word processor or text editor that creates ASCII text (such as Windows' Notepad) to create a file with the extension .WBT. After you've created the file, you run it by choosing the file with the Run command from the File Manager.

For example, if you were to write a simple batch file to run Word for Windows, it would read like this:

```
Run ("\winword\winword.exe", "")
```

The text in the first set of quotation marks defines the program to run; that in the second set is a parameter to pass to the program. Thus if you wanted your batch file to run Word for Windows and open the file MAKEMY.DAY, the line would read

```
Run ("\winword\winword.exe", "makemy.day")
```

Or, let's say you wanted to display a message box reading "Go ahead ... click on it!" for eight seconds before Word for Windows loaded and opened MAKEMY.DAY. The batch file would then read

```
Display (8, "Go ahead ... click on it!")
Run ("\winword\winword.exe", "makemy.day")
```

This is just the most basic use of the program's batch language. With it, you can create far more sophisticated batch files. WinBatch is the easiest to use of the Windows development tools, and in some ways the most powerful—even compared to commercial products.

WinBatch
Registration fee: $$
Wilson WindowWare
2701 California Ave. SW, Suite 212
Seattle, WA 98116
(206) 937-9335; (800) 762-8383

Window Safe

Many people don't realize that running certain DOS utilities, such as CHKDSK, while you're in Windows can corrupt your hard disk. Window Safe is designed to prevent this from happening. For example, typing **CHKDSK /F** while in Windows sometimes causes damage. Window Safe protects you against trouble by refusing to allow you to run the CHKDSK /F command while you're running Windows.

Running some other DOS utilities while you're in Windows can cause trouble as well. The unregistered version of Window Safe won't help you with them, but if you register the program with its author, you'll get a version that will also stop other utilities from doing damage.

Window Safe
Registration fee: $
Mom's Software
P.O. Box 449
Rockaway Beach, OR 97136
(503) 355-2281

WinCli

Windows may be a great operating environment, but, as anyone who has used it very much knows, to get any system work done, you'll need to get out to the DOS prompt. And while you're there, you won't have any of the bonuses you get from Windows.

Now you can get the best of both worlds, by using WinCli. With WinCli, you can perform many of the same functions you can from the DOS prompt. When you run it, the program looks very much like the DOS prompt. But you get more. You can, for example, run Windows programs from WinCli by just typing their names at the command line, instead of hunting for their icons on the Windows desktop.

You can treat WinCli as you do any other window, so you can easily maximize, minimize, and close it. With WinCli, you also get a scrollable window, as you do with other Windows applications.

WinCli
Registration fee: $
Eschalon Development, Inc.
110-2 Renaissance Square
New Westminster, British Columbia
Canada V3M 6K3
(604) 520-1543

WinPost

Are you tired of sticking Post-it notes all over your monitor and desk to remind you to do certain things? You need do it no more. Instead, get Win-Post. WinPost lets you create reminder notes on your Windows screen and manipulate them any way you wish.

Creating notes is simple: Load the program, and click on Create a Note. You'll be prompted to enter the size of note you want to create. Once you create the note, you can place it anywhere on the screen you wish. Figure 10.19 shows a series of notes created with WinPost.

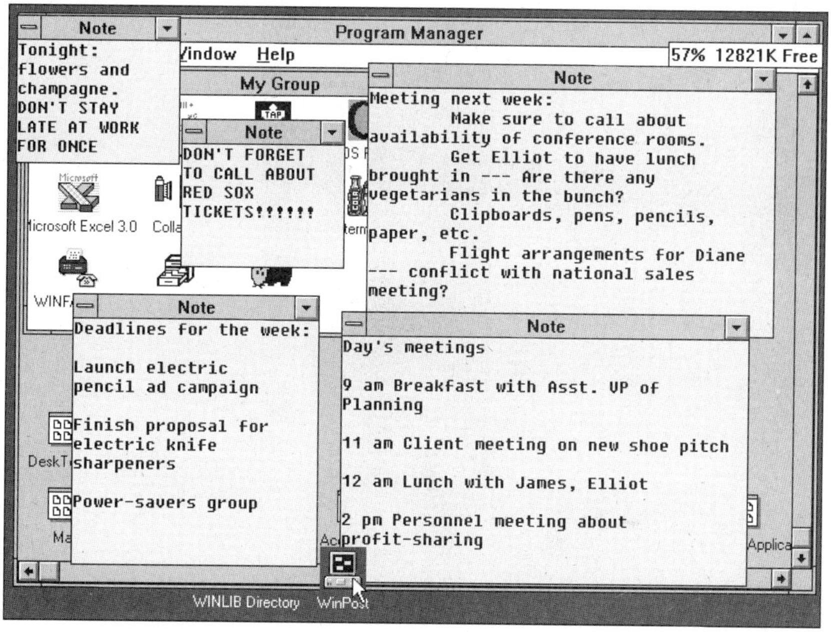

Figure 10.19
A series of notes made with WinPost

You can change your notes' shape, size, color, and style, as well as the size of their type. They can be printed out. You can search through your notes for a specific text string, and the notes can be deleted or hidden.

One of the program's most useful functions is the ability to create "alarm" notes—notes that pop up (and beep if you so choose) at a predefined time to remind you to do things such as attend a meeting . . . or duck one.

WinPost
Registration fee: $
Eastern Mountain Software
P.O. Box 20178
Columbus, OH 43220
(614) 798-0910

CHAPTER

11

Hard-Disk Enhancers, Backup Programs, and Formatters

Hard-Disk Enhancers

Backup Programs

Floppy-Disk Formatters

Miscellaneous Hard-Disk Programs

HOW IMPORTANT IS YOUR HARD DISK? YOU'LL NEVER REALLY KNOW until it begins to malfunction, or worse yet, crashes completely. Then you'll find out that in many ways it's the most important part of your computer. All your work is there—your data, notes, memos, outlines, virtually everything you do while you're at your PC. And all your programs are there as well, probably thousands of dollars worth.

Because your hard disk is so important, there have been countless shareware programs written to make sure it functions at peak efficiency. You'll find programs, such as Disk OrGanizer, that defragment your hard disk and so speed up access time. And there are programs to test your disk for bad sectors, and ones that park the heads of your disk while it's not being accessed, to save wear and tear. You'll even find programs that promise to give you more disk space by compressing your files on the fly.

And, of course, you'll find many programs to help you back up your hard disk, which may be the most important thing you can do for your hard disk.

Since you use floppies as well as a hard disk, many programs have been written to handle floppy disks—primarily to format them, but also to make sure your floppies work at top efficiency.

In fact, there are so many disk utilities available, and they perform such varying tasks, that it's hard to choose the best among them. I've organized this chapter into four parts. The first covers programs that make sure your hard disk functions as efficiently and smoothly as possible. The second part is my pick of the best backup programs. The third part covers programs that make it easier to format floppy disks. And the final part lists miscellaneous programs to help you use your hard disk.

With the programs in this chapter, even if your disk goes sour on you, you'll feel as little pain as possible.

Hard-Disk Enhancers

Hard disks are never fast enough and never big enough. When you had a 20Mb drive, you thought that if you only had a 40Mb one, all your troubles would be over. When you got a 40Mb one, you knew that an 80Mb would do the trick. And even when you get into the 100Mb-and-over range, you'll find that there's just never enough space. The same thing holds true for speed. On the PC, speed isn't dangerous, just addictive. You can't get enough of it.

The following programs will make your hard disk work faster, seem larger, and last longer. Disk OrGanizer and ORG, for example, will speed it up. Several programs will compress files on the fly and make the disk hold more data. Others will help prolong disk life. They all have one thing in common, though: They'll pay for themselves many times over.

Disk OrGanizer (DOG)

Your hard disk ages just like you do. It slows down and gets more crotchety as time passes. That's because as you use it more, the files on it become increasingly fragmented. The data belonging to a given file gets stored across your entire hard disk, rather than contiguously. This means that the disk head has to go to several different places to retrieve data for one file.

The disk also slows down as time goes on because you delete entries in your directories. Although you can't see them, there's still a record of those entries. To access a certain file, your PC has to search through all of the entries—even the ones you can't see.

There's no magic elixir that will stop you from aging, but there is one for your hard disk. It's called Disk OrGanizer (DOG). DOG defragments your hard disk, reorganizing it so that file data is stored contiguously. This means the hard disk can access files more easily and quickly. DOG will also remove deleted entries from your directories.

Before defragmenting your hard disk with DOG, it's a good idea to test your hard disk for problems. To do that, type **DOG /TEST** at the command line and press Enter. The program will report back on any errors it finds. If it finds errors, you should type **CHKDSK /F** and press Enter before continuing. That will run DOS's CHKDSK program and fix the errors. You're now ready to use DOG.

One note about the program: Version 3.12 has a bug that could cause data to be lost if the disk has unmarked bad clusters. Make sure your copy has a different version number before using the program. Also, back up your hard disk before using DOG.

Disk OrGanizer
Registration fee: $
Soft GAM's Software
G. Allen Morris III
P.O. Box 1311
Mendocino, CA 95460
(707) 961-1632

HDTEST

Bad sectors pepper your hard disk; if a file is written to them, you may lose the file. And that's just the beginning. You don't want to know all the problems that you might encounter using your disk—if you knew, you might never want to use it again.

But there's something you can do: Take preventative medicine, in the form of HDTEST. HDTEST does a thorough test of your hard disk's magnetic media. It writes 20 different test patterns to every cluster on your hard disk, and then checks that each pattern can be read back correctly. It marks any bad clusters it finds so that they won't be used in the future.

The program includes a number of companion programs. HDCHEK, for example, will inspect your hard disk and give a short report on what it finds, but won't take any remedial action. Since HDTEST doesn't run on some hard disks and computer systems, running HDCHEK first is also a good way to find out whether HDTEST will run.

Be sure to back up your hard disk before using HDTEST, and don't use it under a multitasking system such as Windows or DESQview. Disable all TSRs when running it. Also be prepared for a wait: Like a careful surgeon, HDTEST takes its time as it goes about its work.

HDTEST
Registration fee: $
P.R. Fletcher
1515 West Montgomery Ave.
Rosemont, PA 19010

NewSpace

NewSpace promises to give you more disk space without making you go out and buy a new hard disk. It does this by compressing files on your hard disk on the fly. But you can still use the files as if they weren't compressed.

There are two steps to using the program. You first install NewSpace on your hard disk and reboot your computer. A line will have been added to your AUTOEXEC.BAT file that will run NewSpace every time you boot your system. Next, you run a program to compress files on your hard disk; NewSpace generally shrinks files down to about half their original size.

After that, there's nothing else you need to do—you just use your PC as you normally would. Whenever you create a new file, it will be compressed automatically. Note that NewSpace will compress only data files—it leaves programs in their uncompressed state. It also will not compress AUTOEXEC.BAT and other system files necessary for your PC's operation.

NewSpace also has a basic file-recovery feature. It will allow you to undelete the last compressed file that you erased.

The program won't work with all backup programs, and if you want to run XTree Gold, you'll need to add some extra switches to the command line. It also won't work with multitasking software such as Windows and DESQview. Before using NewSpace, make sure to back up your hard disk.

Note that the developer, Isogon Corporation, no longer supports the shareware version of this product. Instead, it sells a commercial version by the same name.

NewSpace
Registration fee: None
The shareware version can be found through some disk vendors, such as Public Brand Software.

ORG

ORG does the same thing DOG does—it defragments your hard disk so it will run faster. As with DOG, you should back up your hard disk before using the program, and you should run the CHKDSK /F command first. ORG can also delete unneeded temporary files (created for backup or housekeeping chores) while it defragments your disk.

ORG
Registration fee: $
Greve Computer Systems
Aubrigstrasse 23
CH 8804 Au
Switzerland

SLIM

How would you like to expand your hard-disk space without spending a penny on hardware? That's the promise of SLIM, a unique program that compresses files on your hard disk—both executable and data files—and then lets you work with them as if they weren't compressed.

You run SLIM by typing **SLIM ON**. This causes it to run as a TSR, taking up 72k of RAM. Now you're ready to compress your files. For example, if you want to compress a file called THEBIG.ONE, you'd type **SLIM THEBIG.ONE**. You've now compressed the file, but you can access it just as if it weren't compressed. The amount of space you'll save will vary, but generally runs between 30 and 80 percent per file.

You should only compress files that you work with infrequently, since compression and decompression take some time. Executable files are well suited for compression, as are data files that aren't often written to. You can compress groups of files using the * and ? wildcards.

SLIM is particularly suited for computers with small hard disks and laptops, since its EXE file takes up less than 24k.

SLIM
Registration fee: $$
Dominic Herity
P.O. Box 3038
Dublin 4
Ireland

Time Park

If you want to prolong the life of your PC and its components for as long as possible, is it better to keep it running unused for long hours at a stretch, or should you turn it off when you're not using it and then turn it back on when you need it? This is one of the longest-running debates in the PC world.

Those who say it should be shut off point out that the continuous rotation of the hard disk, even when it's not being accessed, puts undue wear and strain on it and increases the chances of the heads crashing into the disk. But what about the wear and tear put on the rest of your system by turning your PC on and off repeatedly?

Time Park tries to give you the best of both worlds. A TSR program that takes up a mere 0.5k, Time Park *parks* the heads (moves them away from the disk surface) and stops the rotation of a hard disk after a user-specified period of disuse—from one to nine minutes. This way, you can keep your PC running without straining your hard disk, since its heads are parked.

Time Park
Registration fee: None
Time Park is available from disk vendors such as Public Brand Software and the Public Software Library.

Backup Programs

Being told to back up your hard disk is a lot like being told by your mother to eat your vegetables. In both cases you know the advice is undoubtedly sound. And in both cases the advice is often too distasteful to follow.

The following programs won't help you stomach spinach or cauliflower, but they will help make backups more palatable. Point and Shoot Backup/Restore, in particular, makes the task as easy as possible, but each of the other programs here has its strengths as well. The point is not which one you use, but that you use one regularly, so that when your hard disk crashes (which it inevitably will) you'll have saved all your data and programs.

Archive

This simple backup program doesn't come with as many bells and whistles as other programs, particularly commercial ones, but it's free, and will perform all the basic backup tasks.

It puts together a list of all the directories and files on your disk. You then scroll through the directory listing, tagging directories and individual files you want to back up. If you want to back up the entire hard disk instead, tag the root directory, and every file will be backed up. Archive will also let you back up only those files that have been altered or created after a certain date.

As you go through the process of tagging files, Archive keeps a running total of the number of files you've tagged and the number of floppy disks you'll need in order to do the backup.

Restoring files from your floppies to your hard disk is easy. It's done in much the same way as files are backed up from your hard disk to your floppies.

Archive
Registration fee: None
Archive is available from on-line systems and from disk vendors such as Public Brand Software.

File/Archive

You don't use most of the files on your hard disk. They sit there, unused, untouched, taking up disk space. In fact, there are so many of them that you might think you need to buy another hard disk sooner than you actually do.

File/Archive will help. First it looks at every file on your hard disk. Then, based on information you give it, it picks out the files you no longer use. You can erase those files, or archive them if you'd rather. The program will archive specified files to floppy disks, and will keep a log of when and where you put the file so that you can find archived files quickly.

File/Archive
Registration fee: $$
Marcor Enterprises
8857 Commerce Park Pl., Suite D
Indianapolis, IN 46268
(317) 876-9376

File-Safe

File-Safe is a straightforward, easily run backup program, with one especially nice touch: It maintains a catalog of all the files you've backed up, and tells you to which disk you've copied them. This makes it easy when you'd like to get at just one or two files—or a certain group of files—without having to restore your entire hard disk from floppies.

File-Safe is run from a menu, so it is quite simple to use. The main screen has options for choosing which files to back up and then backing up those files; for reviewing the files you're going to back up, and making any changes; for restoring files by viewing a catalog of files you've backed up; and for printing the catalog to paper, so that you can look at a hard copy of it instead of reviewing it on screen.

When you choose the Analyze/Backup Files option from the main menu, it will list all the files in all the directories you've chosen to back up, as shown in Figure 11.1. You can deselect files and directories from this screen before doing a backup. Pressing Enter twice begins the backup process.

Figure 11.1
A partial list of files to be backed up

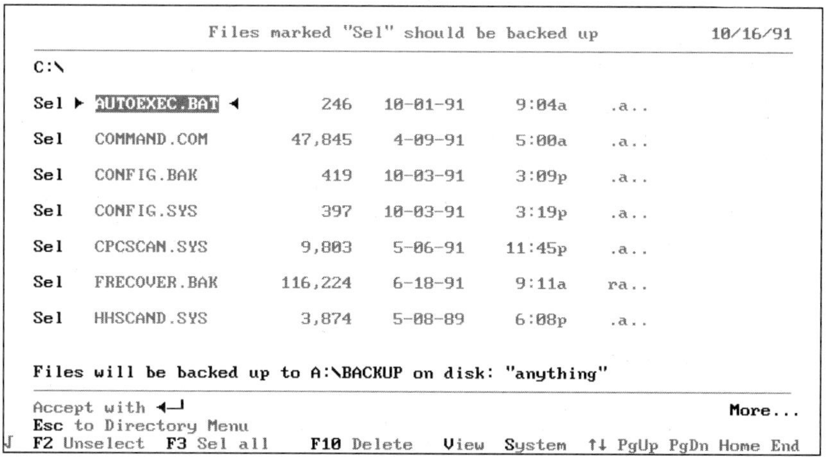

Once you've backed up files, restoring them is simple. Choose Restore from Catalog from the main menu and you'll be presented with a list of the files you've backed up, the date you backed them up, and the floppy disk(s) you've backed them up to. Choose the files you want restored, and the program goes to work. It's that simple.

File-Safe also has a built-in virus detector. When you run File-Safe, it checks the program for the presence of a virus. If it finds one, an X will flash in the lower-left corner of the main menu. Note, however, that its virus detector doesn't check for viruses in any programs other than itself.

File-Safe
Registration fee: $$
Marcor Enterprises
8857 Commerce Park Pl., Suite D
Indianapolis, IN 46268
(317) 876-9376

Point and Shoot Backup/Restore

Point and Shoot Backup/Restore is an exceptionally flexible and easy-to-use backup program, and should make even the laziest among us back up our disks.

When you first load the program, you'll be greeted with a main menu. The menu items you'll be most concerned with are Backup, Compression, and Restore. Backup, as its name implies, backs up your hard disk. The Compression option allows you to compress or decompress individual files on your hard disk without backing them up. Restore will copy the files that were backed up on your floppies to your hard disk.

When you choose Backup, the program looks into your hard disk, cataloging every file in every directory. When its work is done, it brings you to the Backup menu, as seen in Figure 11.2.

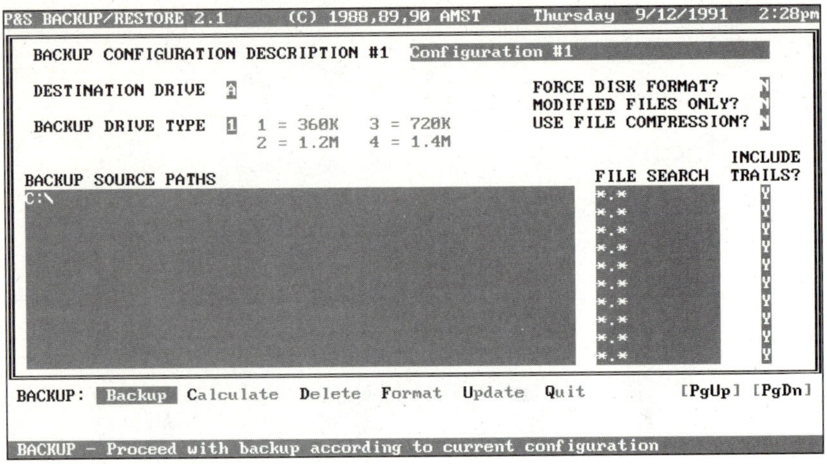

Figure 11.2
Point and Shoot Backup/Restore's Backup menu

There are many specifications you can make for your backups, including the designation and density of the drive you'll be backing up to, whether to use file compression, and whether to back up all files or only those files changed since the last backup. You can also tell the program to back up the entire hard disk, or only certain subdirectories on the disk. You can have it back up only files with certain extensions, such as .DOC.

You can create ten different, customized backup configurations. So, for example, if you want daily backups of only those WK1 files in your \BUDGET directory that have been modified since the last backup, you can do so. Or, if you want to back up all the DOC files on your disk weekly, use that as another configuration. You might also have a configuration for backing up the entire disk once a month.

To choose individual directories to back up, move your cursor to the File Search option on the screen and press F7. A tree directory of your hard disk will appear. Scroll through the directories until you find the one you want to back up and press Enter. You can back up as many as ten different subdirectories, and all their branches, in a single backup, as seen in Figure 11.3.

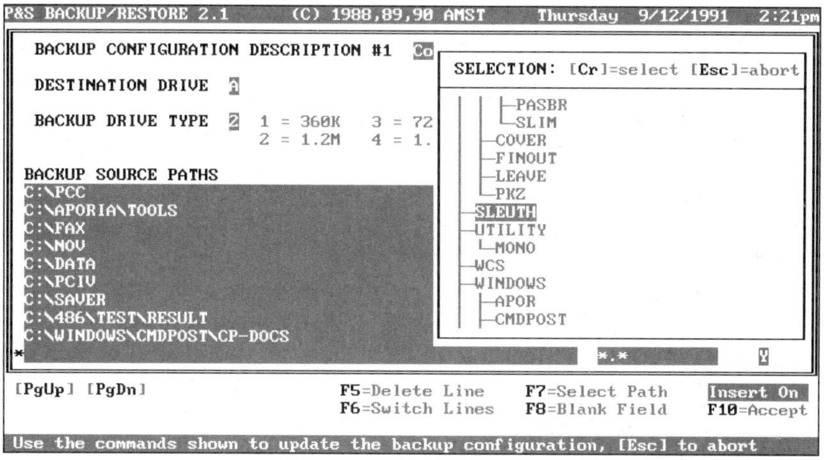

Figure 11.3
Choosing individual directories for a backup

Before backing up, you'll probably want to know how many floppy disks you'll need to have ready and how long the backup will take. Choose Calculate from the Backup screen, press Enter, and the program will estimate how long the backup will take (in minutes) and the number of disks you'll need. It will also tell you the number of files and bytes on your disk.

If you want to restore the files to your hard disk after you've backed them up, the program also offers a number of options. You can restore the entire disk, or only specified files and directories. You can also restore files to a directory other than the one from which they came, as well as a number of other options.

The program will compress and decompress individual files on your hard disk as well. To do so, choose Compression from the main menu. A tree listing of your hard disk will be displayed, as seen in Figure 11.4. Scroll to the file you want to compress or decompress, choose the Compress file or Decompress file option from the menu, and your work is done.

Point & Shoot Backup/Restore
Registration fee: $
Applied Micro Systems Technology
P.O. Box 1784
Stillwater, OK 74076
(405) 377-0444

Figure 11.4
Compressing individual files

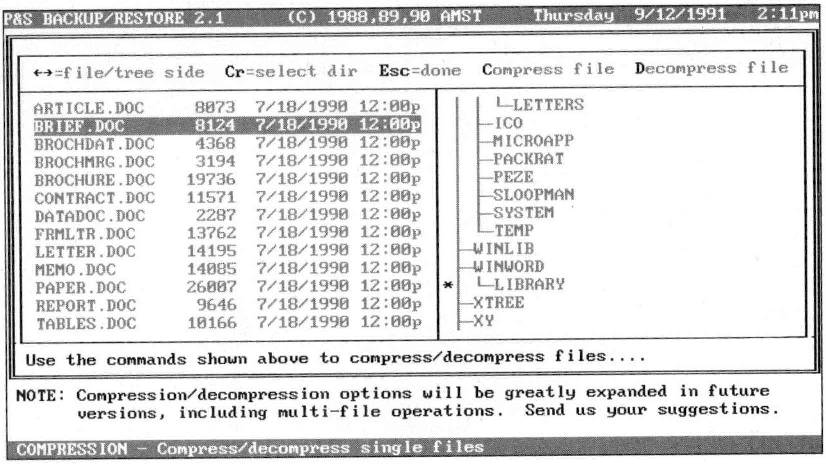

Floppy-Disk Formatters

Nothing could be more mundane than formatting floppy disks. It's perhaps the most tedious task you'll ever perform at the PC. But what could be done to make it easier, or to make the time pass more quickly while you're formatting? Plenty.

AnaDisk will let you copy files to a floppy disk and format the disk for you first. Con>Format will format disks in the background, freeing you up to work on your PC while it formats floppy disks. Other programs will let you copy disks in both drives simultaneously.

None of the following programs are flashy. But they'll all save you time, your most precious computing resource.

AnaDisk

AnaDisk is the most complete floppy-disk utility you'll probably ever come across. It has something for everyone. Whether you're a business professional, only interested in getting the job done; a power user with a special task in mind; or a technical whiz who wants to examine physical sectors on a floppy, you'll find something in here for you.

Nontechnical users will find this program useful for several purposes. The simplest is for making copies of disks. You can copy a disk without first having to format the target disk—AnaDisk will do the formatting for you, before it does the copying.

AnaDisk will also search through an entire disk for a given string of text, and then report to you on its findings. You can perform case-sensitive or case-neutral searches, and use wildcards and other search criteria. It will even search through files that you've deleted. (It can do this because when you delete a file, you don't actually erase its data. The first character of its name is simply erased from the directory listing. The data stays there until it's overwritten with other data.)

If you have more technical inclinations, the program will do even more for you. It will examine your floppy disk, determine its density and format, and note if any problem areas are found. It also provides you with a report on what it finds, as shown in Figure 11.5.

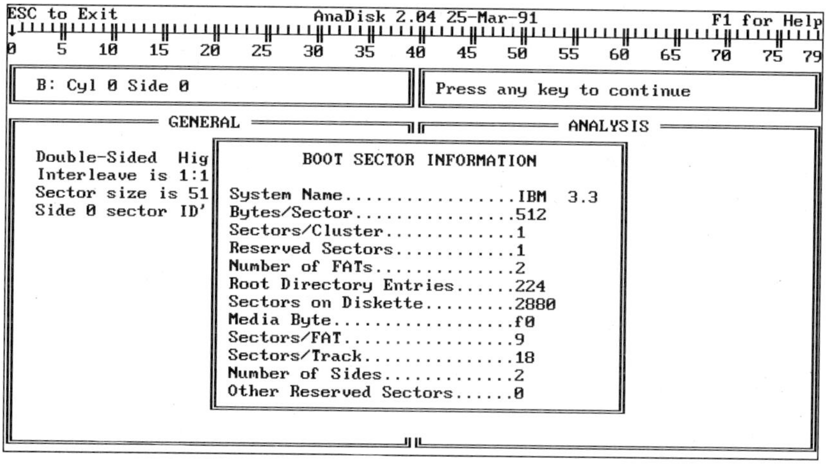

Figure 11.5 The results of an AnaDisk scan of a floppy disk

AnaDisk does more than just report on problems: It fixes them. The program will find data errors, move those data errors off the bad portion of the disk, and mark the bad sectors so they won't be used again. And, as it does this, it doesn't harm your files.

Technical users will find even more uses for AnaDisk. It will, for example, let you edit individual sectors and the File Allocation Table (FAT). Nontechnical users should steer clear of this part of the program, however, since they could easily do irreparable damage to your data with it.

AnaDisk
Sydex
Registration fee: $
P.O. Box 5700
Eugene, OR 97405
(503) 683-6033

Con>Format

How much time do you spend each month waiting while your system formats floppy disks? Likely more than you realize. This job is one of computing's biggest time wasters. There's something absurd about devoting all that 386-power (or 286-, 486-, or even 8088-power, for that matter) on your desk exclusively to formatting chores.

There's a way to get all that time back. Use Con>Format. Con>Format will format a floppy disk in the background while you do other work with your PC. It handles all sizes and densities of disks, runs as an 11k TSR, and, when it's finished formatting, will pop up over the program you're running to ask if you want to format another (it will also use tones in lieu of, or in addition to, the pop-up window if you wish).

It's a well-designed program: For example, it won't let a program access your floppy drive when it's formatting a disk there. Instead the drive will be accessed after the formatting finishes.

Con>Format
Registration fee: $
Sydex
P.O. Box 5700
Eugene, OR 97405
(503) 683-6033

Easy Format Package

You don't have to be a rocket scientist to format a floppy disk. Pop it in your drive, issue the right formatting command, and you're ready to go. Right?

That may be true if you're formatting only a single floppy, and not doing anything fancy to it (like putting on a volume label or making it a bootable disk). But what if you want to format multiple floppies on both your A and B drives? What if you want to format some at 360k, some at 720k, some at 1.2Mb, and some at 1.44Mb? Let's say you also want a few to be bootable, and volume labels on some but not others. How easy is it to format disks now?

Not so easy, unless you have the Format Package. This simple, menu-driven package makes short work of even the hardest formatting chores. When you run it, you'll first be greeted with a menu. Most of your work will be done in the Format Control submenu, the left-hand option on this main menu. This is where you'll control your formatting options.

The first thing you'll do is select the drive or drives in which you'll be formatting and the capacity of the disk you'll format. Choose Drive and Disk Sizes from the Format Control submenu, and type in the letter of the drive you'll format. Another menu will pop up, as seen in Figure 11.6, from which you can choose the physical size of the floppy disk, its capacity, and the type of drive in which you'll be doing the formatting.

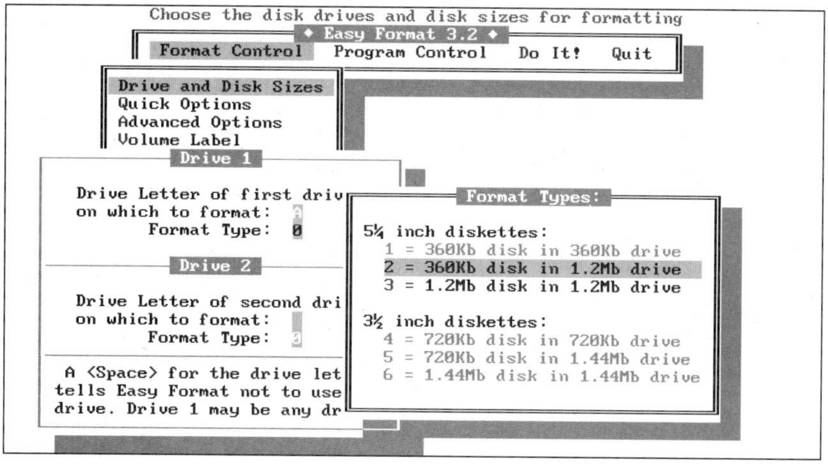

Figure 11.6
Choosing the drive and disk specifications

Next you'll choose the formatting method. For most tasks, you should choose Quick Options from the Format Control menu. From here you'll decide how carefully the disk should be formatted, as seen in Figure 11.7. You can tell the program not to bother to check for bad sectors, or you can choose from a number of different methods for detecting and marking off bad sectors and protecting against future errors. In general, the more protection you ask for, the slower the format will be.

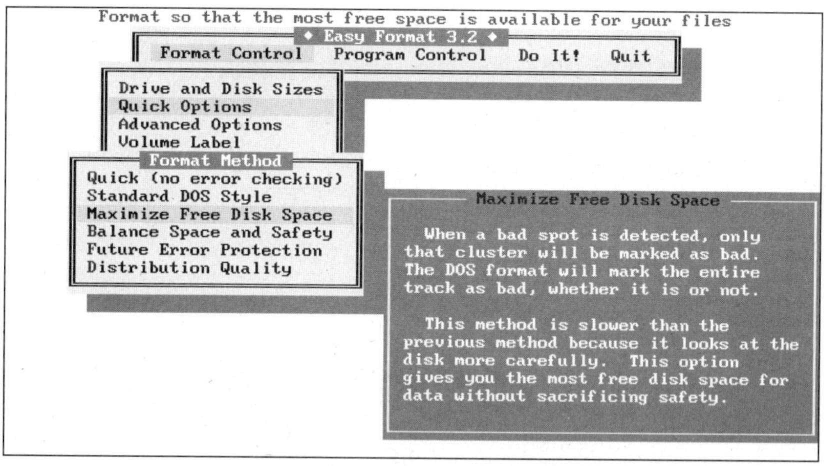

Figure 11.7
Choosing which format method to use

Other options on the Format Control submenu let you create a bootable disk and place a volume label on the disk. The program will even allow you to have a customized message pop up when the disk is used to boot up a computer.

Easy Format Package
Registration fee: $
Falk Data Systems
5322 Rockwood Court
El Paso, TX 79932
(915) 584-7670

FormatMaster

This is a floppy-disk formatter with a twist. Not only will it do all the formatting chores you would expect, such as making bootable, formatted floppies, creating system labels, and the like, but it will also actually let normal 360k disks be formatted to contain 800k of data when formatted in a 1.2Mb drive. It does this using some technical magic that you don't really need to know about—the point is, it works.

Be aware that formatting a 360k disk to contain 800k of data won't work on all systems. Older clones, in particular, may have some trouble with this, as may some versions of DOS. Even on these systems, however, you should be able to format a 360k disk to hold 720k of data.

FormatMaster does more than just give you that extra capacity on floppy disks, however. It's also great for bulk formatting chores. Although you can use the program for formatting floppies in ones and twos, it really comes into its own when you're formatting several at a time. This is because it will let you format floppies in both your A and B drives at once. And the formatting goes on continuously in each drive.

The program has many other options for formatting floppies, such as checking the disk for bad sectors and marking them off if they're bad. Despite the program's many options, it's menu-driven, and so is easy to use.

FormatMaster
Registration fee: $
New-Ware
8050 Camino Kiosco
San Diego, CA 92122
(619) 455-6225

Miscellaneous Hard-Disk Programs

Want to know how fast your hard disk is? Would you like to see displayed, in chart form, the relative sizes of the directories on your drive? And how would you like to have a log detailing how you spend your time at the keyboard?

The following programs will do all that for you, and more. CORE Test, for example, is the standard used for measuring hard-disk speed, so you can see whether the claims your salesperson made when you bought your hard disk are true. Disk-at-a-Glance will let you see which of your directories are largest, and so are ripe for pruning. The other utilities listed below will perform similarly useful jobs.

Bar Graphs

Ever wonder what types of files make up most of your hard disk? Wonder no more: Bar Graphs (also known as Dave's File Usage Graph) will show you. If you have a CGA, EGA, or VGA system, it will display a vertical bar graph showing how many files of each of eight types are on your system: compressed files, executable files, text files, data files, programming-related files, system files, graphics files, and Windows files.

Bar Graphs groups the files into these eight types, and then shows, within each individual grouping, the total number of files with a given extension, as seen in Figure 11.8. For example, in the Windows grouping it will show the number of files with the extensions .BMP, .INI, .ICO, .PIF, .GRP, and so on. You can have Bar Graphs display a single directory or your entire disk.

Bar Graphs
Registration fee: None
David Smith
1104 Mason Dr.
Hurst, TX 76053

CORE Test

How fast is your hard disk? Do you have any idea? Sure, when you bought it, they promised you that it was speedy. Maybe you were told it had an access time of 17 milliseconds, or 19ms, or 21ms. But how can you know whether you were told the truth? Use CORE Test. This fast, simple test is distributed free by CORE International, a well-known hard-disk manufacturer, and has become an industry standard.

To run it, you type **CORETEST** at the C> prompt and press Enter. The program will go to work, showing you a graphic screen detailing how far along it is in its work. When CORE Test is done, it tells you the average transfer rate, the seek time, the track-to-track seek time, and an overall

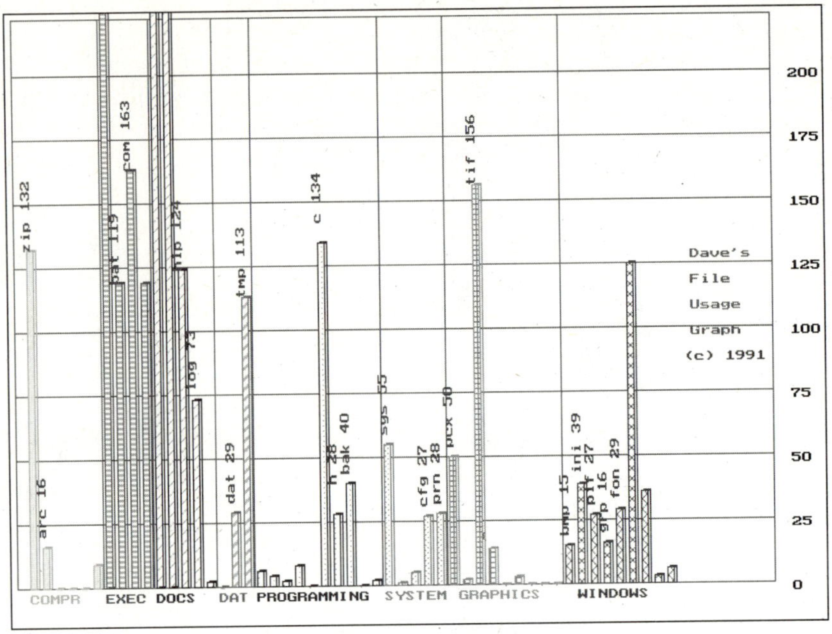

Figure 11.8 Bar Graphs' depiction of all the files on a hard disk

performance index for your disk, as shown in Figure 11.9. Then it compares those results to several common hard disks.

CORE Test
Registration fee: None
CORE International Inc.
7171 North Federal Highway
Boca Raton, FL 33487
(407) 997-6055

Disk-at-a-Glance (DAAG)

If you're like many people, your hard disk is always on the verge of filling up. Directories filled with unused or rarely used data and programs are often the culprit. You need a way to see which are the largest directories, so that you can target them for pruning or splitting into subdirectories.

Disk-at-a-Glance (DAAG) will do the job for you. When you run it, it displays all the directories on your hard disk, including hidden directories, in tree structure. It lists the number of files in each directory, the total number of bytes occupied by each directory, the percentage of the total disk space used that each directory takes up, and the percentage of disk capacity each directory occupies.

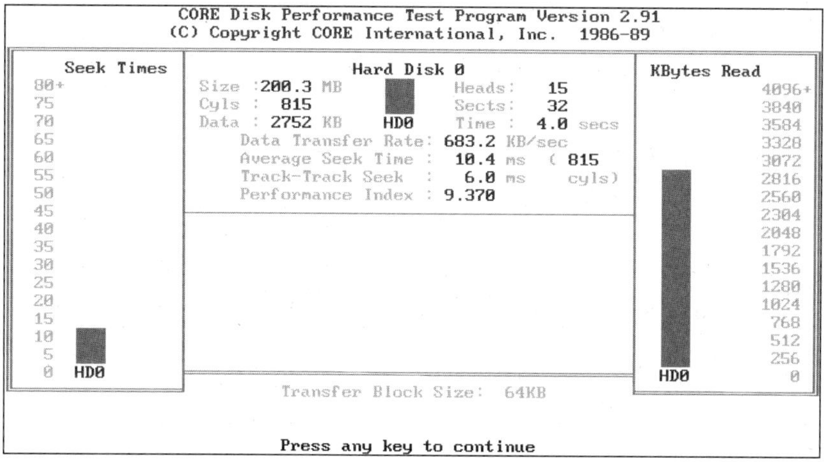

Figure 11.9 The results of a CORE Test

When you move your cursor to a directory and press Enter, you'll be given a rundown on the number, size, and types of files in the directory, by extension. Highlight a file extension listing, and another window will pop up, giving you details on individual files, as seen in Figure 11.10. You can delete files from this window by highlighting a file and pressing the Del key. You can also browse through the file by pressing the Enter key when the file is highlighted.

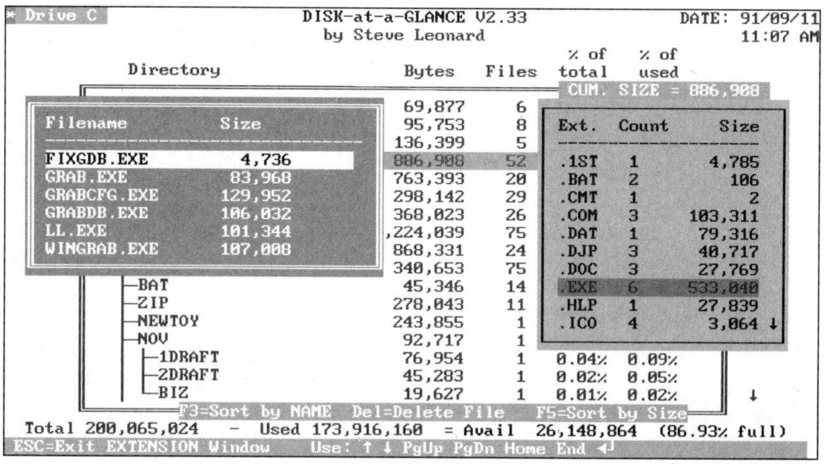

Figure 11.10 A detailed listing of files with .EXE extensions from DAAG

DAAG will also compile a list of duplicate file names on disk for you. Press F3 to get the list. You won't be able to delete files from this listing, but you can create an ASCII file containing the duplicate file names, which you can then print out using your word processor.

The most entertaining part of the program is the pie chart it will display on EGA and VGA systems, as seen in Figure 11.11. The chart shows graphically the largest directories on your disk, and also reports the percentage of occupied disk space taken up by each directory.

Figure 11.11
Pie chart of the largest directories on a hard disk

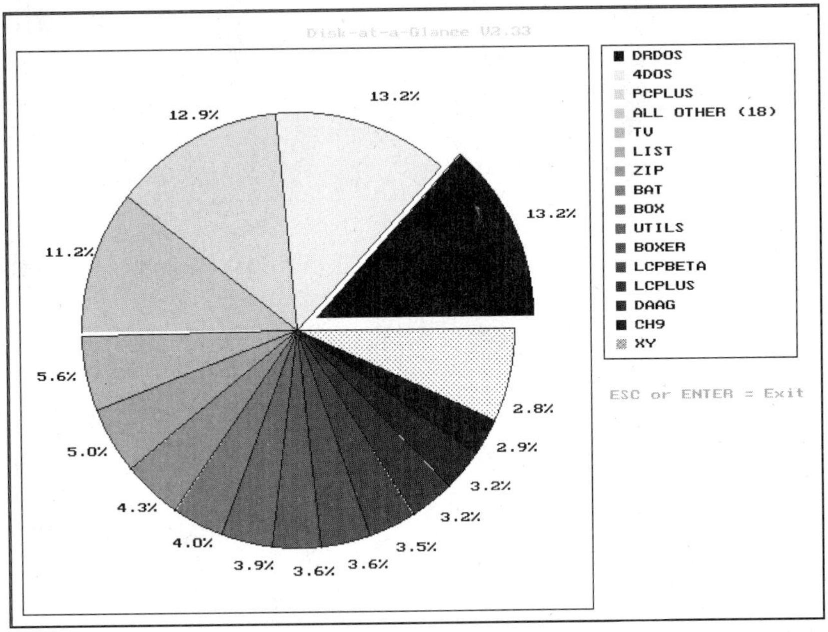

DAAG also includes another interesting utility. Press F2 and a record of your current directory tree listing will be saved to disk, along with the current date.

Disk-at-a-Glance
Registration fee: $ (voluntary donation)
Steve Leonard
260 Dunbar Road
Hilton, NY 14468

LogIt!

This unique program prepares a log of how time is spent on a PC. It records the time you first load each application, the amount of time spent in each application, and the number of keystrokes used while in the application. It also creates reports based on that data.

LogIt! runs as a TSR, silently watching and calculating while you're hard at work. It's useful if, for example, you want to keep a detailed record of your computer use, or if you need to account for your time by project or account. (Although, if you use the same program for different projects, you'd have to exit and then reload the application.) If you have a home business and use your computer for personal as well as business use, it will detail how long was spent on each task, for your tax records.

LogIt!
Registration fee: $
Robertson Software
Dept. LS-3
P.O. Box 576
Geneva, IL 60134

OptiCopy

When you copy a large number of files from your hard disk to a group of floppies, you'll find that a great deal of the space on the floppies is wasted. DOS's COPY command copies files with no thought given to efficient file placement. Many of your backup floppies, therefore, will be nowhere near full, since if there isn't room for the file COPY is trying to write, it just rejects the disk rather than looking for a smaller file.

OptiCopy optimizes the copying process. It checks the list of files you're copying and figures out the most efficient way of storing the files on your floppies. Don't be surprised if you find a "0 Bytes free" message on your floppies after using OptiCopy—it can be that efficient. The same author also makes OptiMove, which does the same thing as OptiCopy, except that it moves files rather than copying them.

OptiCopy
Registration fee: None
Paul Galbraith
275 Alscot Crescent
Oakville, Ontario
Canada L6J 4R5
(416) 844-3770

CHAPTER

12

Antiviral Programs

Virus Detection Programs

Virus Disinfectors

Infection Prevention Software

Antiviral Utilities

ASK AROUND ENOUGH AND YOU'LL PROBABLY COME ACROSS SOMEone who's been hit by a virus, or knows someone who's been infected. Viruses are no longer exceedingly rare—they've spread far and wide.

As explained in Chapter 2, you can get viruses from many sources: shady bulletin boards, pirated programs, even shrink-wrapped software. Some people fear that shareware is more prone than other types of software to be infected, but this isn't the case. I've downloaded hundreds of shareware programs, and have yet to come across one infected with a virus. I know of many people with similar experiences.

Whether you use shareware or commercial software, however, you should always play it safe and regularly use antiviral programs. You'll find that the best of these are shareware. Shareware authors, not commercial software writers, pioneered antiviral programs, and the most comprehensive suite of such programs can still be found in the shareware marketplace.

There are four general types of antiviral software. The first, often called scanning software, will detect the presence of viruses in your system, and then report to you on what it finds. The second type of antiviral programs are disinfectants. These programs kill viruses once they are found. The third type are those that prevent your PC from becoming infected, or at least warn you at the first sign of infection. The final type is composed of utilities. These may simply give you information about viruses, or they might help you use other antiviral software. The four sections of this chapter detail each of the main types of antiviral software.

When comparing antiviral programs, pay no attention to the number of viruses they claim to detect or disinfect. There are many strains of each virus, and one program may count the Jerusalem virus as a single virus, whereas another may count each of its variants—resulting in a much higher, and misleading, number. Instead of such numbers, keep in mind the kind of support you'll receive when you register. Most importantly, find out how often the program is updated. Frequent updates usually mean better support, and also mean that your antiviral program will quickly have a cure for new viruses as they are detected.

McAfee Associates is the industry leader in creating antiviral software, and has a large, comprehensive suite of antiviral tools. Because of that, the next section covers the McAfee series in general. Then, throughout the chapter, individual programs sold by McAfee are discussed.

McAfee Antiviral Series

McAfee Associates was an early pioneer in antiviral software with its shareware product ViruScan. As its name implies, ViruScan is a virus scanner, and a top-notch one at that. But ViruScan is just one in McAfee's family of antiviral products. Taken together, ViruScan and its siblings form a comprehensive, no-frills suite of protection, detection, and eradication products.

Each product in the suite must be purchased separately, but they all work much the same way. ViruScan detects and can also eradicate viruses. Clean-Up kills viruses, and offers a better way of doing so than ViruScan. VShield is a virus prevention program that runs as a TSR and checks programs for viruses before you run them. NetScan is a virus detection program for use on networks. VCopy is a replacement for the DOS COPY command, and checks for viruses as you copy programs from a floppy disk to your hard disk. There are also other products in the line, detailed in the appropriate section.

The McAfee series is supported via telephone if you register (you'll only pay for the toll call, not for support), a bulletin board, and on a CompuServe forum. The programs are usually updated every four to six weeks, and can be downloaded from the bulletin board, CompuServe, and other on-line sources. They can be obtained directly from the company as well. When you register for a particular program, updates are free for one year, though if you want them on disk direct from the company (instead of downloading the software), you'll have to pay for the floppies.

To reach the McAfee Associates bulletin board, call (408) 988-4004 for a 2400 bps connection, (408) 988-5138 for a HST 9600 bps connection, and (408) 988-5190 for a v32 9600 bps connection. To reach the company on CompuServe, type **GO VIRUSFORUM** at a CompuServe prompt.

Virus Detection Programs

The single most useful antiviral tool you can buy is a program that detects viruses; these are often called *scanning software*. If you use scanning software regularly, you can be sure that if you're ever attacked by a virus, the damage will be as minor as possible. That's because the sooner you detect a virus, the less chance it will have to harm your system, and the sooner you'll be able to kill the infection.

Scanning software usually works in one of two ways: It either looks inside programs for specific viruses, or it checks for the general effects caused by viruses. Some scanning software, such as ViruScan from industry leader McAfee Associates, will also disinfect your PC, although most scanning software won't.

Below I've covered the major virus detection programs. You'll find several from McAfee Associates, in addition to ViruScan. Other developers have come up with interesting approaches as well. And these are also worth looking into.

CHECKUP

CHECKUP doesn't check for specific viruses; instead, it examines files subject to infection in a variety of ways, and lets you know when something's amiss. In this way, according to its author, Richard Levin, it should be able to detect any virus, not just those that have already been discovered.

When you first run CHECKUP, it calculates a baseline of data for the files you want checked. It keeps a record of the file size, of mathematical calculations performed on the file, and other information. Although you can keep this baseline data on your hard disk, it's safer to store it on a floppy, where it can't be accessed by a virus.

Whenever you run CHECKUP subsequently, it compares files against the original baseline data. The program actually dissects the files into data blocks, then scans and compares each byte on the file with the original baseline data. If it finds discrepancies, it tells you that the file has been changed, and so may be infected.

CHECKUP
Registration fee: $ (home use); $$ (office use)
Richard B. Levin
Levin & Associates
9405 Bustleton Ave.
P.O. Box 14546
Philadelphia, PA 19115

CKCOM

This extremely small virus-checking program takes the minimalist approach to virus detection. It assumes that viruses will attack your COMMAND.COM file, so that's the only file it looks at. It doesn't look for specific viruses, and it won't kill viruses. Rather, it checks to see if your COMMAND.COM file has changed size. The author wrote it after getting attacked by the Yankee Doodle virus.

Running the program is exceptionally easy. First look at the size of your COMMAND.COM file. My version of DOS 5, for example, has a size of 47,845 bytes. After you know the size, type the command **CKCOM**, followed by the size of your COMMAND.COM file (in my case, **47485**), on the command line and press Enter. CKCOM checks the current size of your COMMAND.COM file. If it has changed, the program warns you that you might have a virus.

CKCOM
Registration fee: $
Russell Hildreth
P.O. Box 72431
Davis, CA 95617

NetScan

ViruScan is a great program, but it lacks one important feature—it won't work on a network. If you want to check network drives for viruses, you'll have to get NetScan, instead.

If you're familiar with ViruScan, you already know how to use NetScan. You run it from the command line. Its syntax and use are virtually identical to ViruScan's, except that NetScan has some added command-line switches for scanning network drives for viruses.

Network users can use NetScan to scan any network drives to which they have privileges (you can't scan a drive you're not privileged to use). You'd probably use it most frequently to scan the portions of the network that a network administrator has set aside for your files.

As with ViruScan, make sure to run it from a write-protected floppy disk. This way, it won't become infected.

The program will be more useful to network administrators than to individual users. Administrators can use it to scan entire file servers. To do so, the program will have to be run under an account with global read, write, and create privileges. It works with 3Com, 3/Share, 3/Open, Novell NetWare, Banyan VINES, DEC DECNet, Microsoft LAN Manager, PC/SA, and NFSNet as well as IBMNET- and NETBIOS-compatible networks. It should be run only while the supervisor account is active. The program scans about 1,000 files in three minutes. Registration and update procedures are the same as for ViruScan.

NetScan
Registration fee: $
McAfee Associates
4423 Cheeney St.
Santa Clara, CA 95054
(408) 988-3832

PC Canary

Well before the existence of more high-tech safety systems, the canary was miners' early warning system. One of the greatest dangers to miners is the presence of deadly, underground gas pockets. Miners took canaries with them down into the mines because the small, hypersensitive birds would die when minute amounts of gas were in the air. When a canary died, the miners knew poison gas was around, so it was time to leave, quickly.

PC Canary takes the same tack with your PC. You install and run the program, and hope that it's one of the first programs to be infected by a virus that enters your system.

The program doesn't check for specific viruses. Instead, it checks for telltale signs of virus activity, such as an attack on its data files, and warns you if it detects an attack. It checks only its own executable file and data files for signs of attack, not any other files. And although PC Canary warns of possible virus infections, it won't let you clean up infections, and it won't stop an infection from starting.

PC Canary
Registration fee: $
Compass/New England
P.O. Box 117
Portsmouth, NH 03802
(603) 431-8030

Sentry

This is one of the lesser-known tools in the McAfee antiviral toolbox. The way it checks for viruses is rather arcane; it has to do with the manner in which viruses attach themselves to programs.

When you first run the program, it creates a log of your system, detailing such things as boot sector instructions, hidden DOS files, device drivers, and programs on your disk. Every time you turn on your PC after that, the program checks this log to see whether there are any signs of infection. Sentry generally takes about 10 minutes to go through its initial installation on a drive with many files on it. After that, however, it runs much more quickly.

You'll have to reinstall Sentry every time you install a new DOS version, remove or add a device driver, delete a program, or replace a program with a different version.

Sentry
Registration fee: $
McAfee Associates
4423 Cheeney St.
Santa Clara, CA 95054
(408) 988-3832

Validate

This program, which is shipped with selected McAfee antiviral programs, is used to make sure that when you download or receive a piece of new software, it is uninfected. It calculates validation data for a given program by performing a mathematical operation on it. When you get a new program, you use Validate to calculate the validation data against data about the program maintained by its author. If the data you calculate matches that data, then you can be assured there's no virus infection.

The program will report to you on the size of the program in bytes, the date it was created, and two validation numbers. If any of the numbers don't match the author's numbers, there may be a problem.

Increasingly, shareware authors are using Validate to assure users that they're getting virus-free software. Some software documentation includes the validation figures to check. If you don't find them in your documentation, you can dial into a bulletin board to get the information at (408) 988-4004.

Validate
Registration fee: Free (with other McAfee programs)
McAfee Associates
4423 Cheeney St.
Santa Clara, CA 95054
(408) 988-3832

Viral

This program will detect viruses, but not kill them. It runs as a 4k TSR and checks programs before you run them to see if they've been altered in any way since you last ran them.

Viral doesn't actually look for specific viruses. Instead, it looks for changes to your executable files. Before loading Viral as a TSR, you first run a file called CHEKER.COM. CHEKER builds a database of the executable files on your disk, and performs calculations on those files. You can have CHEKER list every executable file, or only some of them.

When Viral runs as a TSR, it checks an executable file, and compares what it finds against the calculation in the database. If the numbers match, you can run the program. If they don't, Viral warns you. Note that it does not kill the viruses it finds.

Viral
Registration fee: $
NeuralSoft Systems
P. O. Box A3083
Chicago, IL 60690

ViruScan

ViruScan (also referred to as Scan) is the centerpiece of the entire McAfee antiviral shareware series. It may be the most powerful and accurate virus detection program available, not just among shareware programs, but among commercial software as well. McAfee was an antiviral pioneer, and the company keeps on the cutting edge of viral detection and cure, constantly discovering new viruses and updating ViruScan so that it will detect them.

ViruScan checks for viruses in several ways. It looks through your PC's hard disk and memory for instruction sequences or patterns that are distinct to specific viruses. When it finds these patterns, it reports that you have a virus. The program is updated every four to six weeks, so that you're protected against any recently discovered viruses. If you happen to know the patterns created by viruses not on the current list of viruses detected by ViruScan, you can add them to the program, and it will scan for those viruses as well.

The program can also search for new, undocumented viruses, both in program files and in the boot sector. It does this by attaching validation codes (called CRCs) to COM and EXE files, and then checking the codes to see if they've been altered.

Always run ViruScan from a write-protected floppy disk. If you ran it from your hard disk, the program itself might become infected. You should make sure to write-protect the floppy it's on so that it can't be attacked by viruses while you're running it.

ViruScan, like all McAfee programs, has no interface to speak of. You run it from the DOS prompt. For basic detection and cleanup chores, its syntax is simple.

To scan a hard disk for a virus with ViruScan, for example, type **SCAN C:** at the command line. The program then begins to check your hard disk for viruses. It first looks in RAM to see if any viruses are there, and then looks through the hard disk, checking all your executable files and the overlay files necessary to the execution of those files. When it checks RAM for viruses it looks only for the most common ones. You can tell it to do a more comprehensive search by adding the command line switch **/M**, although that search will take a bit more time.

When ViruScan encounters a virus, or viruses, it reports to you, on screen, the name of the infected file, and the name of the virus, as shown in Figure 12.1. It also summarizes the number of files it checked, and the number of files found to be infected.

If you'd like, you can have the program create an ASCII file with a report on its findings by adding the **/REPORT** command-line switch.

The program is exceptionally flexible. It can search individual directories, individual files, multiple directories and files, and multiple drives at a single pass. You can tell it the extension of specific overlay files, and it will check those as well. It can also scan inside executable files compressed with PKWARE's PKLITE program.

Figure 12.1
ViruScan reporting on a virus-ridden disk

```
  Found 12 Tricks Trojan [Tricks]
Scanning A:\VIRUS\VIR_11.COM
  Found Ah Virus [Ah]
Scanning A:\VIRUS\VIR_12.EXE
  Found Spanish April Fool [D28]
Scanning A:\VIRUS\VIR_13.COM
  Found 1661 Virus [1661]
  Found 1701/1704 Virus - Version B [170X]
Scanning A:\VIRUS\VIR_15.COM
  Found RMIT Virus [RMIT]
  Found 1701/1704 Virus - Version B [170X]
Scanning A:\VIRUS\VIR_16.COM
  Found Cracker Jack Virus [CRJ]
  Found Yap Virus [Yap]
Scanning A:\VIRUS\VIR_17.EXE
  Found 512 Virus [512]

Disk A: contains 2 directories and 20 files.

 Found 16 files containing viruses.


SCAN 7.8V82 Copyright 1989-91 by McAfee Associates.  (408) 988-3832

 More? ( H = Help )
```

When you use these functions, however, the program becomes a bit more difficult to use. For example, let's say you want ViruScan to do a comprehensive search of RAM for viruses. You also want it to search for viruses in the \PROGRAM subdirectory and check overlay files with an .ADD extension, in addition to the files it normally checks. Finally, you'd like a report of the results placed in your \VIRUS subdirectory, and given the name INFECT.RPT. To do all this you'd type

```
SCAN C:\PROGRAM /M /E .ADD /REPORT C:\VIRUS\INFECT.RPT
```

ViruScan can eradicate viruses as well as detect them, but it does so by deleting the file in which the virus is found. To scan for viruses and then delete infected files as they're found, you'd type **SCAN C: /D**. When the program encounters an infected file, it asks whether you want to delete it, as seen in Figure 12.2. To delete the file, press Y.

A better bet for virus eradication is to use McAfee's Clean-Up (see "Virus Disinfectors"), which kills the virus, and then attempts to reconstruct the file where the virus had lodged.

CAUTION! *There are no versions of ViruScan with version numbers 78 and 79. Trojan horses disguised as these versions of ViruScan were written; if you download one, delete it from your disk, and check your disk for viruses. If you find it on a bulletin board, alert the board's system operator (SYSOP).*

Figure 12.2 ViruScan deleting files infected with viruses

```
Scanning A:\VIRUS\VIR_2.EXE
  Found Invader Virus [Invader]
  Do you want to overwrite and delete "VIR_2.EXE" [Y/n] ? Yes
Scanning A:\VIRUS\VIR_3.EXE
  Found Invader Virus [Invader]
  Do you want to overwrite and delete "VIR_3.EXE" [Y/n] ? Yes
Scanning A:\VIRUS\VIR_4.COM
  Found Horse Boot Virus [H-B]
  Do you want to overwrite and delete "VIR_4.COM" [Y/n] ? Yes
Scanning A:\VIRUS\VIR_5.COM
  Found ETC Virus [ETC]
  Do you want to overwrite and delete "VIR_5.COM" [Y/n] ? Yes
Scanning A:\VIRUS\VIR_6.EXE
  Found Hero Virus [Hero]
  Do you want to overwrite and delete "VIR_6.EXE" [Y/n] ? Yes
Scanning A:\VIRUS\VIR_7.EXE
  Found Klaeren Virus [Kla]
  Do you want to overwrite and delete "VIR_7.EXE" [Y/n] ? Yes
Scanning A:\VIRUS\VIR_8.EXE
  Found Damage Virus [Dam]
  Do you want to overwrite and delete "VIR_8.EXE" [Y/n] ? Yes
Scanning A:\VIRUS\VIR_9.COM
  Found CD Virus [CD]
  Found Datacrime II-b Virus [Crime-2B]
  Do you want to overwrite and delete "VIR_9.COM" [Y/n] ?
```

ViruScan
Registration fee: $
McAfee Associates
4423 Cheeney St.
Santa Clara, CA 95054
(408) 988-3832

VIRx

This stripped-down version of the commercial virus protection program Virex is useful for virus detection rather than for disinfection and cure. It scans your hard disk for the presence of viruses and alerts you if it finds any. It will also allow you to delete the infected file, but it won't reconstruct that file—the file will be lost. In order to be able to kill viruses and recover the original, uninfected file, you'll need the commercial version, Virex.

VIRx will check for viruses not only on your hard disk but on network drives as well. It can detect viruses in EXE and COM files, even if those files are compressed with the PKLITE or LZEXE compression program. You can tell it to do a normal scan, or a longer scan that checks files for viruses much more thoroughly. It will also allow you to create an ASCII file that contains a report of its findings.

Be aware that VIRx is not supported as shareware—in order to get support, you'll have to buy the Virex virus protection program.

VIRx
Registration fee: None
Available on many bulletin boards, including CompuServe

Virus Disinfectors

Detecting a virus is the first step in keeping yourself free of infection. But once you've found a virus, you need to kill it—and you'd like to kill it without also destroying the programs the virus invaded.

That's where virus disinfectors come in. They'll exterminate viruses for you, and salvage your files whenever possible. These programs usually can't detect the presence of viruses; you have to find them first, using scanning software. Although some scanning software will also kill viruses, they do so by deleting the infected files.

The two disinfectors below are both from McAfee Associates. Clean-Up will kill most viruses wherever they've set up shop. Some particularly stubborn infections that attack the boot sector and partition table may respond better to MDISK.

Clean-Up

If you run ViruScan or some other virus-detection program and encounter viruses, this is the program to use to eradicate them. Often, virus-detection programs don't do a good job of killing viruses—they're much better at finding them. Clean-Up, on the other hand, can usually kill the viruses without destroying the infected files.

In order to use Clean-Up, you will have to identify the virus you wish to kill. It searches through files, the partition table, and boot sector for the virus. When it finds it, Clean-Up eradicates the virus and restores the infected file to its pristine state.

Like all the other McAfee programs, Clean-Up is command-line driven. Its syntax is similar to that of ViruScan and other programs in the McAfee series.

For simple cleanup operations, it's quite simple to use. For example, let's say that you've used ViruScan and discovered that the Jerusalem virus has infected the OHNO.EXE file in the \PURITY subdirectory of your C drive. You'd simply put a write-protected floppy in your A or B drive with the Clean-Up program on it and type the following command at the C prompt:

```
CLEAN C:\PURITY\OHNO.EXE [JERU]
```

What if, however, you are worried that the virus has gone elsewhere, and not just stayed in that one file? You have a variety of options. You can have Clean-Up look through the entire \PURITY subdirectory in search of the virus, or you could have it look through the entire hard disk. To disinfect the entire hard disk, you'd issue the command

```
CLEAN C:\ [JERU]
```

There are a great number of other Clean-Up options available as well. It can clean multiple floppy disks, create an ASCII report of its actions, and look for viruses in program overlay files (files that certain executable files need in order to run) with extensions you specify.

Clean-Up
Registration fee: $
McAfee Associates
4423 Cheeney St.
Santa Clara, CA 95054
(408) 988-3832

MDISK

Clean-Up will be able to kill most viruses and still keep the infected files intact. But it can't always do the job. Viruses that infect the boot sector and partition table, such as Pakistani Brain, Stoned, and Ping Pong, may be especially difficult—Clean-Up may not be able to save the files after killing the viruses.

MDISK will do the job: It can remove the viruses from the boot sector and partition table, and will keep your files intact.

MDISK
Registration fee: $
McAfee Associates
4423 Cheeney St.
Santa Clara, CA 95054
(408) 988-3832

Infection Prevention Software

Scanners and disinfectors are effective tools against viruses, but in the ideal world you wouldn't have to use them. What you'd like is a program that can actually prevent your PC from becoming infected. That's what the next three programs do.

Often, prevention software runs as a TSR sitting in your PC's memory until a virus is detected. Then it warns you that you might be infected, or else automatically shuts down your system. That's the approach taken by Secure and by McAfee's VShield program.

Flu_Shot+ takes a different approach—it uses a series of prevention tools in an attempt to lock viruses out of your PC.

Flu_Shot+

Ross Greenberg, the creator of Flu_Shot+, takes a slightly different approach to virus detection than the McAfee series of shareware products. Flu_Shot+ doesn't check for specific viruses, as do most of the McAfee programs. Instead, it uses several different tools—most of them designed to prevent infection. It lets you write-protect programs and files so that they can't be altered, protecting you against viral infections. It checks programs to see if they've been altered in any manner. It then runs as a TSR, waiting to see if any unknown TSRs attempt to run. If one does, it warns you that you might have a virus on your hands.

Using this program takes more work than the McAfee series—you don't just run it and let it do the work. You'll have to do a fair amount of customization to use it to its full effect, as follows.

The program is built around a table called FLUSHOT.DAT, like the one shown in Figure 12.3. Flu_Shot+ bases all its operations on the instructions given to it in this file.

Figure 12.3
A typical FLUSHOT.DAT file

```
P=*.bat
P=*.sys
P=*.exe
P=*.com
P=*FLUSHOT.DAT
P=*AUTOEXEC.BAT
R=*FLUSHOT.DAT
R=*AUTOEXEC.BAT
C=C:\COMMAND.COM[35421]
C=C:\IO.SYS[14958]
C-C:\MSDOS.SYS[19411]
T=C:\SIDE\SK.COM
```

In FLUSHOT.DAT are file names, and next to those files are numbers enclosed in brackets. When you run Flu_Shot+, it performs calculations on the files listed in FLUSHOT.DAT and compares what it comes up with against the numbers in the brackets. If there's a difference between the numbers, Flu_Shot+ warns you that a virus might be present.

The program comes with a FLUSHOT.DAT file already built in. However, the first time you run Flu_Shot+, you'll have to customize FLUSHOT.-DAT for your system. First you run the program by typing **FSP** and pressing Enter. Flu_Shot+ then checks the data listed in the FLUSHOT.DAT file. The file will already include some file names—primarily system files like

COMMAND.COM. The bracketed numbers next to those file names, however, will be incorrect, since they will vary with every system.

Flu_Shot+ will calculate what the proper numbers for those files should be, but you must then use a text editor that reads and writes clean ASCII text to insert the proper numbers in the brackets.

You can have Flu_Shot+ check many other files and programs in this way, not just those listed in the FLUSHOT.DAT file shipped to you. You simply add the file name to FLUSHOT.DAT, have Flu_Shot+ do a calculation on that file, and put the proper number next to the file name in brackets. Whenever Flu_Shot+ runs, it will do a calculation, check to see if the result matches the number in the FLUSHOT.DAT file, and will warn you if there's no match.

Flu_Shot+ has other tools in its arsenal as well. You can have it write-protect or read-protect important files such as your COM, EXE, and SYS files, so that viruses can't alter them. You do this by using the FLUSHOT.DAT file to indicate which files to write- or read-protect. In a similar manner, you list in that file which programs you commonly run as TSRs. When Flu_Shot+ comes across a TSR that isn't listed in the file, it will issue a warning.

Flu_Shot+
Registration fee: $
Software Concepts Design
P.O. Box 908
Margaretville, NY 12455
(607) 326-4422

Secure

Secure is a small (4k) memory-resident program that is designed to stop a virus from infecting your PC. It sits in your computer's memory, watching for any signs of infection.

In essence, it will not allow anything to be written to your executable files. If it detects a virus attempting to do that, it will halt the execution of the program.

Secure
Registration fee: $
Mark A. Washburn
4656 Polk St. N.E.
Columbia Heights, MN 55421

VShield

VShield is McAfee's virus prevention program—it will actually stop viruses from spreading throughout your system. When you run it, it checks the boot sector, partition table, system files, and RAM for any viruses. It then loads itself as a TSR. When you issue a command to run an application program, VShield checks the program for viruses. If it finds a virus, it won't let the program run. It also won't allow you to warm-boot your system from a floppy disk that has a boot-sector virus. If VShield detects an infected program attempting to load, it will show the name of the file and the virus infecting it, and won't allow the file to run.

VShield can also check for viruses it doesn't know about. It does this by looking at programs in which ViruScan has placed validation codes. If it finds those codes altered—indicating the probable presence of a virus—it won't let the program run.

When used with the /COPY command-line switch, VShield will check files as they're copied to see if those files contain viruses.

There are two versions of the program. The first, VSHIELD.EXE, checks for viruses it knows about by looking for their tell-tale signatures, and also checks programs with validation codes put in by ViruScan. This version takes up 31k as a TSR, but that overhead can be reduced to 3k if you specify that it can be swapped to disk. The other version of the program, VSHIELD1.EXE, only does validation checking. It takes up 6k as a TSR.

VShield can also be used to allow only certain programs to run on a system, programs which you "certify" can be run. This feature would be used primarily by system administrators worried about users spreading viruses.

VShield
Registration fee: $
McAfee Associates
4423 Cheeney St.
Santa Clara, CA 95054
(408) 988-3832

Antiviral Utilities

The utilities listed below help you in the fight against viruses in a number of different ways. McAfee's VCopy, for example, is used in place of DOS's COPY command, and checks for the presence of a virus whenever you copy a file to your hard disk. HyperText VSUM, on the other hand, is an informational program about viruses. If you know you've been infected, it will help you figure out what infection has hit you and how to cure it.

There are other useful antiviral utilities as well. Several of them, particularly Virus Central, will help you use the sometimes difficult-to-master McAfee programs. Especially interesting is Virus Simulator, which will create COM files that mimic viruses. You can use it to see just how well your scanning software works.

HyperText VSUM

This program will tell you everything you ever wanted to know about viruses—and then some. It's not a virus detector, an antiviral vaccine, or a virus killer. Instead, it's a program that contains a great deal of detailed information about viruses. It will tell you not only what symptoms are caused by specific viruses, but also which detection programs can best detect them and which are best used for disinfecting them.

The program is organized in hypertext format, which means that finding information is exceptionally easy. On any given screen of text, there are certain words that you can highlight, either by clicking on them with a mouse or by moving your cursor to them and pressing Enter. When you do, you'll get a screen of information about the word you've highlighted. In this way, you can easily navigate through tremendous amounts of information.

There are many ways in which you can look up viruses. You can choose the Virus Index item from the main menu. Then choose a letter of the alphabet, and you'll be presented with a list of all the viruses that begin with that letter. Choose a virus from the list, and you'll get information about that virus.

If you're interested in browsing, an even more interesting way to use the program is to choose the Relationship Chart item from the main menu. When you do this, you'll be shown a family tree of every known virus, including the name of the original virus and its variants, as seen in Figure 12.4.

Figure 12.4
Some virus family trees

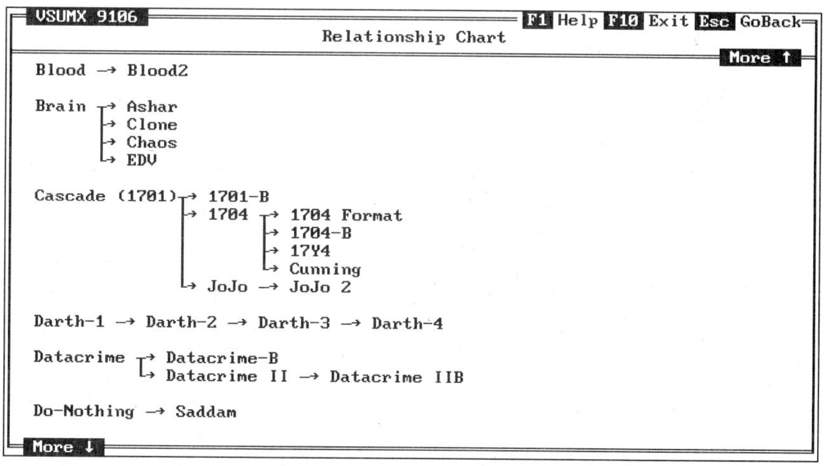

Choose any individual virus from this listing, and you'll be shown information about the virus: its aliases, how common it is, when it was discovered, its symptoms, programs that will detect it and those which will eradicate it, as well as general comments about the virus. An information screen for the common Cascade virus is shown in Figure 12.5.

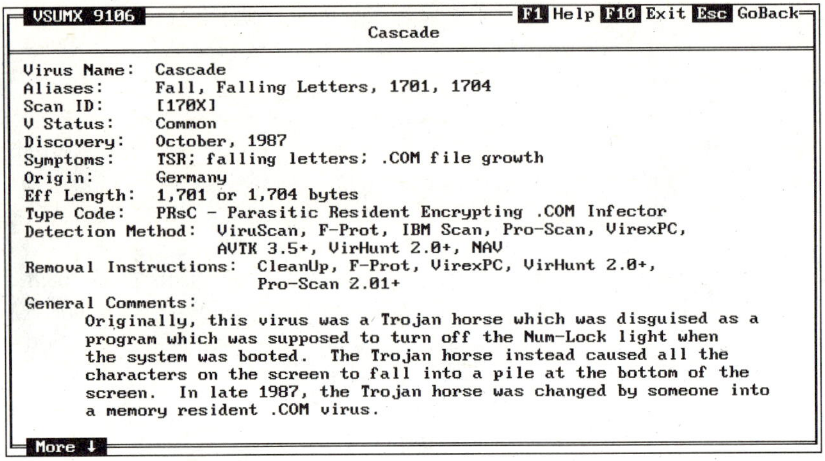

Figure 12.5 Information about the Cascade virus from HyperText VSUM

There are many other ways to search for virus listings. You can, for example, search for boot sector viruses only, you can search by country of origin, and you can search by the size of the virus itself.

The program is updated regularly, so new viruses can be added as they are discovered. For anyone interested in viruses, or for those, such as system administrators, who need to be up-to-the-minute about virus infections, this is a must-have program.

HyperText VSUM
Registration fee: $
Patricia M. Hoffman
3333 Bowers Ave., Suite 130
Santa Clara, CA 95054
(408) 988-3773

SCANTOOL

This menu-driven program simplifies the use of the McAfee antiviral programs ViruScan, Clean-Up, VCopy, and MDISK. From its main menu, you choose which of the programs to run. You also select from the many options the McAfee series uses. It greatly simplifies the use of the sometimes complex programs, as shown in Figure 12.6.

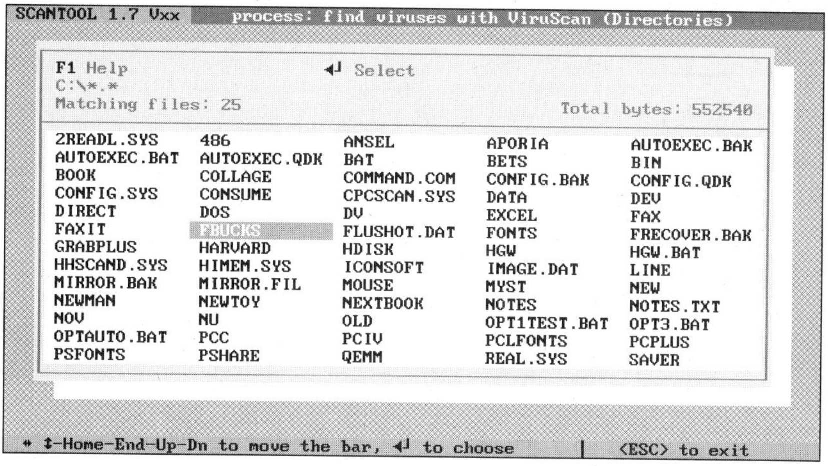

Figure 12.6 Choosing files to be scanned for viruses with SCANTOOL

SCANTOOL works with a mouse, allows you to use shortcut keys, and includes a built-in screen saver. Of course, you'll also have to get the ViruScan, Clean-Up, VCopy, and MDISK programs from McAfee to use this program.

SCANTOOL
Registration fee: 5.5 DM (money orders in Deutsche marks only)
Dirk Zender
Dudenhoferstr.64
6720 SPEYER
Germany
Phone: (0623) 98148

VCopy

VCopy uses an interesting tactic in the war against viruses. It's a replacement for the DOS COPY command. When you use VCopy to copy files, it searches your PC's memory for viruses, and then checks the boot sectors and partition tables of the source and destination disks. Finally, it checks the files you're copying. In this way, it makes sure that no infected files and viruses enter your system. If VCopy finds a virus, it reports the name of the virus and the name of the file that's been infected. You're then given the options of not copying the file, or instead going ahead and letting the file be copied.

There are a couple of things to keep in mind when using VCopy. It will slow down your copying by about 10 percent. And although you use the same syntax with VCopy as you do with the MS-DOS 3.3 COPY command, you can't use the COPY CON function.

> **VCopy**
> Registration fee: $
> McAfee Associates
> 4423 Cheeney St.
> Santa Clara, CA 94054
> (408) 988-3832

Virus Central

The McAfee series of antiviral programs is probably the most comprehensive set of tools you'll find to detect and clean up viruses. There's one problem with it, however—it's not particularly easy to use.

That's where Virus Central comes in. Like SCANTOOL, this program puts a pretty face on three of the major McAfee antiviral products, making them easier to use and customize. It gives you access to: ViruScan, NetScan, and Clean-Up, and it has an optional, built-in screen saver.

When you load the program, a menu will appear across the top of your screen. You can use a mouse or the arrow keys to move the cursor to the option you want. From here, you'll be able to set the program defaults, get information about viruses, exit to a DOS shell, and run ViruScan, NetScan, and Clean-Up. You can also execute certain functions by pressing the function keys.

You configure and run ViruScan and NetScan from the same option on the menu. That's because the programs are essentially the same. (NetScan is the version of ViruScan that allows you to scan network drives for viruses.) Virus Central will know which of the programs to use by the letter of the drive you tell it to scan.

When you choose to run ViruScan or NetScan from the menu, you'll be greeted with a submenu, seen in Figure 12.7. This submenu has 22 items on it, each of them an option for running the ViruScan or NetScan program. From here you can specify preferences, such as which drive and subdirectory you want to scan, whether you want to overwrite and delete infected files, whether you'd like a report generated of the program's findings, whether you want to scan for viruses presumed to be extinct, and which overlay extensions you need to check. When you've configured the program to run the way you want it to, you select the OK option, and the program will do the scan.

If your scan detects viruses, you run Clean-Up by choosing it from the main menu. (You can also configure the program to run Clean-Up automatically when ViruScan detects a virus.) The Clean-Up submenu includes options for the name of the virus or viruses to clean up, the drive and directory to look in, and whether to generate a report.

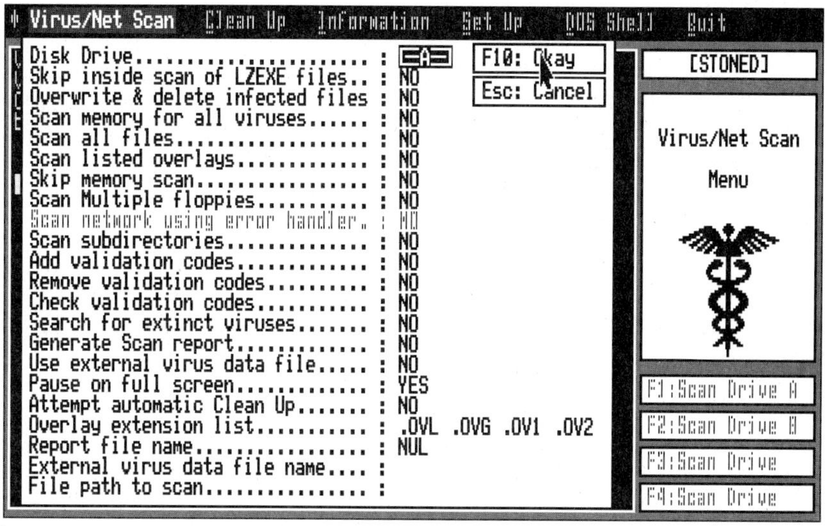

Figure 12.7 The ViruScan submenu

Another choice from the main menu gives brief descriptions of viruses. Choose from a list, and you'll be given information such as the virus name, its characteristics, and the damage it causes.

Note that Virus Central is only a shell for the McAfee programs. In order for it to work, the McAfee ViruScan, NetScan, and Clean-Up programs must be located in the same directory in which it resides.

Virus Central
Registration fee: $
Alejandro L. Abello
2937 Sherwood Dr.
San Carlos, CA 94070
(415) 369-1811

Virus Simulator

Using a virus-detection program requires a great leap of faith. There's no way for you to know whether the scanning program is working—you have to take the author's word for it. It would be nice if there were a way to tell whether the program works. Better yet, it would be nice if you could test each of the virus detection programs to see which worked the best. But the only way to do that would be to infect your PC with a virus—something you certainly don't want to do.

Actually, there is another way: Use the Virus Simulator. It generates files that have tell-tale signatures usually associated with specific viruses. The files it creates aren't actually viruses, of course. They simply mimic viruses by showing the viruses' unique signatures. When a virus-detection program comes across one of these files, it should identify it as a virus. You can test how well your virus scanner works by generating these false viruses and seeing whether your scanner can detect them.

To run the program, put the file VIRSIM.COM on a disk in your A drive. Then type **VIRSIM** and press Enter. First the program will test itself, and make sure it hasn't been infected with a virus. It will then ask you what types of simulated viruses it should create. It can create three kinds: those that infect COM and EXE files, those that infect the boot sector, and those that are memory resident. Choose the type you'd like created, and the program will generate files that will look like viruses to scanning programs. Figure 12.8 shows Virus Simulator creating files simulating viruses that infect COM and EXE files.

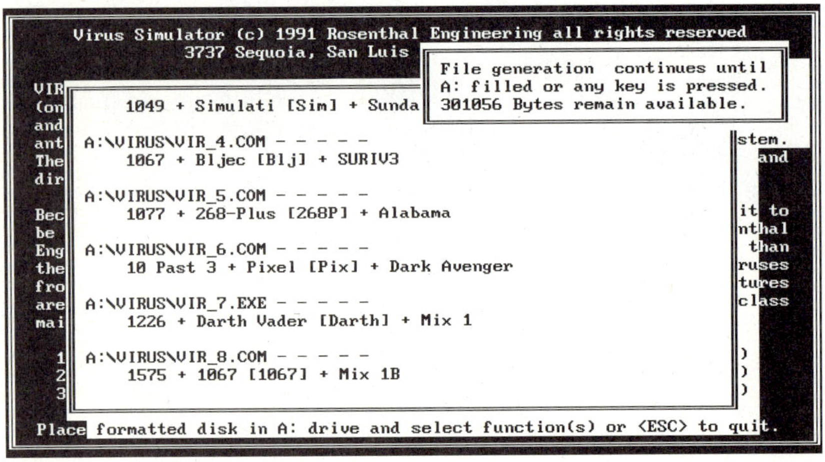

Figure 12.8 Virus Simulator creating simulated viruses

When you choose to create simulations of viruses that infect COM and EXE files, the program will randomly create them, and keep creating them until you press a key, or until your floppy disk is full. It will also create a text file that details which virus simulations it created, so you can check whether your virus-detection program uncovers the proper ones.

To test your virus-detection program, have it scan your A drive, and see what it finds. Or, you can copy the simulated-virus files to your C drive and use your virus-detection program to look for viruses there.

Devious network administrators might find a use for the program as well. If they've asked all users on the network to regularly check for viruses, they can make sure that people are in fact checking for them by creating a simulated virus and putting it into different network subdirectories.

The authors of Virus Simulator claim the program can simulate the signatures of every known virus. As new viruses are created and uncovered, simulations of them are added to the program.

Virus Simulator
Registration fee: $
Rosenthal Engineering
3737 Sequoia
San Luis Obispo, CA 93401

CHAPTER

13

Printer Programs and Utilities

General Printer Programs and Utilities

Envelope, Label, and Letterhead Print Programs

Font Utilities

POSSIBLY THE MOST UNDERUTILIZED COMPONENT OF YOUR COMPUTER setup is your printer. Sure, you print out documents and letters with it. You might even use it for creating graphics or newsletters. But there's much you haven't used your printer for, because you haven't known it could do the work.

For example, did you know you could use your laser or inkjet printer to create fully paginated booklets, with printing on both the front and back sides? 4Book (shipped with another program called 4Print) will let you do that. You can easily solve the most dreaded of PC problems—addressing envelopes—with a shareware utility called Grab Plus. And you can create oversized banners and all kinds of graphics with a program called PrintPartner.

There are far more shareware printer utilities available than commercial ones. You'll find one for just about any specific printing need you have. Included below are some of the best, to give you a taste of what's out there.

I've organized the chapter into three general categories. "General Printer Programs and Utilities" includes a variety of programs, such as 4Book and PrintPartner, that do many different kinds of printing tasks. "Envelope, Label, and Letterhead Print Programs" focuses on the best programs to accomplish those three jobs. And "Font Utilities" covers programs that will help you get the most out of type fonts, particularly if you have a laser printer.

You'll find something here to make your printer more powerful, whether you have an 9-pin dot-matrix printer or a Hewlett-Packard LaserJet with 4Mb of memory.

General Printer Programs and Utilities

Most of your printer's power is probably going to waste, because it's so hard to control. You'd be amazed at the tricks your printer can do for you, if you only knew how to tame it.

The following programs will soon have your printer jumping through hoops. You can make it print booklets for you with 4Book or BOOKLET. You can create banners with it using PrintPlus. And if you have a dot-matrix printer, you can make it do remarkable and marvelous things with Image-Print—things that you thought only a laser printer could accomplish.

There's more here as well, from general purpose programs to make all your printing easier to more specialized programs that will reduce the time your PC is tied up with printing tasks.

BOOKLET

BOOKLET will create booklet-sized ($5\frac{1}{2}$-by-$8\frac{1}{2}$-inch) documents using a Hewlett-Packard or compatible laser printer. It will print four columns of text per sheet of paper, in landscape mode—two columns on the left side and two on the right. In this way, you can fold the paper in half to create a booklet. You can also print on the back of the paper, to make double-sided booklets.

To use BOOKLET, you first use your word processor to create a formatted, single-column document. You then print that file to disk, rather than to a printer, and finally you use BOOKLET to print the file in booklet form.

Be aware that BOOKLET doesn't come with any fonts. In order for the program to work, your laser printer must have the fonts BOOKLET supports, either in cartridge form or as a soft font. Because the program is menu-driven, it's relatively easy to use.

BOOKLET
Registration fee: $
Sympathetic Software
9531 Telhan Dr.
Huntington Beach, CA 92646

DMP

How many hours do you think you've spent sitting at your PC's keyboard, waiting for a file to print? When you tell most programs to print a file, you can't use your PC while it's printing. With some applications, that can take a while. And things only get worse when you want to print multiple files.

DMP has a solution—*spool* the files you want to print. Spooling means that you take the file created by the printer and put it in memory or somewhere on disk. The printer then prints from that location, freeing up your PC so that you can use it while the printer churns away in the background. DMP will allow you to put files in a number of different places. You can spool them to your hard disk, a RAM disk, or to extended and expanded memory if you have any on your PC.

You can also use DMP to print a file to disk. Then at a later time, you can print from that disk file. This would be useful if you have a laptop and don't want to carry a printer along. You could print a file to disk on your laptop, and then print out that file when you get back to your office or home.

DMP takes up 16k as a TSR. (The files you'll print, however, will take up much more than that.) DMP works with both serial and parallel printers.

DMP
Registration fee: $
DMP Software
204 East 2nd Ave., Suite 610
San Mateo, CA 94401

4Print

If you have a Hewlett-Packard or compatible laser printer, you need 4Print—it's that simple. This remarkable utility will save you reams of paper, let you see up to four pages of a document at one time, and let you print oversized spreadsheets.

How does it do this? In several ways. First, it will print two columns of text in landscape mode on each side of a sheet of paper. That means each sheet of paper can hold the equivalent of four pages of text. It also includes a special condensed font that lets you print three columns of text on each side. If you regularly print out shareware documentation, 4Print is especially helpful, because you'll get six pages of documentation onto a single sheet. Figure 13.1 shows 4Print's README.DOC files printed three columns to a side in 4Print's condensed type.

Figure 13.1 Creating three columns of text on a page with 4Print

4PRINT 4.1 LAST-MINUTE NOTES AND INFORMATION
SHAREWARE VERSION
Last Updated August 1991
Korenthal Associates, Inc.

This file contains last-minute notes and instructions on installing and using 4Print 4.1, including notes on how to eliminate paper-shuffling on non-duplex printers, using 4Print with a DeskJet, and using the shareware fonts included with this package.

We welcome all disk vendors and BBS sysops who wish to distribute 4Print, and invite them to refer to VENDOR.DOC and SYSOP.DOC for complete information relating to them. Individuals who wish to share 4Print with their friends and colleagues, or to upload 4Print to their favorite BBS's, are also welcome; please see LICENSE.DOC for details. Sample descriptions of 4Print suitable for BBS file listings and vendor catalogs are available in DESCRIBE.DOC.

Information on registering 4Print and other KA products can be found in REGISTER.DOC and PRODUCTS.DOC.

Introduction:

4Print 4.1 is a paper-saving utility for HP LaserJets, DeskJets and compatibles. 4Print prints two or three fully readable pages of text sideways across the page, and by printing on both sides, it can yield four, six, or even more pages of text on each sheet!

4Print allows programmers to view four pages of source code at a time, writers to read four pages of text, and spreadsheet and database users to print wide reports all the way across the page. 4Print's reduced paper consumption means lower paper costs and less shelf space taken up for storing printouts, and it's also good for the ecology!

New with version 4.1 of 4Print is the companion utility 4Book, which makes it easy to produce handsome booklets. Other new features include printing 1-4 columns of text, variable number of lines per page, automatic line numbering, compression of excess blank lines and page breaks, intelligent word wrap, improved DeskJet and LaserJet-compatible support, reverse printing options to eliminate the need for paper-shuffling, and support for A4 paper. An optional Windows interface is also available; see REGISTER.DOC for details.

The User's Guide and Addendum:

The 4Print 4.1 documentation comes in two parts: the User's Guide (4PRINT.DOC), which covers all program features up through version 4.0, and the Addendum (ADDENDUM.DOC), which describes features new to version 4.1 and contains the 4Book User's Guide. The Addendum also covers topics such as printing on legal size paper, running 4Print under DESQview, using 4Print with the HP LaserJet IIISi, and additional trouble-shooting information.

Though 4Print and 4Book come preset for most common uses, both are rich with features (in other words, they've got a bad case of option-itis), and it's worth the time to at least glance through the User's Guide and Addendum to familiarize yourself with some of what these programs can do. That way, when you have some special application in the future, you'll get that nagging feeling that somehow 4Print can do what you want, and then you can go back and read the docs carefully.

Installation:

The installation process is slightly different depending on whether you've got the shareware version of 4Print as a self-extracting archive (with a .EXE extension) or in zipped form (.ZIP extension).

> If you received your 4Print shareware disk from a disk vendor or directly from KA, you should have a file named 4PR410.EXE. This is a self-extracting archive containing all of the shareware distribution files. To install 4Print, create a 4Print subdirectory and then extract all the files into that directory:

```
C>md \4print
C>a:4pr410 \4print
```

> Alternatively, if you downloaded 4Print from a BBS or CompuServe (or any of the other online services), you will have a file called 4PR410.ZIP, and you'll need PKUNZIP to extract the files. (If your copy of 4Print was compressed using one of the other file compression utilities, such as ARC or LHARC, for example, you'll need the extraction program that goes with that utility.) Install 4Print by creating a 4Print subdirectory and then extracting all the files into that directory:

```
C>md \4print
C>pkunzip 4pr410 \4print
```

Once you've uncompressed the archive, please check that none of the files are missing. The complete list of files can be found in the text file PACKING.LST.

To access 4Print from any drive or subdirectory on your computer, you need to add the 4Print directory to your DOS search path. Type "path" at the DOS prompt to see your current path, and then add 4Print to it:

```
C>path
PATH=C:\DOS33;C:\MYPROGS                (for example)
C>path c:\dos33;c:\myprogs;c:\4print
```

Tip for advanced users: You only need 4PRINT.EXE and 4PRINT.OVL to use 4Print. (The 4Book utility also requires 4BOOK.EXE; you'll probably also want 4BOOK.CFG and SAYINGS.TXT.) Instead of changing your path to include the 4Print subdirectory, you can simply copy these files to any subdirectory in your search path.

Quick Start:

Type the following at the DOS prompt:

```
C>4print
```

The program will provide several screens of information on how to use most of its options. You can use the <PgUp> and <PgDn> keys to page through the help screens, or press <Esc> to return to DOS.

The best thing to do first is to 4Print any ASCII file single sided to get a feel for the program. To print this file, for instance, type:

```
    C>4print readme.doc -s
or  C>4print readme.doc -dj -s    (if you are using a DeskJet)
```

Next, you might try double sided printing:

```
    C>4print readme.doc
or  C>4print readme.doc -d        (if you are using a IID or IIID)
or  C>4print readme.doc -dj       (if you are using a DeskJet)
```

Unless you are using a duplex printer (IID or IIID), 4Print will pause between passes and ask you to reinsert the paper in the paper tray (or manually if you include the "-m" switch) to print the reverse side.

4Print has many advanced formatting and paper handling features. For now, you might try three column, "maximum output" mode like this:

```
C>4print readme.doc -max     (add -d for duplex, -dj for DeskJet)
```

All documentation files, including PACKING.LST and all files ending with the .DOC extension, make likely candidates for 4Print. In fact, we recommend that the User's Guide, 4PRINT.DOC, be printed by typing the following:

```
C>4print 4print.doc -doc     (add -d for duplex, -dj for DeskJet)
```

4Book Quick Start:

To get started with 4Book, type the following at the DOS prompt:

```
C>4book
```

The program will provide several screens of information on how to use most of its options. You can use the <PgUp> and <PgDn> keys to page through the help screens, or press <Esc> to return to DOS.

To get a feel for what 4Book does, try creating a booklet using a small text file. To print this file, for instance, type:

```
    C>4book readme.doc
or  C>4book readme.doc -d         (if you are using a IID or IIID)
or  C>4book readme.doc -dj        (if you are using a DeskJet)
```

The program will pause after it scans the file, and prompt you to press "Y" to print the booklet. 4Book will then call 4Print with the name of the file and any options you've specified. Unless you have a duplex printer and have included the "-d" option on the command line, 4Print will pause after printing the front side and ask you to reinsert the paper in the paper tray to print the reverse side.

You can use 4Book to print the 4Print 4.1 Addendum, ADDENDUM.DOC, by typing the following:

```
C>4book addendum.doc -bn-    (add -d for duplex, -dj for DeskJet)
```

Reverse Printing Options:

(If you have a duplex printer such as the IID, IIID, or IIISi with the duplex option, this section does not apply to you. Use your printer's duplex capability for all double-sided printing by specifying the "-d" or "-ds" option in both 4Print and 4Book.)

4Print and 4Book now have advanced paper handling features which will allow you to obtain perfectly collated, double-sided printouts without manually shuffling any pages, even on non-duplex printers.

The new options are "-r" (reverse print back side) and "-rf" (reverse print front side). We have included a file called TESTPRIN.BAT on the 4Print distribution disk which will automatically determine the set of options appropriate to your needs. To run the batch file, simply make sure your printer is online and type TESTPRIN at the DOS prompt.

See "Advanced Paper Handling Features" in the 4Print Addendum for more information about using these options.

DeskJet Users:

4Print has special handling for the HP DeskJet, DeskJet Plus, and DeskJet 500. If you are using any of these printers, you *must* specify the "-dj" switch every time you run 4Print. Alternatively, you may put "SET 4PRINT=-DJ" (don't forget the dash after the equals sign) in your AUTOEXEC.BAT and omit the "-dj" switch from your subsequent 4Print runs.

By default, 4Print prints in the DeskJet's draft mode which is faster and uses less ink. If you wish to use the DeskJet's letter quality mode with 4Print, specify "-djl" instead of "-dj".

No special font is required to use 4Print with the DeskJet, but if you have the original model (not Plus or 500), your printer must be equipped with the optional landscape cartridge. In addition, the original model DeskJet does not accept landscape soft fonts, so you may not use the shareware fonts described below. Note that DeskJet Plus and 500 printers require a 128K or 256K RAM cartridge in order to use soft fonts.

Additional Fonts For Use With 4Print:

We have provided a collection of shareware soft fonts from Elfring Soft Fonts which you may find useful. To access these fonts, type this at the DOS prompt:

```
C>fonts#
```

The following files will be added to your 4Print directory:

```
GOO8OR17.PCL      Normal font / for all LaserJets
GOO6OR25.PCL      Tiny font   \ except the LaserJet+

GPO8OR17.PCL      Normal font /
GPO6OR25.PCL      Tiny font   \ for LaserJet+

GOO6OR17.DJL      Normal font /
GOO8OR25.DJL      Tiny font   \ for DeskJet+ and 500

ID1  (see below)
ID2  (see below)
PERM (see below)

REGFONTS.DOC      Shareware font registration information
```

Each of these fonts is a Letter Gothic, sans serif font. They also

README.DOC 8-20-91 4:10a Page 1 of 2

You can also use 4Print to print anything that can't fit on a normal page, such as extra-wide spreadsheets or program listings. 4Print will print them in landscape mode, so that they can fit on the paper.

4Print controls almost every aspect of the printing process. You can control the number of columns you want on each page, which tray the paper should be fed from, the number of lines per page, placement of page headers, and much more. It supports Hewlett-Packard laser printers and compatibles, as well as Hewlett-Packard DeskJets.

The program is command-line driven, so if you're doing complex printing jobs, the syntax can be a bit confusing. For basic printing work, however, it's straightforward. For example, to print the file MANYWORD.DOC onto the front and back of a sheet of paper, with three columns of text per side, you'd issue the following command:

```
4PRINT MANYWORD.DOC -MAX
```

The -MAX switch tells the program to put three columns of text per side.

4Print has a companion program, called 4Book, that is as innovative as 4Print. 4Book will let you create booklets using a laser printer. It takes a text file, rearranges the order in which pages are to be printed, and then prints them so that you can fold the pages in half to make a $5^1/_2$-by-$8^1/_2$-inch booklet.

You can customize the booklet in many ways. You can choose from different cover styles and different fonts for the booklet's name, as shown in Figure 13.2. You can also have it choose a quote from its predefined list, and change the quote every time you print out the book.

Figure 13.2
The front and back pages of a booklet created with 4Book

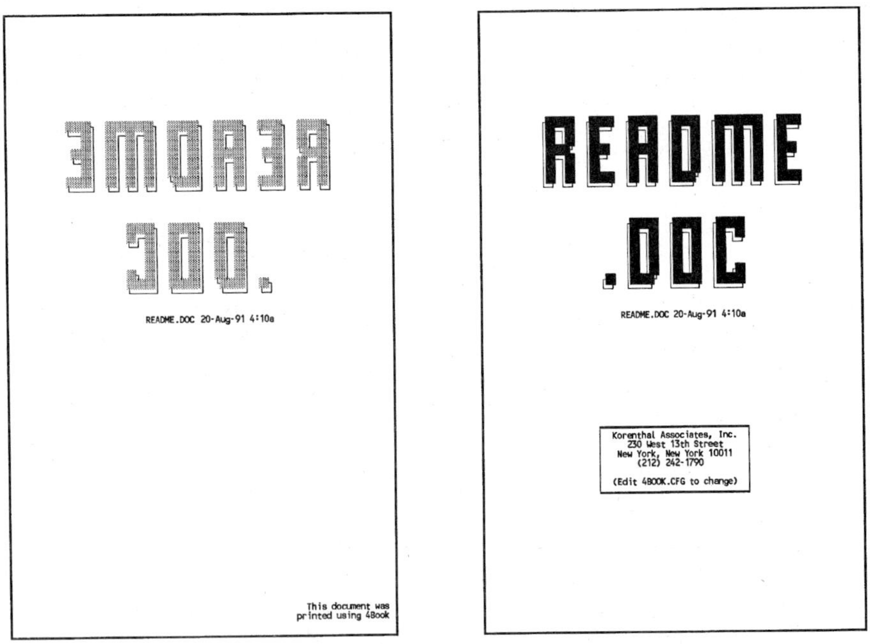

4Book comes with 4Print. (It requires 4Print in order to work, and you can't use it with any 4Print version before 4.0.)

4Print
Registration fee: $$
Korenthal Associates, Inc.
230 West 13th St.
New York, NY 10011
(212) 242-1790; (800) 527-7647 (orders)

4Shell

If you're a Windows user, don't feel left out of the 4Print and 4Book scene; there's a separate program called 4Shell that serves as a Windows-based front end to both programs. In fact, 4Shell makes using both those programs much easier, since it lets you have all their command-line switches within easy reach, as shown in Figure 13.3.

Figure 13.3
Using 4Shell to control printer output via 4Print

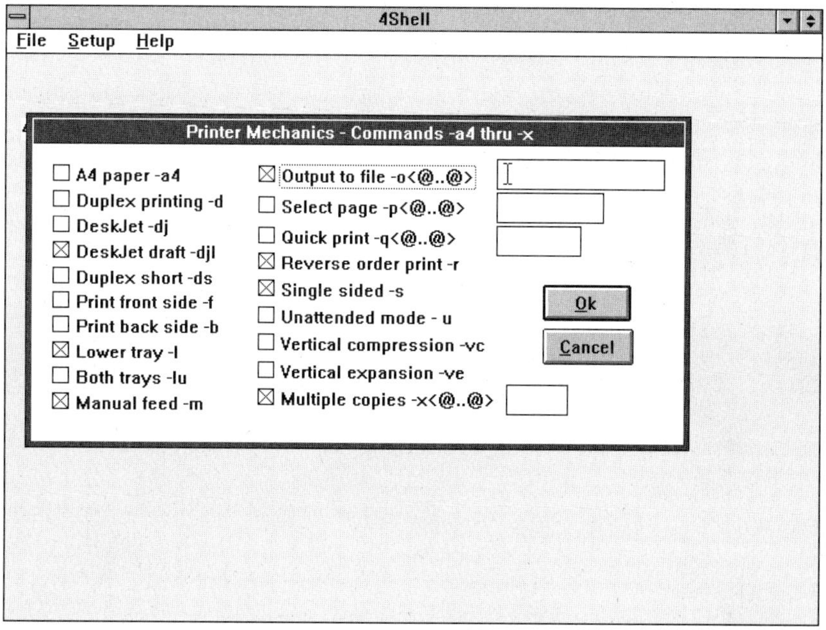

To use 4Shell, install it as you would any other Windows program. Then call it up, fill in several dialog boxes, and you'll be able to get at all the power of the programs without having to remember 4Print's numerous command-line switches. Of course, to use the program, you'll need both 4Print and 4Book, since 4Shell is only a front end to those programs.

4Shell
Registration fee: $
ZPAY Payroll Systems, Inc.
2526 69th Ave. South
St. Petersburg, FL 33712
(813) 866-8233

ImagePrint

Are you a dot-matrix printer owner suffering from laser envy? When you see friends and co-workers printing out pages full of sharp type with exotic, sizable fonts, do you wish that you could too?

You can, and you won't have to spend $800 or more for a laser printer. Instead, you can use ImagePrint. This helpful utility will let you output crisp text in a variety of fonts and sizes using your current dot-matrix printer, whether you have a 9-pin or a 24-pin printer.

With ImagePrint, you can select from five different levels of print quality, beginning with draft mode, the standard output for dot-matrix printers, and ending with high-quality, six-pass printing, in which the printhead passes across each line of type six times for crisp output. The program comes with 25 fonts from which you can choose, including oversized headline fonts.

ImagePrint can be run either from the command line or through the menu shown in Figure 13.4. If your requirements are simple, or if you become an ImagePrint expert, you'll want to use the command line. If you're only an occasional user, however, or if you have any kind of sophisticated printing you plan on doing, you'll be better off using the menu-driven version.

You can use ImagePrint to print a file you've already created with your word processor or text editor, or you can use ImagePrint's text editor to create a file to be printed. The text editor is linked to the main part of the program, so it's easy to change fonts and printing characteristics by moving into ImagePrint from the text editor.

You can preview your text on screen and make sure it's what you want before you send it to the printer. ImagePrint works with a wide range of dot-matrix printers, so the odds are it will work with yours.

ImagePrint
Registration fee: $$
IMAGE Computer Systems
P.O. Box 647
Avon, CT 06001
(203) 678-8771

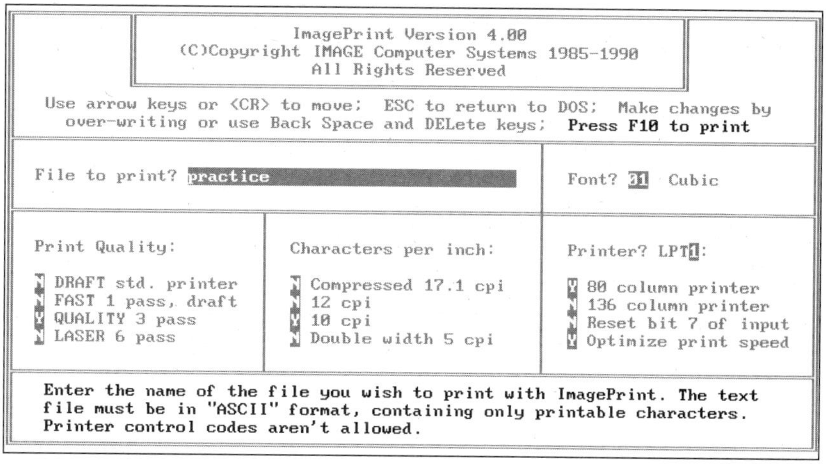

Figure 13.4
The menu-driven mode of ImagePrint

PrintGL

Plotters create great graphics, especially if you're using computer-aided drawing (CAD) or scientific programs. The de facto printer language for plotters is the HP-GL language. But what if you have a program that creates HP-GL output, and you don't have a plotter? You can get PrintGL.

This program will allow you to output HP-GL files on a variety of printers, including laser printers, PostScript printers, and a variety of 9- and 24-pin dot-matrix printers. You can run the program either from the command line or through a menu interface.

PrintGL
Registration fee: $$
Ravitz Software Inc.
P.O. Box 25068
Lexington, KY 40524

PrintPartner

This popular printing program regularly shows up on the monthly list of the ten best-selling shareware programs, and with good reason. It lets you use dot-matrix and laser printers to print banners (both normal- and oversized), signs, and calendars. The program is very easy to use: within minutes of loading it, you'll be able to create customized banners, signs, and calendars with little trouble. It's simple enough for children to use, yet flexible enough so that even veteran PC users won't be bored with it.

Banners can have a graphic at either end (but not both ends), and you can choose from a number of different fonts for their text. Signs can have two graphics, which can be placed anywhere on the sign. Each line of text on the sign can be of a different font and size. Calendars can be created for any year from 1980 to 2098. You can print the name of the month in any supported font.

The program is menu-driven, which is one of the reasons it's so simple to use. When you first load it (type **PP** and press Enter), you'll be presented with a main menu. From this menu you can choose to configure the software or to make a banner, sign, calendar, or picture. When you create a picture, you can use it in the banner, sign, or calendar you create.

When you choose a menu item to create a banner, for example, a sub-menu will come on screen. This menu lets you choose the various options available to you. From here, you'll choose the graphics, if any, to use, and the font in which to print your banner. You'll also use this menu to enter the text you want on the banner, select its height, and to save and print the banner.

To include a graphic, choose the menu item for selecting a graphic. Then scroll through the list of available graphics, shown in Figure 13.5. Press Enter, and the graphic you've highlighted will appear on your banner. You can choose from the many graphics shipped with the program, or you can create and use your own.

You can then continue through the banner-making menu, shown in Figure 13.6, choosing graphics, fonts, and typing in your banner text.

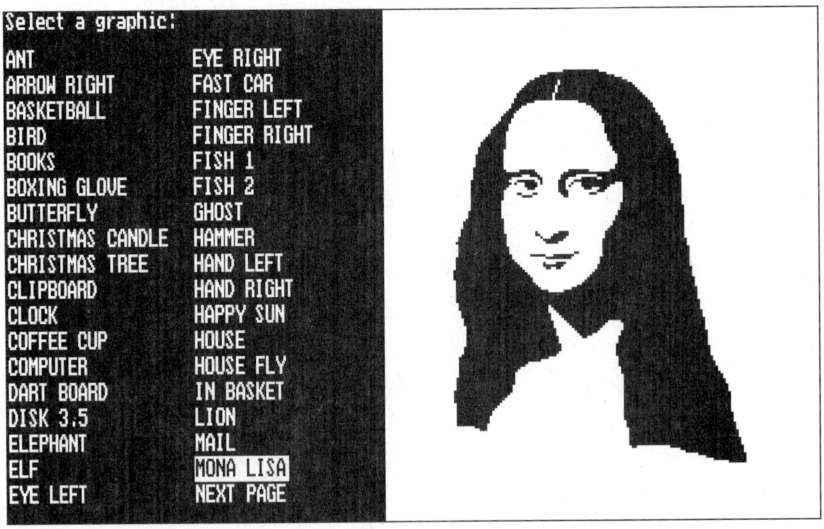

Figure 13.5
Choosing a graphic to be placed on a banner

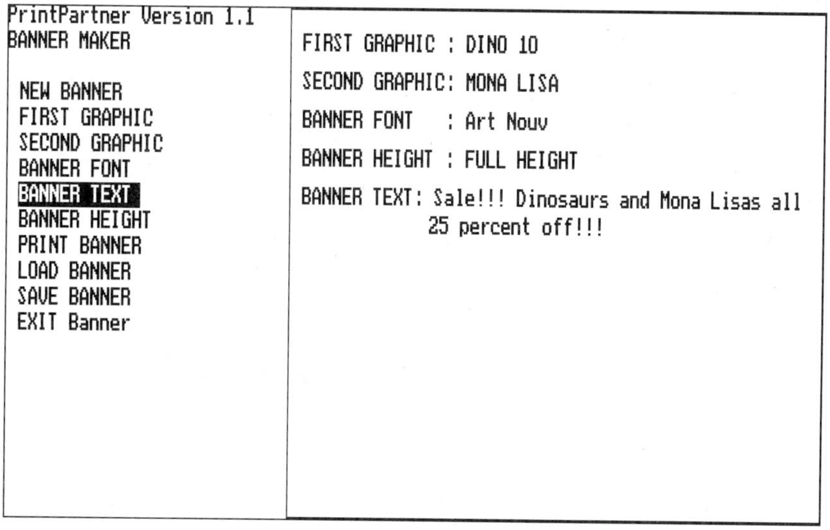

Figure 13.6 Filling out the banner-making menu

You can also create signs and calendars in a similar way, by choosing menu items and, when you're ready, printing your creation.

The program comes with many graphics and fonts, and supports a wide range of dot-matrix and laser printers. Once you have it, you'll be surprised at how many uses you can put it to.

PrintPartner
Registration fee: $
Robert Bequette
Acropolis Software
P.O. Box 5037
Fair Oaks, CA 95628
(916) 967-4791

PrintPlus

PrintPlus is a menu-driven program that lets you easily control the way files are printed. It has a number of options for printing, including the ability to strip out unwanted white space between lines of type. It also has a file viewer, so you can read a file before printing, as well as a helpful preview mode, which will tell you how many pages long any file will be when printed.

PrintPlus will also let you print to an ASCII file rather than to a printer. And you can limit printing to specified pages of a file.

The program is quite easy to use. When you load it, you'll be greeted by a screen that looks more like a hard-disk manager than a printer utility, as seen in Figure 13.7. The left side of the screen shows the files in your current directory. You use pull-down menus to perform a number of functions on those files.

Figure 13.7
PrintPlus's main screen

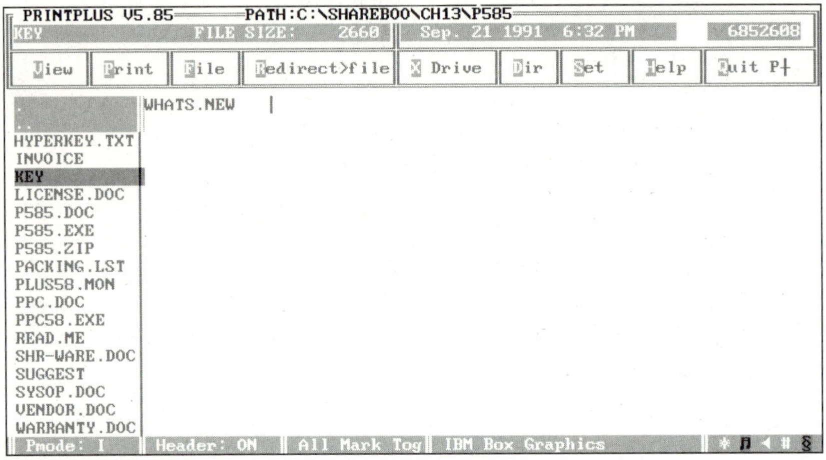

The Print menu, shown in Figure 13.8, is undoubtedly the most useful in the program. From there you can control many aspects of printing. For example, you can print in one of three different modes, including compressed mode. You can put page headers on your printed pages; control a number of mechanical features of your printer, such as lines per page; and set other printing options, such as whether to print line or page numbers. One of the most useful features of this part of the program is that its previewing abilities will tell you how long each file will take to print.

You can use PrintPlus as a basic hard-disk manager as well: You can view, copy, rename, and delete files, and can use it to easily navigate through your hard disk.

PrintPlus
Registration fee: $
Lambert Klein
P.O. Box 611
Wayne, MI 48184
(313) 326-1583

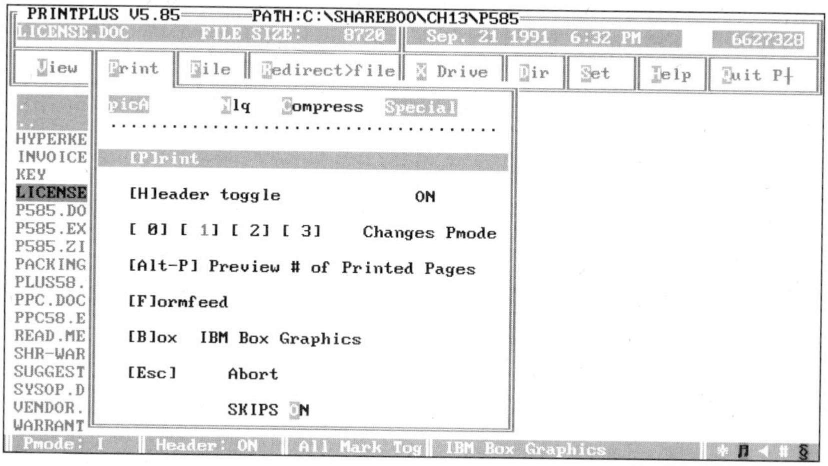

Figure 13.8
The Print menu of PrintPlus

Envelope, Label, and Letterhead Print Programs

More time and discussion is probably spent on figuring out ways to print envelopes than any other printing task. It should be so simple—and it's not. It should be obvious—and it's not. And it should be within everyone's reach—and it's not.

Using the following programs, you'll not only be able to print envelopes: you'll also be able to create your own customized letterhead, logo and all. And you'll be able to print out labels as well. Grab Plus handles the envelope chores; Laser Letterhead Plus does the letterhead; and MR. LABEL makes easy work out of your most complex label-printing chores.

Grab Plus

Every day many thousands of people labor over a task that should be mindless: printing envelopes with a PC. More man- and woman-power has been devoted to that mundane task than you can imagine. Most people just give up after a while, and print addresses by hand. How many times have you gotten a beautifully formatted letter, with fonts galore, only to see a hand-scrawled address on the envelope? Not very impressive, is it?

Grab Plus solves the problem in a snap. Whatever your word processor, whether you're a DOS user or a Windows maven, this nifty little utility will print envelopes for you with ease and style.

The DOS version runs as a 6k TSR. It waits quietly in memory, until you call it up by pressing Alt-Z. When you do so, a shaded rectangle appears on the screen. Move the rectangle over the address you want to print, and adjust its size with the F7, F8, F9, and F10 keys. When it's correctly placed and sized, press Alt-X, and your envelope will be printed. Figure 13.9 shows Grab Plus grabbing an address from a letter.

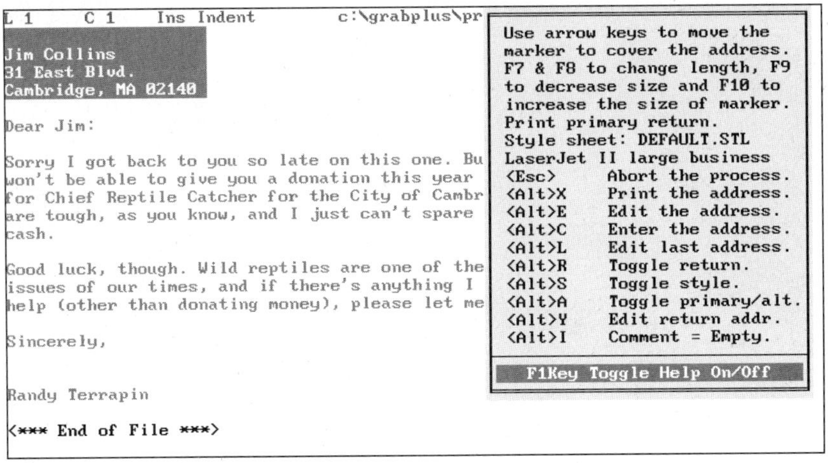

Figure 13.9
Grab Plus capturing an address to send to the printer

The program is quite customizable. You can print to a number of envelope sizes and types in various orientations. You can have your return address printed automatically if you wish, or add comments to the envelope (such as "Personal and Confidential"). And you can use it with downloadable fonts to add more zest to your envelopes. It should work with just about any printer you can name.

But Grab Plus is more than just an envelope printer; it's also a database. You can keep a database of names and addresses, and then easily print envelopes directly from the database. It's simple to search for names, addresses, and phone numbers, and just as easy to add a new listing. The database can be exported to an ASCII file, and Grab Plus can import certain ASCII file formats as well. Figure 13.10 shows an address being grabbed from the database.

Grab Plus also comes with a Windows version, called WinGRAB. It can work in one of two ways: either using the Windows Clipboard, or from within certain word processors directly. To use the Clipboard, highlight the address with your word processor, copy it to the Clipboard, switch to WinGRAB, paste the address, and then issue the Print command.

A much faster way is to run the program directly from within Word for Windows or Ami Pro. In Word for Windows, for example, it will install itself as an item on the Utilities menu. Highlight the address you want to print on an envelope, click on the Print WinGRAB Envelope option, and a

WinGRAB dialog box will appear. If you want to print the envelope with defaults you've chosen previously, tell the program to print. Otherwise, you can customize the envelope as shown in Figure 13.11.

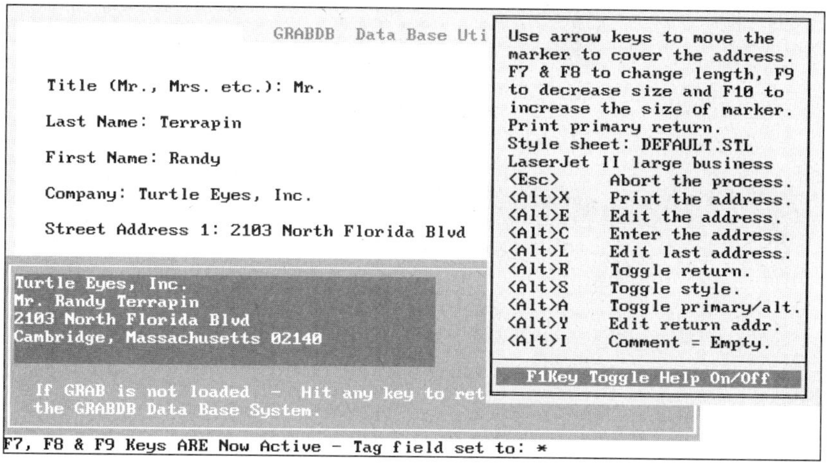

Figure 13.10
Using Grab Plus's database

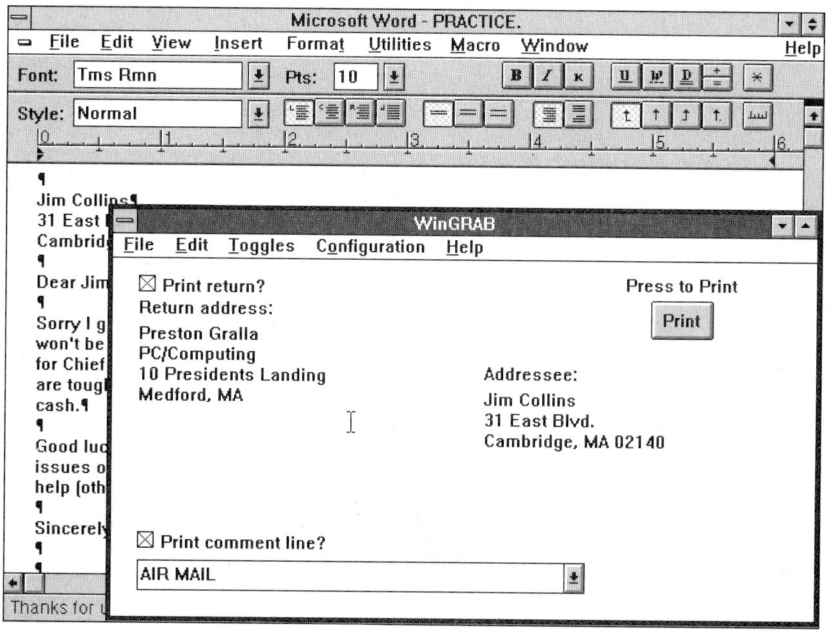

Figure 13.11
Customizing an envelope to be printed with WinGRAB

This program is quite simply the best envelope printer you'll find. If you're tired of hand-addressing envelopes, buy it. As a bonus, a label-printing program for laser printers, called LaserLabel, is included in the package.

Grab Plus
Registration fee: $$
ZPAY Payroll Systems, Inc.
2526 69th Ave. South
St. Petersburg, FL 33712
(813) 866-8233

Laser Letterhead Plus

Every time you take a sheet of preprinted letterhead, or a preprinted envelope, and slip it into your laser printer, you're wasting money. That's because it's expensive to have letterhead stationery made up—and your laser printer can do the job for free.

Laser Letterhead Plus will let you use the full power of your laser printer to create your own letterhead and envelopes. It's an extremely flexible program, and allows you to include graphic images on your letterhead. So you can, for example, include your company logo.

The program, despite its flexibility, is surprisingly easy to use. It's menu-driven, so you need not remember complex commands. Most of the work is done by filling out forms, which contain information such as the fonts you want to use, the placement of the text, the graphics files (in PCX format) to use, and the size of paper and type of envelope you'll be using. Once those options are set, you only need to push a button or two to print your stationery. You can even set up a number of different styles, and easily choose among them.

The program is not WYSIWYG—in other words, you won't be able to design your stationery on screen and see what it looks like. Instead, sit down with a pen and pencil and do a sketch of what you'd like the stationery to look like. With that in hand, use the program to recreate what you've drawn. You'll find that it should be able to print just about anything you can conceive.

How flexible is the program? It will, for example, let you place a "watermark" on your paper. These watermarks are light images or logos that are printed very faintly of a sheet of paper. They look something like the watermarks in expensive paper.

Note that if you want to include graphic images on your stationery, you might need extra memory in your laser printer. To print letterhead using soft fonts, you'll only need 512k, which is the minimum amount of memory most laser printers ship with. But if you want to include a PCX file, you'll need 1Mb of memory. If you want to include a watermark as well, you'll need 2Mb.

When you register the program, you get a number of bonuses. You'll get a free, text-based logo, a free PCX letterhead image, and a PCX watermark image, all based on your initials or business name, or on a PCX file you supply. You can also send along a graphics file in a format other than PCX, and it will be converted to PCX format. Or you can simply send an image that you'd like converted into a PCX file, and it will be done for you.

Laser Letterhead Plus
Registration fee: $
Consultant Pharmacist Services, Inc.
P.O. Box 47097
St. Petersburg, FL 33743
(813) 544-0212

MR. LABEL

Getting your printer to print addresses on envelopes is hard enough. An even more daunting task is to print out labels—either a single one or, worse yet, a whole group of them. You'll generally find it far easier and more efficient to bring out the dinosaur that's been hibernating in the closet—your old electric typewriter.

Get MR. LABEL, though, and you can kiss the typewriter goodbye. This program will allow you to print labels in a variety of configurations on any printer you can name. You can use in it one of two ways: either like a typewriter, to print out a single label; or to print an entire group of labels at a time.

You'll find a great deal of flexibility here. You can print up to nine labels across the page. You can include one of four borders around your labels. And you can use either soft fonts or cartridge fonts, so you can customize your labels' appearance.

The program will also allow you to address envelopes and print letterhead, price tags, labels for file folders, Rolodex cards, and more. It will print U.S. Postnet bar codes as well. You can link MR. LABEL to a database and print out labels from those records, or use its built-in text editor instead.

The program is menu-driven, and so is exceptionally simple to use. The bottom part of the screen is where you'll design or address the label. The top part of the screen contains the function-key menus. To perform a task, bring its menu to the screen by pressing the corresponding function key, and then follow the program's prompts. Figure 13.12 shows the label settings menu.

To type a new label, you simply press Enter at the main menu and start typing, as shown in Figure 13.13.

If you use common types of labels, you'll find that a good deal of your work has been done for you. Included are formats for a number of different label sizes. For example, the program includes preconfigured settings for all of Avery's laser labels. If you need to address labels, you'll find this program an enormous time saver.

MR. LABEL
Registration fee: $
DataWave Software
P.O. Box 42213
Mesa, AZ 85274
(602) 820-8041

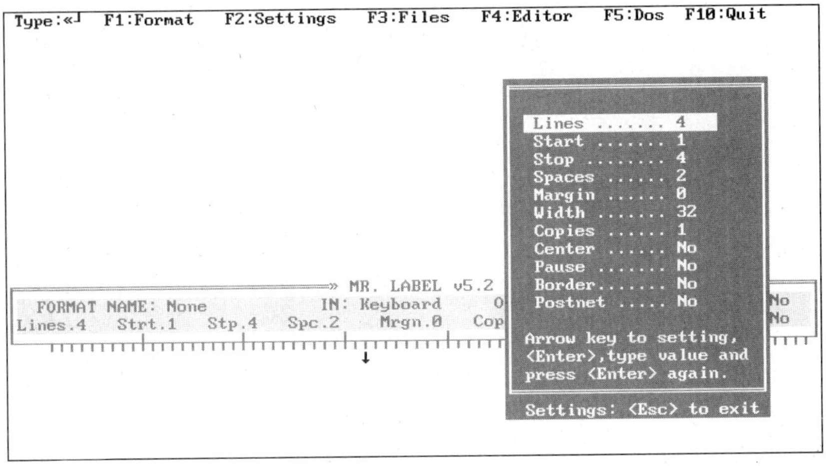

Figure 13.12 Using MR. LABEL's Settings menu

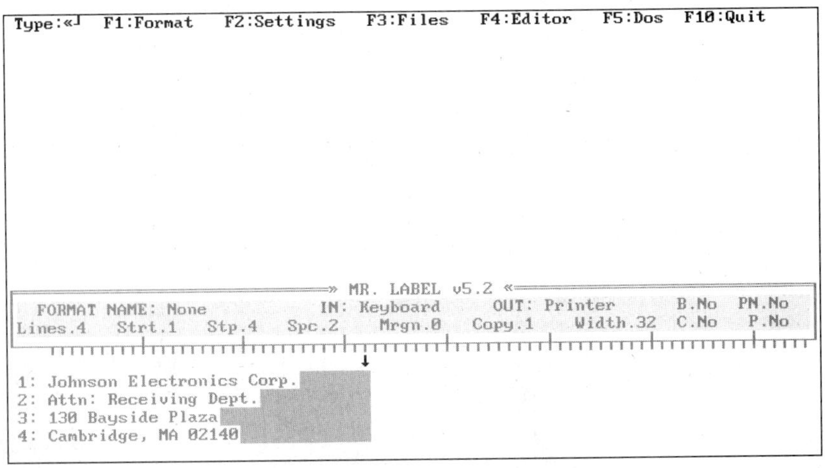

Figure 13.13 Creating the text for a new label

Font Utilities

If you own a laser printer, in particular one in, or compatible with, Hewlett-Packard's LaserJet series, you know how addictive fonts can be. Fonts to a printer are like memory is to a PC: You can never get enough.

The problem is that fonts are expensive. You can buy font cartridges to plug into your printer, but when you shop for them, be prepared for sticker shock: cartridges generally have a list price of several hundred dollars and up. You can also buy soft fonts for your printer—fonts that you download from your PC. These fonts are kept on your hard disk, and downloaded to your laser printer when they're needed. When fonts are downloaded, they exist in your LaserJet's memory, and so when the printer is turned off, they'll vanish. The next time you need to use them you'll have to download them again.

To use soft fonts you'll generally need the fonts themselves and some way to download them to the printer. Commercial fonts and downloading software are available, but there's also a vast amount of shareware available to do the task as well. On any bulletin board, you'll find hundreds, perhaps thousands, of different fonts—in fact, if you're not careful, you'll find yourself going font-crazy and filling your hard disk with them.

As you read about these programs, remember the correct definitions of the terms *font* and *typeface,* since these words are sometimes, incorrectly, used interchangeably. A typeface is a particular family of type: for example, Times Roman or Gill Sans. A font is a particular typeface, at a particular size, in a particular style or weight. So, for example, type that is 12-point Times Roman bold is one font; 12-point Times Roman italic is another, separate font; and plain vanilla Times Roman 12-point is yet another.

This section won't concentrate on individual fonts, since there are far too many available to cover. Instead, it covers some of the various font utilities to make using and managing your font library easier.

Elfring LaserJet Soft Font Package

This all-purpose starter kit from fontmeister Gary Elfring contains everything you need to build, use, and manage a font collection. It includes a font downloader, a collection of 21 soft fonts, and several helpful utilities.

The 21 fonts include several styles and sizes of Roman and Helvetica, as well as Century Legal, Broadway, Greek, Script, Flourish, a font of *dingbats* (special symbols), and a font of computer key tops.

The utility you'll use most in this package is called DOWNLOAD. With it, you'll be able to download your fonts from your hard disk (or floppy disk, if that's where you keep them) to your printer. It works with Hewlett-Packard LaserJets and compatibles, and with Hewlett-Packard DeskJets.

DOWNLOAD lets you send individual fonts or groups of fonts to the printer at one time. The fonts are sent through the parallel port (LPT) connected to the printer. You can send through either LPT1, LPT2, or LPT3. (The default is LPT1.) For example, to send a Broadway 18-point soft font named BW180RPN.USP to your LaserJet, which is attached to LPT2, you'd type

```
DOWNLOAD BW18ØRPN.USP LPT2:
```

The font would then be in your LaserJet, available for use.

One of the problems with any font downloader is that you need to know the name of the font in order to download it. You may remember that you have a particular font—12-point Century Legal, for example—but you probably won't remember its name: CE120RPN.USP. Or you may have such a large font collection that you don't even know what fonts you have anymore. Or, possibly, you notice a number of font names on your hard disk, and you don't know what they look like.

There's a utility in this package to help you with all that: DISPFONT. DISPFONT will print out a catalog of your fonts; you can also tell it to print a sample sheet for each font. The sample sheet has four sections. One section gives the file name of the soft font, the name of the typeface, its size and style (bold, italic, and so on), and other information. Another section shows you the entire character set of the font. A third section shows several lines of type printed with the font. The final section shows you a "map" of the font—every character in the font, next to its corresponding keyboard character or the decimal code that will select it. Figure 13.14 shows a sample page for an 18-point Broadway normal font.

Another utility in the package, called FONTINFO, will give you technical information about any font you have on disk. Type **FONTINFO** followed by the font name, and the program will give you the characteristics of the font, including its name, height, size, style, and orientation (landscape or portrait), as well as other technical details. It will also let you know whether the font is for a LaserJet or DeskJet printer.

The package also includes printer drivers for WordPerfect, Microsoft Word, and Microsoft Works. Also included are text files describing how to use the fonts with Ventura and PageMaker desktop publishing software and with Windows 3.0.

A full collection of soft fonts and other font utilities is available from Elfring Soft Fonts as well.

Elfring LaserJet Soft Font Package
Registration fee: $
Elfring Soft Fonts
P.O. Box 61
Wasco, IL 60183
(708) 377-3520

Figure 13.14 A DISPFONT font sample sheet

```
File: bw180rpn.usp, Broadway: normal 18 pts, portrait
```

abcdefghijklmnopqrstuvwxyz |[]{};:'"
ABCDEFGHIJKLMNOPQRSTUVWXYZ
0123456789`~!@#$%^&*()-_=+\,.<>/?

The quick brown fox jumped over the lazy dog. Register shareware!

33=!	34="	35=#	36=$	37=%	38=&	39='	40=(	41=)
42=*	43=+	44=,	45=-	46=.	47=/	48=0	49=1	50=2
51=3	52=4	53=5	54=6	55=7	56=8	57=9	58=:	59=;
60=<	61==	62=>	63=?	64=@	65=A	66=B	67=C	68=D
69=E	70=F	71=G	72=H	73=I	74=J	75=K	76=L	77=M
78=N	79=O	80=P	81=Q	82=R	83=S	84=T	85=U	86=V
87=W	88=X	89=Y	90=Z	91=[	92=\	93=]	94=^	95=_
96=`	97=a	98=b	99=c	100=d	101=e	102=f	103=g	104=h
105=i	106=j	107=k	108=l	109=m	110=n	111=o	112=p	113=q
114=r	115=s	116=t	117=u	118=v	119=w	120=x	121=y	122=z
123={	124=|	125=}	126=~					

FONTVIEW

Wouldn't it be nice to have an idea of what a particular HP LaserJet soft font would look like before you actually used it? It would also be helpful if you didn't have to print out the font first. What if you could instead view the characters on screen?

That's what FONTVIEW will do for you. Type **FONTVIEW** and the file name of the font you wish to view, and the program will display on screen, individually, each character that makes up the font, as seen in Figure 13.15. You can scroll through the entire character set, pressing a key when you want to view the next character; you can have the program automatically show you each character for a predetermined number of seconds; or you can ask to see specific characters only.

The program will also give you a great deal of technical detail about the font: its size and characteristics, precise measurements, vertical placement on the line, and much more.

FONTVIEW works only with EGA or higher-resolution graphics cards and monitors. Included with it is a program called FONTCLEAN, which cleans up some shareware fonts so that they can be easily used with font downloading and viewing utilities.

> **FONTVIEW**
> Registration fee: $
> S.H. Moody & Associates, Inc.
> 1810 Fair Oaks Ave.
> South Pasadena, CA 91030

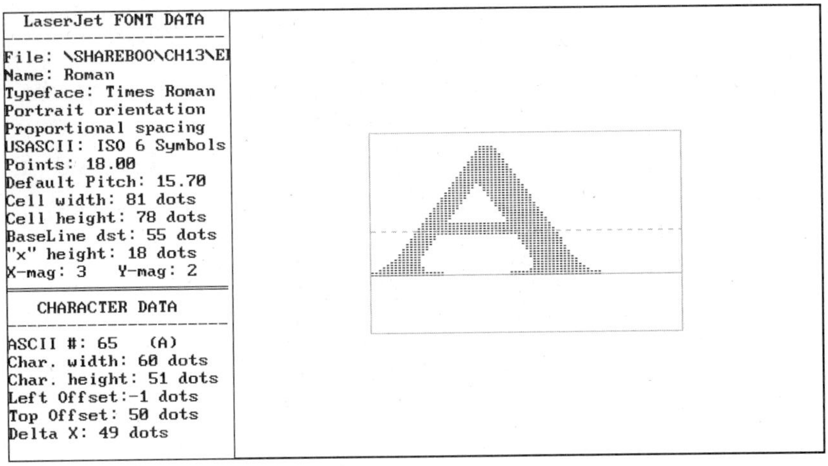

Figure 13.15 FONTVIEW displaying an 18-point bold Times Roman font

TSR Download

This exceptional utility from Elfring Soft Fonts is the best font downloader you'll find in the world of shareware. It can run as a TSR or from the command line. Using it as a TSR, however, is far more powerful, because you have access to your fonts and can control your printer even from within an application such as a word processor.

Unlike the Elfring DOWNLOAD font utility (see "Elfring LaserJet Soft Font Package," above), this program has prompts, menus, and help screens, so it's quite easy to use. Just press Ctrl-Alt-D, and TSR Download pops up over the program you're running. You'll then be able to download and manage your fonts.

After you pop up the program, downloading fonts is quite easy. A list of fonts appears in a window. One by one, move your cursor to the fonts you want downloaded and press Enter. Once you've marked all the fonts you want downloaded, type **D** or press F10, and they'll be downloaded to your printer.

If you have a long list of fonts and don't want to have to scroll through all of them for the one you want, you can use a built-in searching capability to quickly find the font you need.

TSR Download also lets you control your printer in a variety of ways by sending form feeds, telling your printer which of its internal font sizes should be used, sending disk files to the printer, and more.

If you use a great many fonts, you'll soon find that they take up a great deal of disk space—in fact, they can quickly consume an entire hard disk. TSR download has a solution for that. It includes a font compression program that will reduce the amount of disk space your fonts take up. When you tell it to download a particular font, TSR Download will decompress the font as it's sent to your printer.

The program will also let you know when your printer's memory is too full to handle more downloaded fonts, and can show you a list of all the fonts you've already downloaded to your printer.

When TSR Download is configured to swap to a hard disk, a RAM disk, or EMS memory, it takes up only 7k of memory. The program can work with Windows 3.0 as well as DOS.

TSR Download
Registration fee: $$
Elfring Soft Fonts
P.O. Box 61
Wasco, IL 60183
(708) 377-3520

REFONT

If you have a Macintosh computer as well as a PC, you've undoubtedly wished you could use your Mac's excellent font collection on your PC—and you've probably thought you couldn't. In fact, however, you can. If you use Windows 3.0 and the Adobe Type Manager (ATM), REFONT will allow you to use Mac Type 1 fonts on a PC. It's exceptionally easy to use. Type **REFONT**, tell it the name of the font you want converted, tell it what you want to call the converted font, and you're done. It's quick, it's easy, and it works.

REFONT
Registration fee: $
Acute Systems
P.O. Box 37
Algonquin, IL 60102

CHAPTER

14

Educational and Entertainment Programs

Non-Windows Programs

Windows Programs

COMPUTER GAMES HAVE BEEN WITH US FROM BEFORE THE DAYS OF the PC revolution. The earliest hackers used minicomputers to create games which they'd play for hours on end, deep into the night, fueled by cola and Chinese takeout food. More often than not, these games were outer space war games.

When the PC came along, games multiplied. Space war games and Pong, a game in which two players knocked a square ball across the screen with paddles, were early favorites.

There's always been a great number of shareware games. In the earliest days of the PC, however, these games were rather crude, and their graphics rudimentary at best—and often nonexistent. Sometimes the cursor keys couldn't control motion; you had to use letter keys instead. As often as not, the spacebar would fire a missile, usually at an incoming alien.

Recently, however, shareware games have grown up. Some of them, such as Commander Keen, rival anything the commercial world has to offer, and have a Nintendo-like feel. Others, such as Mines, offer a more intellectual challenge. You'll find shoot-em-ups, text adventure games, games of logic, games based on non-PC games (chess and Monopoly, for example), and far more. In fact, you could fill many large books with listings of all the shareware computer games available. A few of the best are listed here, to give you a taste of what's available.

There's more to this chapter than just games, however. The PC is a great educational tool—partly because it blurs the line between work and play. Consequently, some of the programs here could be seen as educational, though they're all fun. Others are entertaining without being either educational or competitive.

The chapter is divided into two sections. The first covers programs for standard DOS use. The second part covers Windows programs only. That environment is drawing an increasing number of games writers, and so merits a section all its own.

Non-Windows Programs

Whether you like space wars, missile attacks, logic games, or the PC equivalent of board games, you'll find a non-Windows shareware game to your liking. Games for standard DOS use are getting remarkably sophisticated these days. Some, such as Moraff's Elite Game Series, support Super VGA resolutions, for example. And the makers of the arcade game Commander Keen are developing games that will only run on 386 PCs and VGA monitors. That's not to say you need that kind of system to play games. Numerous games, such as PC-Monopoly, require only modest systems.

For the most part, the programs here are intended for adults. But I did include two of the hundreds of shareware programs available for children: Animated Memory Game and EGA Coloring Book.

The programs listed below comprise a survey of the kind of games you're likely to find on bulletin boards and from disk vendors. Check them out, and then look around—there are countless others available to entertain you.

Animated Memory Game

This game is a good way to test and improve your child's memory. It's like the traditional game of Memory played with cards and boards, except that here there's the added benefit of animation to engage your child's attention.

Playing the game is simple. There are a number of tiles on the screen, and beneath each tile is a picture. The child uses the mouse or keyboard to click first on one tile, revealing its picture, then on another, to try to match them. If there is no match, the tiles cover the pictures again, and the child can try again. If there is a match, the pictures hidden beneath the tiles become animated. There are differing levels of difficulty, so that even adults can be challenged.

To test the game, I turned to my in-house expert, my six-year-old daughter, Mia. Her report: "Kids who are good at thinking would like this game. The moving balloons were the best."

The author of this game has a number of other animated educational games, including the Animated Alphabet, Animated Shapes, Animated Mother Goose, and Animated Math.

Animated Memory Game
Registration fee: $
Tom Guthery IV
Rt. 1, Box 601
Del Valle, TX 78617

BassTour

Let me be straight about this: I hate fishing. I hate baiting hooks with worms, waiting around while the fish decide whether to bite, landing fish, and taking the hooks out of their mouths. Cleaning them has never been a favorite occupation, either.

There is an enjoyable way to fish, however. When I get the urge to test my mettle against the denizens of the deep, I play BassTour, a simulation of a bass-fishing tournament. First you rig a boat for fishing and choose any one of half a dozen lakes; then you're ready to go. The object of the game is to catch the five largest bass that you can in six hours.

The game is surprisingly realistic. You decide what kind of rod to fish with and the type of bait to pack. You'll also have to watch how much gas your boat uses while playing. The graphics are lifelike, too, as you can see in Figure 14.1.

Figure 14.1
A view of Crystal Lake in BassTour

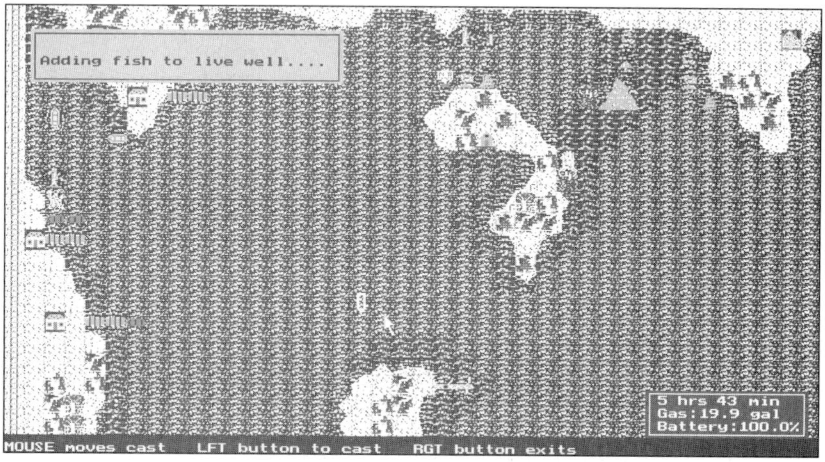

While you're fishing, keep an eye out for Lulu, a gargantuan bass hidden in every lake. If you catch her, you get to print out a certificate commemorating the event.

This game has developed such a large and devoted following that there are a number of add-ins for it. Another author, Nels Anderson, sells a program called BassMap that allows you to create your own lakes to fish in. You'll also find a lot of lakes created with that program on bulletin boards, so that you can download and fish in them.

BassTour
Registration fee: $
Richard Olsen
68 Hartwell Ave.
Littleton, MA 01460

BassMap
Registration fee: $
Nels Anderson
92 Bishop Dr.
Framingham, MA 01701

Commander Keen

If your idea of a shareware game is a simple-minded monochrome shoot-em-up in crude CGA resolution, you'll be stunned by what you find in Commander Keen. This game works only with EGA-level graphics and above, and features crisp animation and speedy controls. It's absolutely addictive: Make sure you load it at the end of the day, because work is over for the day, if not the week, once you load this program.

Commander Keen is very much in the arcade tradition, and will remind you of Nintendo games, such as Super Mario Bros. Like those games, there are a number of different versions, or *episodes*, of Commander Keen. All the episodes share the same high-energy action, and the idea behind them is similar: You have to go through a series of challenges to reach your final goal. Using a joystick or the keyboard, you run, jump, leap, use a stun gun, and do anything you can to avoid the aliens while pursuing your mission. Sound effects, of course, add to the pleasure of destruction. They're witty, playful, entertaining games that you won't want to stop playing.

The first episode is Invasion of the Vorticons. Billy Blaze, an eight-year-old genius, builds an interstellar starship in his backyard out of odds and ends, including old joysticks, a car battery, rubber cement, and plastic tubing. He then blasts off to Mars as soon as his baby-sitter falls asleep. The game begins on Mars, where the Martians have stolen vital parts of Blaze's spaceship and hidden them in various Martian cities. Billy has to find them, put his ship back together, and get off the planet to repel a Vorticon invasion of Earth, fighting off robots and beasties along the way. Worse yet, he has to do it all before his parents get home!

In Episode Two, Billy has blasted off from Mars to find the Vorticon mothership hovering above Earth, ready to destroy it. Billy has to sneak into the ship and neutralize it before Earth is destroyed. In Episode Three, he travels to the planet Vorticon VI, where the entire population of the planet awaits him, bent on his destruction.

Only Episode One is available as shareware. Episodes Two and Three can only be purchased commercially, from Apogee Software; they're not available as shareware. Apogee has a number of other top-notch games as well. These include Duke Nukem (see below) and the KROZ series, in which you maneuver through a series of mazes, avoiding bad guys along the way. By the early part of 1992, the company will also have released its first game for 386 machines or better with VGA graphics cards. It will be a sci-fi flight game, with fully bit-mapped, 3-D backgrounds instead of the polygon-type backgrounds found in many flight games.

Commander Keen
Registration fee: $ (all three for the price of two)
Apogee Software Productions
P.O. Box 476389
Garland, TX 75047
(214) 278-5655; (800) 852-5659 (orders)

CURSES!

You plague-ridden pond scum! You deliriously unlikable, enormous excuse for a wimp! You're suffering from bulbous soul rot, you and all your crudely prudish, impotently slobbering shabby swindlers!

Those are just a smattering of the insults you can create with this shockingly uncontrollable, internally repetitive, amazingly egomaniacal... sorry, that was the program talking again. Anyway, use this program to create the most creative, off-the-wall insults imaginable. Just type **CURSES** at the command line, press Enter, and you're ready for lists and lists of the most bizarre insults you'll ever come across.

The program doesn't stop at creating insults. It will also generate compliments as well. Need to curry favor with your boss? Call him or her a "highly-thought-of miracle." Courting someone? Call him or her a "noticeably long-lasting kind dream." Or if you want to be gender-specific, call her a "miraculous woman," or him a "significant boy."

For either compliments or insults, you can add new words to a master list, take away old ones, and have the program create new terms at random.

CURSES!
Registration fee: $
Rosemary West
R.K. West Consulting
P.O. Box 8059
Mission Hills, CA 91346

Duke Nukem

Duke Nukem is a macho kind of guy. How can you tell? Well, just look at the name of the first Duke Nukem episode: Shrapnel City. It says it all.

But Duke has to be macho. It's 1997, and Doctor Proton (née Blunderwitz) has created a techbot army and conquered Earth's largest city. Proton used to be a nice guy, but a horrible radiation accident changed all that. Now he wants to conquer the world, and taking over Earth's largest city is only the first step.

Only one person stands between Proton and his evil aim—Duke Nukem, a heavily muscled commando hired by the CIA to waste Proton. Duke is dropped onto a skyscraper in the city, and has to find his way to the underground lair of Dr. Proton. Using just a pistol, an enormous set of muscles, and a can-do attitude, our fearless Duke must battle techbots, nuclear waste, and other nasty things in his search.

Like Commander Keen, this is a top-notch arcade game. The action is fast and the animation's superb. It's less playful than Commander Keen, but for those who like Rambo-style shoot-em-ups, it's top of the line.

In Episode Two, you travel to the moon in pursuit of Dr. Proton, to make sure he doesn't invade the earth. In Episode Three, you travel to the future for similar reasons.

The registration policy for Duke Nukem is the same as for Commander Keen—only the first episode is available as shareware. The other episodes can be purchased commercially from Apogee Software.

Duke Nukem
Registration fee: $ (all three for the price of two)
Scott Miller
Apogee Software Productions
P.O. Box 476389
Garland, TX 75043
(214) 278-5655; (800) 852-5659 (orders)

EGA Coloring Book

If you have a child over the age of three, and you want to introduce him or her to the computer with a really enjoyable program, you need EGA Coloring Book. As the name implies, it's a coloring book. It's fun, it's colorful, and it's exceptionally easy to use. Your kids will learn basic computer skills, such as using the mouse and following menus, while they're having fun.

The program comes with a number of pictures. Your child calls the picture onto the screen, and then uses the mouse to color the picture. Coloring is quite simple; with the picture on the screen, click the right mouse button to display the color palette. There are over 500 different colors and patterns to choose from. Then move the mouse pointer, which is in the shape of a crayon, over to the color desired, and click the left mouse button. Then move the crayon where the color should go, and click the left button again. The color is automatically filled in. Figure 14.2 shows a picture that has been colored in with EGA Coloring Book—in black and white. Naturally, the original picture was in vivid color.

Figure 14.2
A picture colored in with EGA Coloring Book

I again asked my expert tester and games reviewer, my six-year-old daughter, Mia, to check out this program. Here's what she had to say: "It's better than coloring with a crayon because when you color with a crayon you're using your hand and you have to color hard. But when you're coloring on a computer, all you have to do is press a button and then it puts in that color. That's what I like about it. And the colors are good."

As the name says, you'll need an EGA monitor to run the program. You'll also need to have a mouse.

EGA Coloring Book
Registration fee: $
Kinderware, Inc.
P.O. Box 1068
North Bend, OH 45052
(513) 941-7295

EGA Trek

The grandaddy of all computer games is Star Trek, named for the ever-popular, multigenerational TV show. Variations of it have been around since the early 1970s, when they ran on minicomputers and mainframes. When PCs made their appearance, Star Trek began voyaging with them as well. The author of this version has been hooked on the game since 1974, and has written different versions for a number of different computers.

The game follows the conventions of the original TV show. You command the U.S.S. Enterprise, a battle-ready starship with 430 officers and crew members. The Federation is at war with the Klingon Empire following the collapse of the Organian Peace Treaty of 3199.5, and a Klingon invasion fleet is on its way. Your mission: Make safe a 64-quadrant section of the galaxy, and do it fast, by destroying marauding Klingon vessels.

Be forewarned that this game is much more an intellectual exercise than a starblaster's delight. You won't find flashy special effects, exploding missiles, and the like; your hand-eye coordination won't be tested. Instead, you'll sit at your command center (pictured in Figure 14.3), controlling every aspect of the Enterprise's operations. You don't use a joystick or a mouse; you issue commands from the keyboard instead, such as **M** for move.

Figure 14.3
The U.S.S. Enterprise's command center

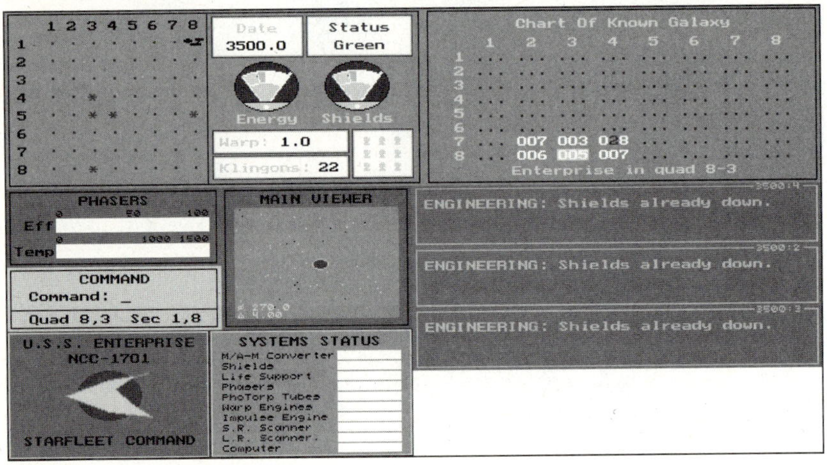

You tell the ship where to go; shift energy among its various systems; ask that repairs be made; fire phasers, experimental death rays, and torpedoes; decide on the speed of your flight; and put the ship in orbit around planets. If things get really out of hand, you can even order the ship to self-destruct.

Hard-core Trekkers will be delighted. Those who favor outer space shoot-em-ups won't. Note that this version of the game features EGA graphics, so you'll need at least an EGA card to run it.

EGA Trek
Registration fee: $
Nels Anderson
92 Bishop Dr.
Framingham, MA 01701

Mines

You'll find this a thoroughly addicting game of logic. On the surface, it's simple: Your screen is a grid. Hidden under each square may, or may not, be a landmine. Your goal is to make it from the upper-left corner of the grid to the lower-right corner without being blown to bits.

You move with the Home, PgUp, PgDn, and arrow keys. When you move to a new space, you're told how many mines touch that space, but not in which direction those mines lie. Based on that, you have to wend your way through the hidden mine field.

To make life more complicated, you can choose to play with a grid with mines only, mines and normal walls, mines and metal walls, or mines and a mixture of normal and metal walls. Normal walls merely impede your progress as you make your way through the minefield, and can easily be stepped around. Metal walls, however, are a more serious problem. When you move next to them, your mine detector doesn't work, so you won't be told whether you're next to a mine or not.

This game proves that the best games are often the simplest, and that the games that engage us the longest are based more on logic than reflexes.

Mines
Registration fee: None
Available from Public Brand Software.

Missile

There's nothing fancy here—just an old-fashioned defense against a missile attack. You have a city to defend, using your antimissile missiles, which you control with a mouse. Missiles rain down from the sky, and you have to keep as many buildings as you can standing. Make sure to defend your radar center, because once it goes, it's more difficult to control your weaponry—you'll feel like a fish in a barrel. The game is over quickly, so if you need a short break from work, it's ideal.

Missile
Registration fee: $
William Soleau
163 Amsterdam Ave., Suite 213
New York, NY 10023

Moraff's Elite Game Series

This excellent series of games has something for just about every type of game player. Whether you like role-playing adventure games, games that test your reflexes, gambling games, math games, or logic games, you'll find something here for you.

The Elite Game Series is made up of four games, all of which are designed to run on Super VGA monitors, a rarity in the game world, commercial or otherwise. They can also run on normal VGA monitors, EGA monitors, and monitors that support Hercules graphics.

Moraff's World is a Dungeons and Dragons type of game. There's a 16-level dungeon through which you travel, making your way around obstacles and fighting dragons and monsters along the way. There are also spells to beware of, as well as spells you can cast, and much more. For those who revel in this type of fantasy world, it's a top-notch game.

Moraff's Stones is an off-beat gambling game, where you gamble against monsters. You'll find yourself easily beating them at first, but as each goes broke, a new, slightly more ferocious and intelligent one takes its place. Soon you're playing nasty, vicious creatures that would as soon stab you in the back as look you in the eye.

Moraff's Super Entrap is a maze game. You have to make your way through an enormous maze that stretches off into the horizon. Blocking your way are enemy robots. As you make your way across the maze, you can first alter the maze and easily avoid the enemy robots. Soon, however, the robots become more intelligent and can alter the maze as well, so avoiding them becomes increasingly difficult.

Moraff's Super Blast is my favorite one of the four. In it, you have a paddle at the bottom of the screen. A bouncing colored square is launched at the multileveled and multicolored ceiling above you. Sometimes the ceiling vanishes when it's hit, other times the square bounces off of it. You have to use your paddle to hit the square when it bounces back toward you.

When you destroy a certain number of squares or objects, you move into higher levels, which become increasingly complicated. These levels may have multiple squares flying at you, and have corridors and other objects spread throughout your screen. Sometimes the corridors and ceilings allow the bouncing square to go right through them, other times the square destroys them, and still other times, the square bounces off. As the square bounces it can change speed and direction, and sometimes splits into as many as 17 bouncing squares. Your paddle may shrink or grow, the square may split into several pieces... almost anything may happen. It's hypnotic, a test of your reflexes and of how well you judge speed and angles. Once you start playing this game, you won't want to stop.

If you have work to get done, the safest thing for you may be to delete these games from your hard disk. Otherwise, you may blow an afternoon—or more.

Moraff's Elite Game Series
Registration fee: $$
MoraffWare
815-A Brazos, Suite 317
Austin, TX 78701
(512) 335-6399; (800) 842-4263 (orders)

PC-Monopoly

Whether you want to journey back to your favorite childhood game or try to become a modern real estate magnate, you'll want to play PC-Monopoly. This computerized version of the old-time favorite is faster than the board version of the game—you won't have to count out money or calculate financial transactions. Instead, the computer does it for you. Unlike the board game, it's also easy to stop playing and resume the game later on.

Up to six people can play. You're given $1,500 to spend in your travels around the board and encounters with good and bad luck. The board itself looks much like the version you're familiar with, as you can see in Figure 14.4.

The rules are like the traditional game, and so is the pleasure of winning.

PC-Monopoly
Registration fee: $
Foothills Software
1515 Shenandoah Dr.
Boise, ID 83712

PICTURE PUZZLE

Jigsaw puzzle fans, rejoice, you have a reason to be at the computer screen. This puzzle game will give you hours of pleasure or frustration, depending on how much you enjoy puzzles.

The game is very much like a jigsaw puzzle. You call a picture onto your screen, look at it for an instant, and then the program cuts it up into rectangular pieces and scrambles it on the screen. You can move pieces with either a mouse or the keyboard, although it's much more direct using the mouse.

You control how many pieces the picture will be sliced into; it can be as few as four, or as many as 1400. When you move a piece into its proper position, the computer will generate a beep, and the piece will stay locked in that position. If it's next to another piece that is in the proper position, the grid lines will be removed between the two pieces. See Figure 14.5 for a partially completed puzzle with 32 pieces.

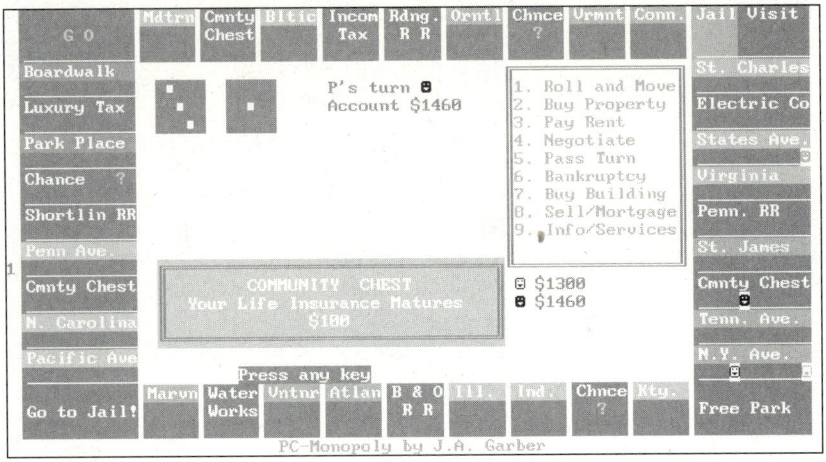

Figure 14.4 A bit of good luck in PC-Monopoly

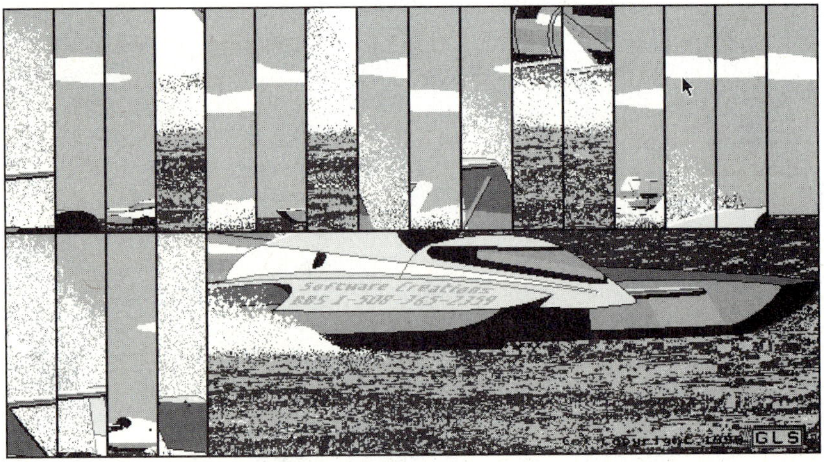

Figure 14.5 A partially completed jigsaw puzzle

While you're in the middle of a puzzle, you can ask the game for help. It will display the complete picture for you, either in the corner of your monitor or on the whole screen.

The game comes with several puzzles, but you can also make your own by creating a graphics file with a painting or drawing program or importing an existing graphic. The game will use PCX and GIF file formats as well as its own PUZ and SAV formats. You'll have to make sure, however, that the resolution of your graphics file is one that the game supports. PCX files, for example, can be at a number of different resolutions, not all of which will work with the game.

If doing puzzles isn't enough for you, and you have a need to compete—against yourself or others—the game will accommodate you. It will display a screen full of statistics for you about your playing. You'll find the total number of moves you've made, the number of those moves that were right and the number that were wrong, the most times a single piece was moved, how many times the help screen was used, and more.

You'll need at least an EGA monitor for the game and 640k of memory. If you have EMS memory, PICTURE PUZZLE will use it.

PICTURE PUZZLE
Registration fee: $
Software Creations
26 Harris St.
Clinton, MA 01510

PowerChess

This is an excellent chess-playing program with many options. Whether you're a beginner, just learning the game, or an advanced player trying to fine-tune your strategy, you'll find much to like here.

There are many levels of play, depending on how long you let the computer calculate each of its moves. For a fast-paced game, give it ten seconds per move. For a slower, more difficult game, allow it longer periods of time. It can ponder up to 36,000,000 seconds on a single move, but at that glacial speed, you won't play a game in your lifetime. The display is clean and crisp, as you can see in Figure 14.6.

The game shows the amount of time you and the computer have each used, has an index of the last 21 moves, and can tell you about all the possible moves on the chessboard. It also has a library of instructive chess games you can replay, and a library of standard openings. Unlike in real-life chess, you can take back a move when you blunder. The program also offers hints when you ask for them.

A particularly nice feature is that you can set up the board however you want—you don't always have to start from the beginning of a game. So, for example, if you want to practice your endgame, you can set up the type of endgame you'd like to work on and start from there.

When you're about to be checkmated, PowerChess tells you it is about to beat you. It recognizes stalemates. All in all, this is a top choice if you're a chess player.

Figure 14.6
PowerChess at work

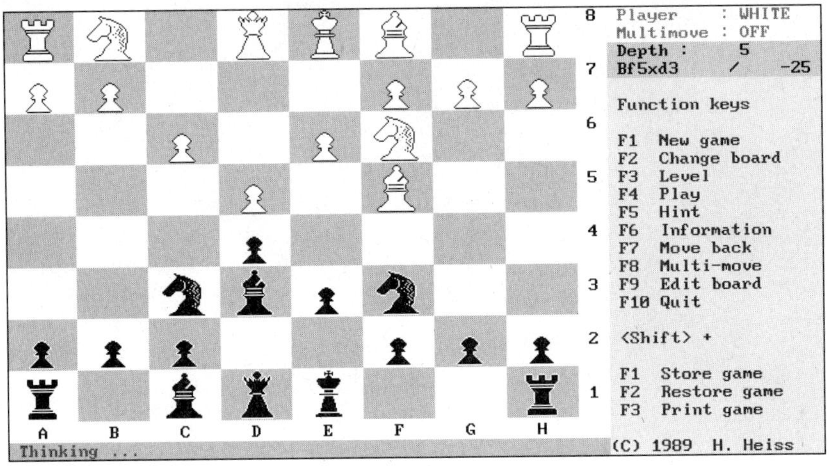

PowerChess
Registration fee: $
New-Ware
8050 Camino Kiosco
San Diego, CA 92122
(619) 455-6225

SkyGlobe

If you've ever looked up at the sky and stared in wonder at the stars, then SkyGlobe is for you. This excellent program does more than just provide you with an easily accessible planetarium—it's also just plain fun to use.

SkyGlobe displays an animated picture of the stars rotating through the sky. The constellations are all marked, as are all the major stars and planets. When you run the program, you tell it from which city you'd like to view the sky. It then shows the sky just as it appears in that city on the day you run the program. Figure 14.7 shows the sky as seen from Boston in October.

As the stars move through the sky, you can control the display to get a great deal of information about the heavens. To change the view, use the cursor keys. To view the heavens as seen from the North Pole, type **N**. To move forward a month in time and see how the sky would look then, type **M**. To increase the speed of movement, type **F**. And to zoom in, type **Z**.

You'll be able to do more than just alter the display, however. You can also search for individual stars, planets, or constellations and print out a star map.

Figure 14.7 SkyGlobe displaying the heavens

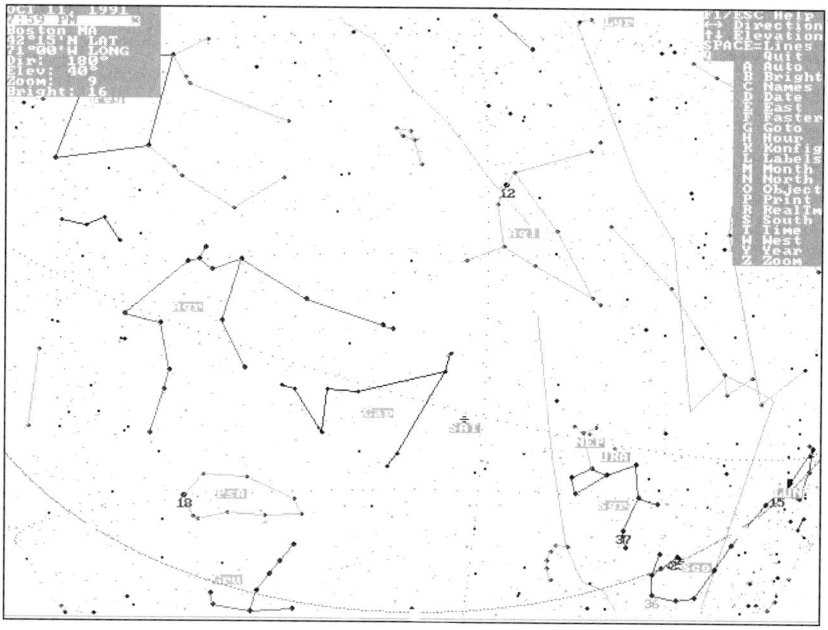

Almost anyone could get a great deal of pleasure out of this program. But if you've ever been bitten by the astronomy bug, you'll absolutely have to have it.

SkyGlobe
Registration fee: $
Klassm Software
284 142nd Ave.
Caledonia, MI 49316

ZZT

This cross between an action and an adventure game is one of the more intriguing games you'll find. It exercises your intelligence as much as it does your ten digits. ZZT comes with 43 game boards, or *rooms,* as the program calls them, each of which is filled with odd creatures, strange objects, and ingenious puzzles.

You travel through a series of these rooms, some of which are mazes, picking up objects along the way for use on your journey. As with many adventure games, you'll meet different characters and have to decide how best to conquer or use them. As in action games, you'll also have to use your reflexes to dodge dangers.

To journey through all 43 rooms will take you some time—the author estimates that it takes a total of about 40 hours to finish them all. If you get stuck, he'll send you a sheet of advice and hints.

A couple of tips for you: Whenever you see an object, touch it to pick it up. You'll probably find a use for it sooner or later. To exit the room you're in, you can usually just head off the screen into the next one.

ZZT
Registration fee: $
Potomac Computer Systems
10406 Holbrook Dr.
Potomac, MD 20854

Windows Programs

Windows and games were made for each other. It's been that way ever since Windows 3.0 was released, and it continues that way today. In fact, the most popular application initially run on Windows 3.0 may well have been the solitaire card game shipped with the product.

You'll find many more shareware Windows games than you'll find commercial Windows games: Aside from Microsoft's Entertainment Pack, there aren't that many commercial games for Windows. Interestingly, one of the games in the Entertainment Pack, Taipei, was written by a shareware author, who sells his own shareware version of the game.

Shareware Windows games range from Windows versions of traditional games, such as WinChess, to artificial "biological" systems, such as Life. In between, you'll find shoot-em-ups, card games, and much more. The Windows interface makes them easier to learn than non-Windows games, and ensures that they all have nice graphic touches. Since you can multitask with them, you'll also be able to run them in the background. Switching between a Windows game and work is that much easier, which makes them all the more seductive. To again paraphrase what Microsoft once said about its own Entertainment Pack, "Now you can use the incredible power of Windows—to goof off."

Backgammon

The name says it all. This game lets you play Backgammon against the computer. You control the difficulty of play (beginner, intermediate, or advanced).

You can have the program suggest moves for you. And you can undo moves—effectively cheating—something you can't do against a human opponent!

Backgammon
Registration fee: None
Available from Public Brand Software

Bandit

Do you like Las Vegas, but not the pricey air fares and hotels? Are you risking your bankbook in low dives, nightclubs, or casinos?

Fret no more. Now dedicated gamblers can play the slots in the safety of their own homes, with Bandit. Playing it is just as easy as throwing quarters down the maws of the ever-hungry, one-armed bandits in Las Vegas.

To play the game, run the program, then click on the Play menu item. The computer pulls the slot machine's arm to send the wheels in the machine spinning. It'll stop on a random combination of symbols, just like it does in Vegas. And you'll generally lose, just as you would there. But you won't have to put up with polyester-clad neighbors, Wayne Newton, and watered-down drinks. And, at the price of this program, you won't lose any real money. Your arm won't even get tired.

Bandit
Registration fee: None
Wicked Witch Software Company
P.O. Box 3452
Reno, NV 89505

Lander

You're the captain of a lunar excursion module, making its final approach to the moon's surface. Your mission: Land the ship without digging a hole halfway to the center of the moon.

You start a thousand meters above the moon. Below you is a craggy landscape, full of mountains and craters. Your task is to find a flat surface, maneuver your craft over to it, and gently land upon it. You control the module's movement by clicking on one of three buttons. You get both vertical and horizontal thrust using rockets, but you have only a limited amount of fuel. Figure 14.8 shows the Lander in midflight.

You can customize a great deal in this game. For example, you can change the force of gravity: less force makes it easier to land, and more force makes it more difficult. You can also alter the amount of thrust given by your rockets and the amount of fuel you have.

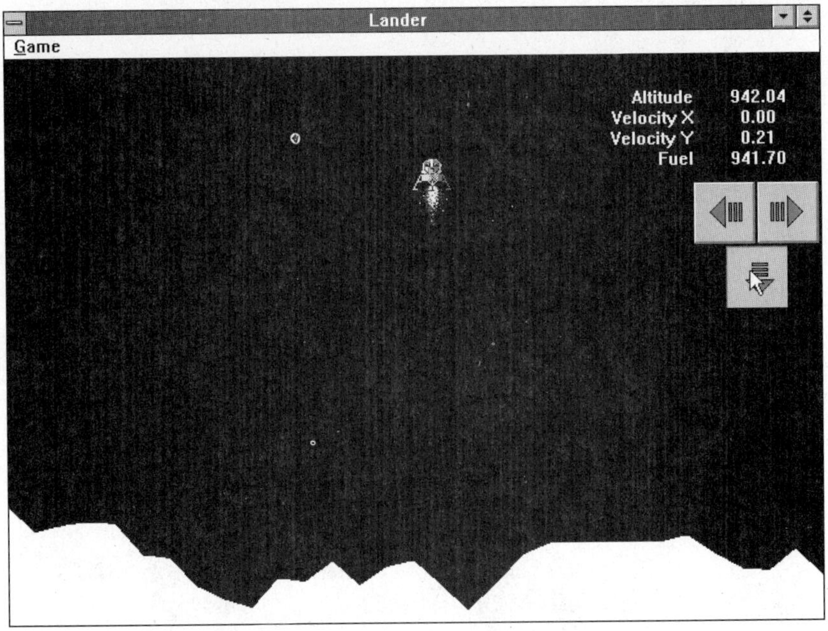

Figure 14.8 Lander descending to the moon's surface

Don't expect it to be easy. And every time you crash, you'll get either a bit of advice or a snide remark from your PC.

Lander
Registration fee: None ($ for source code)
TMA
15 Whittier Road
Natick, MA 01760
(508) 655-5823

Life

This is more an intellectual exercise than a game, but it's one of the more addicting programs you'll ever run. What it does, in essence, is create little cells of artificial life, which are represented as colored squares on a grid background. These squares interact with each other, age, and grow, just as cells do in real life. The net effect is a hypnotic, kaleidoscopic view of life being born and dying in front of your eyes.

The simulation has a simple set of rules. If a cell has less than two neighbors, it promptly dies (of loneliness?). If it has more than three neighbors, it dies as well (overcrowding?). If an empty space on the grid has three live neighbors, that empty space suddenly springs to life.

Additionally, every ten cycles that a cell is alive, it ages, turning a different color. After it reaches old age—eight color cycles—it dies.

You can do more than watch all this—you can control some of the conditions as well. For example, you control the speed with which the program cycles through life. You can also kill cells and give birth to cells by using the mouse. You can create patterns of cells and see how they cycle through life, or have the computer create random patterns for you.

Life
Registration fee: None
Tom Wheeler
31294 Morlock
Livonia, MI 48152

PolyAnna

File this one under "kaleidoscopic entertainment." Run this program, and your screen is filled with an endlessly changing polygon; it snakes around your screen, changing shape and color. You can do more than watch it, though: You're given control over virtually every aspect of the kaleidoscope. For example, you can alter the way it changes shapes and colors.

PolyAnna
Registration fee: None ($ for source code)
David Bennett
1100 Liggett Court
Blue Springs, MO 65015

SPS Games Pack

This collection of three games should keep you away from your work for a good amount of time. The first game, called Mines, has you sweeping a mine field. The other two games—Arachnid and Towers—are variants on solitaire.

Mines is similar to the Mines game contained in Microsoft's Entertainment Pack. You're faced with a grid of tiles. Hidden beneath some of the tiles are landmines which you must avoid. You start in the upper-left corner, and have to find a path through the minefield to get to the field's lower-right corner.

You're given information about where the mines might be located, so you can mark which squares you think are safe and which aren't. Then you carefully work your way through the mine field. If you reach your destination safely, you win (you generally don't). You'll find this game thoroughly addicting (not to say disarming), and you'll play that "one last game" for hours on end.

If you find the version of solitaire shipped with Windows too easy, then you'll love the Arachnid card game. You're dealt ten stacks of cards in the game, as shown in Figure 14.9. Your object is to build complete stacks of cards from the King to the Ace in the same suit. When you complete a stack, you remove it to the top of the screen. After you've built eight such stacks (in your dreams!) you've won. Luckily, Arachnid allows for two levels of cheating—otherwise you might never win. There are also even more difficult variations of the game, but unless you're a serious cards masochist, I wouldn't suggest trying them out.

Figure 14.9
A hand of cards in Arachnid

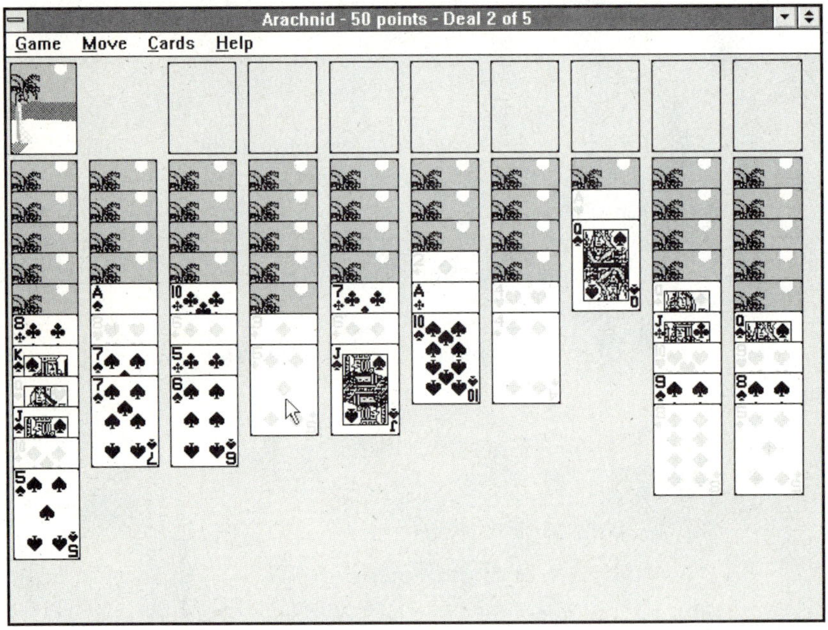

Towers is another card game. The program's author readily acknowledges that it's taken directly from a Macintosh shareware game called Seahaven Towers. You're dealt ten stacks of cards, each of which at first has five cards in it. All the cards are played face up. There are several other types of piles as well, including an aces pile. The object of the game is to get all the cards into the aces pile.

You move cards by placing them on a card of the same suit, and one number higher. For example, you place the two of hearts on top of the three of hearts. The game tracks how many games you've won and lost, and how many in a row you've won and lost. Good luck—you'll need it, playing this killer version of solitaire.

SPS Game Pack
Registration fee: £15
SP Services
P.O. Box 456
Southampton,
United Kingdom
SO9 7XG

Taipei

Taipei is yet another of those Windows games that turns even the most disciplined of us into game-playing goof-offs. Taipei is a solitaire version of the Chinese game of Mah-Jongg. When you load the program, tiles are piled atop one another willy-nilly. Each tile has a picture or Chinese character on it. Your task is to match up tiles with identical pictures or characters. You can only match tiles that aren't covered or blocked by other tiles. To win you'll need a combination of skill and luck; it's like solving a complicated crossword puzzle.

This version of Taipei is pretty much identical to the version that Microsoft sells as part of their Windows Entertainment Pack. There's good reason for that: The same author wrote both programs. If you get it as shareware, though, you can try out the program before buying it—and then pay a fraction of the commercial price if you like it.

Taipei
Registration fee: $
David Norris
17911 NE 101st Court
Redmond, WA 98052

WinChess

If you like chess, and want to play it under Windows, then this is the game for you. You can play against the computer, pit the computer against itself, or play against another opponent at the keyboard.

You control the level of play, that is, how completely the computer looks at all the possible moves. The higher the level of play, the longer the computer takes to move. You can also give the game a chess problem to solve, and it will solve it if it can.

There are many other options as well. You can choose to play with a chess clock showing, and to have the computer show, on screen, all the moves it's considering as it contemplates its next move. Figure 14.10 shows the game with these options enabled.

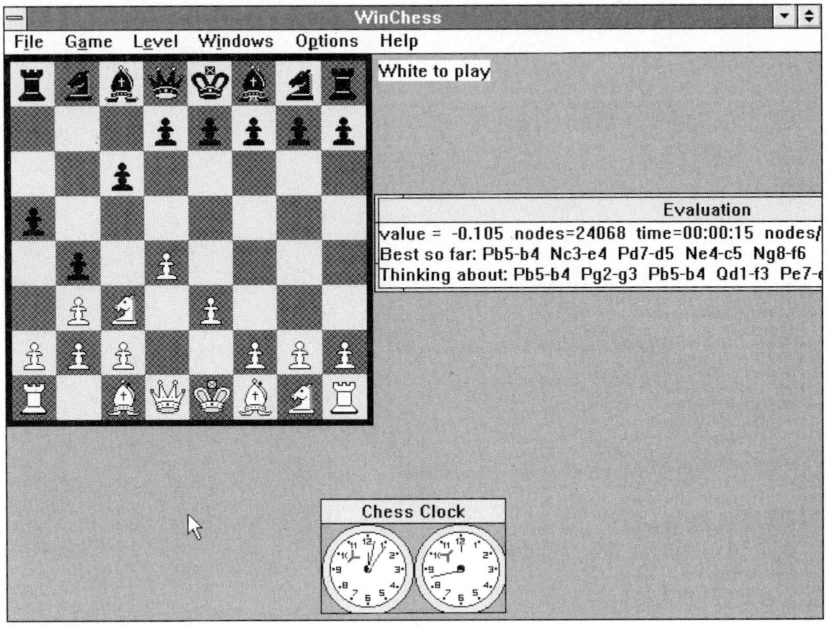

Figure 14.10 WinChess with the clock and evaluation options enabled

You can use sound or not, you can tell the program to follow traditional openings or not, and you can display a list of all the moves in the game. The game will even offer you hints, if you like. In fact, about the only thing the game doesn't do is cackle when it wins, or knock over the board when it's defeated.

WinChess
Registration fee: $
David Norris
17911 NE 101st Court
Redmond, WA 98052

Windows Command

The Klingons, as usual, are up to no good. This time they want to destroy six of your cities. To protect against them, you have Missile Silo Alpha.

The game begins when a missile siren sounds, and the sky fills with missiles headed toward your cities. You destroy the missiles with your mouse. After each wave of missiles, another comes your way. Figure 14.11 shows a missile attack.

Figure 14.11
A Klingon missile attack

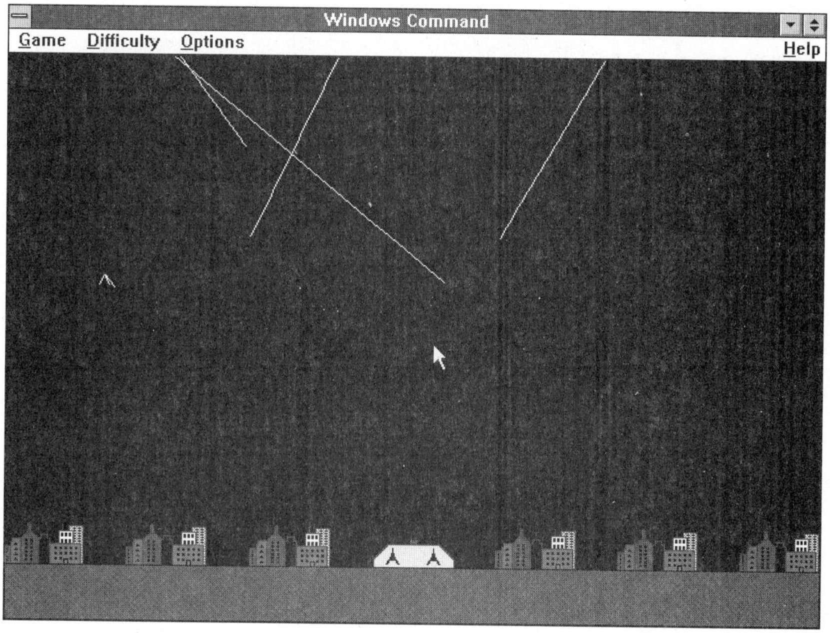

At the end of each round, you get your score, a new set of missiles, and a bonus city for each 10,000 points you've accumulated.

Klingons, fierce fighters that they are, send cloaked bombers into the fray. You can't see these planes, but they'll bomb your cities anyway. And they bring starships in, as well.

The version currently available as shareware ends once you reach 20,000 points. Since the program's author has released a commercial version of the game, he is no longer supporting it as shareware. So if you get really hooked, you'll have to buy the commercial game.

Windows Command
Registration fee: None
Available on CompuServe in the ZENITH forum, library 15.

WinPoker

Have you grown tired of playing solitaire day and night on your PC? Would you like, perhaps, to play a higher-stakes card game?

If so, WinPoker is for you. And if you like poker, you'll really like this game. The normal rules apply: You're dealt five cards. As in regular poker, you can hold them all, or ask for three new ones (four if you have an ace). Mouse clicks control which cards you'll hold, and when to get a new set of cards.

The computer doesn't deal itself a set of cards. So rather than betting, you're given points for certain hands, from 5 for a pair of jacks or better, all the way up to 4,000 for a royal straight flush. If you don't get jacks or better, you lose. Figure 14.12 shows a winning hand.

Figure 14.12
WinPoker deals a winning hand

You can also chart your wins or losses with a nice statistics function. It will tell you the number of hands you've played, the numbers and percentages of those you've lost, and the numbers and percentages of those you won with which hands.

WinPoker
Registration fee: $
Dean Zamzow
P.O. Box 55761
Phoenix, AZ 85078

CHAPTER

15

Miscellaneous Programs

Graphics Programs

Memory Utilities

Personal Information Managers

Grab Bag Programs

THE BREADTH OF THE TYPES OF SHAREWARE IS TRULY REMARKABLE. AS you've seen in the preceding chapters, there's a piece of software for just about any task you can name. This chapter looks at shareware that is difficult to categorize. These programs don't fit easily into one of the major types of software, or are not in widespread use. That doesn't mean they are second-rate. In fact, some of the programs below are among the best-written software available as shareware, and often top the shareware best-seller lists.

I've divided the chapter into four sections. The first part covers graphics programs. The second section details memory utilities. The third is about personal information managers. And the last section is a grab bag of excellent programs that nevertheless defy categorization.

Spend the time to browse through what's below—more than likely you'll find at least one program you can't live without.

Graphics Programs

For a long time, the PC has been primarily a text-intensive tool; traditionally, it hasn't done well when handling graphics programs. This is partially because the memory requirements of graphics were too great for the earliest PCs, and their processors were too slow and monitors too fuzzy to make working with graphics anything other than a tedious chore.

But as the hardware became faster, memory cheaper, and high-quality color monitors and cards more common, that began to change. You can now find many graphics programs, for every purpose from drawing and painting to creating presentations, slides, and entire screen shows.

In general, shareware has lagged behind its commercial brethren when it comes to graphics software; there aren't many graphics shareware programs available. Increasingly, however, shareware authors are turning their attention to graphics, with good results.

Following are descriptions of two high-quality shareware graphics programs. Desktop Paint allows you to create or alter images. Show Partner Lite is for those who want to create presentations on the PC. Each is a solid, sophisticated program that makes the most of your computer's graphics capabilities.

Desktop Paint and Desktop Paint 256

These two programs are paint programs—that is, programs that can create and modify graphic images in a variety of different formats.

The programs are largely the same. The difference is that Desktop Paint works only with monochrome files, whereas Desktop Paint 256 works with color files. The monochrome version works with various bit-mapped formats, including MAC and PSF MAC (MacPaint files), IMB (Ventura Publisher files), PCX (PC Paintbrush files), WPG (WordPerfect files, if they contain bit-mapped images), and TIFF files. The color program works with bit-mapped files in various formats including PCX (PC Paintbrush), GIF (CompuServe), IFF/LBM (Deluxe Paint), and TIFF.

With these programs, you'll be able to create and edit graphic images either to use on their own, or to include in other documents, such as those produced with desktop publishing software.

The programs work much like popular commercial painting programs such as PC-Paint. To edit an image, you call it up to the screen, and then use a variety of painting and drawing tools on it. There are two sets of tools available. The first is accessed from a drop-down menu across the top of the screen. From there, you can invert, flip, and rotate the image; modify the image's colors or its gray values; choose text and fonts; open, close, and print files; use a clipboard to transfer portions of images between files; and choose images from a picture gallery. Figure 15.1 shows Desktop Paint with one image displayed, while another is being chosen from the picture gallery.

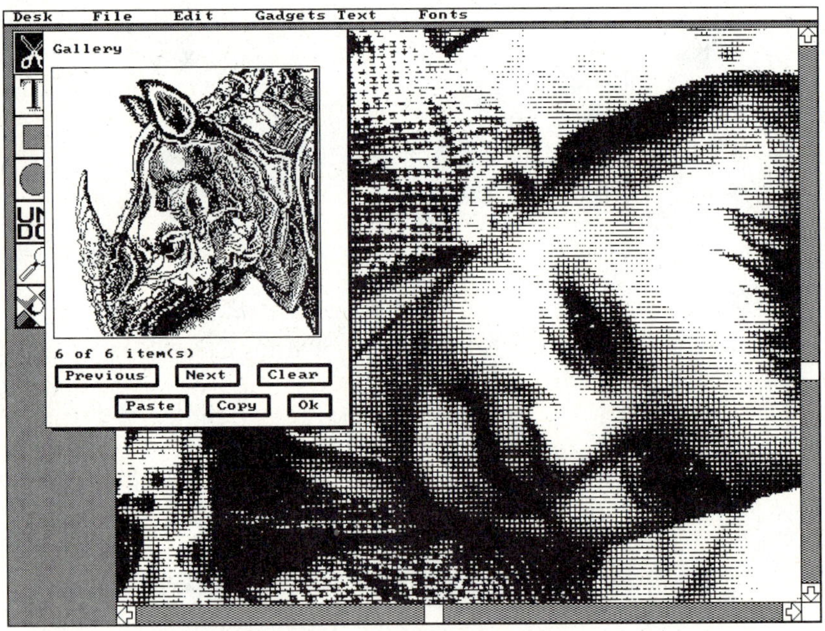

Figure 15.1 Desktop Paint in operation

The other set of tools is accessed from what's called the Toolbox, which runs down the left-hand side of the screen. They are chosen by clicking on the corresponding icon with the mouse. With these tools you can select, cut, and move areas of the drawing; "airbrush" and erase portions of the image;

draw lines, ellipses, and rectangles; and fill in images with color or patterns, among other drawing and painting tasks.

Desktop Paint requires a mouse and a Hercules, EGA, or VGA card. Desktop Paint 256 requires a mouse, a VGA monitor, and either the Paradise Plus (256k on board), Paradise Professional (512k on board), ATI VGA Wonder card (256k or 512k on board), or Headland Video7 or 1024i card (256k or 512k on board) in order to run. It will also run on graphics cards that are fully compatible with one of these cards.

As with the author's other graphic program, Graphics Workshop, covered in Chapter 9, Desktop Paint has one of the strongest registration offers you'll ever find. Instead of paying a registration fee, you can buy the novel *Coven: A Novel* by Steven William Rimmer. Send comments about the book, or a photocopy of its cover, and you'll be registered.

Desktop Paint
Registration fee: $ (or purchase of the book *Coven: A Novel*, by Steven William Rimmer)

Desktop Paint 256
Registration fee: $
Alchemy Mindworks, Inc.
P.O. Box 500
Beeton, Ontario
Canada L0G 1A0

Show Partner Lite

One of the most underused powers of your PC is its considerable ability to give graphic presentations on screen. These presentations are very much like slide shows—one image following another in succession. The difference is that you can also add many special effects to your PC "slides." You can have screens fade in and fade out, weave in and weave out, and much more.

You can even give a screen show that displays what you've created on your PC with several different programs. For example, you can show a spreadsheet screen, then a 3-D bar chart created with a graphics program, then a database report.

Show Partner Lite allows you to create these kinds of presentations. The program began as commercial software, and became one of the better-known presentation programs. Recently, and fortunately for shareware users, it was released as shareware.

The program has everything you'll need to create on-screen presentations; each step in the process has a separate module. The first module, called CAPTURE, will let you capture any screen displayed on your PC into a file. In essence, a snapshot of your screen is saved, in its own graphics format —GX2.

To use it, you first load CAPTURE as a TSR. Then you run an applications program, create a screen you wish to capture, and use CAPTURE to capture that screen to a disk file. The images you've captured form the heart of your presentation—the equivalent of slides in a slide show.

After you've captured those images, you can edit them; for instance, you can change their colors, draw on top of them, and erase pieces of them. These and other changes can be made using the Grafix Editor (GED) portion of the program. Figure 15.2 shows an image being edited with GED. You can also use GED's drawing tools to create images from scratch.

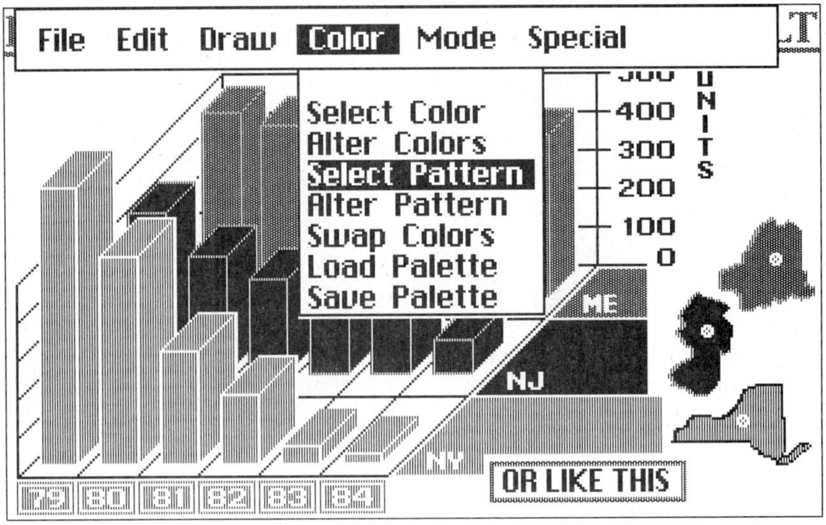

Figure 15.2 Editing an image with the Grafix Editor

Once you have captured, edited, and created the images you want to display, you're ready to create a screen show. To do that, you use the Slide Show Editor (SLED). With SLED, you list the screens you want displayed in your screen show. You also specify the special effects, if any, you want to use—that is, how to handle the transition from one slide to the next. This is done quickly, by filling in a form about each image. Figure 15.3 shows SLED being used to create and edit a screen show.

You can use SLED to view the show you've created, and then edit it further, if you wish. You can also use a module called the Script Editor to further refine your presentation. The Script Editor uses a powerful script language, which allows you to add many more special effects to your shows, including the use of sound.

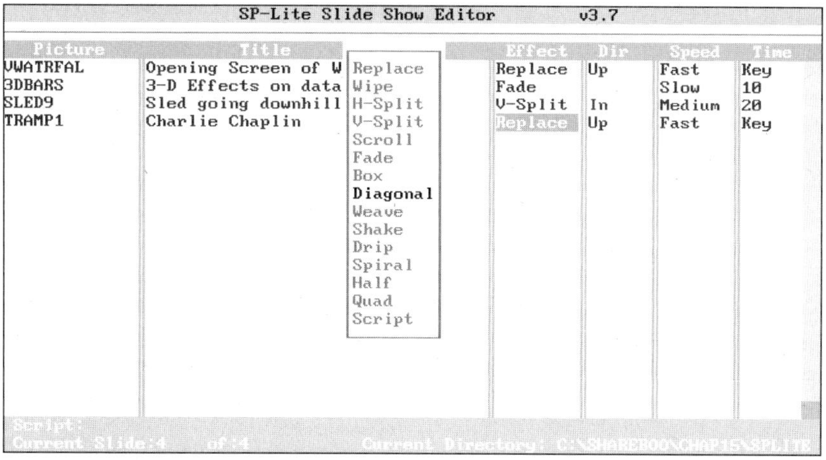

Figure 15.3
Creating a screen show with the Slide Show Editor

Once you've finished the presentation, you use the Show module to run the finished presentation. You can even create self-running presentations that you can give out on disk. The recipients won't need Show Partner Lite in order to see your presentation—they'll only need the file you've created.

Show Partner Lite
Registration fee: $$$
Attn: Ed Bailey
Brightbill-Roberts & Co.
421 University Building
Syracuse, NY 13202
(800) 444-3490

Memory Utilities

Perhaps the PC's greatest limitation is the way in which it handles memory. Because of the way DOS was built in the earliest days, programs usually have been limited to using a maximum of 640k of memory—an enormous amount in the dawn of the personal computing era, but a piddling figure today.

There have been many schemes through the years to get around that limitation. One was the creation of Terminate-and-Stay-Resident (TSR) programs. These programs, once loaded, stay in memory all the time, so you can use them even when you're in another program. TSRs help you make more efficient use of your PC's memory, because they let your PC do more than one task at a time. However, they use up memory quickly, and can cause other problems as well. A number of shareware programs have been written to make them work more efficiently, however. The TSR Utilities, detailed below, are a particularly good tool for doing this.

Another memory-manipulation scheme is to allow device drivers, TSRs, and other programs to be "loaded high" into the memory found above 640k. This memory is usually reserved for a variety of housekeeping chores; but in fact, much of it goes unused. Therefore, software authors have written programs that allow certain computers to use that memory. Commercially, the first, best-known ones are QEMM and 386 To The Max; DOS 5 also added this ability to DOS itself. Shareware programs have also entered the market with similar capabilities, including the DOS 5 Memory Management Kit, covered below.

One note about memory utilities: They're generally only for those who feel comfortable with tinkering. You'll have to play around to get them to work right, and you'll find there are always new ways in which you can fine-tune your memory configuration—in fact, for many people, this tinkering is an end unto itself.

DOS 5 Memory Management Kit

The introduction of DOS 5 was a great leap forward for DOS. It introduced a raft of features and utilities that users have been repeatedly asking for, in some cases for years.

Key among those features was an improvement in the way DOS handles memory. First off, DOS 5 freed up more of the lower 640k of memory for applications programs. It also included memory-management utilities to load TSRs, device drivers, and other programs into the memory between 640k and 1 Mb (called high memory), keeping the lower 640k of memory as free of memory-clogging resident programs and device drivers as possible.

But DOS 5 doesn't go the whole distance—there are still a number of memory utilities it lacks. The DOS 5 Memory Management Kit gives them to you. With it, you'll be able to control just about every aspect of memory under DOS 5.

One of the more important of these utilities is HRAM. This utility improves upon DOS 5's memory management in a number of ways. First, it lets owners of 8088- and 80286-based PCs load programs into high memory—something that DOS 5 doesn't allow (it performs that function only for those who own 386 PCs). HRAM also optimizes the location and order of the programs it loads high, determining their most efficient placement. DOS 5 leaves that to trial and error. HRAM also looks into high memory for areas that DOS 5 overlooked, potentially giving you more high memory.

Min-mem is another utility that will free up your PC's memory. It does this in a different way than HRAM. Min-mem is a TSR handler. TSRs, as mentioned before, are programs that are loaded into memory and stay there until called up with a certain key combination, called a *hotkey.* They can be accessed and run while you're running other applications.

Normally, when you run several TSRs simultaneously, they will eat up a good deal of your RAM. For example, if you load three TSRs, and one of them takes up 25k, another takes up 42k, and another takes up 51k, they'll take up a total of 118k of your RAM. Min-mem, however, will reduce that total significantly—when it's running, those TSRs would only use a total of 15k of memory. Min-mem does this by running as a 15k TSR itself. In essence, it takes the TSRs out of memory and places them on your hard disk. Then, when you need access to one of them, you call up Min-mem by pressing a hotkey, and tell Min-mem which TSR you want to run.

The final utility in the bunch, VRAM, converts extended memory to expanded memory, or creates up to 32Mb of simulated expanded memory from your hard disk space. This is helpful because extended memory can only be used when running an 80386 chip in protected mode, whereas expanded memory can be used in a wider variety of ways.

DOS 5 Memory Management Kit
Registration fee: $$
Biologic Company
7950 Blue Gray Circle
Manassas, VA 22110
(703) 368-2949

TSR Utilities

This set of 11 utilities gives you every tool you'll need to manage TSRs. The most famous utilities in the group are MARK and RELEASE, which allow you to remove TSRs from your PC's memory without having to reboot your system. But there are other useful utilities in the bunch, too, especially those that let you peer into your PC's memory.

Using MARK and RELEASE is quite simple. You run MARK by typing **MARK** at the command line and pressing Enter. Then run your TSRs. This will mark the location of the TSRs in your system's memory. When you want to take the TSRs out of your system's memory, type **RELEASE** and press Enter. All the TSRs will be released from memory.

You can also use these utilities to load and unload TSRs one at a time instead of all at once. For example, let's say you want to load three TSRs, and have the option of unloading them individually. For this example, suppose the three TSRs are called 1TSR, 2TSR, and 3TSR, and they are all loaded by typing their file names. To mark their locations in memory and load the programs, you would type the following commands:

MARK
1TSR

MARK
2TSR
MARK
3TSR

Then, when you run RELEASE, the last-loaded program (3TSR) will be removed from memory, while the other two remain. If you type **RELEASE** again, 2TSR will be removed, and so on.

There are a number of command-line options for running these programs, which are even more complex and let you manage TSRs in more sophisticated ways. Also included in TSR Utilities is a program called FMARK, which takes up less memory than does MARK.

Three other utilities of note are MAPMEM, FREERAM, and DEVICE. MAPMEM shows a map of your memory. It details what programs are running, how much memory they use, and other technical information, as seen in Figure 15.4.

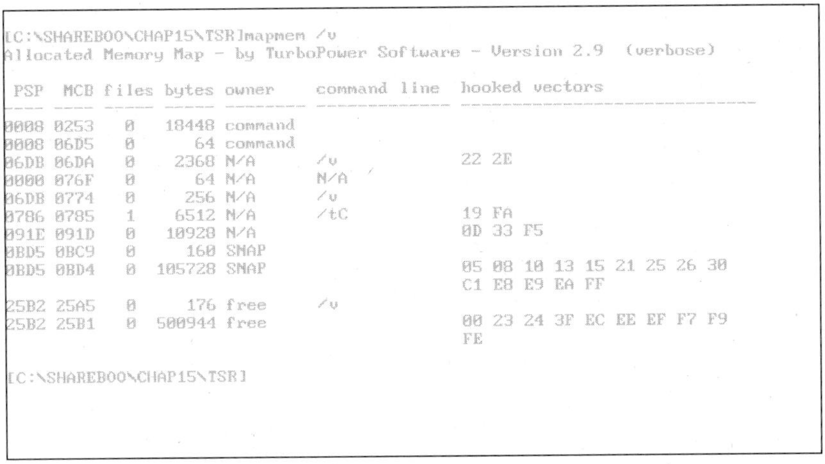

```
[C:\SHAREBOO\CHAP15\TSR]mapmem /v
Allocated Memory Map - by TurboPower Software - Version 2.9  (verbose)

 PSP  MCB files bytes owner    command line  hooked vectors
---- ---- ----- ----- -------- ------------- ------------------------------
0008 0253   0   18448 command
0008 06D5   0      64 command
06DB 06DA   0    2368 N/A      /v            22 2E
0000 076F   0      64 N/A      N/A
06DB 0774   0     256 N/A      /v
0786 0785   1    6512 N/A      /tC           19 FA
091E 091D   0   10928 N/A                    0D 33 F5
0BD5 0BC9   0     160 SNAP
0BD5 0BD4   0  105728 SNAP                   05 08 10 13 15 21 25 26 30
                                             C1 E8 E9 EA FF

25B2 25A5   0     176 free     /v
25B2 25B1   0  500944 free                   00 23 24 3F EC EE EF F7 F9
                                             FE

[C:\SHAREBOO\CHAP15\TSR]
```

Figure 15.4
MAPMEM reporting on the status of a PC's memory

RAMFREE will tell you how much memory you have free for use with an application. It does exactly what DOS's CHKDSK command does, with one difference: You won't have to wait while your hard disk is analyzed in order to get a memory report.

The DEVICE program gives you a full, technical report on the device drivers you've loaded in your CONFIG.SYS file.

The newest version of the TSR Utilities allows MARK and RELEASE to load and unload TSRs under DOS 5 in high memory, located above 640k.

TSR Utilities
Registration fee: None
TurboPower Software
P.O. Box 49009
Colorado Springs, CO 80949
(719) 260-6641

VGARAM

If you have a VGA graphics card and monitor on your system, you probably have a gold mine of memory, just waiting to be used. If your graphics card has at least 256k of memory (and virtually all VGA cards do), if your PC has at least 640k of RAM, and if you don't always use your PC for graphics, you can get up to 96k of extra memory for your programs.

VGARAM works by converting RAM from your VGA card into memory that your PC can use in main RAM. But it's able to get at the RAM only if you're not using your PC in graphics mode; when you run a graphics application, you'll have to temporarily disable VGARAM. Then you re-enable it when you return to a text-based application.

VGARAM works with some EGA cards as well as VGA cards. Be aware, however, that it won't work on all systems and setups.

VGARAM
Registration fee: $
Infinite Technologies
11403 Cronhill Dr., Suite D
Owings Mills, MD 21117
(301) 363-1097

Personal Information Managers

Personal Information Managers (PIMs) are among the least understood of PC applications, and often the most loosely defined. They run the gamut from calendars to scheduling software to phone-and-address programs, on up to programs that can do all those tasks and more, including keeping track of files on disk and popping up reminders about meetings.

I've covered just a few shareware PIMs below. Each is suited to different preferences. Active Life is for those who like a graphical approach to scheduling, whereas My-Desk is heavily text-based.

Active Life

Active Life is primarily a scheduler and calendar program. There are two versions of the program, but they look and work very much alike. One works under Windows, the other under DOS.

The Windows version, because it uses the common Windows menus and commands, is quite easy to get started. You create a schedule for yourself every day, noting down things such as appointments, deadlines, and other things that must be done. You can then view that schedule in a number of ways: day by day, an entire week at a time, even alphabetically. You can also have several such views active at once on your screen.

Active Life for Windows includes more than just a scheduler, though. You can also display a calendar and a "pad" for taking notes. Figure 15.5 shows the daily view, with the Calendar and Notebook items open.

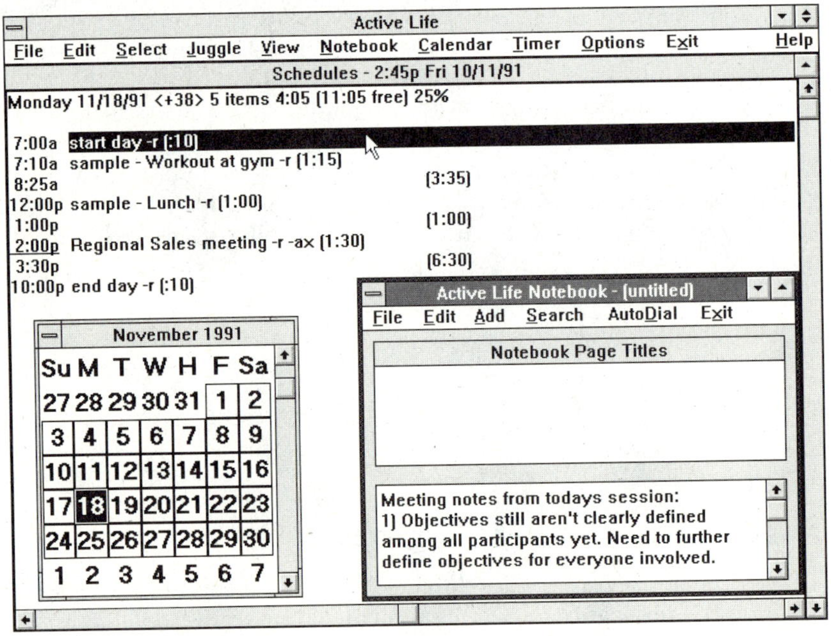

Figure 15.5 A daily listing in Active Life for Windows

Additionally, the program has other useful utilities, including one that times how long you spend on various tasks.

The DOS version is similar to the Windows version, in that it also runs in a graphical environment—one that looks and feels very much like Windows.

Active Life
1Soft Corporation
Registration fee: $$$$
P.O. Box 1320
Middletown, CA 95461
(707) 987-0256; (800) 326-4391

My-Desk

This is an interesting calendaring program, with a difference—almost all of its functions are accessed using a text editor. It can work either in stand-alone mode or as a TSR.

There are several modules to the program, most of which can be gotten to from the text editor. There's an appointment calendar, which has pop-up alarms that warn you when an appointment is pending. The calendar will also issue daily reminders about tasks that need to be done. The program has a calculator, for doing math problems; a table listing ASCII characters; and ways to perform DOS functions from within the program.

The editor, even just by itself, is useful. Since you can run it as a TSR, you can always pop it up over your current application in order to take notes. The calendar looks like a traditional monthly calendar, with large rectangles representing each day of the month. Within each rectangle, you can note things that must be done on that day.

My-Desk isn't the prettiest of programs, but if you're more comfortable with text editors than you are with graphics-based programs, it should serve you well.

My-Desk
Registration fee: $
Nelson Ford
Public Software Library
P.O. Box 35705
Houston, TX 77235
(713) 524-6394; (800) 242-4775 (orders)

Personal Calendar

This is a simple calendar program that keeps track of your daily appointments. Using it, you display the current month, the previous month, and the next month on screen, as well as all of the day's appointments and a clock showing the time of day. A typical daily listing is shown in Figure 15.6. There's also a note-taking capability, so you can jot things down throughout the day.

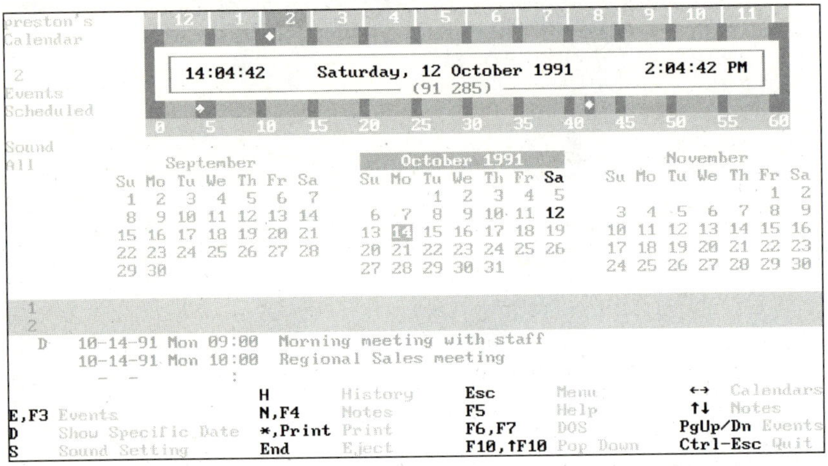

Figure 15.6
A typical listing in Personal Calendar

What lends Personal Calendar much of its power is that it can be run as a TSR, not just as a stand-alone program. That means you can always have your calendar at your fingertips, since you can pop it up over other programs. In this mode, Personal Calendar will pop up to remind you when you have an appointment by sounding an alarm. When run as a TSR, only a 6k kernel of the program remains in memory. The rest of the program is swapped either to your hard disk or to expanded (EMS) memory.

You can also print your schedule and calendar with the program, so that you can refer to them when you're away from your PC, and you can create an ASCII file of your appointments for export to other programs. Your appointments may be password-protected if you wish, so you are the only one who has access to all your records.

Personal Calendar
Registration fee: $
Paul Muñoz-Colman
11645 Charter Oak Ct., #201
Reston, VA 22090
(703) 435-1110

Grab Bag Programs

No matter how many categories you come up with for shareware, there will always be a number of excellent programs that refuse to be classified. I've listed a few of these below.

The programs do a wide variety of things for you. Back & Forth lets you run several programs at once on your PC. METZ Lock and PC-Vault are security systems. Newkey is a macro program and all-around keyboard enhancer. And ZIPKEY keeps zip codes and area codes always near at hand. Every one of these programs is excellent. They're aimed at specific tasks, and they do what they set out to do exceptionally well.

Back & Forth

There are many ways in which computers don't mirror the way we truly work and think. For example, we commonly switch between different tasks throughout the day, often spending only a minute or two on one before switching to another. But to switch between tasks on a PC can take a great deal of time, especially if you only want to do one small thing. You have to exit one application, load another, exit the second one, and load a third, and so on.

Back & Forth solves the problem for you. It will allow you to have up to 20 programs loaded at one time on your PC, and then let you switch instantly among them. So if you're in your word processor, and need to look at a piece of data from your spreadsheet, you'll only have to press a key combination, and you'll be instantly in your spreadsheet. You'll even be able to cut text from one program and paste it into another. Back & Forth resembles DESQ-view, a commercial program that allows you to do similar tasks.

The more memory you have, and the larger hard disk you own, the better this program will work for you. It operates by switching programs from memory to either another portion of memory or to disk when they're not in use, and then back to memory when you call them up. Because of that, a PC with larger memory will allow you to run more programs simultaneously, and a PC with a fast disk will speed up things.

You'll have to spend some time setting up the program to work properly with your system. Although things will go quicker and easier for you if you have a good working knowledge of memory and DOS, it's not required. To set it up, you fill out forms that allow you to specify how much memory you want to devote to certain tasks and the kind of memory you have on your system, among other things. After you've done the basic setup, you fill in other forms to allow your software to run under the program, supplying information such as the program's name, the directory it's stored in, and the command needed to execute it from the command line. You also define a key combination—a hotkey—that will allow you to instantly switch to that program when you're in another program. Figure 15.7 shows the form for allowing the word processor XyWrite to run under Back & Forth.

Figure 15.7
Customizing Back & Forth to run XyWrite

The program itself takes up from 14k to 20k of conventional memory. If you load it into high memory, however, between 640k and 1Mb, it will take up only 1k of lower memory. It makes use of extended memory, expanded memory, RAM disks, hard disks, and conventional memory.

If you've ever been frustrated that you can't easily do several jobs at once on your PC, this program is worth a look.

Back & Forth
Registration fee: $$
Progressive Solutions, Inc.
Box 276125
San Antonio, TX 78227
(212) 794-9341; (800) 833-4400 (orders)

METZ Lock

If you're a Windows user, and want to be able to lock your system so that only you or someone you authorize can access it, consider METZ Lock. Whenever you run the program, your system will be locked—only someone who knows the password will be allowed to use it. You can also configure the program so that it automatically runs whenever your system is started. In this way, only someone who knows your password can use your PC.

METZ Lock is quite flexible. You can have it automatically lock your system at the same time every day, so that, for example, it will be locked every day when you leave work. The program also includes an optional screen blanker, to preserve your monitor.

If you run only Windows programs within Windows, you'll only need to run METZ Lock from within Windows, and it will lock your system when you tell it to. However, if you run DOS programs in a DOS window, you'll have to intall a TSR program from the DOS prompt before a Windows session. This TSR program will also allow you to disable the Ctrl-Alt-Del keystroke sequence, so that those keystrokes can't be used to reboot your computer.

METZ Lock
Registration fee: $$
METZ Software
P.O. Box 6042
Bellevue, WA 98008
(206) 641-4525; (800) 447-1712 (orders)

Newkey

This is an exceptionally powerful and useful keyboard macro program. It can save you much time and wasted energy at the keyboard.

With Newkey, you assign keystroke sequences to particular key combinations. Subsequently, those sequences will be replayed whenever you hit that key combination, whether you're at the DOS prompt or within a program. So, for example, you could assign the text string "Greetings and Felicitations" to the key combination Alt-G, and then whenever Alt-G was struck, the phrase "Greetings and Felicitations" would be typed in.

That is about the simplest type of macro you can create. You can also create much more complicated macros with this program, especially since you can create macros that will pause and take in keyboard input. The macros can accept input in several ways, using both fixed fields and variable fields. When a fixed-field macro stops to accept input, you enter a specified number of characters, and the macro uses those characters and then resumes. With a variable-field macro, the number of characters you enter can vary. The macro waits for you to press Enter before taking in that input and using it.

But even the latter just touches the surface of what's here. You can nest macros within each other, copy macros to each other, and much, much more.

Newkey also has a screen blanker, and can also enhance your keyboard in other ways, including speeding up the *typematic rate*—the speed and responsiveness of your keyboard.

Newkey has several different modules, with differing memory requirements. As you might expect, he most powerful module requires the most memory, whereas less powerful modules require less.

Newkey
Registration fee: $$
FAB Software
P.O. Box 336
Wayland, MA 01778
(508) 358-6357

PC-Vault

Do you have sensitive information on your computer that you'd like to keep from prying eyes? Or are you simply worried that some otherwise well-intentioned person might sit down at your keyboard and do some serious harm to your system or software setup?

If you're worried about either of these things, or if you have other reasons to keep other people from using your computer, then you owe yourself a look at PC-Vault, a security system that will keep unauthorized people from using your PC.

PC-Vault does its work by forcing you, or anyone who uses your PC, to enter a password every time the computer is booted from the hard disk. If the password doesn't match the password you've put into the program, the computer won't boot. If someone tries to get around the security system by booting from the A drive instead of from the hard disk, they'll be able to boot the PC, but won't be able to access the hard disk.

The program also includes what it calls a LunchBreak feature. When you use the LunchBreak portion of the program, your screen is blanked, and your keyboard is locked, so that no one can use or interfere with your PC, but your computer will continue to process whatever task you've asked it to do. This means that you can set a large database operation into motion, for example, put the PC in LunchBreak mode, and then go out to lunch. While you're gone, your computer will finish the database operation, but no one will be able to use the PC.

You can use passwords of up to 16 characters. Additionally, you can set a user name as well, so that someone trying to use your PC will have to know both the password and the user name you've chosen. If someone without the proper password and user name tries to use your PC after a user-specified number of times, an alarm will ring on the PC's speaker. After another user-specified number of attempts, an alarm will ring on the speaker, and the system will lock up for five minutes.

Be aware that the unregistered version of PC-Vault program is crippled: It only allows for passwords of one character, and that character has to be a letter from A to G. Also, make sure to back up your hard disk before using the program for the first time.

PC-Vault
Registration fee: $
Johnson Computer Systems, Inc.
20 Dinwiddie Pl.
Newport News, VA 23602
(804) 872-9583

ZIPKEY

How much time (and money) have you spent calling directory assistance for the area code of a city outside your state? And how much time have you spent similarly trying to find out the zip code of a particular place, so you could mail a letter there?

If you're like most of us, you've spent a fair amount of time at those tasks. With ZIPKEY, you'll need do those no longer—zip codes and area codes will always literally be at your fingertips.

You can run ZIPKEY as a stand-alone or a memory-resident program, although you might be better off running it as a TSR. Then the information will always be close at hand.

When you call the program up, a screen pops up on your screen. If you want to find out the area code and zip code of a particular city or state, you first type the two-digit postal code for the state (**NY** for New York, for example). You then see all the area codes located within that state. To see the area code and zip code of a city within that state, you then type in the name of the city, and you'll be shown the area code and zip code or codes for the city.

You can also use the features in a reverse way. You can, for example, type in a zip code, and be shown the city that matches it, or type in an area code, and see the region covered by that area code.

ZIPKEY
Registration fee: $
Eric Isaacson Software
416 East University Ave.
Bloomington, IN 47401
(812) 339-1811

CHAPTER

16

PC/Computing's Ten Top Shareware Picks

Top Word Processor: PC-Write

Top Communications Program: QModem

Top Spreadsheet: As-Easy-As

Top Database: PC-File

Top DOS Shell: Hard Disk Director

Top General Utility: 4DOS

Top Windows Utility: IconMaster

Top Printer Program: 4Print

Top Game Program: Commander Keen

Top Miscellaneous Program: ZIPKEY

IT'S IMPOSSIBLE, WHEN LOOKING AT HUNDREDS OF SHAREWARE PROGRAMS, not to come up with favorites. Although every program I've written about in this book is worthy of note, some are better than others—and some stand out head and shoulders above the rest. Those programs are what this chapter is about.

I've used a number of different criteria here for choosing the top programs—notably usefulness, elegance of design, and raw power—and added one more to the mix: gut instinct. When two programs were close in all else, I used subjective means to determine the best of the best.

By necessity, choosing the ten top shareware programs means some great software is going to be left out. Just because a program isn't on this list doesn't mean it isn't an excellent piece of software. You may well find that programs not included here suit your own purposes better than those that are listed.

With all that said, the following programs are the best in each of ten categories, corresponding to several of the preceding chapters. Each of the programs below displays an excellence far beyond what one might expect from shareware—or any other software, for that matter. Take the time to try out each of these programs. They will give you a true taste of the best that shareware has to offer.

Top Word Processor: PC-Write

The only thing more dangerous than talking about religion or politics with friends is debating word processors. For a number of reasons, it's an emotional subject, one that touches raw nerves and sets off extended monologues. Some of the most extended on-line debates held on PC/Contact, PC/Computing's on-line forum, have been about the various merits, or lack thereof, of popular word processors such as WordPerfect, Word for Windows, and WordStar.

That emotional attachment to a word processor is just as prevalent in the shareware world as it is among commercial programs. So I'm fully aware of the consequences of putting forth an opinion (in print, yet) on the best shareware word processor.

I must say, though, that it wasn't a difficult choice. The only hesitation I had was in whether the choice should go to a full-fledged word processor or to a text editor instead. The text editor QEdit has long been a favorite of mine, and Boxer, a powerful new text editor, is gaining many adherents as well.

I decided, though, that the award should go to a full-fledged word processor. Text editors are fine for doing simple editing chores, but when you really need writing or editing done, and especially if you care what your output looks like, you'll need a word processor.

And so PC-Write gets the nod. The award is for the entire PC-Write family of programs, which includes the original PC-Write, PC-Write Lite, and PC-Write Standard Level.

PC-Write is clearly the most powerful of shareware word processors. You'll find everything here you need in a word processor, and more. It offers powerful editing functions, solid printer control, a macro-writing facility, and the ability to work in multiple windows. It even has features that some commercial word processors lack, such as the ability to create indices and tables of contents. Also noteworthy is that it allows you to edit one file while you print another, something that many word processors can't do. Figure 16.1 shows two open windows in PC-Write.

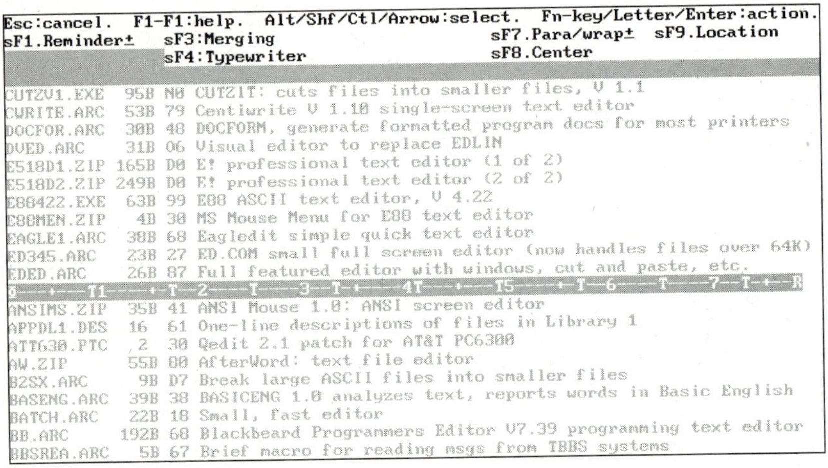

Figure 16.1
Editing in two windows in PC-Write

Despite all this power, it's straightforward and easy to use. It also has an excellent help facility that's always near at hand. Press F1 twice, and you'll be brought into the help system. Move your cursor through the categories on the top part of the screen, and the bottom part of the screen shows you the help text.

PC-Write Lite is a stripped-down version of PC-Write. It's faster and easier to use. It also takes up less disk space than PC-Write, so it's ideal for taking along on a laptop.

The newest member of the family, PC-Write Standard Level, is in some ways the most intriguing. It's more powerful than PC-Write Lite, but less powerful than PC-Write. What's innovative about it is that it allows you to customize it to a great extent. By creating a "profile," you decide what features to include, what to leave out, and how the program should look and feel.

Individually, any of these programs are top of the line. Taken together, they're a superb word processing trio. For more information about PC-Write and other word processors and text editors, turn to Chapter 3.

PC-Write
Registration fee: $$$$

PC-Write Lite
Registration fee: $$$

PC-Write Standard Level
Registration fee: $$$$
Quicksoft
219 First Ave. North, #224
Seattle, WA 98109
(206) 282-0452; (800) 888-8088 (orders)

Top Communications Program: QModem

Shareware and communications software have always been intimately tied. Without communications software there would never be the number of shareware programs available, since there would be no easy way to get at those programs. And without shareware, PC communications wouldn't be as widespread as it now is, because many people use communications software primarily to download shareware.

Because of this symbiotic relationship, there are numerous top-notch shareware communications programs. Choosing among them was one of the most difficult tasks I had in writing this book. I know there's no way to win—my choice is bound to raise hackles. There are so many favorites out there, that choosing any single program is bound to anger those who favor others.

Several programs vied for the top honors. I considered ProComm, that time-honored shareware favorite, but finally decided against it. Datastorm, ProComm's author, adds new features only to the commercial version of the product, not to the shareware version. Because of that, the shareware version is starting to show its age.

I also considered a Windows communications package, Unicom. Unicom is an excellent program, and in some ways is better than commercial Windows communications programs because it tends to be easier to use and more straightforward. But I decided against it for two reasons. The first reason is that Unicom is limited to a smaller number of people than would be a DOS-based program since Windows hasn't yet overtaken DOS. And secondly, Unicom has some of the worst nag screens I've come across in the world of shareware.

I finally decided on QModem. It has everything you need for sophisticated communications, yet is also quite easy to use. It has many file-transfer protocols, many different terminal emulations, and can work with a wide variety of modems.

Even beginners will be able to write communications scripts easily with QModem, because the program's QuickLearn scripting facility can be used by those with little or no on-line experience. The program also has a text editor and a good phone-log facility for tracking incoming and outgoing calls. It has a host mode as well. Figure 16.2 shows how you edit an entry in the dialing window.

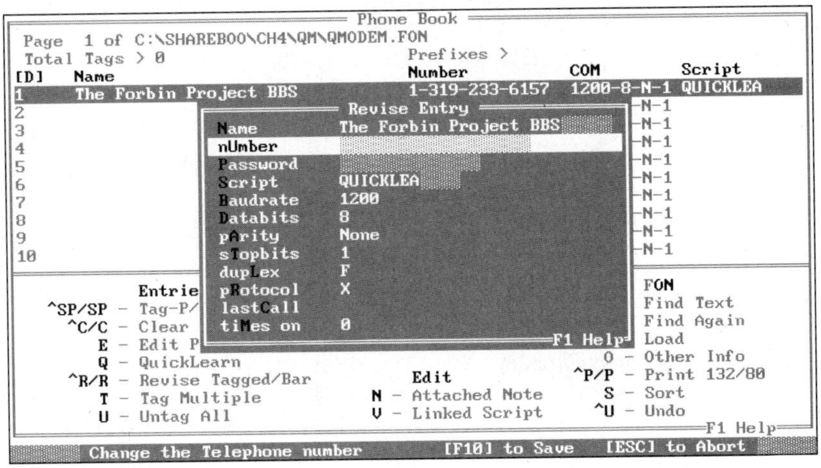

Figure 16.2
Editing an entry in QModem

You can also easily split the program's screen, and it has a particularly powerful batch upload feature. In fact, there's very little that this program won't do.

A commercial version of QModem lists for $99. But Mustang Software also makes available a less powerful version of the program for free from a variety of shareware sources. This version, called a "test drive," carries no registration fee—it's yours for free forever. Mustang will continue to upgrade the "test drive" version. It will, however, always be less powerful than their commercial package.

For more information about QModem, other communications programs and utilities, and compression programs and utilities, turn to Chapter 4.

QModem
Registration fee: Free
Mustang Software
P.O. Box 2264
Bakersfield, CA 93303
(805) 395-0223

Top Spreadsheet: As-Easy-As

Shareware spreadsheets tend not to have as many bells and whistles as their commercial brethren. And possibly because of the longtime popularity of spreadsheets such as Lotus 1-2-3, Microsoft Excel, and Borland's Quattro Pro, there isn't an overabundance of shareware spreadsheets.

That doesn't mean, however, that there aren't excellent shareware spreadsheets—there are. They generally offer more power than the average user—even the advanced user—will ever need. And they're much less expensive than commercial spreadsheets, usually costing less than $100, compared to list prices of $500 for commercial packages.

Several shareware spreadsheets are worthy of note, but the best one, and the most popular, is As-Easy-As. The power of this spreadsheet will surprise you, and its modest registration fee makes it one of the best values in all of sharewaredom.

How powerful is it? As-Easy-As can create spreadsheets with up to 8192 rows by 256 columns. It can create ten different types of graphs. It will solve equations. It can import and export dBASE III and dBASE IV files. It supports CGA, Hercules, and EGA cards. And it will import Lotus .WKS and .WK1 worksheets.

And if that's not enough for you, there's more. As-Easy-As can link spreadsheets and has database functions as well. You'll be able to export your spreadsheets and graphs in PIC format so that they can be used with desktop publishing and word processing programs. There's a built-in word processing module. And it includes all the spreadsheet formulas and calculations that you would expect from a top-level spreadsheet.

When using As-Easy-As, a slash (/) key brings a menu on screen, as show in Figure 16.3. The menu can be a pull-down vertical menu on either side of the screen, or it can be configured in Lotus 1-2-3 fashion so that it goes horizontally across the top of the screen.

The program has become so popular that a number of shareware add-ins will work with it, including several from the program's developer, Trius. Some of the add-ins will let you do sophisticated printing with the program, allowing you, for example, to print spreadsheets sideways. Other add-ins allow you to create 3-D graphics.

There are also many templates available for As-Easy-As, which will allow you to do such things as choosing among different types of life insurance. When you register As-Easy-As, you get several add-ins and templates for free.

For more information about As-Easy-As and other spreadsheets and spreadsheet utilities, turn to Chapter 5.

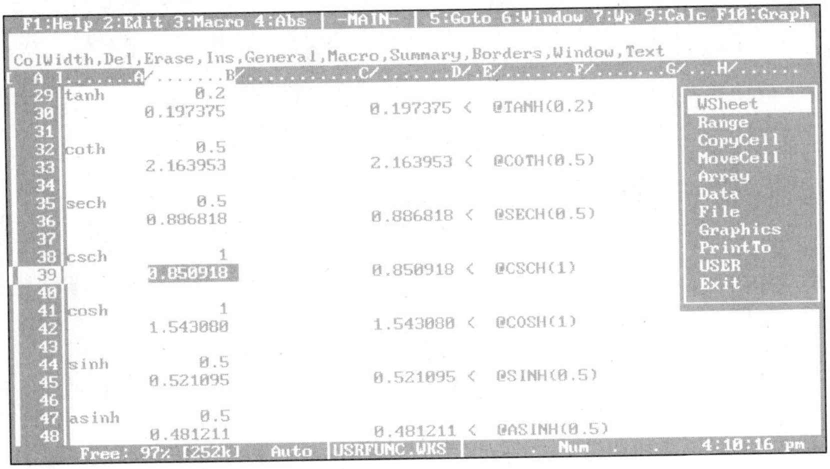

Figure 16.3
As-Easy-As with an on-screen menu

As-Easy-As
Registration fee: $$
Trius, Inc.
231 Sutton St., Suite 2D-3
North Andover, MA 01845
(508) 794-9377

Top Database: PC-File

There are many excellent shareware databases. In general, they balance two ideals: giving you the most power and being as simple to use as possible. It's not always easy to maintain that balance; in general, programs stress one or the other. Some, such as WAMPUM, fall on the side of being powerful, but aren't as easy to use as other shareware databases. Others, such as FastFile, are quite easy to use, but don't offer the same amount of power as do other, more difficult programs.

That's what makes PC-File so remarkable, and why it's my choice as the top shareware database. It's simple enough for database novices to use, yet powerful enough that even experienced database users won't be dissatisfied. In some other categories of shareware it was difficult to choose a top program, because there were so many top contenders. But when it came to databases, the choice was simple. PC-File is without peer.

PC-File is menu-driven, so those new to databases need not feel uncomfortable or intimidated when first using it. To create a new database from scratch, you fill out a series of on-screen forms. Even relatively inexperienced users should be able to create a new database within ten minutes.

Using the database you've created is similarly simple. Again, the menus mean that even users without database experience will be able to get at the program's many features.

Just because it's easy to use doesn't mean that power has been sacrificed. It hasn't. Its files are dBASE compatible, it has password protection and LAN support, and has a macro language. Its searching features are sophisticated and include Boolean logic operators. You can sort on up to ten fields at once. And you can bypass the menus in many instances, and use the keyboard instead. You can create mailing labels, perform mail-merge tasks, generate reports, and create and print graphics based on your data. You can also use it to dial your telephone and keep track of your phone calls.

As an example of how the program balances ease of use and power, look at its search capabilities. For simple searches, or for users not greatly experienced with databases, there's a simple search mode, in which you fill in the blanks in an on-screen questionnaire, shown in Figure 16.4. For more experienced users, or more complicated searches, you can type in a search formula.

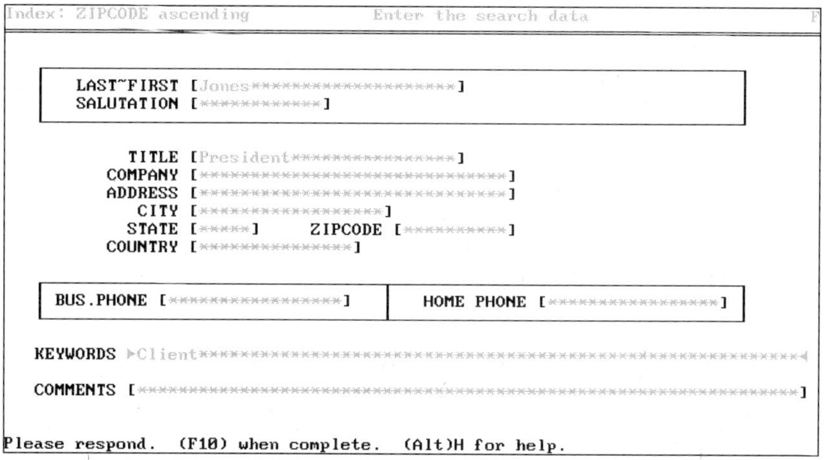

Figure 16.4
Searching for a record in PC-File the simple way

The last version of PC-File available as shareware is version 5.0. PC-File 6.0 and above, and a Windows version of the product, are only available as commercial software. ButtonWare, however, will continue to support the shareware versions of PC-File.

For more information about PC-File and other shareware databases and database utilities, turn to Chapter 6.

PC-File
Registration fee: $$$$
ButtonWare
ButtonWare, Inc.
P.O. Box 96058
Bellevue, WA 98009
(206) 454-0479; (800) 528-8866 (orders)

Top DOS Shell: Hard Disk Director

DOS shells are absolutely invaluable programs. Without them, you're left to the vagaries of DOS, something I wouldn't wish on my worst enemy.

Shells do several things for you. They'll show you, in a tree structure, the organization of your hard disk's directories. They'll allow you to manage your directories and files without resorting to cryptic DOS commands. And they'll let you easily get at other DOS commands as well.

There are many DOS shells available, many of them quite good. And recently Xtree, a long-time commercial favorite, was made available as shareware, adding yet one more solid DOS shell to the ranks of try-it-before-you-buy-it software.

It wasn't a particularly difficult decision to come up with the best DOS shell. There were a number of worthy contenders, notably Xtree and Stupen-DOS. But the best of the bunch is definitely Hard Disk Director. That's because this shell goes well beyond what you expect from a DOS shell. Not only will it let you manage your directories, hard disk, and files with ease, but it also includes a menuing system. And it has many other helpful features, such as a utility that will let you change to any directory with just a few keystrokes.

When the program is loaded it shows you, in tree form, all the directories on your disk. This is where you'll do most of your work. The program will let you copy, move, delete, and rename files and directories. You'll be able to move entire directories, with all the files in them, to a different directory. And its utilities are superb as well. The program will tell you, for instance, what percent of your hard disk is full, and how many disks you'll need to back up individual directories or your entire hard disk.

Hard Disk Director is actually a set of four related programs. The overall DOS shell, named DL.EXE, is the one you'll use for global work on your hard disk. A streamlined version of the program, DB.EXE, lets you manage individual directories rather than an entire hard disk. A file named DA.EXE lets you work on your files without using the tree-like listing of DL.EXE. And DM.EXE is the menuing program. While the menuing portion of Hard

Disk Director isn't as sophisticated as some of the shareware that's devoted exclusively to menuing, it's a solid, useful program.

For more information about Hard Disk Director and other shareware DOS shells and menuing programs, turn to Chapter 8.

Hard Disk Director
Registration fee: $$
Helpware
1537 Fourth St.
San Rafael, CA 94901
(415) 453-9779

Top General Utility: 4DOS

Shareware excels in utility programs. Many people, in fact, think only of utilities when they think of shareware, because this is one area where the breadth and usefulness of the programs available outstrip what you'll find in the commercial world.

There are literally thousands of utilities to solve just about any problem you can name. You'll find a dizzying choice of file searchers, batch-file enhancers, command-line utilities, and far, far more. Choosing the single utility among them as the best leaves out dozens of exceptional programs.

This was the closest call of any I had to make. The choice boiled down to two utilities: List Plus and 4DOS. List Plus is a superb file viewer, directory lister, DOS shell, and more. 4DOS is a complete replacement for COMMAND.COM.

In the end, I chose 4DOS. This exceptional program is everything that DOS should have been. Pick any command-line problem you have, and the odds are that 4DOS will solve it for you.

You can use 4DOS instead of COMMAND.COM, or can instead load it on top of COMMAND.COM. The program does a number of things. It enhances many DOS commands, such as DELETE and COPY. You can, for example, erase files with a number of different extensions at once with it, and can have the program force you to confirm that you want to delete the files.

It also includes many commands that DOS simply doesn't have. Noteworthy among them is a MOVE command that allows you to move a file easily between directories or drives. With DOS, you would first have to copy the file to another drive or directory and then erase it from the original drive or directory. You'll find dozens of other commands not found in DOS as well.

4DOS also has a rich batch-command language. With it, you'll be able to execute nested batch files, accept input from the keyboard, draw boxes and lines in color, beep the speaker at a certain tone for a certain duration, and more.

The program also has alias commands, which let you issue a lengthy command with only a few keystrokes. To do this, you simply tell 4DOS to issue the long command every time you type a simple command that you've previously defined as an alias.

4DOS has an excellent help system that is accessed by pressing the F1 key. The most recent version also features commands specifically geared to DOS 5. The program, in fact, is such a good one that Symantec licensed it from its shareware author, tweaked it a bit, and includes it in the Norton Utilities as its NDOS replacement for COMMAND.COM. Symantec knows a good thing when they see it, and so should you.

For more information about 4DOS and other general utilities, turn to Chapter 9.

4DOS
Registration fee: $$
JP Software
P.O. Box 1470
East Arlington, MA 02174
(617) 646-3975; (800) 368-8777 (orders)

Top Windows Utility: IconMaster

Nowhere is there more vitality and creativity in the shareware world today than in those developers writing programs and utilities for Windows. When Windows first came out, shareware authors rushed out with numerous utilities to make up for Windows shortcomings, and to do things that Windows simply couldn't do.

That rush of software continues today. The range of special programs devoted to making Windows easier to use is astonishing. You'll find a shareware program to make just about any aspect of Windows work better.

In picking the best Windows utility, I steered clear of Windows applications such as the communications package Unicom and the text editor WinEdit. I looked only at utilities and other programs designed to make Windows easier to use, that enhanced Windows in some unique way, or that provided a system utility that Windows didn't provide.

There are so many excellent utilities that coming up with a clear winner was difficult. METZ Software has several noteworthy ones, in particular the METZ Task Manager, an excellent replacement for Windows Task Manager. And Sloop Manager, from Sloop Software, makes an interesting, unique replacement for the Windows Program Manager. Chapter 10, on special Windows shareware, details other top programs.

In the end, though, I decided upon IconMaster as the best shareware utility. There are several reasons for the choice. First, what it does can be found nowhere in Windows as it is shipped. In this, IconMaster is unlike replacements for the Task Manager and Program Manager—they only improve on things shipped with Windows, whereas IconMaster gives you features that the shipped version of the program lacks.

Second, the program is simply so well done. It's exceedingly simple to use, and is designed intelligently and elegantly. It's a joy to use.

IconMaster manages every aspect of your icons under Windows. Begin by using it to see what icons you have on your system. IconMaster will let you view every icon you have, whether the icon is in ICO format or it's found in a file with an .EXE or .DLL extension. Using it, you can view an entire icon collection found in an .EXE file, and you can also view icons embedded within individual Windows applications.

You can do more than view the icons, however. You can extract any icon from an icon collection, either for use with a program or to edit. You can even extract an icon from an application such as Excel, and use that icon in application.

IconMaster lets you create new icons from scratch, too. And you don't have to be an artist to create a new icon. I'm ham-handed at best when a pencil or paintbrush is put in my grasp, but even I can create Windows icons. And if I can, you certainly can. Figure 16.5 shows IconMaster with an icon library in the background and a seasonal icon being created in the foreground. When it is placed, in its proper size, on the Windows desktop, it will look just like a Jack O' Lantern.

Even if you're not icon crazy, you owe it to yourself to take a look at this program. Your sudden icon mastery may surprise you. For more information about IconMaster and other special Windows programs, turn to Chapter 10.

IconMaster
Registration fee: $
Phillip Kaufman
19987 Moran Lane
Saratoga, CA 95040

Top Printer Program: 4Print

Printers aren't the most exciting pieces of computer hardware. In general, they sit there, waiting silently for you to press the proper button, and then they spring to life, spitting out pages.

Most software doesn't take full advantage of all the power hidden in printers. Word processors may give you access to fonts, and graphics software may let you print out images, but in general, few programs really exercise printers fully. And you'll find practically no commercial programs that let you train your printer to do what *you* want it to.

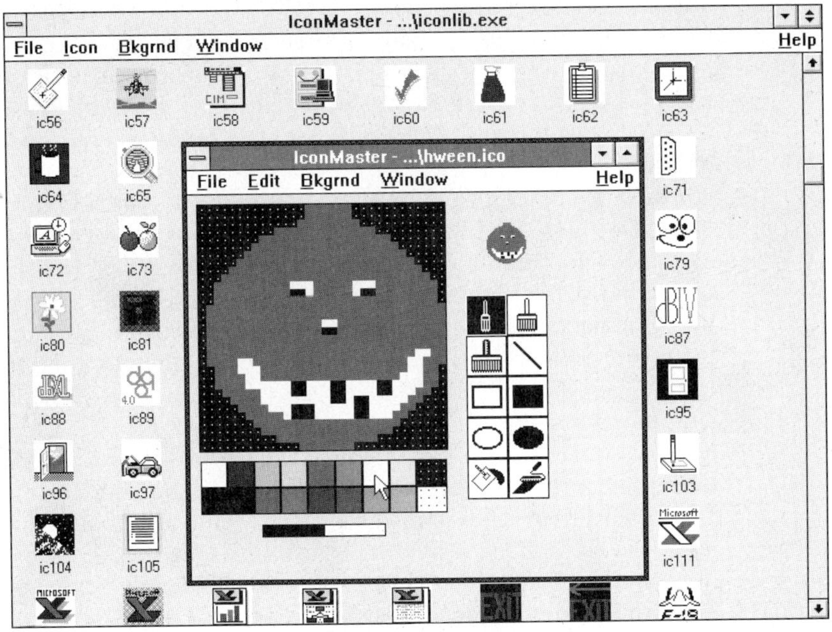

Figure 16.5
Creating a new icon with IconMaster

Luckily, there are a great many shareware programs that tame your printer. And whereas many of them are quite useful, the most innovative and useful of all is 4Print. This unique program lets you use your laser printer to print up to three pages of text, side by side in columns, on a single sheet of paper, saving you reams of paper. You can also print on both sides of the paper, giving you six pages of text on a single sheet. If you regularly print out shareware documentation, you'll find this an invaluable resource. And if you care about the environment, this is a useful program as well, since it cuts down on paper waste by squeezing so much text on a single sheet. You can tell your printer the number of columns you want on each page, the number of lines per page, the page header, which tray to feed the paper from, and more. It will also print in landscape mode so that you can, for example, fit oversized spreadsheets onto a single sheet of paper.

Shipped with the package is an equally innovative program called 4Book, which lets you use your laser printer to create booklets. It takes a text file and reorganizes the order in which the pages will be printed. It then prints the pages two columns to a side, front and back, so that you can fold the pages in half to make a $5^1/_2$-by-$8^1/_2$-inch booklet. The booklet can be easily customized in a number of ways, letting you choose from different cover styles and fonts, for example, as seen in Figure 16.6.

Figure 16.6
A front and back page of a booklet created with 4Book and 4Print

And Windows users need not feel left out. A separate program called 4Shell is a Windows-based front end to both 4Print and 4Book, and makes them much easier to use. Because the programs have so many options and command-line switches to remember otherwise, this is a particularly nice way to go.

For more information about 4Print and other printer programs and utilities, turn to Chapter 13.

4Print
Registration fee: $$
Korenthal Associates, Inc.
230 West 13th St.
New York, NY 10011
(212) 242-1790; (800) 527-7647 (orders)

4Shell
Registration fee: $
ZPAY Payroll Systems, Inc.
2526 69th Ave. South
St. Petersburg, FL 33712
(813) 866-8233

Top Game Program: Commander Keen

Choosing the best shareware game is a difficult proposition. It's not just that there are so many shareware games, but that there are so many different *types* of shareware games. Adventure games, text-based games, strategy games, Windows games, arcade games—the list could go on for some time. The problem was how to choose the best from so many types.

I used one overriding guideline in choosing the best game—which one is the most fun? Which game would I start just to pass a few minutes between phone calls, and find that an hour had passed when I looked up at the clock again?

When I looked at it that way, the answer was really quite simple. The arcade game Commander Keen is the best of the bunch. Normally, I don't play a great many computer games. But Commander Keen is a cut above: The animation and controls are of arcade quality; the characters are funny; and the play witty and challenging. It's one game that I'll keep for some time.

The game is also excellent because it makes full use of the most recent technology. You'll need an EGA or VGA card to play Commander Keen, and though that might keep some people from playing it, it also means it's up-to-date and visually attractive.

If you get the game, here are a couple of hints. First, if your computer beeps for no apparent reason or the game refuses to accept input from your keyboard, type **KEEN1 /K** and press Enter to start the game.

Also, some places in the game can be reached only by using a pogo stick, which you pick up along the way. Even then, how to get at these spots isn't immediately obvious—you'll have to practice the Impossible Pogo Trick. To do this, move in a direction, press the Pogo key (the Alt key), release it quickly, and then press the Jump key (the Ctrl key). You'll move in remarkable ways.

Also, when you finally make your way to the Vorticon Commander's Castle, look for hidden bricks in the entrance hallway. If you find these, you'll get bonus points.

If you're really stumped, or are just looking for even more hints and tricks, call the Commander Keen hints line at (214) 240-0614.

The first episode of Commander Keen is available as shareware for $15. The next two episodes, however, are not available as shareware; they must be purchased directly from the author. They're available for $15 each, and are well worth the cost, especially if you get hooked on this game, as I did. You can buy all three episodes for $30.

One final note: A developer is turning this game into a Nintendo cartridge, so if you get the PC version now, you can say you knew the game before it became *really* famous.

For more information about Commander Keen and other games, turn to Chapter 14.

Commander Keen
Registration fee: $ per episode (all three for the price of two)
Scott Miller
Apogee Software Productions
P.O. Box 476389
Garland, TX 75047
(214) 278-5655; (800) 852-5659 (orders)

Top Miscellaneous Program: ZIPKEY

It may seem odd to choose the best miscellaneous program, because the programs covered in that chapter were all so dissimilar. How can you, for example, compare the quality of a graphics program to a memory utility?

It's not easy, but it can be done. In deciding on the best miscellaneous program, I took several factors into account. First, I looked at how useful the program was. Second, I considered how widely it would be used—a truly phenomenal program that only four people might find of use shouldn't get the award. Third, I judged the program's quality. Finally, I used my gut instincts and went on intangibles: Which one was flat-out the best?

The choice narrowed down to two programs, Desktop Paint and ZIPKEY. Desktop Paint is an excellent graphics program that allows you to create and edit graphic images. ZIPKEY puts zip codes and area codes just a keystroke away whenever you're at your keyboard.

I ended up choosing ZIPKEY for one overriding reason: its usefulness. With it, you'll no longer have to consult the phone directory to get the area code for a specific city; you'll be able to do it at your keyboard. You'll no longer need to wait on hold with the Post Office to find out a town's zip code—that zip code is only a keystroke or two away.

The program can be run either as a TSR, or in stand-alone mode. When used as a TSR, you can copy zip codes directly into an underlying application.

When you call up the program, a screen appears. To see a listing of area codes by state, type the two-letter postal abbreviation for the state's name. You'll see every area code found in the state. To see the area code and zip code of a specific city or town, type in the name of the place. You'll then see the area code and zip code or codes for that location.

The features can also be used in reverse. When you type in a zip code, you will be shown the city or town that matches it. And if you type in an area code, you'll be shown the region that area code covers.

For more information about ZIPKEY and other miscellaneous programs, turn to Chapter 15.

ZIPKEY
Registration fee: $
Eric Isaacson Software
416 East University Ave.
Bloomington, IN 47401
(812) 339-1811

APPENDIX A

Programs on the Disks

At the back of the book, you'll find two 5 1/4-inch, 360k disks filled with six shareware programs for you to try. Even used individually, the programs are quite useful; taken together, they're a comprehensive package that will help you download and use shareware, manage your hard disk, and get the most out of Windows, if you use that operating environment. The programs have been chosen for their high quality as well as general usefulness.

The programs on disk include the popular compression program PKZIP, the communications program {COMMO}, the hard disk manager Treeview, the superb file viewer List, the antiviral program ViruScan, and the innovative replacement for the Windows Task Manager, the METZ Task Manager. In this appendix I'll first give brief descriptions of each of the programs. Then I'll explain how to get the programs from the attached floppy disks onto your hard disk. Finally, I'll give details on how you might use the programs best in order to find and make use of other shareware programs.

Note that the normal rules of shareware apply to these programs—they're free only on a trial basis. If you like them and plan to continue using them, register them with their authors.

Program Descriptions

Below are brief descriptions of the six programs on the attached disks. For more information about these programs, turn to the chapters in which they're covered.

{COMMO}

This communications package's strengths are its small size, speed of execution, and flexibility. The program can be used to upload and download files with the Xmodem and Xmodem-1k (old Ymodem) communication protocols. It can also upload and download ASCII files. For other types of file transfers, {COMMO} can be linked via built-in macros to external protocol drivers. The program's small executable size (about 35k) makes it ideal for taking along on a laptop. {COMMO} also has a macro-writing facility and a host mode. For more information about {COMMO}, see Chapter 4.

List

This remarkable utility should be a vital part of everyone's software toolkit. It's a file viewer, a directory lister, a DOS shell, a phone dialer, and far more.

It excels as a file viewer, which is what it's used for most. Use it to quickly view files, without having to wait while your word processor or text editor loads. To view a file called MANUAL.DOC, type **LIST MANUAL.DOC** on the command line, and you'll be able to view the file on screen. Scroll through the file by using the cursor and Page Up and Page Down keys.

List will also display a directory listing of all the files within a subdirectory. You can display the directory in one to six columns and toggle among the type of display at will.

List will also let you view, copy, delete, rename, move, sort, tag, and untag files. If you hook a word processor or text editor to the program, you can also edit files. You can run programs from List as well, and use it to dial your telephone if you have a modem. For more information on List, see Chapter 9.

METZ Task Manager

This innovative program has the power that Windows' familiar Task Manager lacks. Run it instead of the Task Manager to see how much more helpful it can be.

When you click on the background portion of your screen, or press Ctrl-Esc, the METZ Task Manager pops up. You can now customize your Windows screen layout; configure your system, by choosing a default printer, for example; check on your system status; and run a screen saver.

One especially useful feature allows you to launch your favorite applications without having to double-click on their icons on the desktop. Instead, you can customize the program so that your applications can be launched directly from the METZ Task Manager. For more information about the METZ Task Manager, see Chapter 10.

PKZIP

If you're interested in shareware, PKZIP may be the most important utility you can have. It has only two purposes: to compress files and to decompress files.

When you're working with shareware, you'll mainly use it to decompress files. That's because most shareware on bulletin boards or on-line services has been compressed using this program. This allows bulletin board operators to save hard-disk space, as well as saving you time on the telephone downloading files. Typically, several files are compressed and combined into one file. PKZIP "unzips" the files, while keeping a copy of the original zipped file intact.

PKZIP is run from the command line. Although its syntax can get complex when you're doing sophisticated chores, it's quite easy to use for doing simple things, such as decompressing a file. To decompress a file called SHWARE.ZIP, for example, you'd type the command **PKUNZIP SHWARE** and press Enter.

The program is also quite useful for compressing files. By compressing files or programs you don't regularly use with PKZIP, you'll save quite a bit of disk space. When you want to use them, simply use the program to decompress the files again.

There are far more tricks PKZIP will do for you. Spend some time with it, and you'll find yourself using it for many other things as well.

For more information about PKZIP, compression programs that make PKZIP easier to use, and alternative compression programs, turn to Chapter 4.

Treeview

This all-purpose disk manager and DOS shell lets you manage your hard disk with ease, and gives you instant access to the most common DOS commands.

Treeview gives you a tree-like listing of your entire hard disk or of individual directories. You'll find it quite easy to navigate, using pull-down menus across the top of the screen or keyboard shortcuts.

Macro commands, the ability to split the screen into multiple directories, and the availability of "hooks," which let you run external programs from within Treeview's menus, are just a few of the program's more useful features. For more information about Treeview, see Chapter 8.

ViruScan

ViruScan is the best antiviral scanning utility you can find. It may be the most powerful and accurate virus detection program available, not just among shareware programs, but among commercial software as well. ViruScan can check for viruses on your floppy disks as well as in your PC's RAM.

Remember to run ViruScan from a write-protected floppy disk; if you ran it from your hard disk, the program itself might become infected.

If ViruScan encounters a virus, it gives you an on-screen report listing the files that were infected and the name of the virus or viruses infecting them. It also summarizes the number of files it checked, and the number of files which have been found to be infected.

The program can search individual directories, individual files, and multiple drives at a single pass. You can tell it the extension of specific overlay files, and it will check those as well. ViruScan can also use several methods for looking for viruses it has never heard of, and scan inside executable files compressed with PKWARE's PKLITE program.

ViruScan can eradicate viruses as well as detect them, but it does so by deleting the file in which the file is found. A better bet for virus eradication is to use McAfee's Clean-Up, which kills the virus and then attempts to reconstruct the disinfected file.

For more information about ViruScan, see Chapter 12.

Installing the Programs

The six programs are on two disks: Disk 1 and Disk 2. Disk 1 contains the programs PKZIP, Treeview, and the METZ Task Manager. Disk 2 contains List, {COMMO}, and ViruScan. All of the programs on disk are in compressed format. Some of them are self-extracting—that is, you'll need no extra software in order to decompress them. You just type the name of the file that contains the programs and they will automatically decompress. The other programs are in ZIP format, and need to be unzipped using PKZIP. Therefore, you'll want to install PKZIP first, so you can use it to extract the .ZIP files for the other programs.

After you've installed the programs, use them as you would any shareware program. For more information on how to use shareware that's new to you, turn to Chapter 2.

Installing Programs on Disk 1: PKZIP, Treeview, and the METZ Task Manager

You'll find three programs on Disk 1: PKZIP, Treeview, and the METZ Task Manager. Both PKZIP and Treeview are self-extracting files. The METZ Task Manager is in ZIP format, so its files must be unzipped with PKZIP before it can be used.

Installing PKZIP

To install PKZIP, first put Disk 1 in your A or B drive; in our example, we'll assume the drive is A. Now make a directory on your hard disk where you want to put PKZIP. Call it whatever you'd like. If your hard disk drive is C, and you're going to call the new directory \ZIP, for example, you would make the directory by entering **MD \ZIP** at the C prompt.

Now you'll need to copy the PKZIP file, PKZ110.EXE, from the disk to the new directory. Using the directory and drive from our example, you would copy the file from the A drive by entering

```
COPY A:PKZ110.EXE C:\ZIP
```

at the C prompt. After your computer finishes copying the file, you should get a prompt telling you the file has been copied.

Now switch to the \ZIP directory by entering **CD \ZIP** at the command line. Check to see that the PKZ110.EXE file was copied to the directory by typing **DIR** and pressing Enter. The PKZ110.EXE file should be listed.

To extract the PKZIP program from the file, just enter **PKZ110** at the command line. All the files that make PKZIP work will be extracted from the PKZ110 file.

You can now use PKZIP to compress and decompress files and to make self-extracting files. Before using the program, be sure to read the

README.DOC and MANUAL.DOC files, using your word processor or text editor.

Installing Treeview

To install Treeview, put Disk 1 in your A or B drive. In our example, we'll again assume the drive is A. Now make a directory on your hard disk where you'll put Treeview. Call it whatever you'd like. If your hard disk drive is C and you're going to call the new directory \TREE, for example, you would make the new directory by entering **MD \TREE** at the C prompt.

Now you'll need to copy the Treeview file, TREEVU.EXE, from the disk to the new directory. Using the drive and directory from our example, you would copy it from the A drive by entering

```
COPY A:TREEVU.EXE C:\TREE
```

at the C prompt. After your computer finishes copying the file, you should get a prompt telling you the file has been copied.

Now switch to the \TREE directory by entering **CD \TREE** at the command line. Check to see that the TREEVU.EXE file was copied to the directory by typing **DIR** and pressing Enter. You should see the TREEVU.EXE file listed there.

To extract the Treeview program from the file, type **TREEVU** at the command line and press Enter. You'll be greeted by a screen that gives a brief description of the program and lists the files that can be extracted from TREEVU.EXE. You'll be asked whether you want to extract the files; type **Y**, and all the files will be extracted.

You can now use Treeview to manage your hard disk, issue DOS prompts, and more. Before using the program, read the READ.ME and TV.DOC files, using your word processor or text editor.

Installing METZ Task Manager

Before installing the METZ Task Manager, you'll need to have first installed the PKZIP program, since the METZ Task Manager is in ZIP format. Follow the directions above for installing PKZIP, if you haven't already done so.

After PKZIP has been installed, put Disk 1 in your A or B drive. In our example, we'll assume the drive is A. Now make a directory on your hard disk where you'll put the METZ Task Manager. Call it whatever you'd like. In our example, we'll assume the hard disk drive is C, and that you're going to call the new directory \METZ. Make the directory by typing **MD \METZ** and pressing Enter at the C prompt.

Now you'll need to copy the METZ Task Manager compressed file, TASKMA.ZIP, from the disk to the new directory. Copy it from the A drive to the directory and drive from the above example by typing

```
COPY A:TASKMA.ZIP C:\METZ
```

at the C prompt and pressing Enter. After your computer finishes copying the file, you should get a prompt telling you the file has been copied.

Now switch to the \METZ directory by typing **CD \METZ** at the command line and pressing Enter. You should now be in the \METZ directory. Check to see that the TASKMA.ZIP file was copied to the directory by typing **DIR** and pressing Enter. You should see the TASKMA.ZIP file listed.

Before you can use the program, you'll need to unzip the file. Assuming that the program PKZIP is in a directory called \ZIP and that the TASKMA.ZIP file is in the directory you're in now, enter

```
\ZIP\PKUNZIP TASKMA
```

at the command line. All the files you need to run the METZ Task Manager should now be extracted from the TASKMA.ZIP file.

You're now ready to use the METZ Task Manager as a replacement for Windows's Task Manager. Before using it, read the file TASKMAN.DOC, using your word processor or text editor.

Installing Programs on Disk 2: List, ViruScan, and {COMMO}

You'll find three programs on Disk 2: List, ViruScan, and {COMMO}. List is a self-extracting file, but {COMMO} and ViruScan are in ZIP format. Before they can be used, they must be decompressed with PKZIP.

Installing List

To install List, put Disk 2 in your A or B drive. In our example, we'll assume the drive is A. Now make a directory on your hard disk where you'll put List. Call it whatever you'd like. For example, if the hard disk drive is C and you're going to call the new directory \LIST, make the directory by entering **MD \LIST** at the C prompt.

Now you'll need to copy the List file, LIST76.EXE, from the disk to the new directory. For example, to copy it from the A drive to the \LIST directory on hard disk drive C, enter

```
COPY A:LIST76.EXE C:\LIST
```

at the C prompt. After your computer finishes copying the file, you should get a prompt telling you the file has been copied.

Now switch to the \LIST directory by typing **CD \LIST** at the command line and pressing Enter. Check to see that the LIST76.EXE file was copied to the directory by typing **DIR** and pressing Enter. You should see the LIST76.EXE file listed there.

To extract the List program from the file, enter **LIST76** at the command line. A screen will appear, telling you what files are about to be extracted and other information. To continue extracting the files, press **Y**. All the files you need will be extracted from the LIST76.EXE file.

You can now use List to view files and manage your hard disk. Before using the program for other tasks, use it to read the LICENSE and LIST.DOC files.

Installing ViruScan

Before installing ViruScan, you'll need to first install the PKZIP program, since ViruScan is in ZIP format. Follow the directions above for installing PKZIP, if you haven't already done so.

After PKZIP has been installed, put Disk 2 in your A or B drive. In our example, we'll assume the drive is A. Now make a directory on your hard disk where you'll put ViruScan. Call it whatever you'd like. For example, if the hard disk drive is C and you're going to call the new directory \SCAN, make the directory by typing **MD \SCAN** and pressing Enter at the C prompt.

Now you'll need to copy the ViruScan file, SCAN84.ZIP, from the disk to the new directory. For example, to copy it from the A drive to the \SCAN directory on hard disk drive C, enter

```
COPY A:SCAN84.ZIP C:\SCAN
```

at the C prompt. After your computer finishes copying the file, you should get a prompt telling you the file has been copied.

Now switch to the \SCAN directory by typing **CD \SCAN** at the command line and pressing Enter. Check to see that the SCAN84.ZIP file was copied to the directory by typing **DIR** and pressing Enter. You should see the SCAN84.ZIP file listed there.

Before you can use the program, you'll need to unzip the file. If the program PKZIP is in a directory called \ZIP and the SCAN84.ZIP file is in the directory you're in now, type

```
\ZIP\PKUNZIP SCAN84
```

at the command line and press Enter. All the files you need to run ViruScan will now be extracted from the SCAN84.ZIP file.

You're now ready to use ViruScan to check your disks for viruses. Before using it, read the README.1ST and the SCANV84.DOC files, using List or your word processor.

Installing {COMMO}

Before installing {COMMO}, you'll need to first install the PKZIP program, since {COMMO} is in ZIP format. Follow the directions above for installing PKZIP, if you haven't already done so.

After PKZIP has been installed, put Disk 2 in your A or B drive. In our example, we'll assume the drive is A. Now make a directory on your hard disk where you'll put {COMMO}. Call it whatever you'd like. For example, if the hard disk drive is C and you're going to call the new directory \COMMO, make the directory by typing **MD \COMMO** and pressing Enter at the C prompt.

Now you'll need to copy the {COMMO} file, COMMO501.ZIP, from the disk to the new directory. To copy it from the A drive to the \COMMO directory on hard disk drive C, type

```
COPY A:COMMO501.ZIP C:\COMMO
```

at the C prompt and press Enter. After your computer finishes copying the file, you should get a prompt telling you the file has been copied.

Now switch to the \COMMO directory by typing **CD \COMMO** at the command line and pressing Enter. Check to see that the COMMO501.ZIP file was copied to the directory by typing **DIR** and pressing Enter. You should see the COMMO501.ZIP file listed there.

Before you can use the program, you'll need to unzip the file. If the program PKZIP is in a directory called \ZIP and the COMMO501.ZIP file is in the directory you're in now, type

```
\ZIP\PKUNZIP COMMO501
```

at the command line and press Enter. All the files you need to run {COMMO} will now be extracted from the COMMO501.ZIP file.

You're now ready to use {COMMO} as a communications program. Before using it, read the READ.ME and COMMO.DOC files, using List or your word processor.

Using the Programs Together

Several of the programs on this disk—notably {COMMO}, List, ViruScan, and PKZIP—have been chosen not only for their general usefulness, but because they're particularly helpful to shareware aficionados. Used together, they form the basis of a powerful toolkit for finding and using shareware.

The best use of {COMMO} is obvious—use it to dial into a bulletin board or an on-line service, and to search for and download shareware. Note that {COMMO} has two protocols for downloading shareware, XModem and Xmodem-1k (old Ymodem). These protocols, especially XModem, should work on most bulletin boards you'll dial into. If they won't, you can attach protocol drives to the program, which will allow you to download files with other protocols. Also note that some files on bulletin boards are meant to be read, not used as programs. These can be downloaded with {COMMO}'s ASCII downloading facility.

Once you've downloaded the shareware, use ViruScan to take basic antiviral precautions and to make sure the shareware contains no viruses. (See Chapters 2 and 12 on the best way to use ViruScan.)

Next, it's time to use PKZIP. The majority of shareware available from on-line sources is in the ZIP compression format. You'll know that a file is in that format by its file extension, .ZIP.

Create a directory to hold the software you've downloaded. For example, if you've downloaded the MINDIT program in its compressed form, MINDIT.ZIP, create a directory called \MINDIT, and put MINDIT.ZIP in that directory. If you already have PKZIP in a directory called \ZIP on your computer, all you need to do to decompress MINDIT.ZIP is to move to the \MINDIT directory, type

```
\ZIP\PKUNZIP MINDIT
```

and press Enter. PKZIP will now decompress all the files in the MINDIT.ZIP file. It will keep the original MINDIT.ZIP file intact, too, however. If you wish, you can delete MINDIT.ZIP from your hard disk after you've begun using the decompressed MINDIT program.

Now that you've unzipped the files, List takes over. Use List to read the MINDIT's documentation. Look first for a file such as READ.ME, README.TXT or README.1ST. To view the file called READ.ME, for example, assuming you've put List in the \LIST subdirectory, type

```
\LIST\LIST READ.ME
```

and press Enter. You'll now be able to view the file. Similarly, you can use List to view the program's documentation.

Treeview can also be helpful when downloading and using shareware. Since it can create and delete directories, and copy, move, and delete files, you can use it to create directories for your shareware, and to manage your shareware files.

Putting a Shareware Toolkit Together

If you're planning on downloading and using shareware, you should have a basic hardware and software toolkit at the ready. The hardware component of your toolkit is a modem. The software tools include a communications package, as well as programs that will simplify and speed up the downloading process. Below are the basics of putting together such a toolkit.

Choosing a Modem

The most important piece of hardware for downloading shareware is your modem. These days, there are two practical choices: a 2,400 bps modem or a 9,600 bps modem.

The choice between the two comes down to cost. Modems that run at 2,400 bps are significantly cheaper than those that run at 9,600 bps. 2,400-bps modems are pretty much a commodity item, and so can be quite inexpensive. You'll find many for under $200, and it's not uncommon to find them under $100.

If you have the money, though, you'll be far better off with a 9,600 bps modem. Prices on these high-speed modems have been dropping quickly, and so they're now within reach of the average user. Choosing a 9,600 bps modem isn't as easy as picking a 2,400 bps model; there can be significant differences among them. Workmanship, warranty coverage, and effective throughput vary widely among brands.

Most important are the kinds of communications standards the modem follows. When you're buying a modem, make sure that it adheres to the V.32/V.32bis and V.42/V.42bis standards. Essentially, the V.32 standards define how modems connect to one another at 2,400, 9,600, and 14,400 bps. The V.42 standard controls the way in which modems make sure that there are no transmission errors when information is transferred between them. Finally, the V.42bis standard determines the data compression between modems. When you have a V.42bis modem, data can be compressed fourfold when communicating with another V.42bis modem. This means you can get an effective throughput of 38,400 bps on a 9,600 bps modem—sixteen times the speed of a 2,400 bps modem.

When buying a 9,600 bps modem, also make sure that it carries as long a warranty as possible. Some makes carry warranties for only one year, while others carry warranties for up to five years.

Your best value in a high-speed modem, in my opinion, is Intel's 9600 EX modem. It was awarded PC/Computing's award for the best modem in 1991, with good reason. It's built solidly, adheres to the V.32/V.32bis and V.42/V.42.bis standards, and carries a five-year warranty. Be forewarned, though, that it's not cheap. As of this writing, you can find it for about $500 through the mail. If you spend a lot of time on-line, however, it's well worth it. You'll save in on-line costs; more importantly, you'll save enormous amounts of your time. It's the modem I used for downloading shareware for this book: Without it, I'd probably still be on-line somewhere, waiting for a download to end.

Software Toolkit

You'll also need a good software toolkit when going on-line to get shareware. In addition to {COMMO}, PKZIP, and the other programs included on the disks enclosed with this book, you'll definitely want to sample the following helpful programs. (Registration information on these programs can be found at the end of this section.)

For instance, there are many different kinds of communications protocols you can use to download software, and not all communications programs have all those protocols. If you want to add more protocols to {COMMO} or other communications software, a program called DSZ can help. DSZ adds several protocols, including Xmodem, Ymodem, and Zmodem. Another helpful program, called OZBEXT, will add CompuServe B and B+ file transfer protocols to your program.

If you have a complicated hardware setup, you may run into problems using your COM ports. For instance, what do you do when you need to use COM3 for communications, and your communications software can only use COM1 or COM2? The answer is to get PortFinder, which will let you use COM3 and COM4.

Finally, before you begin a file transfer, it would be handy to know how long you'll be on-line. You can do that with a program called TransferTIME. The program will estimate how long it will take to download a file using Xmodem, Ymodem, ZModem, or CompuServe B+ protocols at 1,200, 2,400, and 9,600 bps. It will also estimate how much the file transfer will cost in connect time.

DSZ
Registration fee: $ (specify 5 1/4- or 3 1/2-inch disk)
Omen Technology
P.O. Box 4681
Portland, OR 97208
(503) 621-3406

OZBEXT
Registration fee: None
Available on CompuServe in IBMCOM, Library 10.

PortFinder
Registration fee: $
mcTRONic Systems
7426 Cornwall Bridge Lane
Houston, TX 77041
(713) 462-7687

TransferTIME
Registration fee: $
RGH Software
Route 1, Box 24
Reed City, MI 49677
(Also available on CompuServe on the IBMCOM forum.)

APPENDIX C

Where to Get Shareware

There are many sources of shareware: on-line sources (which include bulletin boards and on-line services), disk vendors, user groups, and friends. Below I've listed the two most popular sources—bulletin boards and disk vendors.

The listings below were compiled by the Association of Shareware Professionals (ASP). In order to be listed with the ASP, bulletin boards and disk vendors have to abide by certain standards of ethics. For more information about the ASP, about shareware in general, and for the most recent version of the listings, you can write or call

Association of Shareware Professionals
545 Grover Rd
Muskegon, MI 49442
(616) 788-5131

Foreign bulletin boards listed here are English-language unless noted otherwise. Subscription rates are approximated in U.S. dollars, except in the case of Canadian boards, where rates are given in Canadian dollars. It is also important to note that phone numbers given here for non-U.S. boards and disk vendors include the U.S. international access code, 011. To dial these numbers from countries outside the U.S., please substitute the appropriate access code for your location.

Bulletin Boards

Downloading shareware is probably the most common way of finding it. Look below for bulletin boards near you, dial in, and start your search. The following list was compiled by Bob Ostrander, ASP BBS Membership Committee Chair.

The entries are listed alphabetically by state in the U.S., and then alphabetically by country for foreign boards. There are three columns in each listing. The first column gives the name of the board, the name of the person who runs it, and the board's mailing address. The second column lists the type of bulletin board software used; the number of phone lines the board has; information about the speed of the board and special communications protocols the board handles; and the board's phone number. The third column gives you miscellaneous information about the board, starting with its subscription cost, if any; nodes it accesses; its specialty or emphasis; and the system operator's direct telephone, FAX, or CompuServe ID numbers (CIS), where available. Happy shareware hunting!

ARIZONA

Community Resources Bryan Woody 1802 West Grant Rd, 11-6 Tucson, AZ 85745	Wildcat! 3 lines 9600 MNP HST V32 V42 602-628-7994 (2400) 602-628-8082 (9600)	$35/yr 602-628-8083 (voice)

ARKANSAS

ST COM-Link Clint McBee Route 1, Box 806-C Mena, AR 71953	Remote Access 2 lines 9600 501-394-1454	Free RIME node (ASP conf host) BBS of Ouachitas User Group on-line games and publications 501-394-3853 (voice) 73710,514 (CIS: Emmett McBee)
The Grapevine Jim Wenzel/Greg Wilson 5324 Camp Robinson Road North Little Rock, AR 72118	PCBoard 5 lines 9600 MNP HST V32 V42 501-753-8121	$25/yr RIME, NANet nodes Amiga, C64, Mac
Data Point! Gary Funk 1729 Cortland Fayetteville, AR 72703	TBBS 5 lines 9600 MNP HST V42 501-442-8777	$30/yr FidoNet, AlterNet, UUCP node On-line games and magazines SDN SDS TDN dist.

CALIFORNIA

Modem's Delight of LM Ronald Dishon 14503 Sabine Dr. La Mirada, CA 90633	Telegard 1 line 9600 MNP HST V32 V42 213-944-1221	$12/yr Fidonet node On-line games 213-944-7499 (voice)
Pacific Rim Information Brenda Donovan 4580 Mount Alifan Dr. San Diego, CA 92111	Fido 4 lines (2 pub, 2 sub) 9600 MNP HST V32 V42 619-278-7361	$35/yr (opt.) Fidonet node On-line games 76276,742 (CIS)
La Palma/Western Kelly Tompkins 161 Hillcrest Dr. Fullerton, CA 92632	Wildcat! 3 lines 2400 MNP 213-865-7374	$40/yr (opt.) RIME, Intelec nodes Specializes in desktop publishing 714-870-4356 (voice) 76556,224 (CIS)
The Kandy Shack Mike Bernstein 12531 Strathmore Dr. Garden Grove, CA 92640	PCBoard 5 lines 600 MNP HST V32 V42 714-636-2667	Free ILink, LuciferNet, SharkNet nodes On-line games 714-638-7308 (voice)

The Board Edward Jeffers 2828 Cochran St., #271 Simi Valley, CA 93065	Wildcat! 1 line 2400 818-366-8874	818-366-0997 (voice)
Mount Kerkis Mike Sisk P.O. Box 2107 Sausalito, CA 94965	Waffle 1 line 2400 MNP 415-289-2338	$9/mo UseNet mail link Specializes in AutoCAD 75300,1253 (CIS)
CompuServe IBMNET Don Watkins 749 Parkside Dr. Santa Rosa, CA 95404	Custom-written Quite a few lines 9600 V32 Local phone numbers	Per minute connect charges Parent company in Columbus, OH. Please mail disks to Sysop at this address. 76703,750 (CIS)
24th St. Exchange Don Kuhwarth P.O. Box 188263 Sacramento, CA 95818	TBBS 9 lines 9600 MNP HST V32 V42 916-451-7179 (2400)	$25-35/yr (opt.) On-line games; PC and Mac 916-454-2992 (voice) 916-451-5829 (9600) 76347,1646 (CIS)

COLORADO

George's Computer Room George Clifford 343 Nome St. Aurora, CO 80010	PCBoard 1 line 9600 MNP V32 V42 303-344-9547	Free Ilink node
Circuit Board Jack Dean 1112 Balmora Dr. Lafayette, CO 80026	Remote Access 2 lines 9600 HST 303-666-0304	$25/yr Fidonet node 303-665-7434 (voice)
Boardwatch Magazine Jack Rickard 5970 South Vivian St. Littleton, CO 80127	TBBS 6 lines 9600 MNP HST V32 303-973-4222	$60/yr FidoNet node Boardwatch Magazine/ USA Today; on-line games 303-973-6038 (voice) 71177,2310 (CIS)
Microlink B Girard Westerberg P.O. Box 620247 Littleton, CO 80162	TBBS 7 lines 9600 MNP HST 303-972-9600 (2400) 303-978-9301 (9600)	$50/yr Fidonet node USA Today; large adult file section
Comm-Post Brian Bartee 540 Acoma St. Denver, CO 80204	TBBS 6 lines 9600 HST V42 303-534-4646	$50/yr Fidonet node 303-534-4538 (voice)

Computer Security BBS Calvin Cline 1108 Elbert Ave. Loveland, CO 80537	Wildcat! 1 line 9600 MNP HST V32 V42 303-962-9536	Free McAfee satellite PC/MAC/Amiga; specializes in security/virus 303-669-4183 (voice)

DELAWARE

DTEL Sam Guccione 1832 North duPont Highway Dover, DE 19901	Major BBS 6 lines 9600 MNP HST Compucom 302-739-2818	Free Delaware Tech. & Community College On-line games IBM- and Amiga-supported 302-739-2802 (voice)

FLORIDA

R Fringe Forum Wyatt Cox P.O. Box 520624 Longwood, FL 32752	Tritel 1 line 9600 MNP 407-331-7754	Free On-line magazines; Home of Home Legal Guide 76177,1421 (CIS)
Miami PC Users Group Don Mackai 10448 SW 49th Pl. Cooper City, FL 33328	PCBoard 1 line 9600 MNP HST 305-680-9481	$24/yr (club membership) RIME node 305-434-2976 (voice)
Computer Hut Gene Davis 1825-F1 Tamiami Trail Port Charlotte, FL 33948	TBBS 3 lines 9600 MNP HST V32 813-624-6129	$25/yr Fidonet node On-line games; Home of Lotto Prophet 813-624-2123 (voice) 71251,2123 (CIS)
Action-Link Systems Jim Davie 2905 6th St. East Bradenton, FL 34208	PCBoard 2 lines 9600 HST 813-747-9295	$25/yr RIME node 813-746-3144 (voice)
Toy Shop Chuck Curtis 4195 Elwood Road Spring Hill, FL 34609	Remote Access 1 line 9600 MNP HST 904-688-9124	Free Fidonet node Amiga 904-683-5684 (voice)
Studio PC Ralph LoBianco 10411 Paula Court Port Richey, FL 34668	RBBS 2 lines 9600 HST 813-862-8850	Free Fidonet, Eggnet, SDN nodes 72517,3004 (CIS)

GEORGIA

COM1 Atlanta
Stan Plager
5143 Oakleaf Terrace
Stone Mountain, GA 30087

PCBoard
5 lines
9600 V32
404-879-5985

$30/yr
BBS of Atlanta PC Users Group
404-469-8711 (voice)

ILLINOIS

Uncle Bob's BBS
Jerry Witwicki
924 Apache Trail
Lake Villa, IL 60046

Spitfire
1 line
9600 MNP HST V32 V42
708-265-0698

Free
On-line games
708-356-1820 (voice)
76427,1764 (CIS)

[Parameters]
Robert Pauls
513 West Walnut St.
Carbondale, IL 62901

Wildcat!
1 line
9600 MNP HST V32 V42
618-549-8448

$2/mo or 20 min/day and UL/DL ratio
RIME node
70023,1064 (CIS)

INDIANA

Mail Room
Scott McPheeters
903 College Dr., Apt. 1
Anderson, IN 46012

Fido
1 line
2400
317-644-5029

$10/yr
On-line games
70142,2754 (CIS)

Microcosm
David Burton
3201 East 38th St.
Indianapolis, IN 46218

Wildcat!
1 line
2400
317-545-0930

Free
On-line games

ClassiComputerFieds
Jim Green
5610 East Washington St.
Indianapolis, IN 46219

Custom-written
21 lines
2400
317-359-5199 (IN)
615-883-4700 (TN)

$25/yr; $40/yr (download)
Part of Shareware Testing Laboratories; disk vendor classifieds, movies, more
317-352-0021 x5550 (voice)

The RoadHouse
Richard Holler
4095-B Creek Way
Indianapolis, IN 46227

Remote Access
1 line
2400 MNP
317-784-2147

Free
Fidonet node (ASP conf. host)
Home of Unicorn Software
73567,1547 (CIS)

PBS-BBS
Tony Moleta
3750 Kentucky Ave.
Indianapolis, IN 46241

PCBoard
20 lines
9600 MNP HST V32 V42
317-856-2087

$50/yr
Part of Public Brand Software; Home of Professional Master Key
317-856-2085 (voice)
76635,1670 (CIS: Bob Ostrander)

Ya! WebeCad! Don Habegger 556 East Parkland Ave. Evansville, IN 47711	Wildcat! 1 line 9600 MNP HST V32 V42 812-428-3870	$25/yr Specializes in CAD and engineering 812-428-3927 (voice)

KANSAS

The Motherboard Marty Sadowsky 318 East 8th Newton, KS 67114	TBBS 1 line 9600 HST 316-284-2421	Free On-line Bible study and games 316-284-2078 (voice)
A.C.S. BBS Ken Collins 817 Southern St. Coffeyville, KS 67337	RBBS 1 line 2400 MNP 316-251-2761	Free On-line games 316-251-3328 (voice)

LOUISIANA

Southern On-line Service Russell C. Jackson 5116 Highland Road, Apt. 75 Baton Rouge, LA 70808	PCBoard 1 line 9600 MNP HST V32 V42 504-766-4174	$40/yr Specializes in Windows 70534,56 (CIS)
PUMA Wildcat! Chuck McMillin - CCS P.O. Box 13231 Alexandria, LA 71315	Wildcat! 2 lines 9600 HST 318-443-1065	Free RIME node On-line games
Linking Rings Don Hutson P.O. Box 238 Tioga, LA 71477	Spitfire 3 lines 9600 MNP HST V32 V42 318-442-5694	Free Fidonet node 318-442-0818 (voice)

MARYLAND

Hollywood News Brandon Hayden P.O. Box 366 Hollywood, MD 20636	PCBoard 3 lines 9600 MNP HST V42 301-373-3530	$15-35/yr (3rd line) RIME node USA Today 301-373-5132 (voice)
CBUG BBS Bob Weber P.O. Box 125 Columbia, MD 21045	PCBoard 2 lines 2400 301-750-1253	Free BBS of Columbia Baltimore Users Group 301-750-2435 (voice)
Rosedale Data Line Gordon Malone P.O. Box 9561 Rosedale, MD 21237	TPBoard 2 lines 9600 MNP HST V32 V42 301-866-4554	$70/yr 301-866-2006 (voice)

MASSACHUSETTS

Total Access Scott Lagos 109 Massachusetts Ave. Lunenburg, MA 01462	PCBoard 6 lines 9600 MNP HST V32 V42 508-342-5998	$40/yr RIME node USA Today; on-line games
Software Creations Daniel Linton, Jr. 26 Harris St. Clinton, MA 01510	PCBoard 3 lines 9600 MNP HST V32 V42 508-365-2359	$30/yr (opt.) RIME node Home of Picture Puzzle; on-line games 508-368-8654 (voice) 73230,3254 (CIS)
Xevious BBS Nels J. Anderson 92 Bishop Dr. Framingham, MA 01701	PCBoard 4 lines 9600 MNP HST V32 V42 508-875-3618	$30/yr (opt.) Home of Mah Jongg, etc. 71020,2613 (CIS)
The Open Window Mike Riley 30 Broadway Beverly, MA 01915	TPBoard 2 lines 9600 MNP V32 V42 508-927-7224	$20/yr (opt.) Windows, OS/2, and Case tools 508-927-8808 (voice) 70164,2065 (CIS)
Channel 1 Tess Heder P.O. Box 338 Cambridge, MA 02238	PCBoard 60 lines 9600 MNP HST V32 V42 617-354-8873	$40-85/yr RIME, Ilink, Smartnet nodes Multilanguage 617-864-0100 (voice)

MICHIGAN

HAL 9000 Victor Volkman 5145 Pontiac Trail Ann Arbor, MI 48105	PCBoard 3 lines 9600 MNP V32 V42 313-663-4173	$15/yr (opt.) W-Net Headquarters Also Mac
Wolverine Rick Rosinski 4702 Jefferson Midland, MI 48706	Searchlight 2 lines 9600 HST 517-695-9952	$20/yr or UL/DL ratio BBS of Midland Computer Club 517-631-7162 (voice)

MINNESOTA

PC-ProFile Wayne Evans 2108 22nd St., NW Rochester, MN 55901	RBBS 3 lines 9600 MNP HST V32 V42 507-288-6347	$35/yr

MISSOURI

Planet ><
Tim Kilgore
2601 South Providence, #40
Columbia, MO 65203

Wildcat!
2 lines
9600 MNP V32 V42
314-443-0319

$20-40/yr
Fidonet node
On-line magazines

NEBRASKA

Hawg Wild!
Nate Chase
1612 North 152nd Plaza
Omaha, NE 68154

Wildcat!
3 lines
9600 MNP V32 V42
402-493-2737

$10-30/yr
72105,1700 (CIS)

NEVADA

Public Access
Shareware Unlimited 900
Rick Cross
2511 Stewart Ave.
Las Vegas, NV 89110

RBBS
13 lines (total)
9600 MNP HST V32 V42
702-383-9939
900-933-0024 (2400)
900-933-0096 (9600)

$45/yr or $1/call + .39/min for 900 numbers
On-line games; USA Today; PC, C64/128, Amiga
702-385-0877 (voice)
70700,2760 (CIS)
800-659-8750 (9600 bps line for author uploads

NEW HAMPSHIRE

Nor'Easter Premium
Gardiner Jones
67 Bayberry Lane
Londonderry, NH 03053

PCBoard
1 line
9600 MNP HST V32 V42
603-432-6711

$25/yr
RIME, Newlife nodes
73700,470 (CIS)

NEW JERSEY

Visions InfoLine
Jeffrey Morgan
885 Sterling St.
Plainfield, NJ 07062

Wildcat!
1 line
9600 MNP HST V32 V42
908-769-1779

$20/yr (opt.)
RIME node
Specializes in media/broadcast
908-769-1778 (voice)
71106,276 (CIS)

Evergreen BBS
Bob Lawton
104 Evergreen Ave.
Hopatcong, NJ 07843

Wildcat!
3 lines
9600 MNP HST V32 V42
201-398-2373

$5-50/yr (opt.)
On-line games
201-770-3461 (voice)

Collectors' BBS Eric Marks P.O. Box 861 Chatham, NJ 07928	TBBS 1 line 2400 201-635-4519	Free Specializes in collecting on-line games 201-635-3509 (voice) 70771,2741 (CIS)
Data-Base Michael Walter 19 Grandin Dr. Annandale, NJ 08801	PCBoard 3 lines 9600 V.32 908-735-2185	$30-45 (opt.) Smartnet node 73260,3622 (CIS)

NEW MEXICO

Albuquerque ROS Steven Fox P.O. Box 13711 Albuquerque, NM 87192	ROS 4 lines 9600 MNP HST V32 V42 505-299-5974	$20/yr (opt.) On-line games 70366,755 (CIS)
Construction Net #6 Pam Trexler 505 Oppenheimer, #209 Los Alamos, NM 87544	Opus 1 line 9600 MNP HST V32 V42 505-662-0659	Free Fidonet node

NEW YORK

The Invention Factory Michael Sussell 321 Greenwich St. New York, NY 10013	PCBoard 44 lines 9600 MNP HST V32 V42 212-431-1194	$15-100/yr On-line games PM 5am-6am daily 212-431-5555 (voice)
Red Phone Info Sys Chris Welber 215 West 11th St. New York, NY 10014	PCBoard 5 lines 9600 MNP HST V32 V42 212-924-1138	$45/yr (1 free line) RIME, Intelec, Smartnet nodes Specializes in LANs 212-924-6899 (voice) 71147,1670 (CIS)
Gooey (GUI) BBS David Shapiro 217 East 85th St. New York, NY 10028	PCBoard 3 lines 9600 MNP HST V32 V42 212-876-5885	$50/yr RIME node
Smart Office Solutions Bob Browne 84 South Division St. New Rochelle, NY 10805	PCBoard 2 lines 9600 MNP HST 914-576-6139	Free RIME, Intelec, PSA-Net nodes 914-632-1496 (voice) 70062,3536 (CIS)
The Consultant Jay Caplan JAF P.O. Box 8571 New York, NY 10116	Prologon/Prodoor 2 lines (1 pub, 1 sub) 600 MNP HST V42 718-837-3236	$40/yr (opt.) 70421,17 (CIS)

<<Prism
Janis Kracht
30 Bedford Ave.
Middletown, NY 10940

Maximus
2 lines
9600 MNP HST V42
914-344-0350

Free
On-line games
70267,2777 (CIS)

Apartment 2
John Rogers
260-32 74th Ave.
Glen Oaks, NY 11004

WWIV
1 line
2400
718-347-1075

Free
WWIVnet node
73447,3127 (CIS)

Albany Computer Entertainment
Mike Gunderloy
6 Arizona Ave.
Rensselaer, NY 12144

Major BBS
10 lines
9600 MNP V32
Compucom
518-479-2051

$10/mo (cheaper by year)
RIME node
On-line conferencing
518-479-3707 (voice)
72771,275 (CIS)

Ulysses Systems Network
Joseph Aquino
735 South James St., #37
Rome, NY 13440

RBBS
3 lines
9600 MNP HST V32 V42
315-339-5591

$10-25/yr (opt.)
On-line games
315-336-4509 (voice)
70033,2175 (CIS)

Excalibur Systems
Ed Gray
42 Beechnut Terrace
Whitesboro, NY 13492

RBBS
1 line
9600 MNP HST V32 V42
315-736-3792

Free
FidoNet, RBBSNet nodes
On-line games
15-736-3842 (voice)

NORTH CAROLINA

Big Byte
Tom Curtis
609 Rogers St.
Rockwell, NC 28138

Searchlight
1 line
9600 MNP HST V32 V42
704-279-2295

Free
Fidonet node
704-279-4433 (voice)

NORTH DAKOTA

City Lites
John Lundel
2498 30th Ave. South, #123
Grand Forks, ND 58201

PCBoard
4 lines
9600 MNP HST V32 V42
701-772-5399

$30/yr or 1/5 UL/DL ratio
RIME node
701-775-5601 (voice)

OREGON

Random Access Info Net
Jeff Clark/Jan Stevens
P.O. Box 136
Corbett, OR 97019

Wildcat!
16 lines
9600 MNP V32 V42
503-695-3250

$35/yr
Internet, Newsnet nodes
On-line games; USA Today; PC/MAC/Unix/Amiga/Atari
503-695-2120 (voice)

PENNSYLVANIA

PGHSouth Dan Deady P.O. Box 14853 Pittsburgh, PA 15234	PCBoard 2 lines 9600 HST 412-563-5416	$25/yr RIME hub 76060,1743 (CIS)
Bad Attitude BBS Gay Ann Dearbeck P.O. Box 89 Erie, PA 16512	Spitfire 2 lines 9600 HST Compucom 814-456-6209	Subscription or UL/DL ratio (opt.) On-line games
SataLink Info Systems Ron Brandt P.O. Box 449 Huntingdon Valley, PA 19006	PCBoard 9 lines 2400 MNP 215-364-3324	$60/yr (9600 HST access) RIME, SDN, WinNet, SDS, ILink, DVNet, SmartNet, FidoNet, DataNet nodes 215-364-8963 (voice)

RHODE ISLAND

Connections BBS Eric Robichaud P.O. Box 748 Woonsocket, RI 02895	Remote Access 1 line 9600 MNP 401-658-3465	Free Home of Blank-It 401-658-4217 (voice) 73770,1633 (CIS)

SOUTH CAROLINA

The B.I.B.S. System Taine Gilliam P.O. Box 1441 Charleston, SC 29402	Maximus 1 line 9600 MNP HST V32 V42 803-577-0545	Free Adult Link, SDN, PDN nodes 72047,473 (CIS)
East Bay X-Change Mike Ratledge 995 Buck Hall Landing McClellanville, SC 29458	Remote Access 2 lines (1 pub, 1 sub) 9600 MNP HST V32 V42 803-556-7485	$25/yr (opt.) Fidonet, SDS nodes PM 3am-4am daily 76666,1512 (CIS)
Pee Dee Exchange Erwin Reyer Route 2, Box 317-A Florence, SC 29501	WWiV 1 line 9600 MNP V42 803-393-7399	Free 75106,3700 (CIS)

TENNESSEE

PC Junction Douglas Carpenter 323 Tennessee Nursery Rd. Cleveland, TN 37311	PC Board 1 line 9600 HST 615-478-2890	$5-25 (opt.) or 1/20 UL/DL ratio Intelec, Smartnet, Throbnet nodes Multilanguage interface; on-line games

For Nashville, TN: see also ClassiComputerFieds, under Indiana

TEXAS

Mother Board II Doug Scoggins 1102 Enterprise Dr., Ste. 209 Grand Prairie, TX 75051	GAP 3 lines 9600 MNP HST V32 V42 214-642-1287	$25/yr RIME node
DFW Programmer's Exchange Ric Naff 2023 Shortal Dr. Dallas, TX 75217	SpitFire 1 line 9600 V32 V42 214-398-3112	Free RIME node On-line games 1600,2611 (CIS)
Collector's Edition Leonard Hult 3733 Rockdale Dr. Dallas, TX 75220	PCBoard 2 lines 9600 MNP HST V32 V42 214-351-9859	$15-25/yr or 30 min/day RIME node
Turning Point Info Paul Tischler 12511 Turkey Ridge Austin, TX 78729	TBBS 2 lines 9600 MNP HST V32 V42 512-219-7828	$40/yr (512) 258-7861 (voice)
CompuSystems Larry Hickerson 714 North Weatherly St. Borger, TX 79007	Wildcat! 1 line 2400 806-274-4054	Free 806-274-5866 (voice)

UTAH

Rocky Mountain Software Raymond Snow P.O. Box 18279 Salt Lake City, UT 84118	PCBoard 4 lines 9600 MNP HST V32 V42 801-963-8721	$40/yr 801-963-8720 (voice) 71441,2410 (CIS)

VIRGINIA

Elusive Diamond Gregg Snyder 9922 Coffer Woods Road Burke, VA 22015	RBBS 3 lines 9600 MNP HST 703-323-6423	$25/yr (opt.) RIME node 703-250-0242 (voice)
The Break (East) Bruce Jackson 4660 Whitaker Pl. Dale City, VA 22193	RBBS 2 lines 9600 MNP HST V32 V42 703-680-9269	Free 703-878-0790 (voice)

GLIB Jon Larimore P.O. Box 636 Arlington, VA 22216	TBBS 17 lines 9600 HST 703-578-4542	Free Gaycom node USA Today; specializes in gay/ lesbian issues 703-379-4568 (voice) 75766,3135 (CIS)
Blue Ridge Express Webb B. Blackman, Jr. P.O. Box 34446 Richmond, VA 23234	RBBS 23 lines 2400 804-790-1675	$30/yr (30 min/day free)
Club PC BBS Jim Kreyling 1217 Crescent Dr. Smithfield, VA 23430	GT Power 1 line 9600 MNP HST V32 V42 DS 804-357-0357	$30/yr or UL/DL ratio GT Global hub, RIME node Home of OZ & QB/PDS software; on-line games 804-357-9190 (voice)
Windows BBS John Champion 155-H Pinewood Crescent Yorktown, VA 23693	Wildcat! 1 line 9600 MNP HST V32 V42 804-766-0553	Free RIME node On-line games; mainly Windows programs

WEST VIRGINIA

Mindless Ones Frank Salerno 117 South Bellview Dr. Weirton, WV 26062	PCBoard 3 lines 9600 MNP HST V32 V42 304-723-0263	Free ILink node BBS of Tri-State Comp Association On-line games

WISCONSIN

Byzantine Empire Jeff Frawley, Sr. 1109 Manson St. Wausau, WI 54401	Wildcat! 1 line 2400 715-848-2833	$15/yr. On-line games 715-842-8998 (voice)
The Twilight Zone John Hrusovszky 1119 East Main St. Auburndale, WI 54412	RBBS 2 lines 9600 MNP HST V32 715-652-2758	Free Fidonet node BBS of Central Wisconsin Users Group; on-line games 715-652-2887 (voice)
Rapid River James Suzda, Sr. 6848 Highway 34 Rudolph, WI 54475	RBBS 1 line 2400 715-435-3855	Free 715-435-3495 (voice)

INTERNATIONAL LISTINGS

CANADA

Canada Remote Systems Jud Newell #D 1331 Crestlawn Dr. Mississauga, Ontario Canada L4W 2P9	PCBoard 108 lines 9600 MNP HST V32 V42 1-416-629-7000	$100/yr (Canadian) English or French interface Many services & users group libraries 1-416-620-1439 (voice) 71625,1404 (CIS)
T-8000 Info System Brian G. Simpson 3324 49th St., SW Calgary, Alberta Canada T3E 3Y3	TBBS 4 lines 9600 MNP HST V32 V42 1-403-246-4487	$35/yr (Canadian) On-line games; Boardwatch, other magazines & DBs; PC & TRS I/III/IV/Coco 70245,1215 (CIS)
AIS Multiline Chris Pinnell P.O. Box 182 Cranbrook, British Columbia Canada V1C 4H7	Major BBS 2 lines 9600 MNP HST V42 1-604-489-4206	$48/yr (Canadian) On-line games 1-604-489-5015 (voice)
Cyberstore Bruce Woodward #390 - 720 Sixth St. New Westminster, British Columbia Canada V3L 3C5	CoCoNet 15 reg, 31 Tymnet lines 9600 MNP V32 V42 1-604-526-3676 Tymnet DPAC 302083501030	Free USA Today & other magazines; PC & Unix/Xenix
CompuSpec Ken Polsson 1143 Burnside Road West Victoria, British Columbia Canada V8Z 1N4	PCBoard 2 lines 9600 MNP HST 1-604-727-2362	$20/yr (Canadian) Specializes in graphics; on-line games 1-604-479-5870 (voice)

PORTUGAL

CATS-BBS Vitor Marques Rua Carlos Jose Barr. 6 C/V Lisbon 1000 Portugal	PCBoard 9 lines 9600 MNP 011-351-1-352-64-22	Approx. $50/yr U.S. 3000 users 011-351-1-352-80-65 (voice) (268)005-229-048 by packet or Tymnet (Portugal)

SPAIN

Icaro BBS Emilio Castellano c/ Luis de Salazar 9 5C Madrid 28002 Spain	Remote Access 1 line 2400 011-34-1-519-46-45	Approx. $30/yr U.S. Spanish language interface LucasFilm support section 100021,176 (CIS: Jose Moro)

TAIWAN ROC

DaemonWorld BBS Raymond Lee 5/fF, 593 Tun-Hwa South Rd. Taipei 10654 Taiwan ROC	Major BBS 16 lines 9600 MNP V32 V42 011-886-2-703-5180	RIME node 011-866-2-708-2125 x172 (voice)

UNITED KINGDOM

Bath BBS Malcolm Burridge 43 Midford Road Bath, Avon BA2 5RW England	Michtron 3 lines 2400 MNP 011-44-225-840060	Approx. $18/yr U.S. PC and Atari
Shareware Support BBS Adrian Mardlin 26 Stanley Hill Ave. Amersham, Buckinghamshire HP7 9BD England	Wildcat! 1 line 9600 MNP HST V32 V42 011-44-494-431861	Free Home of Flexibak Plus 011-44-494-729236 (voice) 100012,1222 (CIS)

Disk Vendors

Another popular way to obtain shareware is from disk vendors. Disk vendors charge a fee for shareware disks that you order from them. Note that their fee does *not* cover the shareware registration fee; it's only for the disk itself. If you decide you like the program, you should register it with its author.

The following is the ASP's list of approved vendors. The list is arranged alphabetically, first by state within the United States, and then alphabetically by country. As before, telephone numbers for foreign locations include the U.S. international access code. If you're dialing from outside the U.S., please substitute your own access code.

ARIZONA

Tammy Tung
Softec Plus
P.O. Box 22885
Tucson, AZ 85734
602-296-6933 (voice)

ARKANSAS

Joe K. McKeel
Shareware Today
P.O. Box 291
Brookland, AR 72417
501-932-9035 (voice)

Robert Reynolds
Data Software
602 4th Ave., Suite 3
Conway, AR 72032
501-327-0388 (voice)

CALIFORNIA

James Carvin
CWI Inzoformation Services
P.O. Box 4851
Anaheim, CA 92803
714-879-7917 (voice)
714-879-1036 (FAX)

Jim Thompson
Jim Thompson Enterprises
150 South Magnolia Ave., Suite 248
Anaheim, CA 92804
714-821-5090 (voice)

Bob Huebschwerlen, Floyd Littrell
Software Source, Inc.
165 Cristich Lane, Unit C
Campbell, CA 95008
800-443-3475 (voice)
408-371-6522 (FAX)

Michael Zanussi
Micro Star
1945 Camino Vida Roble, Suites A & B
Carlsbad, CA 92008
619-931-4947 (voice)
619-931-4950 (FAX)

Christine Harris
PD Software House
6456 Tupelo Dr., Suite 363
Citrus Heights, CA 95621
800-359-1985 (voice)

Cliff Drumeller
Generic Computer Systems
22612 Foothill Blvd., Suite 200-C
Hayward, CA 94541
415-581-1494 (voice)

James F. Summers
Kennen Publishing
2650 La Cienega Ave.
Los Angeles, CA 90034
213-836-0338 (voice)

Jim Horowitz
The Software Labs
3767 Overland Ave., #112
Los Angeles, CA 90034
213-559-5456 (voice)
213-559-3405 (FAX)

Carmen Fiore
Ceramics & Crafts by Marjorie
P.O. Box 424
Morgan Hill, CA 95038
408-683-2240 (voice)

Gil Gilgen
The $5 Computer Software Store
177 Riverside Dr.
Newport Beach, CA 92663
714-751-2667 (voice)
714-751-0914 (FAX)

Ken Schneider
Nuclear Computing
(Windows products only)
7667 Shadyglade Ave.
North Hollywood, CA 91605
818-764-5374 (voice)

Laura Sol
Computers International
P.O. Box 566085
Oceanside, CA 92058
619-630-0055 (voice)
619-630-0520 (FAX)

Clark Oden
Rainbow Software
P.O. Box 3908
Ontario, CA 91761
714-923-1047 (voice)

John Dibble
D-K Distributing
1057 West Philadelphia, Suite 243
Ontario, CA 91762
714-590-1038 (voice)

Linda Bartholf
Barbara's Choice
38438 20th St. East
Palmdale, CA 93550
805-949-7887 (voice)

Geraldine Eby
Computer Bin
P.O. Box 1826
Perris, CA 92370
714-928-9656 (voice)

Soliman Shebani
ACL
1601 Fulton Ave., Suite 10
Sacramento, CA 95825
916-973-1850 (voice)

J. Cagney France
Next Stop Computing
P.O. Box 1467
San Carlos, CA 94070
415-592-6735 (voice)

Carole Cruz
PC Shareware
1763 Garnet Ave.
San Diego, CA 92109
619-272-6673 (voice)

Rekha Shah
ReejTech
P.O. Box 969
Cupertino, CA 95015
408-973-0352 (voice)

Craig Smith
Sunshine Shareware
1630 South Diamond, Suite B
Santa Ana, CA 92704
714-754-4577 (voice)

George Pulido, Library Manager
PC-SIG
1030D East Duane Ave.
Sunnyvale, CA 94086
408-730-9291 (voice)

Herbert Davis
Best Bits & Bytes
P.O. Box 8245
Van Nuys, CA 91409
818-764-9503 (voice)

John Nicholson
Bear Ware
P.O. Box 11603
Marina Del Rey, CA 90295
213-822-1376 (voice)

Georgianna Fox
Paradise Software
7657 Winnetka Ave., Suite 328-A
Winnetka, CA 91306
818-700-0784 (voice)

COLORADO

Vincent Creazzo, Jr.
Mega-Byte PC Software Supply
8110 West Colfax Ave.
Lakewood, CO 80215
303-239-9224 (voice)

Angie Neverburg
Mile High Software
5149 West 69th Pl.
Westminster, CO 80030
303-426-0465 (voice)

Frank Bushey
The Generic Software Place
5491 West 88th Ave., #113-B
Westminster, CO 80033
303-427-3621 (voice)

CONNECTICUT

Wilfred Desaulnievs
Bright Futures, Inc.
P.O. Box 1030
East Windsor, CT 06088
203-745-5322 (voice)

David Wood
Computer Solutions
181 B Route 37
New Fairfield, CT 06812
203-746-6372 (voice)
203-746-1894 (FAX)

Kevin Tran
PC Arcade
14 Moreland Ave.
Oakville, CT 06779
203-798-3318 (voice)

FLORIDA

George Ryan
Florida PC Library/Shareware+
PO Box 491070
Leesburg, FL 34749
904-728-8088 (voice)

Rodney Lampert
Shareware Depot
12261 SW 132 Court
Miami, FL 33186
305-378-9282 (voice)
305-378-9857 (FAX)

Steven Woas
Celestial Press/Software
4424 Dohrcrest Dr.
New Port Richey, FL 34652
813-845-8522 (voice)

Suz Benge
Simply Software
2989 Sarletto St.
North Port, FL 34287
813-426-2568 (voice)

Robert L. Gilmore
N4ZDU Shareware
Route 3, Box 1151
Oldtown, FL 32680
904-542-9348 (voice)

William Rogers
Public Domain Users Group
1263 Grove Park Dr.
Orange Park, FL 32073
904-264-3512 (voice)

Roger Jones
Shareware To Go
P.O. Box 574575
Orlando, FL 32857
407-679-5159 (voice)

Marvin Graff
Intelligent Resources Corp.
3386 State Road 584, Suite 301
Palm Harbor, FL 34684
813-785-0614 (voice)
813-787-8717 (FAX)

Herb Friedman
The Software Peddler
551 SW 135 Ave., Suite B-111
Pembroke Pines, FL 33027
305-435-9330 (voice)
305-431-8995 (FAX)

Steven J. Robertson
Southern Data
6820 Charleston St.
Hollywood, FL 33024
305-963-0587 (voice)

Elizabeth A. Colontonio
Computer Hut
1825-F1 Tamiami Trail
Port Charlotte, FL 33948
813-624-2123 (voice)
813-624-2191 (FAX)

Sara Cohen
Mom and Pop's Software
3431 Dow Lane
Spring Hill, FL 34609
904-686-1746 (voice)

Rick Olson
Advantage Plus Distributors
7113 Halifax Court
Tampa, FL 33615
813-885-1478 (voice)

Randy Barlow
House of Barlow
6612 South Kisimmee St.
Tampa, FL 33616

Fred Owens
Fred's Software
8502 Wayland Court
Tampa, FL 33634
813-884-2448 (voice)

Ray Cook
Whitecat Software
1958-37th Ave.
Vero Beach, FL 32960
407-569-6634 (voice)

GEORGIA

Donald Spero
Data Outlet Shareware
P.O. Box 776
Macon, GA 31202
912-743-3732 (voice)

Robert Pope
Personal Computer Creations, Inc.
P.O. Box 2201
Peachtree City, GA 30269
404-304-1304 (voice)

HAWAII

Isaac Leonard
I. Leonard & Company
1875 Kalaniandole St.
Hilo, HI 96720
808-935-1273 (voice)

B. Michael Tagawa
Vista Photographic L&P, Inc.
95-106 Huaala Pl.
Mililani, HI 96789
808-625-7512 (voice)

ILLINOIS

Charles Strusz
Infoquest
Route 1, Box 157
Carbondale, IL 62901
618-549-3414 (voice)
618-457-7057 (FAX)

Susan E. Chomyok
that Disk company
P.O. Box 634
Glen Ellyn, IL 60138
708-858-8357 (voice)

Mr. & Mrs. Ron Gafron
PeakSoft
865 North Dexter
Hoffman Estates, IL 60194
708-843-1225 (voice)

William Dickson
Shareable Software International, Inc.
P.O. Box 59102
Schaumburg, IL 60159
708-397-0381 (FAX)

Michael Lauria
Airline Computer Supplies
869 East Schaumburg Road, Suite 200
Schaumburg, IL 60194
708-619-8182 (voice)

INDIANA

Ron Hermann
Generic Software Place, Inc.
P.O. Box 1177
Carmel, IN 46032
317-846-8474 (voice)

Shawn Berg
Bee Software Publishing, Inc.
P.O. Box 1179
Hammond, IN 46320
219-931-3761 (voice)

Jim Green
Shareware Testing Laboratories
5610 East Washington St.
Indianapolis, IN 46219
317-351-0021 (voice)
317-357-8505 (FAX)

Bob Burns, Librarian
Public Brand Software
3750 Kentucky Ave.
Indianapolis, IN 46241
317-856-2091 (voice)

Jennie Harvey
SaturnSoft, Ltd.
2120 Ohio St., Box 8909
Michigan City, IN 46360
219-874-6398 (voice)
219-874-9670 (FAX)

KENTUCKY

Dr. Donald Bodley
FF & P Enterprises
Dr. File Finder's Shareware Collection
2050 Idle Hour Center, Suite 106
Lexington, KY 40502
606-266-9958 (voice)

Laura D. Falk
Software Shopper
Falsoft, Inc.
9509 U.S. Highway 42, P.O. Box 385
Prospect, KY 40059
502-228-4492 (voice)
502-228-5121 (FAX)

LOUISIANA

Charles J. Tekippe, Ph.D., Librarian
Sizzleware Shareware Library
P.O. Box 6429
Lake Charles, LA 70606
318-474-1548 (voice)

MARYLAND

William Barb, Jr.
Software Connection
816 South Highland Ave.
Baltimore, MD 21224
301-276-8302 (voice)

MASSACHUSETTS

Dominic Mariano
Discovery Software
P.O. Box 1056
Attleboro, MA 02703
508-226-5541 (voice)

Mark A. Connor
Software Shoppe
P.O. Box 785
Ayer, MA 01432
508-772-7909 (voice)

William Mitchell
Mitchell Disk Software Library
P.O. Box 96
Bradford, MA 01835
508-372-1779 (voice)

Shareware Librarian
Argus Computerized Exchange
20 Mall Road, Suite 210
Burlington, MA 01803
617-674-2354 (voice)
617-674-2360 (FAX)

Denis R. Bergeron
New England Shareware
116 Memory Lane
Orange, MA 01364
508-575-0742 (voice)

MICHIGAN

June Lee
Softshoppe
P.O. Box 3678
Ann Arbor, MI 48106
313-763-8721 (voice)

Patrick R. Rygiel
HYTech, Inc.
P.O. Box 805
Dearborn, MI 48121
313-837-1796 (voice)

Gary Berg
Sofsource/Digital By Design
4241 Southport Circle
Okemos, MI 48864
517-349-3560 (voice)
517-349-3419 (FAX)

MINNESOTA

Duane Franke
Sherburne Knowledge Systems, Inc.
12220 Riverwood Dr.
Burnsville, MN 55337
612-895-6099 (voice)
612-895-1792 (FAX)

MISSOURI

Larry Myers
Infinity Data Products
1404 Old Cape Road, #3
Jackson, MO 63755
314-243-8483 (voice)

Glen Roper
The Datapak Library
1226 South Plaza
Springfield, MO 65804
417-865-9641 x4118 (voice)

MONTANA

W.R. Richardson
Prairieware
P.O. Box 265
3101-1st Ave. North
Great Falls, MT 59401
406-727-4675 (voice)

NEW HAMPSHIRE

James C. Richards
Simple Series
P.O. Box 1167
Plaistow, NH 03865
603-642-3828 (voice)

NEW JERSEY

Dixon Yee
Micro Technology
21 Vistage Dr.
East Windsor, NJ 08520
609-426-0465 (voice)

Bruce A. Fulda
Cheap Disks
P.O. Box 224
Kearny, NJ 07032
201-762-3014 (voice)

Alex Hahn
Bureau of Electronic Publishing
141 New Road
Parsippany, NJ 07054
201-808-2700 (voice)
201-808-2676 (FAX)

Art Wengel
Princeton Software, Inc.
200 Wall St.
Princeton, NJ 08540
609-924-4900 (voice)

NEW YORK

George M. Hurley
GVH Computer Services
768 East 222nd St.
Bronx, NY 10467
212-798-7738 (voice)

Richard Graham
Night Owls Computer Service
219 Potomac Ave.
Buffalo, NY 14213
716-886-2726 (voice)
716-886-0545 (FAX)

Leo Patterson
HYPER.DOC Business Information Systems
9119 Skinner Road
Fredonia, NY 14063
716-672-4254 (voice)

Bill Shor
Pik A Program
13 St. Marks Pl.
New York, NY 10003
212-598-4459 (voice)
212-228-5879 (FAX)

Craig Kerwien
Ziff Communications
1 Park Ave.
New York, NY 10016
212-503-3554 (voice)
212-503-4415 (FAX)

NORTH CAROLINA

Dave Cohen
DBLinx
1117 Manchester Dr.
Cary, NC 27511
919-469-5196 (voice)

Catherine L. Adams
Adams Computer Sales
7322 Avalon Dr.
Fayetteville, NC 28303
919-867-6181 (voice)

Michael Wester
Shareware Solutions
Route 6, Box 34
Fuquay-Varina, NC 27526

E. Richard (Dick) Hefner
PD Select, Inc.
P.O. Box 1884
Gastonia, NC 28053
704-868-2664 (voice)

Mile Champion
Treasure Chest Software
5010 Pecan Dr.
Shelby, NC 28150
704-487-8447 (voice)

NORTH DAKOTA

Conrad Kulesza
Midwest Software Library
P.O. Box 6184
Grand Forks, ND 58202
800-333-7614 (voice)

OHIO

Donald R. Hein
Ultimate Data Technology
7751 Hickory Lane
Findlay, OH 45840
419-423-3920 (voice)

Anthony Saliba
Most Significant Bits
13733-B Madison Ave.
Lakewood, OH 44107
216-221-9836 (voice)

Gregg W. Flagg
Flagg's Floppy
26929 Tall Oaks Trail
Olmsted Township, OH 44138
216-235-9407 (voice)

Frank Garber
Shareware & More
2037 Key St. #F
Maumee, OH 43537
419-347-4065 (voice)

Chris Williams
Accusoft
14761 Pearl Road, Suite 309
Strongsville, OH 44136
216-225-2340 (voice)
216-225-2340 (FAX)

OREGON

Bethy Cuozzo
Software Excitement
6475 Crater Lake Highway
Central Point, OR 97502
503-826-8086 (voice)
503-826-8090 (FAX)

Robert C. Johnson
Reasonable Solutions, Inc.
2101 West Main St.
Medford, OR 97501
503-776-5777 (voice)
503-773-7803 (FAX)

PENNSYLVANIA

Laird Bonn
Bonware
P.O. Box 246, Pine Maple Street
McAllisterville, PA 17049
717-463-3030 or 717-463-2300 (voice)

Charles S. Percherke
Computer Bug
4110 Brownsville Road, Suite 50
Pittsburgh, PA 15227
412-882-3374 (voice)
412-882-8523 (FAX)

Lawrence Delaney
$ave On $oftware
P.O. Box 2837
Wilkes Barre, PA 18703
717-824-5452 (voice)
717-822-9767 (FAX)

RHODE ISLAND

Jim Martin
Pendragon Software Library
75 Meadowbrook Road
East Greenwich, RI 02818
401-884-6825 (voice)

SOUTH DAKOTA

Rolin Welch
SELECTaWARE
602 NW 9th, Box D16
Madison, SD 57042
605-256-9600 (voice)

TENNESSEE

Anton F. Sedelmeier
T & D Electronics
Route 1, Box 65
Big Rock, TN 37023
615-232-7934 (voice)

Alvin F. Lowe
AFL Industries
213 Ward Circle
Brentwood, TN 37027
615-383-1459 (voice)

Chuck Breazeale
People's Choice
235 Germantown Bend CV. #1
Cordova, TN 38018
901-753-0148 (voice)
901-753-1429 (FAX)

Glenn Smith
Bullseye Distributing
315 Mountain High Dr.
Antioch, TN 37013
615-256-0185 (voice)
615-255-9513 (FAX)

Chip Mincey
Mr. Disk Software
5915 Casey Dr.
Knoxville, TN 37909
615-584-3954 (voice)
615-584-8025 (FAX)

Dean Winegardner
ValueWare
400 Midshipman Road
Knoxville, TN 37922
615-675-7958 (voice)
615-675-0657 (FAX)

TEXAS

Gregory N. Wilson
Big Byte Software
2111 Arkansas Lane, #207
Arlington, TX 76013
817-265-2007 (voice)

Roger Arnold
Arnold Company
Highway 1528, Route 2, Bldg. 231
Cooper, TX 75432
903-395-2922 (voice)
903-395-2340 (FAX)

George Croft
Printers Shareware
5019-5021 West Lovers Lane
Dallas, TX 75209
214-350-1902 (voice)
214-350-2610 (FAX)

Scott Lipsky
Babbage's, Inc.
10741 King William Dr.
Dallas, TX 75220
214-401-9000 (voice)
214-401-9002 (FAX)

Steve Casey
Graematter
P.O. Box 874
Greenville, TX 75401
903-454-3366 (voice)

Nelson Ford
Public Software Library
P.O. Box 35705
Houston, TX 77235
713-721-5205 (voice)

Kenneth Finto
Finto Software
Route 2, Box 44
Rosebud, TX 76570
817-583-2151 (voice)
817-583-2151 (FAX)

UTAH

Mr. Alan C. Heiner
Winners Edge Computer Software
3531 West 5000 St.
Roy, UT 84067
801-825-4229 (voice)

VIRGINIA

Lana Chapman
B.L. Software
P.O. Box 13474
Chesapeake, VA 23325
804-420-8380 (voice)

Kouok Law
Romy Informa Tech
301 East Second St.
Farmville, VA 23901
804-392-8784 (voice)

Paul K. Kirk
Elite Shareware Labs, Inc.
1724 Springhill Road, #C
Staunton, VA 24401
703-885-0726 (voice)

Perry A. Langla, Jr.
Shareware Unlimited
P.O. Box 6303
Virginia Beach, VA 23456
804-471-0882 (voice)

WASHINGTON

Beth Gills
Shareware Outlet, Inc.
713 110th Ave. NE, Suite 206
Bellevue, WA 98004
206-646-3571 (voice)
206-454-3382 (FAX)

Peter Kwan
Gemini Marketing, Inc.
P.O. Box 640
Duvall, WA 98019
206-788-4295 (voice)
206-788-0717 (FAX)

Don Miner
Turbo Users Group
P.O. Box 1510
Poulsbo, WA 98370
206-779-9508 (voice)

Greg Randall
Alpha Systems Computer Software
132-117th St. South
Tacoma, WA 98444
206-535-1995 (voice)

WISCONSIN

Judith C. Brown
Fox Valley Technical College
1825 North Bluemound Dr.
Appleton, WI 54913
414-735-2470 (voice)

Glenn Klein
GK Enterprises
8634 West National Ave.
West Allis, WI 53227
414-546-0111 (voice)
414-546-2371 (FAX)

INTERNATIONAL LISTINGS

ARGENTINA

Daniel Alberto Saban
Estudio Shareware
Riobamba 436 Piso 3 of 5
Capital Federal 1025
Argentina
011-541-583-1570 (voice)
011-541-313-7267 (FAX)

AUSTRALIA

New South Wales

Bill Antill
Seltec Shareware Library
101/29 Newland St.
Bondi Junction, New South Wales 2022
Australia
011-61-2-369-2292 (voice)
011-61-2-369-2201 (FAX)

George Margelis
Budgetware
9 Abermarle St.
Newtown, New South Wales 2042
Australia
011-61-2-519-4233 (voice)
011-61-2-516-4236 (FAX)

Martin S. Utian
Fairware Pty, Ltd.
P.O. Box 411, Rose Bay
Sydney, New South Wales 2029
Australia
011-61-2-371-6623 (voice)
011-61-2-371-0107 (FAX)

Bill Washington
Affordable Software
21 Blaxland St.
P.O. Box 472
Matraville, New South Wales 2036
Australia
011-61-2-311-3539 (voice)

Queensland

Ian Mackay
Manaccom Pty, Ltd.
9 Camford St.
Milton, Queensland 4064
Australia
011-61-7-368-2366 (voice)
011-61-7-369-7589 (FAX)

Mervyn E. Perkins
Alphon Edugames
221 Ridley Road
Bridgeman Downs, Queensland 4035
Australia
011-61-7-263-2744 (voice)

South Australia

David A. Ryan
DKR Software
Box 372
Brighton, South Australia 5048
Australia
011-61-8-377-0049 (voice)
011-61-8-298-7081 (FAX)

Brian W. Stedman
Elite Management
South Mayflower Crescent
Hallett Cove, South Australia 5158
Australia
011-61-8-381-4851 (voice)

Victoria

Linda Burgdorf
PD Software Services P/L
8 Bentley St.
Wantirna, Victoria 3152
Australia
011-61-3-729-9534 (voice)

Alan Siew
AAT Computer Services
P.O. Box 416
Glen Waverly, Victoria 3150
Australia
011-61-3-801-2428 (voice)

West Australia

John A. Chadwick
A Drive Software
7 Waterloo Road
Woodbridge, West Australia 6168
Australia
011-61-9-592-2624 (voice)

Joseph Gazia
Spearwood Shareware Service
22 Sitwell Close
Spearwood, West Australia 6163
Australia
011-61-9-418-5721 (voice)

Benzie Pikoos
Brightspark Computers
4 Richards Pl.
Noranda, Perth, West Australia 6062
Australia
011-61-9-375-1178 (voice)
011-61-9-375-1668 (FAX)

AUSTRIA

Mohiyel-Din Hussein
Husco Austria Handelsgesellschaft m.b.H
Bosendorferstrasse 4
Vienna 1010
Austria
011-43-1/505 94 0621 (FAX)

BELGIUM

Plovie P.
TRAX
Steenstraat 61
8211 Belgium
011-32-50-20-07-35 (voice)
011-32-50-20-07-35 (FAX)

BRAZIL

David James Rotenberg
Maple Informatica Ltda.
Caixa Postal 54201
01296 São Paulo - SP
Brazil
011-55-11-826-4849 (voice)
011-55-11-826-5375 (FAX)

CANADA

Alberta

Distant Markets
Box 1149,
194-3803 Calgary Trail South
Edmonton, Alberta
Canada T6J 5M8
1-403-436-3009 (voice)
1-403-435-0928 (FAX)

British Columbia

Gordon Simmonds
SIM-COM Services
35158 High Dr.
Abbotsford, British Columbia
Canada V2S 4P6
1-604-854-3475 (voice)

Larry Norton
Northern Lights Software
P.O. Box 33026
11198-84th Ave.
Delta, British Columbia
Canada V4C 8E6
1-604-590-3111 (voice)

Kamloops Computer Software
357 Robson Dr.
Kamloops, British Columbia
Canada V2E 1W2
1-604-374-3475 (voice)
1-604-374-0308 (FAX)

Joe P. Kiene
GF Stores Ltd.
RR #1, Davis Bay Road/11
Sechelt, British Columbia
Canada V0N 3A0
1-604-885-5025

Robert Swinhoe
Mike Rowe Services
204-2722 5th St.
Victoria, British Columbia
Canada V8T 4B2
1-604-381-2553 (voice)

Robert A. Reid
Del-Com Services
884-164th St.
White Rock, British Columbia
Canada V4A 4Y5
1-604-535-1300 (voice)

Newfoundland

Paul Squires
Performance Shareware, Inc.
627 Topsail Road
St. Johns, Newfoundland
Canada A1E 2E1
1-709-368-5022 (voice)
1-709-747-3841 (FAX)

Nova Scotia

Claire Farrell
Fred's Favourites
P.O. Box 2542
Dartmouth, Nova Scotia
Canada B2W 4B7
1-902-434-0696 (voice)

Ontario

Amir Khan
Khan's Software
36 Judit Crescent
Brampton, Ontario
Canada L6S 3J4
1-416-458-7360 (voice)

Ralph Kendall
Kencordall Computers
5111 New St.
Burlington, Ontario
Canada L7L 1V2
1-416-333-0444 (voice)

Henri Cousineau
Crazy Horse Software
1249 Second St. West
Cornwall, Ontario
Canada K6J 1J2
1-613-932-6343 (voice)

Dave Pohl
Cross Country Shareware
340 Edinburgh Road North
Guelph, Ontario
Canada N1H 7Y4
1-519-837-0777 (voice)
1-519-836-6043 (FAX)

Paul Fitzpatrick
Alternative Personal Software
269 Springside Dr., Suite C
Hamilton, Ontario
Canada L9B 1P8
1-416-577-4068 (voice)
1-416-577-9861 (FAX)

Hussein Ruda
HRS Software Inc.
145 Royal Crest Court, Unit 41
Markham, Ontario
Canada L3R 9Z4
1-416-470-7669 (voice)
1-416-470-9916 (FAX)

Lawrence Chiabai
Dinsdale Industries
2032 Merivale Road
Nepean, Ontario
Canada K2G 1G6
1-613-723-9532 (voice)

Carlos Dos Santos/Camy Fernandes
CC Supplies
193 Groves Terrace
Newmarket, Ontario
Canada L3Y 8C8
1-416-853-9314 (voice)

Phil Knight
Knightec
35 Robb Blvd., #6
Orangeville, Ontario
Canada L9W 3L1
1-519-942-0624 (voice)
1-519-942-3612 (FAX)

Peter Ellis
Encode Business Systems, Inc.
434 West St. North
Orillia, Ontario
Canada L3V 5E8
1-705-327-7628 (voice)

Greg Dzudz
Software Stop
5211 Grand Blvd.
Windsor, Ontario
Canada N8T 1M2
1-519-974-6731 (voice)

Quebec

Sylvain Gagnon
Logiciels PCS
C.D. 33
Cap Madeleine, Quebec
Canada G8T 7W1
1-819-373-4408 (voice)

Marc Routhier
Marc Routhier Co.
3431, de la Dauversaire
Sainte-Foy, Quebec
Canada G1X 2H6
1-418-653-3705 (voice)

Richard Gaudreault
Logicom
5180 Le Haure
Trois-Rivières-Quest, Quebec
Canada G8Y 5Y9
1-819-378-5013 (voice)
1-819-373-5396 (FAX)

DENMARK

Niels Bjerre
NB-data
Danmarksgade 16
DK-4874 Gedser
Denmark
011-45-53-87-99-75 (voice)

FRANCE

Jean-Marie Guitard
Ordinateurs Utilisateurs France (OUF)
27 Rue des Bluets
Paris 75011
France
011-33-1-4338-0258 (voice)
011-33-1-4338-0873 (FAX)

Nicolas V. Kelemen
DP Tool Club
102 Rue Des Fusilles
Villeneuve D'Ascq F-59493
France
011-33-2084-1963
011-33-2056-5525

GERMANY

Toni Maier-Ennerst
Computer Solutions Software Gm.
Gartenstrasse 2
W-8010 Grafing, Bavaria
Germany

Michael Schlomer
Soft Consult GambH.
Marktplatz 2
6277 Bad Camberg
Germany
011-49-6434-3399 (voice)
011-49-6434-5356 (FAX)

Karsten Windfelder
Josef-Traxel-Weg 4
6500 Mainz
Germany
011-49-6131-368881 (voice)
011-49-6131-368882 (FAX)

Wolfgang Gäbler
CDV - Newsoft
Ettlinger Strasse 5
D-7500 Karlsruhe 1
Germany
011-49-721-385078 (voice)
011-49-721-356437 (FAX)

Camouflage-Soft
Postfach/P.O. Box 761
Sittersweg 85
W-6600 Saarbrücken
Germany
011-49-681-4170330 (voice)
011-49-681-5847397 (FAX)

Nane Jürgensen
Die Deutsche Software Biblioth
Alpenstrasse 52
8038 Groebenzell
Germany

Norbert Zielinski
Zillesoft
Alpener Strasse 67a
D-4134 Rheinberg 1
Germany
011-49-2843-80187 (voice)
011-49-2841-22778 (FAX)

PD-Service-Lage
P.B. 1743
Lage/Lippe
D-4937 Lage/Lippe
Germany
011-49-5232-66912 (voice)
011-49-5232-4039 (FAX)

HONG KONG

Au Mei Fan
Unipub Technologies
4/F, Flat A, Hoi On Building
92-98 Sai Wan Ho Street, Shaukiwan
Hong Kong
011-852-571-5196 (voice)
011-852-566-4487 (FAX)

MALAYSIA

Lee Kim Hye
PC Software Publishing
372-K Lorong 1, Hilir Garden
Ujong Pasir Melaka 75050
Malaysia
011-60-06-244598 (voice)

MEXICO

Adviseware
1211 Sab Dario, Suite 630
Laredo, TX 78040
011-52-5588-0083 (voice)

NETHERLANDS

David Voyle
Tonehalt (Holland) Ltd.
Postbus 13500
2501 Em Den Haag
Netherlands
011-31-70-3658372 (voice)
011-31-70-3616336 (FAX)

NEW ZEALAND

Christopher R. Bennett
23 Tennyson St.
Balmoral, Auckland 4
New Zealand
011-64-9-603-491 (voice)

Robert Logan Cross
Bytes and Nibbles Computer Utilities
24 Leckhampton Court
Dunedin, Otago 9001
New Zealand
011-64-3-455-3669 (voice)

Bill Strauss
Computer Library of New Zealand, Ltd.
Waipopo Road
RD3 Timaru
New Zealand
011-64-3-615-9333 (voice)
011-64-3-615-9333 (FAX)

UNITED KINGDOM

England

Murdoch MacTaggart
The Software Centre
Little Brympton
Brympton d'everycy
Yeoville, Somerset BA22 8TD
England
011-44-935-862609 (voice)

Roland G. Brade
Venus Electronics Shareware
26 Pevensey Way, Frimley Green
Camberley, Surrey GU16 5YJ
England
011-44-252-837860 (voice)

Neil Blaber
P.D. (& Shareware) Software Library
Winscombe House, Beacon Road
Crowborough, Sussex TN6 1UL
England
011-44-892-663298 (voice)
011-44-892-667473 (FAX)

Vincent Paul Cassidy
Disk Park
23 Eagle Dr.
Flitwick, Bedford MK45 1RH
England
011-44-525-713358 (voice)

J.M. Green
Advantage
56 Bath Road
Cheltenham, Gloucestershire GL53 7HJ
England
011-44-242-224340 (voice)
011-44-242-226755 (FAX)

Dr. P.A. Hickling
ShareWare-Elite
25 Cades Parc
Helston, Cornwall TR13 8QS
England
011-44-326-564164 (voice)
011-44-326-564164 (FAX)

Raymond W.G. Harris
ElectronArt Design Ltd. (Pocketware)
78 Kimberley Ave.
Ilford, Essex IG2 7AS
England
011-44-81-590-7979 (voice)

Omicron Systems, Ltd.
45 Blenheim Crescent
Leight-On-Sea, Essex SS9 3DT
England
011-44-702-710391 (voice)

Stewart John Collins
Comopharm Ltd. T/A PC-Sig
111-113 Wandsworth High St.
London SW18 4WY
England
011-44-81-877-1103 (voice)

Larry Rozmaryn
North London Shareware
188 Osidge Lane
Southgate, London N14 5DR
England
011-44-81-361-9811 (voice)

Michael Goodman
Goodman Enterprises
16 Conrad Close
Meir Hay Estate
Longton, Stoke-on-Trent ST3 1SW
England
011-44-782-335650 (voice)
011-44-782-316132 (FAX)

James Wright
PC Independent User Group
87 High St.
Tonbridge, Kent TN9 1RX
England
011-44-732-771512 (voice)
011-44-732-771513 (FAX)

Mark Thompson
MT Software
Greensward House, The Broadway
Totland, Isle of Wight P039 OBX
England
011-44-983-756056 (voice)

M.J. Gearing
Softville Computer Supplies
Unit 5, Stratfield Park, Elettra Ave.
Waterlooville, Hampshire P07 7XN
England
011-44-705-266509 (voice)
011-44-705-251884 (FAX)

Scotland

Don Cuthbert
PC Assist, Ltd.
4/4 Carubbers Close
135 High St.
Edinburgh EH1 1SJ
Scotland
011-44-31-557-6432 (voice)

Peter M. Vass
Vasstec, Ltd.
1485 Dumbarton Road
Glasgow G14 9XL
Scotland
011-44-41-954-6853 (voice)
011-44-41-950-1385 (FAX)

Wales

Alan Marsh
Softcell Services
25 Maywood
Bryna, Pontyclun
Mid Glamorgan CF7 9PZ
Wales

APPENDIX D

Using PC/Contact and ZiffNet

PC/Contact, *PC/Computing*'s on-line service, is an excellent source of shareware, with an extensive shareware library. Many free programs and utilities are also available, including every utility written for *PC/Computing* magazine; all you pay for these programs is connect charges. In addition to utilities and shareware, there are hundreds of macros, spreadsheet templates, batch files, and the like available for downloading.

When you log on to PC/Contact, you'll also be able to talk on line to others interested in shareware or in virtually any other topic you can imagine. *PC/Computing* editors are on line as well, and you can leave messages for them. I'm on line there myself most days, so you can leave messages for me, too.

PC/Computing is actually part of a larger on-line service called ZiffNet, which is owned by the Ziff-Davis Publishing Company. ZiffNet is also home base for the on-line services of other Ziff-Davis magazines, including *PC Magazine, Computer Shopper,* and *PC Week.* These magazines, like *PC/Computing,* also have libraries of shareware, freeware, and public domain software available for downloading. In addition, the popular disk vendor Public Brands Software has its collection of shareware available on line. PC/Contact, along with the rest of ZiffNet, is connected to CompuServe, so once you've joined PC/Contact, you've joined CompuServe, and vice versa.

There are three general places on ZiffNet you'll go to get shareware and free programs and utilities. First, there are the forums of individual magazines, of which PC/Contact is one. The second place to look is through a central searching facility called the Software and Utility Library. Using this facility, you'll be able to locate programs and utilities throughout the different magazines' forums. The final place to try is Public Brand Software's vast shareware collection.

Joining PC/Contact

If you already subscribe to CompuServe, you already have access to PC/Contact, so logging on is easy. Just type

```
GO ZNT:PCCONTACT
```

and press Enter, and you'll have access to the forum. (If you're already in the ZiffNet service, just type **GO PCCONTACT**.) The cost of the forum is $12.80 per hour for 1,200 and 2,400 bps connections, and $22.80 per hour for 9,600 bps connections.

If you're not a CompuServe or ZiffNet member yet, you'll have to join to access PC/Contact. First, you need a local phone number to use when calling PC/Contact. To get this number, call CompuServe at (800) 635-6225. You'll be greeted by a voice-response system, which asks if you want to get a local access number. Tell it that you want that number. Next, you'll be asked to enter your own phone number and area code, and the speed at which you plan to dial into the service. When you have finished entering this information, you'll be given a local access number.

If you prefer, you can get a local access number by modem instead, by dialing into a CompuServe toll-free modem line. Set your communications parameters to 7 data bits, even parity, and full duplex. Then call (800) 346-3247. After your connection is made, press Enter. On your screen, you'll see a prompt that reads "HOST NAME." In response, type **PHONES** and press Enter. A series of on-screen menus will guide you to your local access number.

Once you have the local access number, you'll need to set the communication parameters on your software. Set them at 7 data bits, even parity, 1 stop bit, and full duplex.

Now you're ready to join. Dial the local access number with your modem. When you're connected, press Ctrl-C. A prompt will come onto your screen that reads "User ID." Type **177000,5555** and press Enter. In response, another prompt will appear, reading "Password." Type **ZIFF*NET** and press Enter. You'll notice when you type that no letters appear on your screen. Don't worry, that's the way it's supposed to be—it's set up that way so that no one can peer over your shoulder and see the password you type in.

A prompt will now appear, which will read "Enter agreement number." Type **PCCSHARE** and press Enter. You will now be asked a series of questions. After answering them, you'll be issued a user ID (sometimes referred to as a PPN) and a temporary password. You can now use this user ID and password to log on to the service, following the steps outlined above for joining. When you're prompted for a user ID, enter the ID you've just been given, and when prompted for a password, enter the password you've just been given.

About two weeks from the time you join, you'll get a letter confirming the user ID you've been given and giving you a new password. If you like, you can change your password: Type **GO PASSWORD** when you're on line and follow the instructions you're given.

Finding Shareware on PC/Contact

PC/Contact has several libraries devoted to shareware, freeware, and public domain programs. Here you'll find shareware that has been reviewed in the magazine, as well as templates, macros, utilities, and programs written for *PC/Computing*. First, get to the PC/Contact forum. After typing **GO PCC** from Ziffnet, or **GO ZNT:PCC** from CompuServe and pressing Enter, you'll be greeted with a menu. Type the menu item **1** which corresponds to "PC/Contact Forum," and press Enter. You're now in the PC/Contact Forum. To get to the libraries, enter **LIBRARIES** at a prompt. You'll see a menu listing of all the available libraries. To go to any of the libraries, type the number on the menu and press Enter. You can now browse through the available files by entering **BROWSE** at the prompt. Any of the files you see can be downloaded.

Similarly, you can download software from any of the other Ziff-Davis magazines on ZiffNet. To download a file from the *PC Magazine* forums, for example, you'd enter **GO MAGNET** at a prompt, and you'd be in *PC Magazine*'s on-line service. To access its libraries, follow the same instructions as above.

Finding Shareware with the Software and Utility Library

There are other ways to get shareware from ZiffNet than using the individual libraries of each magazine. One of these is to use the Software and Utility Library, a central repository of shareware, freeware, and public domain software.

To get to the Software and Utility Library, choose that menu option when you log onto ZiffNet, or enter **GO SOFTLIB** at a prompt. You're now in the Software and Utility Library. You'll be greeted by a menu that will help you search for files. If you're not sure how to use the menu, choose the item that gives help on searching.

Using the search information you give it, the Library will look throughout its system for the files you need. When its search is complete, you'll get a list of files that meet your search description. To get a description of any one of those files, type the number that corresponds to it on screen and press Enter. You'll get a brief description of that file; then you'll be asked if you want to download it. If you do, type **Y**, press Enter, and then follow the prompts for downloading the file. If you don't want to download it, type **N** and press Enter.

Getting On-Line Shareware from Public Brand Software

Probably the most comprehensive source of shareware on ZiffNet is from Public Brand Software. Public Brand Software is actually a disk vendor, but it also makes its shareware available on line through its ZiffNet forum, PBSFORUM.

To get there from PC/Contact (or any other ZiffNet forum) type **GO PBSFORUM** and press Enter. If you're on CompuServe rather than ZiffNet, type **GO ZNT:PBSFORUM** and press Enter. You're now in the Public Brand Software forum.

This forum is like any other on CompuServe or ZiffNet—you can use it to exchange messages with people about shareware and to download shareware from Public Brand Software's sizable libraries. To use the software libraries, type **LIBRARIES** and press Enter at a prompt. You'll see a menu listing of all the available libraries. To go to any of the libraries, type the number on the menu and press Enter. You can now browse through the available files by typing **BROWSE** and pressing Enter at the prompt. Any of the files you see can be downloaded.

Using all of these extensive libraries of shareware, freeware, and public domain software is an excellent way to locate and sample the latest programs and utilities at a moderate cost. It is important to remember, however, that you must still register shareware with its owner if you plan on using it regularly, no matter where you get it from; this enables shareware authors to continue writing new and useful programs for you to enjoy in the future.

INDEX

D

E

F

H

I

J

K

T

U

V

W

X

Z

■ TO RECEIVE 3½-INCH DISK(S)

The Ziff-Davis Press software contained on the 5¼-inch disk(s) included with this book is also available in 3½-inch (720k) format. If you would like to receive the software in the 3½-inch format, please return the 5¼-inch disk(s) with your name and address to:

Disk Exchange
Ziff-Davis Press
5903 Christie Avenue
Emeryville, CA 94608

■ END-USER LICENSE AGREEMENT

READ THIS AGREEMENT CAREFULLY BEFORE BUYING THIS BOOK. BY BUYING THE BOOK AND USING THE PROGRAM LISTINGS, DISKS, AND PROGRAMS REFERRED TO BELOW, YOU ACCEPT THE TERMS OF THIS AGREEMENT.

The program listings included in this book and the programs included on the diskette(s) contained in the package on the opposite page ("Disks") are proprietary products of Ziff-Davis Press and/or third party suppliers ("Suppliers"). The program listings and programs are hereinafter collectively referred to as the "Programs." Ziff-Davis Press and the Suppliers retain ownership of the Disks and copyright to the Programs, as their respective interests may appear. The Programs and the copy of the Disks provided are licensed (not sold) to you under the conditions set forth herein.

License. You may use the Disks on any compatible computer, provided that the Disks are used on only one computer and by one user at a time.

Restrictions. You may not commercially distribute the Disks or the Programs or otherwise reproduce, publish, or distribute or otherwise use the Disks or the Programs in any manner that may infringe any copyright or other proprietary right of Ziff-Davis Press, the Suppliers, or any other party or assign, sublicense, or otherwise transfer the Disks or this agreement to any other party unless such party agrees to accept the terms and conditions of this agreement. You may not alter, translate, modify, or adapt the Disks or the Programs or create derivative works or decompile, disassemble, or otherwise reverse engineer the Disks or the Programs. This license and your right to use the Disks and the Programs automatically terminates if you fail to comply with any provision of this agreement.

U.S. GOVERNMENT RESTRICTED RIGHTS. The disks and the programs are provided with **RESTRICTED RIGHTS**. Use, duplication, or disclosure by the Government is subject to restrictions as set forth in subparagraph (c)(1)(ii) of the Rights in Technical Data and Computer Software Clause at DFARS (48 CFR 252.277-7013). The Proprietor of the compilation of the Programs and the Disks is Ziff-Davis Press, 5903 Christie Avenue, Emeryville, CA 94608.

Limited Warranty. Ziff-Davis Press warrants the physical Disks to be free of defects in materials and workmanship under normal use for a period of 30 days from the purchase date. If Ziff-Davis Press receives written notification within the warranty period of defects in materials or workmanship in the physical Disks, and such notification is determined by Ziff-Davis Press to be correct, Ziff-Davis Press will, at its option, replace the defective Disks or refund a prorata portion of the purchase price of the book. **THESE ARE YOUR SOLE REMEDIES FOR ANY BREACH OF WARRANTY.**

EXCEPT AS SPECIFICALLY PROVIDED ABOVE, THE DISKS AND THE PROGRAMS ARE PROVIDED "AS IS" WITHOUT ANY WARRANTY OF ANY KIND. NEITHER ZIFF-DAVIS PRESS NOR THE SUPPLIERS MAKE ANY WARRANTY OF ANY KIND AS TO THE ACCURACY OR COMPLETENESS OF THE DISKS OR THE PROGRAMS OR THE RESULTS TO BE OBTAINED FROM USING THE DISKS OR THE PROGRAMS AND NEITHER ZIFF-DAVIS PRESS NOR THE SUPPLIERS SHALL BE RESPONSIBLE FOR ANY CLAIMS ATTRIBUTABLE TO ERRORS, OMISSIONS, OR OTHER INACCURACIES IN THE DISKS OR THE PROGRAMS. THE ENTIRE RISK AS TO THE RESULTS AND PERFORMANCE OF THE DISKS AND THE PROGRAMS IS ASSUMED BY THE USER. FURTHER, NEITHER ZIFF-DAVIS PRESS NOR THE SUPPLIERS MAKE ANY REPRESENTATIONS OR WARRANTIES, EITHER EXPRESS OR IMPLIED, WITH RESPECT TO THE DISKS OR THE PROGRAMS, INCLUDING BUT NOT LIMITED TO, THE QUALITY, PERFORMANCE, MERCHANTABILITY, OR FITNESS FOR A PARTICULAR PURPOSE OF THE DISKS OR THE PROGRAMS. IN NO EVENT SHALL ZIFF-DAVIS PRESS OR THE SUPPLIERS BE LIABLE FOR DIRECT, INDIRECT, SPECIAL, INCIDENTAL, OR CONSEQUENTIAL DAMAGES ARISING OUT THE USE OF OR INABILITY TO USE THE DISKS OR THE PROGRAMS OR FOR ANY LOSS OR DAMAGE OF ANY NATURE CAUSED TO ANY PERSON OR PROPERTY AS A RESULT OF THE USE OF THE DISKS OR THE PROGRAMS, EVEN IF ZIFF-DAVIS PRESS OR THE SUPPLIERS HAVE BEEN SPECIFICALLY ADVISED OF THE POSSIBILITY OF SUCH DAMAGES. NEITHER ZIFF-DAVIS PRESS NOR THE SUPPLIERS ARE RESPONSIBLE FOR ANY COSTS INCLUDING, BUT NOT LIMITED TO, THOSE INCURRED AS A RESULT OF LOST PROFITS OR REVENUE, LOSS OF USE OF THE DISKS OR THE PROGRAMS, LOSS OF DATA, THE COSTS OF RECOVERING SOFTWARE OR DATA, OR THIRD-PARTY CLAIMS. IN NO EVENT WILL ZIFF-DAVIS PRESS' OR THE SUPPLIERS' LIABILITY FOR ANY DAMAGES TO YOU OR ANY OTHER PARTY EVER EXCEED THE PRICE OF THIS BOOK. NO SALES PERSON OR OTHER REPRESENTATIVE OF ANY PARTY INVOLVED IN THE DISTRIBUTION OF THE DISKS IS AUTHORIZED TO MAKE ANY MODIFICATIONS OR ADDITIONS TO THIS LIMITED WARRANTY.

Some states do not allow the exclusion or limitation of implied warranties or limitation of liability for incidental or consequential damages, so the above limitation or exclusion may not apply to you.

General. Ziff-Davis Press and the Suppliers retain all rights not expressly granted. Nothing in this license constitutes a waiver of the rights of Ziff-Davis Press or the Suppliers under the U.S. Copyright Act or any other Federal or State Law, international treaty, or foreign law.